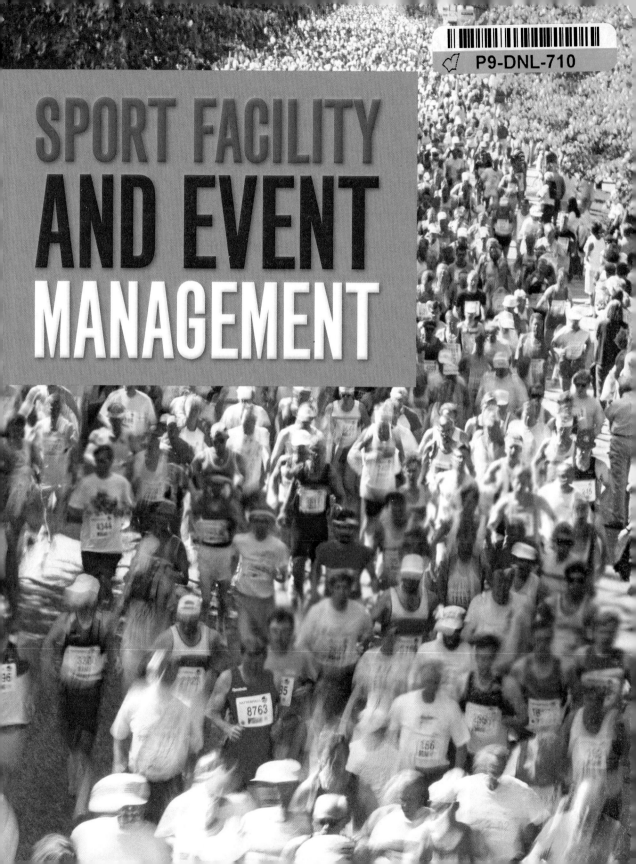

SPORT FACILITY
AND EVENT
MANAGEMENT

SPORT FACILITY AND EVENT MANAGEMENT

Thomas J. Aicher, PhD
Assistant Professor
Program Coordinator of Sport
    Administration
University of Cincinnati

Amanda L. Paule–Koba, PhD
Associate Professor of Sport
    Management
Bowling Green State University

Brianna L. Newland, EdD
Assistant Professor of Sport
    Management
University of Delaware

JONES & BARTLETT
LEARNING

World Headquarters
Jones & Bartlett Learning
5 Wall Street
Burlington, MA 01803
978-443-5000
info@jblearning.com
www.jblearning.com

Jones & Bartlett Learning books and products are available through most bookstores and online booksellers. To contact Jones & Bartlett Learning directly, call 800-832-0034, fax 978-443-8000, or visit our website, www.jblearning.com.

Substantial discounts on bulk quantities of Jones & Bartlett Learning publications are available to corporations, professional associations, and other qualified organizations. For details and specific discount information, contact the special sales department at Jones & Bartlett Learning via the above contact information or send an email to specialsales@jblearning.com.

9846-1

Production Credits

Chief Executive Officer: Ty Field	Media Development Assistant: Shannon Sheehan
President: James Homer	VP, Manufacturing and Inventory Control:
Chief Product Officer: Eduardo Moura	Therese Connell
VP, Executive Publisher: David D. Cella	Composition: Cenveo Publisher Services
Publisher: Cathy L. Esperti	Cover Design: Kristin E. Parker
Acquisitions Editor: Ryan Angel	Interior Design: Publishers' Design and Production
Associate Editor: Kayla Dos Santos	Services, Inc.
Associate Director of Production: Julie C. Bolduc	Rights and Photo Research Coordinator: Mary Flatley
Production Editor: Michael Noon	Cover Image: © Chad Ehlers/Alamy
Production Assistant: Brooke Appe	Front Matter Opener Photo: © Stockbyte/Thinkstock
Senior Marketing Manager: Andrea DeFronzo	Printing and Binding: Manufactured in the United States by RR Donnelley
Manager, Rights and Media: Joanna Lundeen	Cover Printing: Manufactured in the United States by RR Donnelley

Library of Congress Cataloging-in-Publication Data
Aicher, Thomas.
  Sport facility and event management / Thomas Aicher, Amanda Paule-Koba, and Brianna Newland.
    pages cm
  Includes bibliographical references and index.
  ISBN 978-1-284-03479-0 (alk. paper)
1. Sports facilities—Management. 2. Special events—Management. I. Title.
  GV401.A35 2016
  796.06'9—dc23
                                            2014044452

6048

Printed in the United States of America
19 18 17 16 15   10 9 8 7 6 5 4 3 2

I dedicate this textbook to my beautiful wife, Kate. It is because of the love and encouragement you have provided me over the years that I have accomplished such great things in my life.

Thomas J. Aicher

I would like to dedicate this textbook to my amazing family— Brian, Jack, and Logan. Thank you for supporting this endeavor and being there with smiles and hugs when I needed them.

Amanda L. Paule-Koba

I would like to dedicate this textbook to my (soon-to-be) husband, Mike. I cannot tell you how wonderful it is to have your unwavering love and support.

Brianna L. Newland

CONTENTS

CHAPTER 3   **Facility Design and Construction**   **37**
Michael Newland and Brianna L. Newland

CHAPTER 8   **Marketing the Facility and Events**   **139**
Brianna L. Newland

CHAPTER 11 **Traditional Revenue Generation in Sport and Recreation** **205**

Brian Menaker

CHAPTER 12   Customer Service   229
Kevin P. Cattani

CHAPTER 13   Risk Management   247
Thomas J. Aicher, Linda Schoenstedt,
and Amanda L. Paule-Koba

Sport Facility and Event Management focuses on the major components of both facility and event management: planning, financing, marketing, implementation, and evaluation. The text integrates timely theoretical insights with real-world practicality and application to afford the reader a strong foundation in facility and event management. It focuses on a broad range of facilities and events to demonstrate the diversity of the industry, touching on various topics relating to recreation, leisure, health, and fitness.

The objective of this text is to provide a working knowledge of how to manage sport facilities and how to plan, manage, implement, and evaluate sport events. As such, the chapters are designed to focus on various components of the sport facility and event management structures to provide a primer for effectively managing sport, recreation, and leisure facilities and events.

Each chapter begins with an Industry Voice feature, in which a person from the sport industry describes how the chapter topic impacts his or her daily routines. This glimpse into the everyday operations of the sport industry orients readers to the content that follows. As the chapter proceeds, both theoretical and practical considerations relating to the topic are explored. Discussions are backed by current research, and real-world examples and tips are provided to engage readers. The chapter concludes with a Case Study and Discussion Questions to help students apply the content and to assess their comprehension.

Chapter Overview

Each chapter contains various features intended to enhance student learning, including Chapter Objectives, Industry Voices, Vignettes, Case Studies, Discussion Questions, and Tips. A major selling point of this text is that it includes actual examples from the industries covered in the text. No other text on the market successfully employs this strategy.

Chapter 1, *Introduction and History,* provides an overview of the industry and reviews its history. From this foundation, readers will build an understanding of facility and event management as they read the chapters that follow.

Chapter 2, *Management Theory,* examines the functions of the management process, the different management styles and the benefits and drawbacks of each, and the differences between a leader and a manager. A manager is a person whose job involves carrying out the five primary functions of the management process: planning, organizing, staffing, leading, and controlling. These five functions can be the difference between running a successful organization or event and running an unsuccessful one.

The manager will attend to the functions of the management process in his or her own distinct management style. There are many different styles, but a manager will generally fall into one of five categories: democratic, autocratic, persuasive, paternalistic, or laissez-faire. Leaders are individuals who encourage and influence the work of others in a positive approach to achieve the organization's goals and objectives. However, leaders and managers are not the same thing. As will be discussed, a leader does not have to be the manager, and a manager is not always a leader.

Chapter 3, *Facility Design and Construction,* starts with a blueprint, which is a set of plans to develop a facility, and progresses through a series of interrelated steps until the product is completed and the ribbon is cut in the grand opening ceremony. The importance of site selection and evaluation, planning and design, construction costs, and the bidding process is discussed. Further, an examination about green building and how it has increased over the past 10 years is included in the chapter.

Chapter 4, *Finance and Budgeting,* discusses the basic concepts of financing sport facilities. A capital project is a long-term investment that will increase the organization's assets. If an organization wants to build a new facility (or renovate an existing facility), there are many upfront costs, including costs associated with land acquisition, construction, and infrastructure development. Thus, it is important that the project manager(s) understands financial statements and how they can be utilized to develop a budget as a forecasting measure.

Chapter 5, *Bidding and Planning for Different Events,* explains the five main types of events: mega-events, recurring events, traveling events, ancillary events, and community events. When creating an event, the managers need to identify goals and objectives. These will guide all of the forthcoming decisions. When setting goals, the managers should follow the SMART (specific, measurable, attainable, relevant, and time-based) principle. It is important to remember that when creating a new event, in addition to your goals for the event, you must assess where it fits in the current marketplace. Being unique is crucial to attracting sponsors, event participants, spectators, and/or media.

If you are submitting a bid to run an event for a national or international sporting event, you need to follow the bid process provided by the event's rights holder. The criteria of the bid will vary depending on the event, but, in most cases, it is not a solitary process. A multitude of individuals (the organizing committee) will need to come together to gather and present the required information in the most cohesive manner possible.

Chapter 6, *Designing the Event Experience,* outlines the elements of designing the event experience, such as understanding experience characteristics, designing the event concept, co-creating event experiences, and attaching meaning. This process will include identifying unique elements of events; developing a concept, theme, and subsequent experience; and finding ways to tie these elements together to create meaning at the event. Experiences are highly subjective, in that two people can have completely different experiences at the same event. Thus, it is imperative that event managers create an event experience that will appeal to a wide range of individuals.

Chapter 7, *Project Management and Event Implementation,* explores the elements of staging and implementing a sport event. This chapter introduces the five phases of project management (initiation, planning, implementation, monitoring, and shutdown) and the concepts and tools to assist the sport event manager in planning and implementing the event. Concepts such as the work breakdown structure, Gantt charts, and other project management tools will be introduced.

Chapter 8, *Marketing the Facility and Events,* discusses the elements of a marketing plan. The discussion starts with conducting a feasibility study to determine if the facility has the capacity to host the event and that market demands are well matched. Next it reviews developing a marketing strategy and plan. It outlines the value, mission, vision, and goals of the event as offered in the marketing plan and explains how these considerations can help identify the ancillary opportunities associated with the event. These aspects provide sport facility and event managers the information they need to conduct proper segmentation.

The chapter introduces the four common ways segmentation occurs: demographics, psychographics, media preferences, and purchasing behaviors. It examines the value of relationship marketing and the use of customer relationships and data-based management systems to improve customer relations. The chapter then outlines how events can utilize the marketing mix (price, product, place, and promotion) to position themselves in the marketplace. Finally, the chapter covers the different strategies events may pursue to communicate their message to consumers. These strategies include traditional marketing techniques as well as some innovative methods (e.g., guerilla and viral marketing).

Chapter 9, *Consumer Behavior,* outlines three major components of how and why people attend or participate in sport events. First, it develops how people are socialized into sport from three different levels: socialization, involvement, and commitment. Next, it provides several motivational forces that act upon individuals as they select the types of events they would like to either spectate or participate in. Finally, it outlines the seven steps in the decision-making process and highlights how both event owners and participants make their purchase decisions.

Chapter 10, *Sponsorship,* describes an incredibly important and often necessary part of creating an event. The importance of sponsorship in producing successful events and providing revenue for a facility cannot be ignored. This chapter discusses ways in which an event manager can find potential sponsors, the process for creating a sponsorship agreement, and the sponsorship agreement itself. The event manager must understand the process of identifying and targeting potential sponsors and ways of proposing the sponsorship relationship to the company.

Chapter 11, *Traditional Revenue Generation in Sport and Recreation,* reviews the various techniques used to generate revenue through sport and recreation organizations and facilities. Sport facilities and associated events provide owners, operators, managers, and other connected stakeholders the opportunity to generate revenue through numerous forms of creative planning. Techniques and principles of revenue generation from sport, participatory, and recreation facilities and events are categorized and summarized. Further, categories of sources of revenue include venue-related revenue such as ticket sales, concessions, merchandise, event fees, and participatory event monies, such as exposition-related income and registration fees.

Chapter 12, *Customer Service,* reviews the various aspects involved with customer service in the sport marketplace. Customer service is a sequence of activities designed to enhance the level of customer satisfaction. Understanding why customers attend events provides information that allows for the tailoring of an experience to best suit the customers' needs and wants. Being familiar with alternative ways of measuring service quality will not only set an organization apart from competition, but will also save the organization valuable resources in targeting external firms to provide those services. This chapter also discusses various ways to measure and better understand how an organization is attending to customer service. It examines the consequences of customer service and why they are so vital in maintaining a competitive edge in an already saturated marketplace.

Chapter 13, *Risk Management,* discusses the process of examining the uncertainty or chance of loss—usually accidental loss, which is sudden, unusual, or unforeseen—and creating a plan to attempt to reduce any risks to all involved in the event. Implementing a comprehensive risk management plan is vital to a facility and/or event. In today's litigious society, understanding how to mitigate financial loss and negligence should be front and center in minimizing risk and potential lawsuits. The growth of new and renovated sport facilities and the creation of diverse events has made this area of the industry much more difficult for managers.

Chapter 14, *Measurement and Evaluation,* reviews the various techniques to measure the performance of the event or facility from a multi-stakeholder perspective. The facility and event industry faces many challenges and serves a variety of stakeholders who each play a significant role in the success of the organization. It is therefore very important that facility and event organizations measure success based on the organization objectives they have put into place. First, the chapter establishes the importance of continuous evaluation of the organization and its performance from pre-event to post-event to ensure that all stakeholder expectations were met. The chapter then outlines the major components of SERVQUAL, economic, environmental, and social, among other, methods of evaluating the organization's performance.

Chapter 15, *Sustainability and Legacy,* outlines the strategies and techniques that organizations employ to create sustainable facilities and events that have a positive impact on the facility, event, and community. It discusses the economic, environmental, and social impacts that facilities and events generate in their host community, the common methodologies utilized to measure each, and strategies to enhance the positive while minimizing the negative impacts. Positive impacts of hosting events can include new and updated roads, entertainment venues, and other infrastructures, as well as increased tourism revenue, media exposure, commercial appeal, and civic pride. Negative impacts can include overcrowding and increased travel concerns, disruption to the local environment, the building or renovating of uneconomical and unsustainable infrastructures, and unfavorable perceptions of the host community. Further, facilities often are left empty or are underutilized, and events sometimes do not make it past the inaugural year.

Instructor Resources

Several resources have been developed to help the instructor organize the course's content and assess student learning. They include the following:

- Test bank: The test bank provides more than 500 questions, including chapter quizzes and student self-assessments.
- Lecture outlines: These brief overviews of each chapter can help the instructor organize a lecture and ensure key points are covered.
- Image bank: The images provided can be used in quizzes, exercises, or class presentations.
- PowerPoint presentations: These valuable teaching supplements are broken down by chapter to be used as lecture talking points or student study guides.
- Sample syllabus.

First, I would like to thank the world's best coeditors, Amanda and Bri, for your willingness to embark on such an endeavor. I could not have asked for a better pair of colleagues to go through this process with and am thankful you agreed to do so. I would also like to thank our contributors. Without you, this book would not be possible. Your knowledge and expertise elevated the quality of each chapter. I would also like to thank Professor Robert Brinkmeyer, whose encouragement and support allowed me to take a chance as an untenured faculty member to achieve a lifelong goal. To the entire Jones & Bartlett Learning team, I thank you for guiding us through the process. Your patience, support, and reminders allowed us to remain on task and produce a high-quality book. Finally, I would like to thank my friends and family, especially my wife, who supported me through the years and who have always encouraged me to accomplish great things.

Thomas J. Aicher

I would first like to thank my coeditors, Tommy and Bri, for being such great colleagues to work with on this book. This book would not have been possible without our fantastic contributors. Thank you for the time and expertise you brought to each of your chapters. Thank you to all of the reviewers who read drafts of this text and offered so many great suggestions to enhance its quality. Finally, thank you to our team at Jones & Bartlett Learning for your patience, insight, and thoughtful suggestions as we developed this book. We could not have completed this book without your encouragement and deadline reminders.

Amanda L. Paule-Koba

I find myself lucky to have had the opportunity to work so closely with my two coeditors, Tommy and Amanda. Your considerate feedback and support was so welcomed and appreciated through the entire process. I would also like to thank both the chapter authors and the industry contacts for your valuable time and effort. The strength and success of this textbook are due to your fantastic experience and expertise. We all greatly appreciate the giving of your valuable time. Finally, I'd like to thank our Jones & Bartlett Learning team for your insight and suggestions as this book came to fruition.

Brianna L. Newland

Thomas J. Aicher is an Assistant Professor and Program Coordinator of Sport Administration at the University of Cincinnati, where he teaches Sport Facility and Event Management, Diversity in Sport Organizations, and Professional Selling in Sport. Dr. Aicher has been an active scholar, examining the motivations and meanings people associate with participation in events, as well as the social impacts associated with those events in the host communities. He has been published in leading academic journals, including the *International Journal of Sport Management and Marketing*, *International Journal of Sport Management*, *Journal for the Study of Sports and Athletes in Education*, *Journal of Issues in Intercollegiate Athletics*, *Applied Research in Coaching and Athletics*, and *International Journal of Sport Management, Recreation and Tourism*.

Dr. Aicher earned his PhD in sport management from Texas A&M University in 2009. He holds a master's degree in sport management from Texas A&M and a bachelor's degree in marketing management from Virginia Tech. Prior to entering academia, Dr. Aicher worked for several sport organizations, including the Salem Avalanche, the Durham Bulls, and First and 10 Marketing. With the latter two organizations, he managed several sport- and nonsport-related events. He has continued his endeavors in event planning throughout his academic career.

Amanda L. Paule-Koba is an Associate Professor of Sport Management at Bowling Green State University, where she teaches Sport and Event Management, Sport and Gender, and Sport in Higher Education. Dr. Paule-Koba has been an active scholar, examining issues in intercollegiate sport (such as the recruitment process and academic clustering), gender equity policies, and Title IX. Dr. Paule-Koba has been published in leading academic journals, including the *Journal of Sport Management, Research Quarterly for Exercise and Sport, Journal of Intercollegiate Sport, Applied Research in Coaching and Athletics Annual*, and *Women in Sport and Physical Activity Journal*. She also has a chapter in the book *Leisure, Women, and Gender.*

Dr. Paule-Koba earned her PhD in sport sociology from Michigan State University in 2008. She holds a master's degree in sport studies and a bachelor's degree in sport organization from Miami University. Prior to entering academia, Dr. Paule-Koba worked for a company that ran professional athletes' summer youth sporting camps all over the United States, which is where she gained her real-life experience in event management.

Brianna L. Newland is an Assistant Professor of Sport Management at the University of Delaware, where she teaches Sport Event and Facility Management, Foundations of Sport Management, Sport Marketing, Sport Law, and Management of Sport Information. Dr. Newland has been an active scholar, exploring how sport events can be leveraged to develop sport and community, how sport organizations sustain their future by attracting and nurturing participation within the organization and via events, and how particular factors may foster/hinder adult participation in sport. Dr. Newland has been published in leading academic journals, including the *Journal of Sport Management, Sport Management Review, Managing Leisure*, and *Sport Marketing Quarterly.*

Dr. Newland earned her doctorate in sport management from the United States Sports Academy in 2006 and completed a postdoctoral fellowship with the University of Texas at Austin in 2007. She holds a master's degree in exercise physiology and nutrition and a bachelor's degree in exercise science from the University of Nebraska–Lincoln. Dr. Newland has also served as a race director for endurance sports for over 10 years, which is where she gained her real-life experience in event management.

Chapter Authors

Trevor Bopp, PhD
Lecturer, Program Coordinator
Department of Tourism, Recreation and Sport Management
College of Health and Human Performance
University of Florida
Gainesville, FL

Kevin P. Cattani, PhD
Associate Professor of Sport Marketing and Management
Health, Wellness, and Sport Marketing and Management Department
University of Dubuque
Dubuque, IA

Lydia M. Dubuisson, MS
Instructional Assistant Professor
Department of Health and Kinesiology
Division of Sport Management
Texas A&M University
College Station, TX

Kostas Karadakis, PhD
Assistant Professor of Sport Management
Sport Management Department
Southern New Hampshire University
Manchester, NH

Brian Menaker, PhD
Assistant Professor of Sport Management
School of Education and Professional Studies
Lake Erie College
Painesville, OH

Michael Newland, LEED AP
Project Manager
Meltech Corporation, Inc.

Linda Schoenstedt, PhD
Associate Professor, Sport Management, Coaching Education
and Athlete Development
Department of Sport Studies
Xavier University
Cincinnati, OH

Emily Sparvero, PhD
Clinical Assistant Professor
Kinesiology and Health Education Department
The College of Education
The University of Texas at Austin
Austin, TX

Industry Voice Authors

Jennifer Berger
General Manager
Pacific Sports
Columbia, MD

Rick Boethling
Executive Director
Race Across America
Boulder, CO

John Capella
Flying Pig Marathon
Cincinnati, OH

Jennifer Clark
Vice President of Competition and Area Services
Special Olympics Colorado
Englewood, CO

Michael Gilason
Vice President
Main Line Expo and Events
King of Prussia, PA

Lesley Irvine
Senior Associate Athletic Director and Senior Women Administrator
Bowling Green State University
Bowling Green, OH

Lindsay Laurent
Director of Licensing and Strategic Revenue
Bowling Green State University
Bowling Green, OH

Michael Muñoz
President
Muñoz Agency
Cincinnati, OH

Dev Pathik
CEO and Founder
The Sports Facilities Advisory
Clearwater, FL

Jason Percival
Assistant Director
Western Southern Open
Mason, OH

Martin Robertson
Senior Lecturer
Event Management, School of Tourism
Bournemouth University
Dorset, United Kingdom

Rob Runnels
Director of Ballpark Entertainment
Round Rock Express
Round Rock, TX

Melissa Schaaf
Director of Marketing
Wells Fargo Center, Comcast-Spectacor
Philadelphia, PA

Don Schumacher
Executive Director
National Association of Sports Commissions
Cincinnati, OH

Hank Zemola
Chief Executive Officer
Chicago Special Events
Chicago, IL

Gary Bernstein, MS
Instructor, Undergraduate Program Coordinator, Internship Director
University of Louisville
Louisville, KY

Willie Burden, EdD
Professor, Facility and Event Management
Georgia Southern University
Statesboro, GA

David Perricone, MBA
Assistant Professor, Sport Management
Centenary College
Hackettstown, NJ

Brenda A. Riemer, PhD
Associate Professor, Facility Development
Eastern Michigan University
Ypsilanti, MI

Robert G. Thrasher, Jr., PhD
Assistant Professor and Program Coordinator
Lees-McRae College
Banner Elk, NC

Abigail Weber, MBA
Assistant Professor
Lindenwood University
Saint Charles, MO

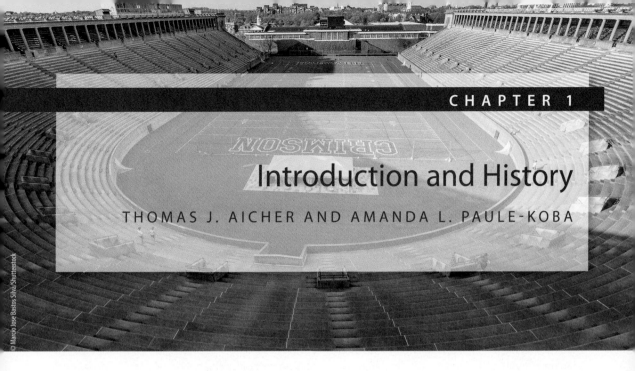

CHAPTER 1

Introduction and History

THOMAS J. AICHER AND AMANDA L. PAULE-KOBA

CHAPTER OBJECTIVES

Upon completion of this chapter, the reader will be able to:

1. Outline the origins of sport facilities and events
2. Explain the evolution of facilities in terms of design, financing, and use
3. Define the main components of the sport facility and event management and main content areas discussed in detail throughout this text

CHAPTER OVERVIEW

This chapter will outline the evolution of facilities and events from the Greek and Roman eras to modern day. It will outline the trends in facility construction, financing, and design over the past few centuries to develop a strong understanding of the evolution to modern facilities. Finally, it will give a brief outline of the entire text to establish an understanding of how to properly navigate the text.

Industry VOICE

Don Schumacher—Executive Director, National Association of Sports Commissions

The National Association of Sports Commissions was created to promote amateur sport and support the Olympic ideals in the United States. As such, we assist the two most important players in the facility and event industry: the event owner and the host communities or facility. We develop best practices for both groups to follow, as well as the opportunity for those two groups to come together to help improve the sporting opportunity and experience. In my current role as Executive Director of the National Association of Sports Commissions, I inform our members of these strategies and assist in developing the relationship between the two groups.

My first position in venue management was Executive Director of the College Football Hall of Fame from 1981 to 1984 in Kings Island, Ohio. As part of the National Football Foundation, the College Hall of Fame built a 10,000-seat football stadium to host various college and high school football events in the stadium and bring in more tourists and visitors to the Hall. My role was to ensure the stadium was constantly in use with either football or nonfootball events. My next position was President of the Cincinnati Riverfront Coliseum, now known as the U.S. Bank Arena. In this role, I managed the relationships with our tenants (e.g., University of Cincinnati basketball team) and also hosted various entertainment and sport events. I later joined the management team at Cinergy Field to help develop events not connected with the two tenants. Other assignments included management of three major seat license and premium seating campaigns before transitioning into my current role.

People who want to work in the sport industry should be motivated by more than just an interest in sports. They should be able to offer something of value to the sport organizations for whom they would like to work. As you begin your career, show management you can make a real contribution while hopefully working toward your goal position. One way to do this is to develop selling skills; doing so is the easiest way to show an organization that you bring value. Developing your communication and selling skills will enhance your confidence and reduce the fear of selling. In my current role, I feel I am selling 90% of the time. I am continually selling new ideas and new concepts. The ability to sell helps us perform as well as we do. Every sport organization needs a great sales staff in order to be successful.

One of the characteristics I look for when hiring a new employee is the willingness to learn. There is always more to learn in this industry, and it is a continuous process, so the willingness to learn is something that will help the individual succeed. I also look for individuals who are proficient with Microsoft Office products, in particular Word and PowerPoint. And personal communication skills are essential. You need to be able to write and communicate well in person, by e-mail, and on the phone. In our business, we are constantly writing reports, bids, proposals, etc., and the ability to do so well is very important. The ability to write and communicate well can be difficult to find among individuals searching for entry-level positions. It is a skill that anyone wanting to enter this industry must develop to better his or her chances.

The sports event travel industry's challenge is that it has received a reputation for being recession-resistant. Because the business grew throughout the recession, it has attracted the attention of organizations that are focused on increased profits over anything. Events are becoming more about the bottom line than offering the opportunity for young athletes to continue to improve. This emphasis on profit can place hotels in the difficult position of agreeing to rebates on each room night. These rebates are passed on to the event owner or facility. The money is used to offset event costs, resulting in higher rates for each room. Hotels are understandably reluctant to participate. Our association works to educate all parties to each transaction on the impact such practices can have.

Event bidding will remain important because there are events that have a steady history of drawing large numbers of visitors to the host community. At the same time, facility owners and host communities are beginning to develop their own events. They do so either by establishing relationships with an existing event and helping the event grow or by creating an entirely new event that will bring people into the community. This level of involvement allows the host organization to control the event and each year strengthen it and increase its beneficial impact. To be able to do this, it is necessary to have strong personal relationships. The sports event travel industry places great emphasis on trust and relationships, which can lead to success for all.

The sports industry is no different than any other industry in that the very word *industry* denotes a commercial activity. Therefore, all of the skills necessary for a successful commercial activity have to translate to sports. Without salespeople, managers, operational staff, risk managers, etc., the sports industry cannot function. It is important to be able to strategically plan to develop organization goals, processes to achieve the goals, and a method to measure success. The remaining chapters discuss these skills in a practical and systematic way so you can develop your skills for a successful career.

Introduction

Throughout history, sport, sport events, and sport facilities have been a major cultural component of our societies. Dating back as long as 30,000 years ago, there is evidence to suggest the enjoyment of sport and sport for leisure, as supported by the prehistoric cave art found in France, Africa, and Australia (Masterman, 2009). The common sports displayed in these renderings are wrestling, running, swimming, and archery. While these renderings do not truly depict sport in a manner in which it is consumed and participated in today, cave paintings in Mongolia dating back to 7000 BC display wrestling matches with crowds of spectators.

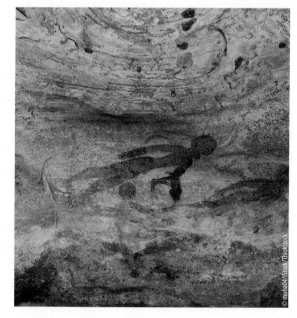

© muha04/iStock/Thinkstock

Combined, these portrayals demonstrate the continued importance of sport participation and consumption within our societies.

This rich history of sport events was largely associated with ceremonies created to honor either religious gods or leaders of the civilization. For example, drawings found on pharaonic monuments depicted individuals participating in various sporting activities (e.g., swimming, boxing, wrestling, running, handball), believed to be designed and governed by ancient kings, princes, and statesmen. In addition, some argue that these events were the first in which basic rules, officials, and uniforms were used during the sport events. While some argue England is the birthplace of football (commonly known as soccer in the United States), the ancient game of cuju was played from 206 BC to 220 AD in China, Korea, Japan, and Vietnam. This game was very similar to football: Players were not allowed to use their hands, points were scored when the ball was passed into a net, and two teams would compete against one another. The games were designed as a method of military training in which the two teams would strive to control the ball to demonstrate their dominance over their opponent. In the United States, lacrosse is considered the country's oldest sporting activity on record. According to records, the game was designed and participated in by Native American men located in the western Great Lakes region. Rules during that time are very similar to the rules of the current version of the sport.

The modern Olympic Games are also rooted in a rich tradition. Originating sometime in the tenth or ninth century BC, the events that would become the Olympic Games were a component of a much larger religious ceremony to honor Zeus, the god of the sky and ruler of the Olympic gods. These ceremonies were held every 4 years, similar to today's Olympics, and included the discus and javelin throws, a foot race, and the long jump. Along with the Olympic Games, these events included the Hera Games, Pythian Games, Isthmian Games, and Nemea Games (Toohey & Veal, 2000), and they are largely considered the first instance of mega-events in which multiple regions participated in and spectated the event. In 393 AD, these events were discontinued by Theodosius I, a Christian Roman Emperor, because of their affiliation with the Greek god. They were revitalized in 1896 AD.

The stadiums used to host the ancient events were located in the Peloponnese region of southern Greece and were combined with religious facilities. It is widely believed that the first Olympic Games were held in 776 BC; however, recent archeological evidence suggests that the original Olympic Stadium and hippodrome were constructed after 700 BC. The stadium held an estimated

40,000 people, and the design was not much different than the U-shaped style commonly used today. The hippodrome, which originally hosted chariot and horse racing events, could host hundreds or even thousands of spectators, depending on the event. The Roman Empire continued to follow a similar design and style of the facilities constructed during the Greek Empire.

The Roman Colosseum, originally named the Flavian Amphitheater after the Flavian Dynasty, was constructed in 80 AD under the order of Emperor Vespasian as a gift to the people of Rome. For those who have seen the movie *Gladiator*, the truth behind the story is that Titus, the son of Vespasian, did in fact host 100 days of games, including the gladiatorial contests; however, it was to celebrate the opening of the Colosseum. Other events that took place during this time included venationes, or wild beast hunts, which placed humans and animals in the Colosseum in a fight to the death, and naumachiae, also called sea battles, in which the arena was flooded and two fleets of ships fought in portrayal of previous naval battles (The Games, 2008). The Romans during this time provided us with some of the same tools we use today to build stadiums. For example, they used one of the first known cranes, consisting of rope, wooden wheels, and a long wooden arm that would lift items to the higher levels. The Colosseum was one of the first structures made from a concrete-type material, and the arched design is still modeled in many modern stadiums. Archeological evidence also shows that the Romans used tickets, numbered gates, and reserved seating during their events. Finally, one of the most impressive features of the Roman Colosseum was that the design allowed for 50,000-plus people to exit the stadium in less than 5 minutes—something most modern facilities are unable to achieve.

Evolution of Facilities

The revival of the Olympic Games in 1896, the addition of collegiate sports in the United States, and the early growth of professional baseball fueled the development of sport facilities in the modern era. From an international perspective, the revival of the Olympic movement facilitated the construction of facilities in Greece, London, and Los Angeles, as these cities hosted the first three editions of the modern Olympic Games. The Panathenaic Stadium was constructed from the remains of an ancient Greek stadium and

TIP

The Colosseum incorporated many other design features still in use today. The History Channel provides several videos discussing the construction of the facility, the events it hosted, and the operations associated with the events. Visit www.history.com/topics/ancient-history/colosseum to learn more about the Colosseum.

is the only stadium in the world constructed of white marble. Recently, the Panathenaic Stadium was renovated to host various events associated with the Olympic Games in 2004, and it is still in use for national and regional events. The White City Stadium in London was constructed to host the 1900 Olympic Games and went through several renovations until it was demolished in 1985. During its time, it housed varying sporting events, but was most recently known for greyhound and auto racing. Los Angeles Memorial Coliseum is the only stadium to host two Olympic Games (1932 and 1984). It has also hosted two National Football League Super Bowls (I and VII) and a Major League Baseball World Series (1959, when the Dodgers hosted three home games). In addition, the Coliseum holds attendance records in international soccer (92,650 spectators during a Chivas vs. Barcelona match in 2006), baseball (115,300 spectators during a Dodgers vs. Red Sox exhibition game in 2008), and special events (134,254 spectators during a Billy Graham event in 1963). In 1984, the Coliseum became a registered landmark, and recently the University of Southern California signed a lease agreement through 2054, which should guarantee its maintenance and upkeep.

Within intercollegiate athletics, Franklin Field in Philadelphia, Pennsylvania, is recognized by the National Collegiate Athletic Association as the oldest university stadium used to host an intercollegiate event. Originally constructed in 1895 for $100,000, the facility hosted the first Penn Relays (the oldest and largest track and field competition in the United States) and the University of Pennsylvania (Penn) football team, with a capacity of approximately 30,000 seats. Since then, the facility has gone through several renovations and has been home to other Penn intercollegiate teams and even the Philadelphia Eagles. Currently, Franklin Field is the home for Penn's football and lacrosse teams, with a capacity of more than 50,000 seats. Even in the early years of intercollegiate athletics, universities participated in what is known as the **arms race**, in which they compete with one another

arms race As it relates to the sport event industry, the competition between sport organizations to have the best facilities, resources, revenue-generating amenities, and other event features to ensure an advantage in the marketplace.

VIGNETTE 1-1

The Arms Race in Intercollegiate Athletics

In 1903, Harvard University in Boston, Massachusetts, constructed the first stadium to use reinforced structural concrete in its design. Seating more than 23,000 spectators, the facility's design was similar to the Panathenaic Stadium in Greece. Not to be outdone by their archrival, in 1912, Yale University in New Haven, Connecticut, built the first stadium designed exclusively to host events. The facility originally hosted 18,000 fans but was quickly expanded to more than 23,000 seats just 4 years later. Since this early period, the two universities have continuously spent money to upgrade their stadiums and increase the capacity. Currently, the Yale Bowl can seat approximately 61,500 fans and is the largest stadium in the Football Championship subdivision. Harvard Stadium is close in number, seating 57,200. What this competition demonstrates is known as the arms race in intercollegiate athletics. While the ideology behind the arms race has not changed over the last 100 years, the amount of money universities are investing in their athletic facilities has substantially increased. For example, Texas is known for its love of both high school and college football. In 2006, Texas A&M completed construction on the second largest video board in college football, the largest board belonging to their archrival, the University of Texas. Recently, Texas A&M developed plans to not only expand its stadium (Kyle Stadium) to 106,511 maximum seating capacity, 6000 more than their rival, but also to enlarge its video board to

7661 square feet, more than 200 square feet larger than the University of Texas's video board (Lester, 2014). The initial cost estimates for this project are $450 million for the entire renovation. The arms race is a constant chase for the best facilities for the athletes and spectators, and it is not limited to football expenditures, as both Texas A&M and the University of Texas spent more than $150 million combined on indoor track and practice facilities.

to have the biggest or best facilities and amenities associated with their athletic programs. Review the vignette for more information about the arms races as well as early and modern examples.

The oldest Major League Baseball (MLB) facility still in use in the United States is Fenway Park (1912), home to the Boston Red Sox, followed closely by Wrigley Field (1914), home of the Chicago Cubs. These two facilities are

TIP

You can view photos of the transformation of these two facilities. For a timeline and photos of Fenway Park, visit mlb.mlb.com/bos/fenwaypark100/timeline.jsp. For Wrigley Field, visit www.chicagotribune.com/videogallery/76640826/.

staples in the sport facility landscape but have gone through several renovations since their inception. Both facilities followed what is known as the jewel box design, which is characterized by the two-tier grandstand; steel, wood, or concrete support beams left exposed and incorporated into the design; seats that are traditionally green; and an unconventionally shaped outfield, as most stadiums in this era were built to fit within one square city block. During this early era of baseball, several facilities were constructed across the country to host teams. In fact, between 1880 and 1920, the MLB lists more than 60 stadiums that were built. The growth in the number of teams and stadiums became a part of the American landscape during this era and was part of the great migration toward the city centers and away from the farmlands during that time.

Trends in Sport Facilities

From this early part of the modern era until the early 1990s, stadiums were constructed and continuously maintained and renovated to remain competitive in the sport facility landscape. However, with changes in the way stadiums were funded, an increase in demand for suites and luxury seating, and a rise in sport-specific stadiums, an estimated 84% of professional sport facilities underwent either major renovations or brand new construction since 1980 (Fried, 2010). The recent construction of Levi's Stadium in Santa Clara, California, the home of the San Francisco 49ers, may be the best example of the various reasons for the changes in sport facilities and will be used as an example throughout the following discussion to highlight these changes.

Howard and Crompton (2002) outlined the trends in sport facility financing. During the early to mid-1900s, stadiums and arenas for professional use were financed and maintained primarily by the owners of the team, a method known as private financing. Starting in the 1960s, team owners began to put increasing pressure on their host community's leadership because of the opportunities to build new facilities in other locations and the support they could get from those new communities. Coined the gestation period, Howard and Crompton (2002) reported that 88% of new stadium construction was done with public funds, meaning municipalities (city and county governments) used tax monies and other resources to fund stadium construction. From 1970 to 1984, nearly all (93%) of the stadiums and arenas that were built were funded and completed with public funds. This era was brought to a halt because of various legislation passed that changed how facilities could be financed using government funds, beginning the era of the transitional phase. The mid-1990s introduced the fully loaded era in which stadiums and arenas were abandoned because they were no longer commercially viable for the teams who used them. This era, ending in 2003, has developed the closest balance between public and private financing, in which a portion of the cost was covered with public financing while the balance was covered by team owners, seat licenses, and sponsorships. Currently, citizens are beginning to call into question the use of public funds for these facilities and are voting down **referendums** to increase taxes to fund their construction. For example, Levi's Stadium in Santa Clara was met with lots of resistance, and several referendums for the use of public funds were voted down. Ultimately, the City of Santa Clara garnered $850 million to attract the San Francisco 49ers away from their current home, demonstrating a possible shift toward public financing. Furthering this possibility, the Atlanta Braves recently reached an agreement with Cobb County in Georgia that the two entities will each cover half of the $672 million stadium.

referendum A direct vote in which an entire electorate (i.e., voting public) is asked to accept or reject a proposal put forward by the community leadership.

Levi's Stadium altered design away from the traditional bowl seating associated with most American football stadiums, which may change the landscape of football stadiums. The design of the stadium includes the traditional bowl seating in the entire facility at the lower and club levels. However, on one side of the stadium, above the lower bowl and club-level seating, four levels of luxury suites are stacked on top of the second tier. This design not only provides the 49ers with a larger amount of premium seating, it reduces the risk of not achieving enough attendance, so they may avoid **television blackout** in the local market, which may have a positive impact on the team's ticket sales. In addition, the bank of suites creates a large flat exterior surface that faces a major transportation artery in the city; this surface could be used to generate additional revenue through sponsorship partnerships.

television blackout The National Football League's policy stating that if the nonpremium or luxury suite tickets have not been sold out, then the game will not be televised in the local market.

The move to Levi's Stadium is a move from Candlestick Park, which was originally designed to host both baseball and football—a design most cities have moved away from in the recent era. For example, the Cincinnati Reds (baseball) and Bengals (football) now each play in sport-specific stadiums.

In the past, they shared Riverfront Stadium. This change in facility provides fans with a much better viewing experience during the events because the two events have different center points. In baseball, the majority of people want to sit near home plate, while in football they prefer to sit closer to the 50-yard line. Because of the manner in which these two fields are constructed, the shared stadium would place football's end zone on either the first or third baseline of a baseball field, with the 50-yard line somewhere behind second base, creating poor sight lines. In San Francisco, the Giants (MLB) moved away from Candlestick Park into what is now called AT&T Park in 2000. This move allowed the Giants to have a baseball-specific facility; however, it came at a cost for the team owners, as it was the first baseball stadium to be 100% financed since Dodger Stadium in 1962. The city did provide a $10 million abatement to improve the infrastructure around the facility, including a connection to the city's metro service.

Trends in Local Sport Facilities

The National Association of Sports Commissions reports annual spending on sport travel has continued to increase in the past decade, with spending greater than $8 billion in the United States alone. To tap into this source of revenue, more and more local municipalities are developing their facility inventory so they can compete in this marketplace. For instance, Carson City, Nevada, invested under $100,000 over a 2-year period in their infrastructure and staffing for sport tourism, which generated approximately $20 million in new economic activity for the community over that period. This new method has shifted local parks and recreation departments from managing local sport leagues and tournaments to competing on a national stage while balancing local facility demands. These new demands have increased the costs associated with maintenance and upkeep of the facilities; however, the new revenue has allowed municipalities to improve the quality of their facility inventory.

Similar to the professional arenas and stadiums, these local facilities need to pass the approval process to receive public funding, and this has proven challenging for some. For example, the Frankenmuth Youth Sport Association (Michigan) developed a plan to develop a self-sustaining recreation center that would include an indoor track, multi-use courts, meeting rooms, 13 outdoor fields, and a splash park that would be free for residents to use. However, even with the breakeven analysis provided by the association, the community residents voted against the facility construction. Alternatively, Elizabethtown, Kentucky, was able to secure $29 million in public monies to invest in the construction of a sports park through a 2% increase in the restaurant sales tax.

Recreation Management recently reported that more than half of the community centers in their survey expected to engage in new construction projects within the next 3 years. Typical features of these recreation facilities include classroom/meeting spaces, fitness centers, bleachers and seating, locker rooms, exercise studios, concession areas, playgrounds, indoor/outdoor sports courts, and open spaces. The common changes or additions to the recreation centers include splash pads, synthetic turf fields, park structures (e.g., shelters and restrooms), and the addition of some of the more traditional items that the facility may be missing from its inventory. Another development is the proliferation of running and biking trails. These two sports have seen considerable growth in participation

VIGNETTE 1-2

Greenways Increase Healthy Living

Greenways are typically paved corridors throughout an urban environment that provide transportation access separated from automobile traffic. In doing so, greenways provide a safer opportunity to engage in cycling, running, rollerblading, and other activities that enhance physical fitness. Federal, state, and local funds have begun to be used for the development and maintenance of these greenways because they provide a marketable value for the community, demonstrating that the community believes in a healthy and active lifestyle. In Denver, Colorado, they developed 81 trails, covering more than 300 miles. In addition, they have developed boat ramps, parks, and other attractions along the South Platte, which was once a polluted river that most residents would not even use for swimming (Crouch, 2009). These developments have led to an increase in tourist activities, including visiting the museums, art galleries, and gardens and shopping along the trails. Since the development of the trails, Denver has been largely considered one of the healthiest cities in the United States. For instance, *Forbes Magazine* recently ranked Denver as the fifth healthiest city, noting the value that the park and greenway system have on the community.

over the past decade (Running USA, 2014; Fineman, 2014), and parks and recreation departments have responded by funding these trails. In addition to the changes in their facilities, centers also plan to add new programming such as nutrition and diet counseling, mind–body programs, sport clubs (e.g., running, swimming, cycling), and sport tournaments and races.

Scale of the Sport Event Industry

The sport event industry may be one of the most challenging industries to define because of the volume and variety of sport event opportunities that could be included in industry estimates. For example, the sport event industry could include something as small as a 50-person 5K (5-kilometer) fun run to raise money for a local charity or something as large as the FIFA World Cup, an event that draws more than 3 million spectators, with another 250 million watching via various international broadcasts. This example highlights two different kinds of events that will be commonly discussed throughout this text: participant led and spectator led. In the first example, the 5K race is considered a participant-led event because the majority of the revenue is generated from those who are participating in the event. In contrast, spectator-led events derive the revenue either directly (e.g., tickets) or indirectly (e.g., sponsorship) from those who are watching the event.

In 2014, the Plunkett Report, a market research organization that provides annual industry reports, estimated that the sport industry is a $435 billion industry, with annual spending of more than $28 billion on sport-related products or services. In the United States alone, the sport industry employs approximately five million people in the broad categories of interscholastic and intercollegiate athletics; professional, community, recreation, and sport organizations; health and fitness organizations; and sporting goods manufacturers. Estimates suggest that the sport industry is expected to eclipse the $450 billion mark in the next 5 years, and sports-related jobs are projected to increase by 23% for the decade ending 2018 (Plunkett et al., 2014). Additionally, the U.S. Bureau of Labor Statistics has reported that 130,570 people work in the spectator sport industry, a small segment of the overall sport industry, with a 9.8% growth rate from 2002.

Who Manages Sport Events?

Sport event management is vastly spreading from the normal professional, collegiate, and parks and recreation governing structures. For instance, chambers of commerce and visitors bureaus have begun to invest in staff and infrastructure associated with hosting sport events to attract tourists to their communities. The National Association of Sports Commissions (www.sportscommissions.org) was developed in 1992 to provide a communication network between event owners and facility owners to increase access to event information and education to best practices. Currently, the membership is at an all-time high, with more than 650 member organizations and 1600 event owners. With this level of growth in the sport event and facility management industry, there is an increased need for individuals who can manage multiple sport events throughout the year, and a need for a better understanding of the event management discipline. For instance, sport event and facility managers need a strong foundation in risk management, finance, human resource management, marketing, customer service, and project management, which leads us to the contents you will find throughout this text.

SUMMARY

For more than 30,000 years, organized sport has been a component of human civilization. As humans and communities have evolved during this time, so have the sport events we participate in and spectate, as have the facilities we use to host those events. While the designs of our facilities have not changed much in terms of structure, the ancillary items we place inside them and the events they host have changed considerably. The remainder of this text will outline the major components of both facility and event management as they pertain to recreational, leisure, and competitive sport events.

DISCUSSION QUESTIONS

1. Explain the relationship between religion and sport in the development of sport events.
2. What is the foundation of sport facilities, and how have the designs and funding changed over time?
3. What role has the "arms race" played in the development of facilities in the United States?
4. What organizations are involved in the management of sport events in your local community? University community?

Case STUDY

Is It Time to Renovate or Rebuild Cameron Indoor Stadium?

Duke University is a private institution located in Durham, North Carolina. With an enrollment of 6600 undergraduate and 6000 graduate students, it is one of the most prestigious universities in the country. Tuition runs about $40,000 a year, making it one of the most affluent schools in the country. Located in what is known as the Research Triangle area of North Carolina, the Raleigh–Durham area has a metropolitan population of 1.5 million people and hosts several headquarters for major corporations.

The Duke University men's and women's basketball teams play their home games in Cameron Indoor Stadium, the crown jewel of college basketball. The stadium was originally built in 1935 and was remodeled in the late 1980s.

Sports Illustrated ranked the stadium fourth on the list of the country's greatest sporting venues of the twentieth century, ahead of Pebble Beach, Wrigley Field, and Fenway Park. The stadium offers little room for concessions and no room for corporate sponsorships. Stadium capacity is 9314, with 3500 of those seats being bleacher seats reserved for students. To say the stadium is antiquated would be an understatement. The Board of Regents thinks a new facility needs to be on par with the other schools in the area; however, they are aware of the public sentiment for Cameron Indoor Stadium. Keep in mind that the University of North Carolina, Wake Forest, and North Carolina State all play in new, modern facilities.

Things to Consider

Take into account that the University of North Carolina sits 8 miles away from the Duke campus, and North Carolina State is about 22 miles away. Wake Forest University is located about 80 miles away. The Raleigh–Durham area is full of graduates and fans from these and other Atlantic Coast Conference schools who would love to buy tickets and watch their school play against Duke, but have been unable to due to Cameron's low seating capacity. Thus, in addition to the opportunity to sell more tickets to its own fans, Duke has the opportunity to sell lots of tickets to visiting teams' fans.

Questions That Need to be Addressed

In determining the fate of the Cameron Indoor Stadium, the following questions must be addressed:

- Who pays?
- Who should pay?
- Who benefits?
- How do you finance this project?

As an agency hired by the Duke athletic department, the athletic director of the university has asked you to evaluate building a new basketball arena or a complete remodeling of the current facility. The athletic director wants you to take into account the number of seats the arena will hold and the added revenue from corporate sponsorship as well as a possible naming rights deal. In theory, a new arena would have many new areas for corporate advertising and hospitality. However, this is debatable because donors might want the new arena to have more of a "campus field house" feel (such as that found in the University of Maryland or Indiana Pacers facilities).

You will have a chance to present your proposal to the Board of Regents. The Board is split on this proposal, and it is a very touchy subject. Some feel that the success of Duke teams in the last 20 years makes this the perfect time to build an arena, while others disagree. Choose whether you would like to renovate or rebuild the arena, and answer the following questions:

1. What part will the Iron Dukes (the athletic department's fundraising/donor group) play in the financial process?
2. What is the Basketball Legacy Fund?
3. Does the Raleigh–Durham area have the corporate infrastructure to support suite/club seat sales?
4. Would a surcharge on student fees work at Duke?
5. How many suites and club seats would you include in a new arena?
6. How would you position a capital campaign for a new stadium?
7. How many seats would this arena hold?
8. Who will own and manage the arena, the athletic department or the school?
9. If remodeling, where does Duke play in the meantime?
10. Would the women's team continue to play in Cameron? Consider this decision from a financial standpoint.
11. Will a new facility be a recruiting advantage or disadvantage?

REFERENCES

Crouch, M. (2009). The Long Good Byway. *Planning, 75*(11), 34–36.

Fineman, D. (2014). The state of bike commuting. *Bicycling Magazine.* Retrieved from http://www.bicycling.com/news/featured-stories/bike-lane-funding

Fried, G. (2010). *Managing sport facilities* (2nd ed.). Champaign, IL: Human Kinetics.

Howard, D. R., & Crompton, J. L. (2002). *Financing sport* (2nd ed.). Morgantown, WV: Fitness Information Technology.

Lester, S. (2014, July). College football's largest video board completed at Texas A&M's Kyle Field. *Dallas Morning News.* Retrieved from http://www.dallasnews.com.

Masterman, G. (2009). *Strategic sport event management.* Oxford, UK: Butterworth-Heinemann.

Plunkett, J. W., Plunkett, M. B., Steinberg, J. S., Faulk, J., & Snider, I. J. (2014). Introduction to the sports industry. *Sports Industry*. Retrieved from http://www.plunkettresearchonline.com.

Running USA. (2014). 2013 annual marathon report. Retrieved from http://www.runningusa.org/marathon-report-2014?returnTo=annual-reports

The Games. (2008). The illustrated history of the Roman Empire website. Retrieved from http://www.roman-empire.net/society/soc-games.html

Toohey, K., & Veal, A. J. (2000). *The Olympic Games: A social perspective*. Cambridge, MA: CABI Publishing.

CHAPTER 2

Management Theory

AMANDA L. PAULE-KOBA

CHAPTER OBJECTIVES

Upon completion of this chapter, the reader will be able to:

1. Define management, sport management, and a manager
2. Understand the functions of the management process
3. Identify the different management styles and the benefits and drawbacks of each
4. Understand the difference between a manager and a leader

CHAPTER OVERVIEW

This chapter will examine the functions of the management process, the different management styles and the benefits and drawbacks of each style, and the differences between a leader and a manager. A manager is a person whose job involves carrying out the five primary functions of the management process: planning, organizing, staffing, leading, and controlling. The manager will attend to the functions of the management process in his or her own distinct management style, which may fall into one of five categories: democratic, autocratic, persuasive, paternalistic, or laissez-faire.

Industry VOICE

Jason Percival—Assistant Director, Western and Southern Open

I currently work as the Assistant Director of Facilities and Operations for the Western and Southern Open tennis tournament in Mason, Ohio. As part of the 13-person team, I work with the other team members to assemble the eighth-largest tennis tournament in the world, hosting the top 40 male and female players, according to the ATP (Association of Tennis Professionals) and WTA (Women's Tennis Association) rankings. Outside of the 9-day Western and Southern Open tournament, I report to a non-profit 501c3 organization, which governs the use of the facility. As such, I work to accommodate many other smaller events to promote the game of tennis, including the Ohio High School Athletic Association boys and girls sectional, district, and state tournaments; various fundraising walks/races; and many youth camps and clinics.

My career path started when as an undergraduate student I was offered the position of Field Manager for the Intramural Sports Department on campus at Ohio University. In this position, I gained a better understanding of facility maintenance. I used this experience to secure a graduate assistantship at the Ohio State University (OSU). While at OSU, I volunteered my free time with the athletic department to help the operations team on game days of many sports. This activity allowed me to meet and develop relationships with many full-time staff members in a relaxed setting (since the work was unpaid). Upon graduation, I focused on an event/facility coordinator position within the Athletic Corporation at California State University. After a few years at California State University, I was

contacted by my former supervisor from OSU, who requested that I apply for an opening at the university. This request led me back to OSU, where I managed three of the recreation centers, including the indoor tennis center, for 3 years.

At this point in my career, I had enough experience to pinpoint my areas of professional strength as well as my areas of enjoyment and aspiration. I realized that the culture and etiquette of professional tennis seemed to most closely match my aspirations. Realizing this, I knew I needed to continue developing myself to become more marketable to a tennis tournament if I was to break back into that field. For that reason, I worked early mornings and weekends at a local country club managing the tennis courts and teaching lessons. This was obviously a huge sacrifice of my free time, but I knew it would pay off as soon as the right job came along. After 3 years of working 60 plus hours per week at OSU and the country club, I received a call from my former supervisor with the Western and Southern Open, who explained that he had a new position opening up on his team and would like me to apply. I applied and was offered the position, which led me to my current role as Assistant Director of the Western and Southern Open. The key throughout this process was that I envisioned my dream job at each step and calculated what the potential hiring manager for this dream job would want to see on an ideal applicant's resume. I then strove to gain that experience, even through unpaid or secondary jobs, in preparation for a job that did not yet exist.

When thinking about the topic of this chapter, management theory, I would recommend that young professionals managing others for the first time realize that time spent with a subordinate is an investment. Good managers must show infinite patience with supervisees, realizing that each minute spent mentoring now will save months' if not years' worth of time in the future. A good mantra for managers is to "be here now," meaning disregard whatever you were doing when a supervisee comes into your office and focus your attention wholly on that person; do not let your mind be preoccupied at that time. Managers must realize that they can always check e-mail or do paperwork at home, but they cannot continue to teach their understudies at the end of the day. As wholehearted time is invested in the people being managed, young managers will begin to see that their supervisees are becoming more self-sufficient, allowing for a far higher level of productivity and efficiency than the manager could ever hope to achieve alone. The ideal supervisor–supervisee relationship is one in which the supervisor knows that her job is to give all the credit to those working under her, and the supervisee knows that his job is to make his boss look good. In summary, nothing will ever be truer than the simple statement by legendary football coach Woody Hayes: "You win with people."

I offer the following five pieces of advice to those hoping to enter the sport industry:

1. Work incessantly in as many varying areas as possible to discover where your passion resides.
2. Define a clear high-reaching goal and determine a potential path to get there.
3. Focus your efforts on what a potential hiring manager for your ideal job would want to see on your resume.
4. Find ways to achieve the desired experience even if it means working a second job or a job at a lower level than you would typically accept; it must be seen as an investment of your time that will pay off when your ideal job is offered.
5. Consider everyone you meet in every position— not just those above you, but also those lateral to and underneath you—to be a possible future hiring manager or potential reference and advocate for you in a future job.

Introduction

The sport manager must carry out the functions of the management process, which are planning, organizing, staffing, leading, and controlling. While the general duties of all managers may be the same, the management style each person uses to carry out the management process can differ. This chapter will examine five different management styles so the reader can begin to form his or her own management philosophy.

What Is Management?

Management is the process of "achieving organizational goals with and through other people within the constraints of limited resources" (Chelladurai, 2001, p. 94). In order to achieve the organizational goals laid out by those in charge, it is necessary to adhere to the functions of

management The process of accomplishing the organization's goals while dealing with resource constraints.

the management process, which include, but are not limited to, planning, organizing, staffing, leading, and controlling. This coordinated and integrated approach to running an organization can have a huge impact on whether or not an organization or an event is successful.

What Is Sport Management?

sport management
The academic discipline that teaches and trains individuals who have a desire to work on the business side of the sport industry.

Sport management is the academic discipline that teaches and trains individuals who have a desire to work on the business side of the sport industry. In this multidisciplinary field, students are taught about event management, marketing, facility management, finance, sales, and sociocultural aspects of the sport industry. In relation to various academic outlets, Dr. Packianathan Chelladurai defined sport management as

> a field concerned with the coordination of the production and marketing of sport services (which have been broadly classified as participant services and spectator services). Such coordination is achieved through the managerial functions of planning, organizing, leading, and evaluating. Thus, sport management, as an area of scientific study and professional preparation, addresses these functions within the specific environment of sport enterprise. (North American Society for Sport Management, 2000, para. 34)

TIP

The North American Society for Sport Management (NASSM) supports and assists professionals working in the fields of sport, leisure, and recreation. For more information about the field of sport management, graduate study in sport management, career services, and the annual conference, visit the North American Society for Sport Management website at www.nassm.com.

Potential areas in which those in sport management may work include, but are not limited to, the following:

- Collegiate athletics
- Professional athletics
- Interscholastic athletics (such as high school, junior high, or elementary athletics)
- State and national sport governing bodies (such as USA Track and Field [USATF] or the Ohio High School Athletic Association)
- The U.S. Olympic Committee
- International sport governing bodies (such as the International Federation of Football Associations [FIFA])

- Community and recreational sport organizations (such as the YMCA or a local recreation and community center)
- Youth organizations (such as the Amateur Youth Soccer Association [AYSO])
- Coaching
- The National Collegiate Athletic Association

Within these different settings of the sport industry, students can obtain a job in the following operations:

- Event management
- Facility operations and management
- Marketing
- Public relations
- Concessions operations
- Ticketing operations
- Financial areas, such as budgeting and accounting
- Event scheduling
- Legal aspects of sport
- Licensing
- Communications and media

Not all of these potential job types will be available in each sport industry setting. For example, a high school athletic department may not have a position solely allocated to public relations. It may be more likely that the school district's public relations representative, the athletic director, or the school principal would be in charge of this area. However, many professional sport teams and event organizations may have a public relations department to handle team and player information.

What Is a Manager?

A **sport manager** is "a person whose job entails planning, organizing, staffing, directing, and controlling, to be performed within the context of an organization whose primary or predominant product or service is sport and sport-related" (Mullin, 1980, p. 3). The sport manager is responsible for achieving an organization's goals while working within the resources that are available.

sport manager The individual who is responsible for the planning, organizing, staffing, directing, and controlling functions that are completed for the organization.

A manager has to possess a multitude of personal skills and characteristics to be successful at the job. Sport managers must be able to effectively communicate to their employees in order to be effective in their position. Good communication skills are a key to success. A manager will constantly be interacting with staff members, customers, patrons, vendors, and sponsors. Being able to keep everyone on the same page and informed about what is occurring in the organization is vital in keeping everyone happy.

Further, a manager must be flexible and organized and have good people skills. Flexibility is essential due to the many unforeseen circumstances and events that can occur when running an event. Being able to roll with the punches and not overreact when things do not go as planned will help staff members also remain calm and positive. For instance, if you are running a youth football camp and the weather suddenly changes from sunny skies to storms, there may be some people who do not know what to do when bad weather arrives. It is important to follow the protocol you have (hopefully) laid out prior to the event. Make sure all of the young athletes are accounted for, and take them inside to the rain location. As the manager, remaining calm and organized will help not only your staff remain calm but the young football players as well.

Organizational skills are necessary to stay on track and meet deadlines. Planning ahead and communicating deadlines to staff members will assist in achieving goals. Organizational skills are also required to be efficient. Efficiency in this case refers to maximizing the resources to produce the greatest result. Resources are often limited, so it is important for managers to be able to get the most out of what they have available to them.

Functions in the Management Process

A manager must carry out the five primary functions of the management process: planning, organizing, staffing, leading, and controlling.

These functions can be the difference between running a successful organization and running an unsuccessful organization.

PLANNING

The planning phase is the initial, and perhaps most important, stage in the management process. Without the planning phase of the management process, managers would not have anything to organize, staff, lead, or control. In this stage, the manager and upper management staff define where the organization wants to be in the future and how to arrive there. The process of setting these organizational goals identifies the direction the organization is heading. This stage is critical for outlining the work that will need to be performed in order to lead the organization to where it desires to be in the upcoming months (short-term plans) and years (long-term plans).

Setting goals during the planning stage should follow the SMART principle. Goals should be **s**pecific, **m**easureable, **a**ttainable, **r**ealistic, and **t**imely. A specific goal should define exactly what is expected and who is involved. Measuring the progress of goals is necessary to stay on track and ensure that all key dates and deadlines are met. Attainable goals should not be too extreme or too easy for the organization to meet. Goals should be realistic and within the organization's capabilities and control. Finally, goals should have a deadline for completion. This time component will help keep the staff on track and discourage them from putting the task off. Having a time frame helps create a sense of urgency, and the employees will work harder to achieve the goal.

The manager must also develop plans to coordinate and implement the work that needs to be done. As the person in charge of completing the project, the manager will have to look to his or her employees to delegate who will be in charge of what aspects of the project. Part of being an effective manager is understanding each employee's strengths and putting the person in a position where he or she can be successful.

Finally, during the planning phase, managers must quickly understand the situation, weigh the pros and cons of each possible decision, and decide on a course of action. Making quick and effective decisions can be the difference between the success and the failure of a project.

As an example of the planning phase, suppose a college athletic department has the goal of increasing student attendance by 10% at home

sporting events by the end of the academic year. This goal is *specific* in that it clearly outlines the expected outcome and the group of people who must be reached (students not currently attending home sporting events) to bring it about. It is *measurable* because the number of students attending athletic events can be tracked via student identification cards being swiped through electronic readers. It is *attainable* and *realistic* because the goal of 10% can be achieved through the hard work of the athletic department staff. Finally, it is *timely* because the goal is to increase attendance by the end of the year. By utilizing the SMART goal principle, managers would be able to effectively create a plan of action to achieve the goal of increasing student attendance at home sporting events.

ORGANIZING

The organizing phase of the management process involves breaking down the total work that has to be completed into different jobs and creating a plan to coordinate how these jobs will be assigned to individuals and completed. This phase includes the creation of a formal structure in the organization that clearly outlines the chain of command and the different divisions of the organization.

The organizing phase involves determining what is needed to meet the organizational goals, who will be responsible for each area, and how it will be effectively accomplished. Often, organizations will create departments that are responsible for certain aspects of the event or organization (i.e., ticketing, marketing and promotions, facility management, concessions, and so forth).

As an example of the organizing phase, consider a YMCA that has decided to create a summer youth soccer camp. Some of the necessary tasks that need to be completed would include creating the marketing materials to recruit participants, hiring coaches, securing fields and checking them for safety, purchasing equipment, dividing participants into equal teams, communicating with participants/parents about practices and games, purchasing jerseys, and ensuring first aid on site in case of emergencies. These tasks would all need to be divided up and given deadlines to ensure the youth soccer camp will occur with minimal problems.

STAFFING

The staffing phase of the management process involves making sure there are enough staff members in the organization to achieve the organizational goals. It is crucial that the manager finds and hires the right people for the job.

When there is a need to hire someone new in the organization, the manager must create a job description to outline the position and the work that will be performed. This phase of the staffing process is known as the recruitment phase. The job description will list all of the candidate requirements, such as education, years of experience, and skills needed. Interested applicants will submit the requested documents (usually a resume, cover letter, and references) to the hiring manager or human resources. Human resource management is "essentially about first, finding the right person for the right job at the right time and, second, ensuring an appropriately trained and satisfied workforce" (Hoye, Smith, Nicholson, Stewart, & Westerbrook, 2009, p. 131). It is important for all managers to take the view that they are also human resource managers. They need to understand that good employees can give a company a competitive edge and can be the organization's greatest asset.

Once the applications have been received, the selection process begins. This process involves narrowing down the applicant pool to the individuals whom the organization would like to interview. Suitable candidates for the job are interviewed, and the manager must choose the individual whom he or she believes is the best fit for the open position. Ultimately, the best candidate is extended a job offer.

After the candidate accepts the job offer, it is the organization's responsibility to train the person to the job specifications, the organization culture, expectations, and so forth. It is the responsibility of the training manager and organization to effectively teach new employees all they will need to know to be successful.

While the employee is working for the organization, it is the organization's responsibility to retain that employee. The manager needs to establish a good work environment where employees are free to ask questions, feel valued, and believe they have the opportunity for growth and advancement. Employees who feel good about themselves and the work they are doing are more apt to stay with the organization than those who do not. Understanding this simple fact is important because it is quite costly to go through the search process for a new employee and spend the time and money associated with training that person. It is much more cost-effective to have employees stay with the organization.

An important part of staffing is securing volunteers to help run the event. A volunteer is "someone who willingly gave unpaid help, in the form of time, service or skills, through an organization or group" (Australian Bureau of Statistics, 2001, p. 44). Green and Chalip (2004) stated that within sport organizations and events, volunteers are "adding several hundred dollars of value per capita to the contribution that sport and recreation make to gross domestic product" (p. 49). Green and Chalip (2004) went on to state, "Volunteers have become particularly vital for the delivery of special events, as most events now depend to some degree on volunteers for event planning and operations" (p. 49).

Once an organization has figured out how many volunteers will be needed to successfully run the event, the focus turns to recruiting volunteers. To attract volunteers, the task must be something that appeals to individuals. Questions such as what is the nature of the event, what benefits will the volunteer receive, what is the level of commitment required, and what will the volunteer be required to do at the event will all need to be answered prior to recruiting volunteers.

After all of the volunteers have been secured, they must be given an introduction to the event, an explanation of what they will be expected to do, and training to be able to complete whatever job is asked of them. Having good volunteers can be an invaluable part of the event.

Staffing is a part of every level of the sport industry. In collegiate athletics, an athletic director must hire the coaches for all of the school's sports. When there is a coaching vacancy, the university must follow proper protocol of announcing the job. After the best candidates are selected for interviews, the athletic director must consider a variety of factors (including the current team, university climate, and previous experience) when deciding who is the best candidate for the job. Choosing the wrong person for the job could further set the program back, cause animosity on the team, and hurt

---

VIGNETTE 2-1

The Importance of Staffing

Hiring entry-level employees can be an exciting and stressful time for any manager. During the staffing phase of the management process, the manager may be in charge of creating the job description. The job description should be clear and thorough enough to provide the potential applicant with a good idea of the job at hand and the necessary qualifications to complete the job.

The following are components that a manager may want to put in the job description.

1. *Job title.* The title of the job should be listed at the top of the job description.
2. *Position description.* A one-sentence description of what the job does within the organization should be included.
3. *Major areas of responsibility.* Using bullet points, the major responsibilities of the position should be listed. For instance, how many people will the person in the position oversee or to whom will the person report? Each of the areas listed should be described in detail. This breakdown will give the potential applicant a good sense of what the job will entail.
4. *Required knowledge, skills, and abilities.* What does the applicant need to know prior to entering into this position? Does the applicant need

to know specific software packages? This section can be divided into required skills and preferred skills. The required skills must be met, and the preferred skills would be a bonus if the applicant possessed them.

5. *Education and experience.* Does the applicant need to have a bachelor's or a master's degree, or is a high school diploma or equivalency test sufficient to be successful in the position? Is it necessary to have experience in the field prior to applying for this position? If so, how many years of experience are required? Does the applicant need to be certified?

There are reasons for including each of these elements, and the organization should realize that including all of these elements may decrease the applicant pool. However, a smaller applicant pool that meets all the desired requirements would be preferred to a larger pool of unqualified candidates.

It is necessary that the manager create a clear job description that gives the potential applicant the required information to decide whether to apply for the position. Writing a thorough job description can be considered one of the first steps of the staffing phase of the management process.

---

future recruiting. And if that coach is fired, the whole process has to start over. This further illustrates the importance of staffing the right people for the job.

LEADING

Leading is the process of using social and informal processes to influence employees' performance. As a manager, you want to encourage and inspire your employees to strive for greatness. Leading involves wearing multiple hats and having multiple responsibilities. In this phase, the manager is responsible for directing, influencing, and motivating the employee. Managers must show their employees what to do and how to do it. Thus being a role model is incredibly important.

In addition, managers need to nurture and mentor their employees. Good managers understand that when their employees succeed, it is a positive reflection upon their managerial skills. Employees, especially new employees, need that mentorship and nurturing in order to flourish in their position and career path.

Communication may be the most important piece of the leading process. If you are not clear in your expectations of your employees or do not give them well-defined directions, the employees will not understand exactly what you expect of them. This could lead to feelings of frustration on behalf of the employees and may result in them losing faith in you as a leader.

Leading is necessary in all aspects of the sport industry. For example, if the Director of Ticket Operations for the Cleveland Cavaliers hires three new entry-level ticket staff employees, it is his or her responsibility to teach each of those employees what the job expectations are. In a position such as ticket sales, where the employee will hear the word "no" dozens of times a day, the manager (in this case the Director of Ticket Operations) will need to find ways to keep up morale and motivate new employees to persevere through all of the nos they hear each day. The manager will also need to teach the new employees his or her "tricks of the trade" and how to win the sale.

CONTROLLING

Controlling is the process of monitoring employees' performance and taking action to effect desired results. The controlling assessment is done in conjunction with the organization's goals, and corrective actions are taken to ensure goals will be met. If the controlling process is done well, it will help align the performance of individuals and groups with the short- and long-range goals of the organization.

This phase is necessary to hold employees accountable and provides the opportunity for the manager to provide feedback to employees about their performance. This feedback is necessary to help the employees grow and develop as industry professionals and to ensure they are progressing toward the overall organizational goals. Feedback is necessary at all levels of the industry and should be used as an opportunity to help the individual and not as a method of punishment. Managers could utilize certain strategies to provide constructive criticism, such as the use of collective language (e.g., "We need to determine . . .". Another option is the pro and con sandwich (e.g., "You are doing a really good job with . . .; however, we need to help you improve in . . . . Finally, you are really shining in . . . ."). In other words, the manager starts the conversation by saying something positive, follows that with something the employee can improve upon, and finishes with another positive statement. This process allows the manager to evaluate the expected performance and compare it to the actual performance of the employee.

The controlling phase is an important part of the management process. Providing oversight and feedback along the way will help keep all employees on task, which should assist the organization in meeting its overall goals. For instance, if you are managing a charity golf scramble, there will be many different areas to consider. As a staff, you will need to recruit golfers to play in the event, secure the golf course, obtain volunteers to help run the event, find sponsors, and obtain prizes for the winners, welcome packages, food and beverages for the golfers, marketing materials, and so on. Many other details also will need to be considered and finished prior to the event. It is important as the manager to make sure each staff member who is assigned to a specific area is on track and has not overlooked anything. Executing this phase of the management process will ensure that your charity golf scramble is a success and that you are proud of the event you executed.

Management Styles

In addition to the functions of management, each manager will have his or her own distinct management style. While everyone is certainly different, there are five specific types of management styles or philosophies that managers may adopt while in the workplace (see **Table 2-1**).

DEMOCRATIC

The democratic management style is a very open and participant-centered approach to management. These managers value their employees' opinions and desire their input in creating new ideas or enhancing current work practices. This approach requires that the manager listen to everyone and give their views consideration. It does not require the manager to do what the employees suggest. The manager is ultimately still in charge of making the decisions.

TABLE 2-1   Management Styles

Type of Style	Definition	Positives of Style	Drawbacks of Style
Democratic	Management is through an open and participant-centered approach.	Employees feel their voice is being heard by management.	This approach may not work well in situations where time is limited.
Autocratic	One person makes decisions for the group or organization.	New employees who do not know which tasks to perform can be more effectively utilized.	Managers may be perceived as bossy or uncaring toward employees' thoughts.
Persuasive	Manager is the decision maker and usually does so with limited input from others.	Decisions are made quickly and managed effectively.	Employees do not like being told what to do and what to believe in without giving input.
Paternalistic	Manager has overall control and expects directives to be followed when given but listens to and cares about the employees' social needs.	Employees feel that their needs are being met and their opinions are valued.	Manager is the one who ultimately makes the decision and may or may not take the advice of the employees when making those decisions.
Laissez-faire	Manager tells the employees what to do and gives them the freedom to go about completing the task.	Employees feel free to take control of a task and feel ownership of it.	Manager cannot provide regular feedback to the employees about their performance.

One benefit of this style of management is that employees appreciate their voice being heard by management. This may make the employee feel more connected and invested in the organization. It is also beneficial for management to hear the opinion of the people who may have the most knowledge. For instance, if a professional sport team has had a decrease in season ticket holder renewals, it would be best to speak directly to those involved in ticketing and sales to see if they have heard from the customers about why they decided not to renew their tickets. These are the employees with direct contact to the customers, so the information they have could be vital to understanding the customers' decision-making process regarding season tickets. It may also inform the organization as to what changes they need to implement to regain the customers who did not renew their tickets.

The democratic style may not work best in situations involving limited time. Due to the nature of this management style, spending too much time asking for input may lead to uncompleted projects or missed deadlines. Also, in some instances, employees may not have the required knowledge to make valuable contributions to the decision-making process.

AUTOCRATIC

The autocratic management style involves one person making decisions for the group or organization. In this style, the manager unilaterally delegates who is doing what task and when it needs to be accomplished. Staff members very seldom have a say or influence in the decision-making process.

This management style is most effective when new employees do not know which tasks to perform or which procedures to follow. Further, this style is useful when employees have not responded to any other leadership style the manager has exhibited.

While the autocratic management style can be very effective, the downside is that it can be perceived as bossy or uncaring toward employees' thoughts. This can foster an environment of resentment. Further, this style of management can lead to less creative solutions to problems since only one person has input.

PERSUASIVE

A persuasive management style is similar to an autocratic style. The manager is still the person making the decision and is usually doing so with limited input or influence from others. The primary difference is that in this management style, the manager spends time with each of his or her employees discussing why the decision was made and why it is the correct one. The manager attempts to convince or persuade the employees to buy into his or her way of thinking about the situation.

An advantage to this style of management is that decisions are made quickly and managed effectively. Employees are also clear on the chain of command and their role within the organization. This reduces any confusion on the part of the employee.

Disadvantages of this management style are that the employees may not trust management, employees do not like being told what to do and what to believe in without giving input, and employees may not feel a vested interest in the company, which may decrease their productivity.

PATERNALISTIC

The paternalistic management style is comparable to the autocratic style in that the manager has overall control and expects his or her directives to be followed when given to the employees. However, a primary difference between the two styles is that paternalistic managers listen to and care about the employees' social needs. The manager will listen to employees and ultimately make decisions that are best for them and the organization. The paternalistic manager will also take the time to explain to the employees why he or she made certain decisions.

A benefit of this approach is that employees feel that their needs are being met and their opinions are valued. Further, the communication that occurs between the manager and employee can lead to increased motivation for the employee.

The main drawback to this management style is that it is still quite autocratic in nature. The manager is the one who ultimately makes the decisions, and he or she may or may not take the advice of his or her employees when making those decisions. Employees who work under a paternalistic manager may also grow to be very dependent on the manager to make all necessary decisions, which can limit their independent or creative thinking.

LAISSEZ-FAIRE

A manager who adopts the laissez-faire management style tells the employees what to do and gives them the freedom to go about completing the task. This management style is best when the employees are highly trained and very competent. Employees must be self-motivated to ensure the work is accomplished in a timely manner.

Benefits of this management style are that employees feel free to take control of a task and feel ownership of it. Using the laissez-faire approach also shows trust in the employees by the manager. Avoiding micromanaging the staff can lead to improved motivation and positive feelings toward the manager and organization.

Drawbacks of the laissez-fair management style are that the manager cannot provide regular feedback to the employees about their performance. Also, employees may feel neglected with this approach since the manager is not consistently around checking in on the progress that is being made on the task.

Leadership

According to Barrow (1977), **leadership** is "the behavioral process of influencing individuals and groups toward a common goal" (p. 232). Thus, leaders are people who motivate and influence the work of others in a positive manner to achieve the organization's goals and objectives. Leadership is a complex set of characteristics and personal attributes that are used to get employees to believe in the leader and want to execute the leader's assignments.

Leaders and managers are not the same thing. A leader does not necessarily have to be the manager, and a manager is not always a leader. While leading is one of the five aspects of the management process, not everyone is able to be an effective leader.

leadership The process of influencing individuals or groups of people to work toward a shared goal.

EFFECTIVE LEADERSHIP GUIDELINES

There are several guidelines that one must follow in order to be an effective leader:

- Lead by example.
- Delegate.
- Communicate.
- Be passionate.
- Demonstrate competence and knowledge.
- Know your staff.
- Be creative.
- Be loyal.

In many ways, leadership is a process that is similar to management. Leadership and management both involve influence, working with people, and effective goal management (Northouse, 2013). However, leadership and management also differ. Management is about "seeking order and stability; leadership is about seeking adaptive and constructive change" (Northouse, 2013, p. 13). While it is not necessary to be the manager to be a leader, it is important that if you are managing a team of individuals, you exhibit leadership characteristics in order to positively influence the people you are working with to achieve the goals you have set forth.

SUMMARY

This chapter has examined the functions of the management process, the different management styles and the benefits and drawbacks of each style, and the differences between a leader and a manager. A manager is a person whose job involves carrying out of the five primary functions of the management process: planning, organizing, staffing, leading, and controlling. These five main functions can be the difference between running an organization or event that is successful and one that is unsuccessful.

The manager will complete the functions of the management process in his or her own distinct management style. Generally, a manager will adopt one of five management styles: democratic, autocratic, persuasive, paternalistic, or laissez-faire. Leaders are individuals who encourage and influence the work of others in a positive approach to achieve the organization's goals and objectives. While some of the characteristics of a leader and a manager are the same, a leader and a manager are not the same thing. A leader does not have to be the manager, and a manager is not always a leader.

DISCUSSION QUESTIONS

1. What are the five functions of the management process? How would a manager working in a YMCA summer camp program implement these functions?
2. Which of the management styles do you feel would be the best method to use when working for a minor league baseball team?
3. Describe your management philosophy. How does this align with your career aspirations?

Case STUDY

Running a Youth Sport Camp

A company that produces youth summer sport camps instructed by professional athletes is looking to hire a new event director to oversee 5 of the 23 youth sport camps. The job description includes planning the camp, recruiting participants, handling the day-of operations of the camp, executing sponsorship agreements, assisting in marketing efforts, and working within the budget.

Although the event director will be new to this organization, he or she will be responsible for executing the youth sport camps to the standard of excellence for which the organization is known. The organization has been around since 2000, runs over 30 professional athlete and collegiate coach youth sport camps, and has annual revenue of over $5 million.

The event director is responsible for leading 5 part-time staff members and approximately 30 volunteers for each camp. While the staff members have a varied amount of experience working with the organization (between 2 and 5 years), each of the volunteers has never worked for the organization or at an event like this. The issue of volunteers is one of great importance because previously there were problems with some volunteers. These volunteers were unprofessional, arrived late, took pictures of the athletes, and asked for autographs, among other things.

Because of the high-profile nature of the athletes whose names are attached to these camps, failure is not an option.

1. Evaluate the pros and cons of using each of the management styles in this situation.
2. What management style do you think the event director should apply in this situation?
3. Do you think the management style needs to change after the event director has been in that role for 3 or more years?
4. How should the event director ensure that all of the volunteers recruited remain professional throughout the entire camp?

REFERENCES

Australian Bureau of Statistics. (2001). *Voluntary work, 2000* (No. 4441.0). Canberra: Author.

Barrow, J. C. (1977). The variables of leadership: A review and conceptual framework. *Academy of Management Review, 2,* 231–251.

Chelladurai, P. (2001). *Managing organizations for sport and physical activity: A systems perspective.* Scottsdale, AZ: Holcomb Hathaway Publishers.

Green, B. C., & Chalip, L. (2004). Paths to volunteer commitment: Lessons from the Sydney Olympic Games. In R. A. Stebbins & M. Graham (Eds.), *Volunteering as leisure. Leisure as volunteering. An international assessment* (pp. 49–67). Wallingford: CABI Publishing.

Hoye, R., Smith, A., Nicholson, M., Stewart, B., & Westerbrook, H. (2009). *Sport management: Principles and applications* (2nd ed.). New York, NY: Routledge.

Mullin, B. J. (1980). Sport management: The nature and utility of the concept. *Arena Review, 4*(3), 1–11.

North American Society for Sport Management. (2000). History. Retrieved from http://www.nassm.com/InfoAbout/NASSM/History

Northouse, P. G. (2013). *Leadership: Theory and practice.* Los Angeles, CA: Sage Publications.

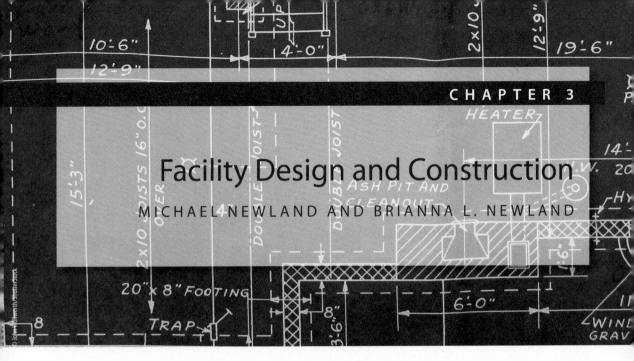

CHAPTER 3

Facility Design and Construction

MICHAEL NEWLAND AND BRIANNA L. NEWLAND

CHAPTER OBJECTIVES

Upon completion of this chapter, the reader will be able to:

1. Describe the process of facility design and construction
2. Demonstrate proficiency in the interrelated steps involved in planning, programming, site selection, and designing
3. Discuss the estimating and bidding processes and the construction of the facility

CHAPTER OVERVIEW

This chapter will explore the elements of sport facility design and construction. Facility development starts with a plan, which creates a program that defines the site selection, develops the drawings, constructs the facility, and progresses through a set of interrelated steps until the product is completed. This chapter will outline the main components of this process, including site selection and evaluation, planning and design, the estimation of construction costs, the bidding of the work, and the construction process. Green construction, design, and issues will also be addressed in this chapter.

IndustryVOICE

Dev Pathik—CEO and Founder, The Sports Facilities Advisory

© Maureen Jeffery

The Sports Facilities Advisory (SFA), based in Clearwater, Florida, provides services to new and existing sport and recreation center operators. SFA's purpose is to serve an array of entities—from private and/or retail developers to educational institutions and government agencies—by providing a range of services to plan, open, manage, or optimize sport facilities. My role in the organization as Founder and Chief Executive Officer (CEO) is to provide strategic guidance and leadership to the organization while offering owners and communities a suite of planning and management services.

My career path was not as linear as that of many students. I graduated from the University of Maryland with a degree in psychology with a focus on team development. I began my career as a corporate advisor working with executive teams to develop senior management and team culture. As I continued to develop team-building centers within corporations, organizations within the youth and amateur sport facility marketplace began to seek my advice and consult on how to create team-building and leadership centers within their facilities. These opportunities exposed a problem in the marketplace in that facility managers and/or owners did not have the adequate skill sets to build and/or maintain these venues. In response to this problem, my team of consultants invested in the creation of SFA, which has now served a portfolio totalling $4 billion.

Students interested in a more entrepreneurial position, or even achieving a high-ranking position like CEO, really need to understand the numbers.

While there is a great deal individuals can learn on the job, one skill set that will benefit the student in the future is a clear understanding of balance sheets, accounting, and other financial statements. As a psychology major, I did not have the opportunity to build this knowledge foundation through coursework. When I started my business, it quickly became apparent just how important financials were in decision making, and I had to learn fast. I would urge students to really focus on basic business knowledge, finance, and accounting for success.

When hiring for entry-level positions, graduates who are proficient in Microsoft Excel and have strong research and analytical skills are attractive to SFA. We also look for hard workers with positive attitudes who are willing to learn. These skill sets allow a new hire to quickly progress from a research assistant or business analyst to a consultant and advisor, which is a great career path. For our organization, graduates really need to understand basic accounting and finance. Interestingly, students don't realize the size and scope of the youth and amateur sport industry. They instead tend to pursue a career in professional and/or collegiate sports. This highly competitive market is saturated with talent, and that marketplace is ultimately smaller than youth and amateur sport. There are billions of dollars in development available in youth and amateur sport. If we were consulting for professional stadiums and arenas only, there would be limited "new" opportunities; there just aren't enough teams! So, in the end, there are a number of missed opportunities if students don't consider the youth and amateur aspect of sport management.

The biggest mistake I see in this industry is the "if you build it, they will come" mentality. The facility managers and municipalities that are often involved with these venues are so driven by a passion for sport that they forget about profitability or the risks involved. They tend to fill the facility with rentals rather than programming. "Rentals" typically bring in $X in revenue, whereas programming consisting of leagues, tournaments, events, etc., that are run "in-house" by facility-paid staff tends to result in $3X in revenue. Further, these facilities take on too much debt and senior management either fails to recognize this as a problem or learns about it too late. The biggest challenge facing facilities in the youth and amateur sports market is that there are a number of people who are passionate about sport but don't have strategic leadership experience or skills. These managers think of sport coaching as leadership, and it *is*, but not the type of business leadership that is necessary to run a $10, $20, or $30 million facility. A challenge for us is to develop leadership skills in managers with sport and/or coaching backgrounds who have limited business experience.

A current trend in the youth and amateur facility management area is the large growth in funding of youth sport facilities and the shift toward privatization and professionalization. In the near future, I foresee a shift of management out of the hands of schools and into those of private operators. A potential problem I expect is that when the organization is driven by profit, it will limit access for low-income and rural athletes. If this shift does occur, we will have to consider access and opportunities for underserved populations. With that being said, privatization can also increase opportunity. There is a great deal of Wall Street money that has found or is finding its way into the marketplace, which will bring higher quality facilities with outsourced professional management. This can have a positive impact on youth sport as the facilities are run more effectively and efficiently via professionally trained staff.

There is much to consider with the design–build of facilities. Our design–build services help customers determine how much physical space is necessary based on proposed sport programs and offerings. Our architect on staff helps develop the plans based on space, programming, and financial forecasting. We then facilitate the process through a local design firm and general contractor who then manages the project to completion. It is important to choose a design firm and general contractor who understand the demands of sport. Because of the seasonality of sport, it is important that deadlines are met so that time is not lost on the season. Firms might also not understand how certain material choices can impact the sport. It is important to choose a firm that has worked on sport facilities to truly understand the intricacies and complexities of sport.

Introduction

Two key elements to the successful construction of a sport facility are controlling costs and keeping the project on schedule. It is imperative that a sport manager not only understand the aspects of facility design and build, but also the cost to maintain the facility once it is built. This chapter will begin to develop a foundation of knowledge by focusing on the facilitation of design and construction.

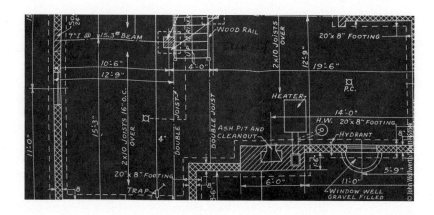

Estimating Costs and Budgeting

pro forma A statement that summarizes the projected future status of a company and that is used as the foundation for financial planning for an organization or project.

fixed cost An expense that does not change as a function of the business activity.

variable cost An expense that changes based on the volume of business activity.

Before a sport facility can be built, the owner must acquire funding for the project. To attain the necessary capital, the owner must estimate the costs to maintain the completed venue. Preparing a budget for a proposed project begins with the basics of weighing the potential expenses against the projected revenue to determine the feasibility of a profitable sporting facility. To calculate the initial costs of a project, all of the estimated costs, including fixed and variable costs, are prepared in a document called a **pro forma** (**Figure 3-1**). Pro forma statements summarize the projected future status of a company and are the foundation for financial planning for an organization or project (Ross, Westerman, & Jordan, 2008). They are vital for determining valuation and are required by the bank to secure funding for the project when there is no financial history. The **fixed costs** are expenses that do not change as a function of the business activity and include such items as the rent, operations, advertising, and insurance. The **variable costs** are volume-related and include labor, cost of goods sold, and raw materials, which are typically managed payouts based on use of the facility and the number of part-time staff and/or subcontractors required at any one time. The pro forma can help managers evaluate new ventures or new strategic initiatives, such as the design and build of a new sporting facility.

The potential revenue streams for the sport facility include monthly rental fees from sport teams and venue rental fees for entertainment events, concession and merchandise sales, and other additional revenue, such as

SAMPLE PROFORMA

Project Name:

	Budget		Actual	SOURCES	Budget		Actual
USES							
Construction				TRF Loan	$ 3,500,000		3,500,000
Demolition	$	150,000	135,750	Other: Investment	$ 250,000		250,000
Environmental Clearances	$	17,000	18,400	Other	$ -		-
Hard Costs	$	3,000,000	3,027,500	Other	$ -		-
Contractor Fee	$	50,000	50,000	Developer Equity During Construction	$ 600,000		600,000
Construction Contingency	$	100,000	125,000				
Construction Management	$	90,000	90,825	**TOTAL PROJECT SOURCES**	$ 4,350,000	$	4,350,000
Other	$	-	-				
Subtotal: Construction	$	3,407,000	3,447,475				
Professional Fees				Developer Equity During Construction:			
Appraisal	$	15,000	16,025	Construction Deferrals (Attorney, Marketing/Advertising, Developer Fee):	$600,000		$600,000
Architect	$	240,000	242,200	Cash needed:	$92,000		$89,750
Attorney	$	10,000	10,000	Interest (assume 50% of loan outstanding during the construction term):	$ 508,000.00	$	$510,250
				Requested Interest Rate (insert a rate 5.5%):			
Cost Cert/Audit	$	7,500	7,500		$ 38,500.00	$	38,500.00
Engineer	$	240,000	242,200				
Environmental Consultant	$	5,000	5,000				
Soil Investigation	$	8,000	7,500				
Surveyor	$	4,000	4,000				
Marketing/Advertising	$	10,000	9,750				
Other	$	-	2,000				
Subtotal: Professional Fees	$	539,500	546,175				
Carrying Costs & Other Project Fees							
Application Fees	$	350	500				
Inspections	$	7,500	7,500				
Interest Costs	$	210,000	192,500				
Bank Fees	$	5,000	4,300				
Property Insurance	$	2,500	2,650				
Real Estate Taxes	$	27,000	21,358				
Title Insurance & Recording	$	800	900				
Other	$	-	-				
Subtotal: Carrying Costs & Other Project Fees	$	253,150	229,708				
Developer Fee	$	72,000	70,000				
TOTAL PROJECT COST	$	4,271,650	4,293,358				

FIGURE 3-1   Example Pro Forma

venue tours. Most commonly, private organizations own and build a sport venue and lease it to sport organizations or even promoters. For example, the Barclays Center in Brooklyn, New York, is owned by the real estate developer Forest City Ratner Companies (FCRC); it is leased by the Brooklyn Nets (basketball) and is the home (leased by) the New York Islanders (hockey) as of 2014. The estimation of revenue streams should be conservative at the outset, as it is common to fall short of reaching goals. This consideration is important if sport managers are also responsible for managing stakeholder expectations for the construction project.

Estimating Construction Costs

soft cost A cost that is not directly related to the physical construction of the project and commonly occurs prior to the project; also called indirect cost.

hard cost A direct cost specifically related to the project.

Once the budget for the facility has been estimated and the preliminary pro forma developed, the construction costs can be estimated. Soft and hard costs are common construction terms used to describe the expenses associated specifically with the construction project and should not be confused with the fixed and variable costs the completed facility will incur, as described previously. The **soft costs**, often referred to as indirect costs, are not directly related to the physical construction of the project and commonly occur prior to the project. These costs can include legal fees, permits, real estate commissions and fees, financing fees, insurance, loans, design fees, and equipment rental fees. The **hard costs**, in contrast, are direct costs specifically related to construction, including land cost, labor, materials, equipment, basic building services, and mechanical and electrical services. These costs are directly affected by the decisions made by the contractor and design team working on the project, so it is very important to closely supervise this process to maintain construction costs overall.

To determine the costs of the proposed construction project, research must be conducted on the costs of available sites (land), building design, building per square foot, materials, labor, and utilities. Due diligence is of utmost importance! It is wise to investigate the costs of similar sites and buildings by visiting other facilities, asking questions, and seeking professional advice from seasoned contractors. A very detailed and accurate assessment of the costs is imperative for an appropriate project budget estimate. Once the pricing of each component is complete and the pro forma presents a profitable project, financing can be acquired to proceed (if necessary).

Site Selection

Site selection is important because a good site location will contribute to the attraction of future patrons to the sport facility. Therefore, a dedicated site search for land and location that has potential to produce anticipated revenues is key to future success.

The planning phase for the facility involves defining the components the facility will offer. Once the facility requirements have been established, a space planner can produce **schematic drawings** that depict the proposed building layout. These schematics exhibit the size of the facility, which then defines maximum capacity and parking requirements. If the facility is not properly planned with defined capacities, it will be impossible to determine the amount of land required to build. For example, the parking lot supporting a building is based on the capacity of patrons permitted in the building. If you do not properly calculate capacity and provide sufficient parking spaces, the amount of patrons able to access the building will be reduced. Having to access off-site parking will inhibit customer service and potentially lead to dissatisfaction from future patrons. Local government agencies provide resources and codes that delineate parking specifications based on capacity for a proposed building. A sound plan and schematics that define the facility's requirements is vital to properly determine the size of your site.

It could prove useful to hire a real estate professional to assist in the search for a site. **Realtors** are not only familiar with the zoning requirements for the proposed facility, but they can also provide the area demographics and traffic volumes around the site location. Accessibility to the site is paramount; a facility that patrons cannot see or easily access can hinder future success!

It is likely that numerous sites are available but are not conducive to building large facilities. The most important function of a site is that it has the capacity to house the building with appropriate parking and the open space that will be designated by local and state stipulations. Another important consideration is patron (and construction) access to the site and traffic flow in and out of the area (Ganaway, 2006). Some questions to consider include the following:

- Is the site near or off major interstates or highways?
- Can the site be accessed from all directions or at least from two opposing directions?
- Can the surrounding infrastructure handle heavy traffic?

schematic drawing
A drawing that exhibits the size of the facility and assists in defining the maximum capacity of land needed to build.

realtor An expert in real estate who can assist in identifying land options, demographics, and traffic volumes of an area, as well as zoning requirements for specific areas.

TIP

It can be very costly to add traffic lights if they are not present and there are code stipulations that require them at the entry/exit points. This cost can be a detriment to the budget if not accounted for in the estimating phase.

topographical report
A survey of the land that identifies any existing buildings, site surface evaluations, and availability of electrical, sewer, water, and gas services.

geotechnical report
A report of the soil conditions that dictate what materials are necessary to support the foundation for the proposed building as well as provisions for drainage of surface and runoff water that can affect the drying time of certain materials.

Furthermore, considering site factors such as multiple entry and exit points, traffic lights, and dedicated turn lanes (or the capability to add them during the construction phase) is extremely important.

There are a few important reports that should be reviewed prior to acquiring the land. First is a **topographical report**, which will show the lot corners, any existing buildings, site surface elevations, finished floor elevations, manholes, storm and sanitary pipes, utility poles, fire hydrants, trees, and any other important objects affecting the site (Ganaway, 2006). The availability of electrical, sewer, water, and gas connections on the site is crucial, as adding them can be a substantial cost. The topographical survey can be compared to the proposed schematics of the proposed site to better understand construction needs.

Second, a **geotechnical report** should also be generated to ensure that the site can support the sport facility foundation. The geotechnical report will indicate soil conditions that dictate what materials are necessary to support the foundation for the proposed building. In addition to the soil conditions, the geotechnical report will provide provisions for drainage of surface and runoff water that can affect the drying time of certain materials (Ganaway, 2006). Nonporous soils may require several days to dry before work can continue (in case of poor weather), and soft/unsuitable soils will incur a greater expense for additional support materials. Knowing the site conditions and/or constraints can provide necessary information to better assess the construction budget estimates, which can help with determining if the site is worth the financial risk.

Once the information is collected, the total value of the site can be assessed to determine if the purchase meets not only the needs for the project, but also the estimates that were presented in the pro forma.

Design Process

By defining the components for the site schematics, a framework is established for the design elements to commence. Once a site that can support the build requirements by accommodating the size of the facility is found, a design firm can be approached to begin the next phase of the project.

Hiring a design firm that is adept in design of sport facilities is essential. A worldwide leader in the field of sport facility design is Populous. Founded in 1983, Populous has built a reputation for designing innovative sport facilities. A few examples of sites/events on which Populous has worked include the 2014 Sochi Olympic Games, the 2012 London Olympic Games, Texas A&M's Kyle Field (redevelopment), the Melbourne Cricket Ground, and Yankee Stadium. It is recommended that you visit the Populous website (www.populous.com) for an extensive (and impressive) list of their projects. Referrals and recommendations from various sources for design firms are helpful, but it is crucial that the firm of choice meet the needs of the sport organization, listen closely, and provide economical services. It is beneficial to interview up to four firms to determine fit and to secure a proposal that includes concept designs and total fees prior to making an informed decision. Reviewing a portfolio of recent and past projects can build confidence that the firm will deliver the right solutions for the project. The pro forma will designate the amount allocated to design the facility. The contract with the design firm must stipulate that the facility will be designed based on the established budget. The designer's contract should include the following:

> **TIP**
>
> Today, storm water (rain water) is required to be held on-site, so building a retention system is a necessary expense that must be built into the project budget. A designer will be able to provide the requirements when laying out the site. A retention system can be an area that holds water in a lake or along the roadways via the construction of a ditch.

- Design costs for schematic, design development, and contract drawings
- Costs for the civil engineer and the topographical and geotechnical reports
- Landscape design costs for landscaping, parking, walks, and retention systems
- Mechanical, plumbing, electrical, and fire protection drawings
- Details regarding acquirement of proper permit issuance
- Details regarding construction administration (i.e., answer contractor questions and provide field verification to ensure the contractor is constructing the building per the drawings)
- Details regarding closeout of the project and final punch list for final repairs prior to acceptance

Once the design firm has been retained, work can begin on the schematic drawings, which determine the function of the building and the layouts, showing the proposed components and required spaces per code. Buildings grow in size as patron counts are established, which then determines the number of elements, such as bathroom fixtures, shower facility sizes (such as for locker rooms), and ancillary spaces, such as mechanical and electrical rooms (which are required). As the building grows in size, costs will also rise. It is important to stay true to the pro forma in order to contain costs and keep the project on track.

After the planning/schematic drawings have been developed and a site has been selected, the architecture and engineering firm can finalize the drawings based on the information attained from the finalized site. This information includes, but is not limited to, the allowable footage distances from the roadway to the front of the property, the side yards, and the rear of the site. Many local codes enforce distances from the road to building. The added space outside of the building footprint is typically used for parking and open space requirements dictated by the local government and community. A good design group will set the building where parking is efficient and allows for easy access to the building as well as in and out of the property.

As the drawings are being finalized, the design firm will confirm and review the components and adjacencies to ensure compliance with the original design plans. Material selections, paint colors, and flooring materials are confirmed and implemented into the drawings. This is typically when modifications are discussed and agreed upon by both parties. Disagreements are often encountered in the design of the exterior of the facility, with the designers possibly wanting to introduce innovative elements and expensive materials to achieve a certain look. Many design firms receive awards for exterior design. While creativity can win awards, it comes at a price. Therefore, it is beneficial to be thorough during the exterior design phase to ensure the original design is conceived to specifications to avoid running over budget and delaying construction.

It can take 8 to 12 months to produce a set of drawings and obtain permits before construction can commence. Acquiring the construction permits varies by local code officials, which can greatly impact the project start date *and* can cause delays if changes have to be made once construction begins. Construction permits generally include a site layout plan that specifically designates the locations of temporary fencing, temporary electrical feeds, temporary toilets, and silt fencing. **Silt fencing** is used to keep any debris from passing from the site to any areas beyond the construction zone. The site

silt fencing Temporary fencing used to keep any debris from passing from the site to any areas beyond the construction zone.

layout plan is submitted early in the design process so that site work can begin before the final construction permits are obtained. Building permits involve an understanding of the local building codes (as determined by the governing entity) and a full review by local officials on all aspects of the design, including the foundations, superstructure (the building itself), façade materials, mechanical elements, plumbing elements, electrical elements, and fire protection. The drawings are checked for compliance with local building codes, and permits are granted once all standards are met. In most cases, the mechanical, electrical, and plumbing elements as well as the fire protection are often delegated to subcontractors who submit and receive their own permits for the project. This task is typically done by the subcontractors because they are required to demonstrate licensure to complete the work as part of the permitting process. Therefore, it is important to build contingency plans and delays into the overall timeline of the project because a number of delays can occur when relying on multiple parties to obtain permits. Keep in mind that any delay or modification to the original plans will cost not only time but money as well.

Construction Process

As the design phase commences, the search should begin for the contractor who will build the facility. As with the design groups, conduct interviews with local contractors that have been recommended or have built a strong reputation for constructing similar projects in the area. It is wise to choose three to four potential contractors to provide a project estimate based on the uncompleted drawings provided by the designer. By requesting this proposal, one can begin to approximate the cost to build as well as management fees and overhead expenses. The fees and allowances for unknown costs not shown on the drawings are generally negotiable with the contractor. A contractor should be selected prior to the finalization of the design to provide recommendations that identify cost reduction, enhance constructability, streamline the construction processes, and improve quality (Arsht, 2003).

A review of the contractor's pricing proposal can highlight when it is appropriate (or necessary) to use higher quality materials and/or when savings can be recouped using lower grade elements. Engineering reviews can provide valuable information on materials if follow-up is necessary. For a high-use venue, like a sport facility, the choice of materials is paramount as they must endure the daily wear and tear and high volume of traffic. The installation of a ceramic tile or stone entry guarantees a greater number of years of use, whereas a vinyl tile or carpet (that will provide an initial clean look) will deteriorate quickly. Therefore, spending more at the outset on materials that can withstand greater wear and tear will provide cost savings in the long term. More durable materials are recommended for locker rooms, showers, sport-specific training areas, swimming pool areas, and other high-use, high-traffic areas within the sport facility. Longevity is key, requiring more costly materials. However, it might be more costly to install new materials earlier than anticipated, so it is important to choose materials wisely. It is advisable to have the architect select the appropriate materials for the project, as this individual will be most educated on the durability and cost of materials.

For the construction of large facilities, it is common to receive a minimum of four contractor bids, with the lowest bid typically winning the project. Often, when the contractor is involved in the final design phase, the outcome is a better project at a lower cost. The contractor provides valuable insight and addresses problematic areas as the drawings are finalized, which tends to minimize the need for redesign; reduce change orders during construction; since many of the questionable areas are addressed early on; and allow for collaboration among professionals early in the project (Arsht, 2003).

As with the design phase, a construction phase is also established in accordance with the terms of a contract that will contain provisions defining the costs and protecting the owner from potential issues that can arise throughout the project (Rounds, 2011). The contract should clearly define that the facility will be constructed according to the drawings for a specific cost over the duration of a set timeline, with agreed-upon materials and high-quality workmanship, all while providing a safe site for workers. Full compliance with the contract terms will lead to a successful project. The drawings for construction typically include the interior layouts for equipment and furniture, but these items are usually not provided by the contractor, which will be noted in the contract. Therefore, during the construction phase, the owner must meet with equipment and furniture vendors to finalize deliveries for installation.

The timeline for the construction of a facility depends not only on the size of the facility, but also on the availability and delivery of supplies, equipment, and materials. Unique building materials can delay the project, so one must consider the lead time for materials and components when reviewing and setting the construction schedule. Construction projects typically take

VIGNETTE 3-1

Qatar World Cup 2022

Many were skeptical when the decision to award the 2022 World Cup to Qatar was made. Not only did the country not have the required infrastructure, it is also not known to have any soccer tradition. With reports of allegations by the International Trade Union Confederation (ITUC) of more than 1200 migrant worker deaths (Manfred, 2014) and rampant corruption, the organizing committee is off to a rough start. It is estimated that Qatar will spend over $200 billion to build the 12 stadiums and supporting infrastructure, which includes complete cities, not just hotels, restaurants, medical facilities, and other necessary structures. Further, the futuristic and innovative designs that won them the bid are not possible, according to the design firm Populous (Associated Press, 2011). Avoiding such problems is precisely why feasibility studies are conducted and well-developed pro formas are necessary before any bids are conducted and building begins!

8 to 12 months to complete, so this time frame, like the design time, must be carefully planned for in the overall schedule in order to meet the deadline for the grand opening of the facility.

As construction commences, there will be a number of meetings on a weekly basis with both the designer and the contractor to review any questions that arise. The owner will be expected to make decisions on how to proceed based on the professional advice and guidance offered by the designer. It is important that any questions be addressed in a timely manner to avoid construction delays. Therefore, it is extremely important to attend project meetings to address these questions and also modify the construction schedule based on the progress (or lack thereof) of the contractor. If the project is lagging, then the contractor should produce tactics to restore the timeline without affecting quality, cost, and worker safety. These meetings are also a means for the designer to review completed work to verify that construction complies with the design plans within the scope of the local codes. On a monthly basis, the owner should conduct a review of the contractor's pay requests with the designer to verify that the work billed has been completed. The designer should approve the invoices with an accurate account of completed work prior to dispensing pay.

As construction reaches completion, the contractor will begin to develop the **operation and maintenance manuals (O&M manuals)**, which will contain pertinent information for the facility manager to maintain the building. These manuals provide detailed information on the management of the new systems in addition to the maintenance and repair of equipment. Additionally, all warranties on materials and components built into the facility will be provided.

The final construction site should be left to the satisfaction of the designer and owner. Once approval is obtained, the designer approves the documents that provide the contractor clearance for final payment. At this time, a final lien waver is issued to ensure the contractor pays all of the subcontractors and suppliers on the project. This is a required document needed to release final payment.

operation and maintenance manual (O&M manual) A collection of documents that contain pertinent information to maintain the building by providing detailed information on the management of the new systems in addition to the maintenance and repair of equipment.

Insurance

Insurance is a necessity to build. The designer and contractor must carry the appropriate insurances when designing and building a project, which can be easily verified in the vetting stages. A design firm is required to have sufficient **liability insurance** to guarantee against failure of the architecture and engineering of the building in the event it collapses after construction. Architects and engineers carry liability insurance to guard against perilous events for which they are at fault. It is in the owner's best interest to have an attorney review these details to ensure there is no liability to the owner prior to, during, and after construction. In addition to liability, contractors also carry insurances that protect against accidents or injuries that may occur during construction for which the contractor is at fault.

The owner must acquire insurance immediately upon purchasing the site. The types of insurance generally include liability insurance and builder's

liability insurance A form of general insurance that protects the insured from risks of liabilities imposed by lawsuits or similar claims.

risk insurance. These two insurance policies protect the owner during construction against theft of materials on the site, fire, and destruction of the constructed building by an **act of God** (which is typically a coverage not provided by the general contractor). This insurance also protects the owner from injuries on the site not associated with the actual construction of the project. The general contractor is also required to carry insurance to protect the owner from any liability of any construction-related injuries of the contracted or subcontracted workers. These insurances protect the owner from injuries incurred on site prior to, during, and following construction. Reducing risk by keeping the site free from debris and anything that can harm a person is important. The contractor in most cases will fence the site as soon as construction begins to alleviate any potential issues from outside parties. Greater detail on risk management is provided in the "Risk Management" chapter.

act of God An instance of uncontrollable natural forces (often used in insurance claims).

Green Construction and LEED Certification

The design, construction, building, and maintenance of facilities involve a great deal of energy, water, and other resources that create considerable waste and impact the environment and ecosystem (Environmental Protection Agency [EPA], 2012). For this reason, green building has been implemented and is now a primary aspect of the design and construction program. A typical green design–build tends to carefully select sites to minimize the impact on the surrounding environment, use renewable and/or energy conservation techniques and natural resources, conserve water, incorporate proper storm water management and limit disruption of natural watershed functions, and use low-volatile organic compound products and proper ventilation practices to improve indoor environment quality (EPA, 2012).

Designers today have a host of specified materials and techniques that are renewable and reusable and often take care to install mechanical and electrical systems that reduce

© Alexey Makushin/iStock/Thinkstock

pervious material
A material that allows water to soak naturally into the ground.

impervious surface
A surface, such as cement pavement, that prevents precipitation from naturally soaking into the ground, causing water to run rapidly into storm drains, sewer systems, and drainage ditches.

Environmental Protection Agency (EPA) The U.S. federal agency responsible for protecting the environment and human health as it relates to the environment.

waste diversion The prevention/reduction of generated waste through recycling, reuse, or composting.

LEED certification A green building certification program that recognizes best-in-class building strategies and practices. LEED stands for Leadership in Energy and Environmental Design.

our carbon footprint and are energy efficient. For example, the design of light-colored roofing materials and use of **pervious materials** on the site are common actions meant to address a green building program. The light-colored roofing materials allow for less heat transfer on the building, which reduces air-conditioning costs. The pervious materials allow water to escape from the building or site, which allows the water to soak naturally into the ground. **Impervious surfaces**, such as cement pavement, prevent precipitation from naturally soaking into the ground, causing water to run rapidly into storm drains, sewer systems, and drainage ditches (EPA, 2012). According to the **Environmental Protection Agency (EPA)**, this can cause a number of problems, including:

- Downstream flooding
- Stream bank erosion
- Increased turbidity (muddiness created by stirred-up sediment) from erosion
- Habitat destruction
- Changes in the stream flow hydrograph (a graph that displays the flow rate of a stream over a period of time)
- Combined sewer overflows
- Infrastructure damage
- Contaminated streams, rivers, and coastal water

Most construction sites also use some type of **waste diversion**, which is the prevention or reduction of generated waste through recycling, reuse, or composting (EPA, 2012). Waste from a construction project is typically divided and parceled into separate containers designated for immediate reuse, potential reuse, and landfill disposal. Waste diversion generates a number of environmental, financial, and social benefits to the owner of the construction site as well as the community, including energy conservation, reduced disposal costs, and a reduced burden on landfills.

Choosing to purchase recycled materials is also a way to incorporate green elements. For example, rubber products and carpeting typically have recycled content. Choosing to buy products and materials within a close proximity of your project reduces the carbon footprint by limiting emissions released through transportation. There are numerous ways to insert green building elements into a project in order to lessen the impact on the environment while developing a strong and economical building program. **LEED certification** is a great way of making sure construction projects maintain environmentally ethical building and waste disposal standards. LEED stands for Leadership in Energy and Environmental Design. This certification is required in most states. The architect will most likely manage the LEED certification requirements for a project.

SUMMARY

This chapter has discussed the importance of proper planning and management of a design–build project. Successful execution of the design–build plan will occur through careful research of contractors who can bid on and deliver the best project based on the owner's pro forma. Considering ways to incorporate green materials and design elements is critical and often required in the building of new facilities. A good sport manager will choose a design firm and contractors who are well versed in these requirements.

DISCUSSION QUESTIONS

1. Your city council has decided to build a new indoor sport facility specifically for basketball, tennis, and soccer. What are the first three steps in the process to consider?
2. What green design–build elements must be considered for a skate park that would not be necessary for a baseball field?
3. There are a number of green aspects to consider when building a new facility. Discuss three main issues that can lead to problems if not considered early in the design–build phase.
4. Why is insurance so important on a job site?

Case Study

Building a Community Sport Facility

You are the director of a sport and recreation center in a midsized suburban city. A member of the city council has approached you with a new vision for sport in the community. The new vision includes developing a new outdoor sport facility that includes softball and baseball fields, soccer fields, hike and bike trails, basketball and tennis courts, and an outdoor swimming pool. There are a number of objectives the city council hopes to meet with this new sport facility. First, the community leaders want to provide more access and opportunity for sport for children, adults, and seniors in the community. The council wants active leagues for all ages for the sports that could be offered in the new facility. Second, the council wants to attract visitors to the community by using the space for competition and tournament play. Finally, when the facility is not in use by the events and/or league play or practice, the space is to be open for general public use to support the council's efforts in creating and sustaining a healthy and active community. The city council member has tasked you with the following to determine the feasibility of such a project:

1. Research the available lots for sale within the community to determine if there is a site with the acreage to develop the outdoor sport facility.
2. Once a few sites have been determined, begin to develop a pro forma to detail the costs to build such a facility.
3. Research the possible green elements that could be incorporated into the design and build of the project.
4. Provide a recommendation as to whether the project is feasible and how the council should proceed.

REFERENCES

Arsht, S. (2003). Construction management: Planning ahead. *American School & University*, *75*(11), 1–18.

Associated Press. (2011, November 8). Qatar urged to scrap air conditioning in stadium. *ESPN Soccer*. Retrieved from http://sports.espn.go.com/espn/wire?section=soccer&id=7206958

Environmental Protection Agency. (2012). Greening EPA. Retrieved from http://www.epa.gov/oaintrnt/index.htm

Ganaway, N. B. (2006). *Construction business management: What every construction contractor, builder, and subcontractor needs to know*. Hoboken, NJ: Wiley & Sons.

Manfred, T. (2014, March 18). The Qatar World Cup is a disaster: 1,200 workers dead, new bribery investigation. *Business Insider*. Retrieved from http://www.businessinsider.com/qatar-world-cup-workers-dead-2014-3

Ross, S. A., Westerfield, R., & Jordan, B. D. (2008). Fundamentals of corporate finance. New York, NY: McGraw-Hill Education.

Rounds, J. L. (2011). *Construction supervision*. Hoboken, NJ: Wiley & Sons.

CHAPTER 4

Finance and Budgeting

EMILY SPARVERO

CHAPTER OBJECTIVES

Upon completion of this chapter, the reader will be able to:

1. Define capital projects and explain why both for-profit and nonprofit organizations undertake them

2. Identify equity and debt funding sources available for a sport organization's capital projects

3. Distinguish between general obligation, revenue, and special tax bonds

4. Compare line-item and program budgets

5. Discuss advantages and disadvantages of zero-based versus incremental budgeting

6. Explain what variance analysis is and how it is used by managers

7. Describe the role of fundraising in charity athletic events

CHAPTER OVERVIEW

This chapter will outline the basic concepts of financing sport facilities. First, it will describe the basic components of financial statements and how they can be utilized to develop a budget as a forecasting measure. Second, it will discuss the types of bonds commonly utilized by organizations to finance the construction or renovation of a new facility. Lastly, it will review the public–private partnerships that facilities create to finance and manage the facility.

Industry VOICE

Rick Boethling—Executive Director, Race Across America

In existence for 33 years, Race Across America (RAAM) is the world's toughest bicycle race. With headquarters in Boulder, Colorado, RAAM is a coast-to-coast bicycle race that starts in Oceanside, California, and finishes in Annapolis, Maryland. It is a continuous race (i.e., no stages like in the Tour de France), and racers can compete in relay teams of two, four, or eight members or as a solo racer. Teams have 9 days to complete the event, while the solo racer has 12 days. The purpose of RAAM is to provide the highest quality endurance bicycling event in the world. Everything we do is aimed at improving the race for all stakeholders involved. Indirectly, we hope we can increase the popularity of cycling as a sport. As the executive director for RAAM, my primary focus is to ensure that everything leading up to the event is in place and ready to go. I also manage the budgetary items and bookkeeping for the event. During the implementation of RAAM, I oversee the operational side of the event.

My career has not taken a traditional path, with my entry into the sports industry happening almost by accident. I majored in finance and international business in college. Afterwards, I managed my own paint contracting business for about 10 years. My father was competing in RAAM as a solo rider, and I decided to sell my company and crew for him (i.e., provide him support) during the race. Upon the conclusion of my father's ride, we were disappointed to learn the owners were going to shut the race down. My father and I decided to purchase it as a side project, and I began assisting with the planning of the event for the upcoming year. We quickly realized that managing an event like RAAM was more complicated than we could have imagined, and I started working full time directing RAAM and other bicycling events.

The first thing I would recommend to students interested in a career in the event business is to seek out a position in something you like doing. Exploring the opportunities available, finding where you fit best and what you like the most, will help steer you in the right direction. You can gain valuable insight by interning or volunteering with several different types of organizations and events. Participating in events is also helpful because it gives you the perspective of the consumer. By working and participating in events, you develop a better understanding of the time commitment and tasks involved, the pay scale, and hopefully whether the event is something you truly enjoy doing.

Aside from the basic qualities you would want from anyone when hiring (e.g., personable, smart, hardworking), the one thing I look for when hiring an entry-level employee is passion. In general, it is not a business designed for high levels of financial success, so having a passion for the sport is very important. I tend to look for people who have worked or volunteered for other events, as well as participated in events. This shows me they have a passion for the sport, understand our customers, and will have the endurance for managing our types of events. Dynamic thinking is critical, as we are continually trying to improve our event and differentiate ourselves from the competition. Oral communication is also very important because we have a lot of interaction with the participants, spectators, and sponsors during the event.

One of the biggest challenges in this industry is the ability to sustain a solid level of growth while maintaining a high level of quality. We are competing against companies with more money and resources for a small segment of customers and potential sponsors. The event business is currently in an expansion cycle, which makes it important to focus on developing a sound business to be able to maintain or grow our market share. Eventually, we will face a time when the event industry matures and potentially declines, which means we need to position ourselves to make it through that time. For RAAM specifically, our biggest challenge is that we host an event that many people do not understand. We have to explain the event to potential sponsors, spectators, and participants so they understand the concept of RAAM. Social media is the primary tool for us to engage and educate the consumers with regard to RAAM and our other events. A secondary strategy we are currently employing is introducing some intermediary distance rides, such as 200- and 400-mile events that could help transition riders from the 100-plus-mile rides to compete in longer distances and eventually RAAM.

Finance and budgeting is vital to our organization. One of the first things we do once the event is over is review the prior year and develop financial projections and budgeting for the next year's race. The budget serves as a guideline for how we plan for everything. It determines how much available we have for marketing, specifies how much we need in sponsorships to support the race, establishes how much staff we can have, and so on. In this industry, there are always issues that arise that cost more than you plan for, so it is important to build in leeway for those occurrences. To manage these expenses, we evaluate the budget and revise our cash flows each month, year round, with extra focus leading up to the event. If you are truly running an event like a business, it is important to set and stay within the budget to ensure financial success of the event and your organization.

Introduction

Financial issues related to facilities and events are often key to the success or failure of a project. If an organization fails to secure the capital funding necessary for a project, or if the organization's budget does not reflect its priorities, the ability of the project to meet organizational goals is in jeopardy. This chapter begins with a discussion of capital funding and the various sources of capital available to different types of organizations. The next section of the chapter provides an overview of facility budgeting, including different budgeting approaches and variance analysis. The chapter concludes with financial issues unique to charity athletic events.

In September 2012, Allen (Texas) High School opened its football season in front of 18,000 fans in Eagle Stadium,

TIP

When the capital funding source requires a referendum, proponents of a bond issue should be willing and have the financial resources necessary to fund a public information campaign to persuade voters to vote for the proposal.

a $60 million state-of-the art sport complex. The stadium was approved as part of a $120 million bond issue and will be paid for through increased property taxes. The Allen stadium attracted attention from various national media outlets, including the *New York Times*, ABC News, and *USA Today*, and was criticized as further proof of misplaced priorities in football-centric Texas. In reality, Eagle Stadium is only one example of the facilities arms race currently underway. In 2012 alone, 28 stadium and arena projects for professional and college sports were scheduled to be completed, with a cumulative cost of more than $3.83 billion (Traiman, 2011). A complete listing of professional and college sport projects from 2012 to 2014 is provided in **Table 4-1**. New facilities are being built to provide spectators with new and/or substantially renovated facilities in which to view sport events at the high school, college, and professional levels. Similarly, facility expenditures are not limited to venues for sport spectatorship. Facilities for sport participation are flourishing, and organizations, including campus recreation departments, public parks and recreation departments, and private, for-profit sport clubs, are renovating or building new facilities. Given the magnitude of facility spending, it is important to understand the mechanisms through which these facilities are funded and the budgeting processes applicable to sport facilities.

Capital Projects

capital project A long-term investment project that will increase the organization's assets

Sport facilities are common capital projects that sport organizations undertake. Capital refers to the funds needed to finance an organization's assets. A **capital project** is a long-term investment project that will increase the organization's assets. If an organization wants to build a new facility (or renovate an existing facility), there are many upfront costs, including costs associated

TABLE 4-1   Professional and College Sport Projects from 2012 to 2014

Facility	Location	Team(s) Hosted	Cost
Barclays Center	Brooklyn, NY	Brooklyn Nets	$1 billion
Madison Square Garden (renovation)	New York, NY	NY Rangers, NY Knicks	$975 million
Marlins Ballpark	Miami, FL	Miami Marlins	$515 million
BBVA Compass Stadium	Houston, TX	Houston Dynamo, Texas Southern University Maroon and Grey Tigers	$80 million
JetBlue Park at Fenway South	Fort Myers, FL	Boston Red Sox (spring training)	$78 million
Tampa Bay Times Forum (renovation)	Tampa Bay, FL	Tampa Bay Lightning	$40 million
Maritime Park Stadium	Pensacola, FL	Pensacola Blue Wahoos	$52 million
Constellation Field	Sugar Land, TX	Sugar Land Skeeters	$35 million
Uni-Trade Stadium	Laredo, TX	Laredo Lemurs	$18 million
California Memorial Stadium	Berkeley, CA	UC Golden Bears	$321 million
The Rose Bowl (renovation)	Pasadena, CA	UCLA Bruins, Rose Bowl	$152 million
Olsen Field	College Station, TX	Texas A&M Aggies	$20.6 million
Griffin Athletics Complex	Florence, SC	Francis Marion Patriots	$10.2 million
Amon G. Carter Stadium	Fort Worth, TX	TCU Horned Frogs	$155 million
UT Arlington Special Events Center	Arlington, TX	UT Arlington Mavericks	$78 million
Hank McCamish Pavilion	Atlanta, GA	Georgia Tech Yellow Jackets	$45 million
Trojan Arena	Troy, AL	Troy University Trojans	$34 million
Convocation Academic Center	New Orleans, LA	Xavier University of Louisiana Gold Rush and Gold Nuggets	$24 million
Kansas State University Basketball Training Facility	Manhattan, KS	Kansas State University Wildcats	$18 million

with land acquisition, construction, and infrastructure development. In order to begin construction, the sport organization needs to have cash available to cover these expenses. Thus, a capital project typically requires large up-front cash outlays. The projects continue to have both cash inflows and outflows over the course of the useful life of the project. In order to determine whether an organization should pursue a capital project, managers need to determine whether the project will increase the value of the organization.

In for-profit sport organizations, this determination is fairly straightforward. Managers can estimate the present value of all revenues that are expected to be generated by the facility (cash inflows) and the present value of all expenses expected to be incurred by the facility (cash outflows). As a simple decision rule, if the present value of the cash inflows is greater than the present value of the cash outflows, then undertaking the facility project will increase the value of the firm. This rule is well illustrated by looking at the values of professional sport team franchises. In 2012, the two National Football League (NFL) teams that realized the greatest increase in franchise value were the Minnesota Vikings and the San Francisco 49ers. What do these two teams have in common? They each recently finalized financing packages for new stadiums.

In nonprofit and public sector sport organizations, decision making about capital projects is complicated by the public service orientation of these organizations. Public sector organizations include federal, state, and local governmental agencies that serve the public good. Nonprofit organizations provide programs and services that the for-profit and public sectors either cannot or are not willing to provide. Public sector and nonprofit organizations do not have shareholders to whom they are accountable. However, they are accountable to their stakeholders (e.g., clients, elected officials, community residents) and, as such, should consider the financial feasibility and sustainability of projects. Specifically, managers should still estimate the present value of the project's revenues and expenses, but the decision of whether to proceed might not be made on solely financial reasons. For example, decisions made by a parks and recreation department might be influenced by the department's commitment to providing a diversity of recreational opportunities to users at all socioeconomic levels. This guiding principle might cause the department to build a new recreation center in an underserved neighborhood, even if the cash inflows from the facility (i.e., membership and program fees) are not sufficient to cover the cost of the facility.

With an understanding of what capital projects are and why a sport organization would choose to undertake such a project, we can now turn our attention to how sport organizations obtain capital needed for these projects. The acquisition, construction, or renovation of a facility will increase the assets of an organization. The increase in the organization's assets is made possible by an equivalent increase in the organization's liabilities, equity, or some combination of the two. We will examine specific ways in which sport organizations can raise the funds necessary to pay for facility projects.

Equity Finance

Equity is ownership interest in an organization, and sport facilities may pursue several different forms of equity financing for capital projects, including sale of stock, retained earnings, and gifts (Brown, Rascher, Nagel, & McEvoy, 2010).

SALE OF STOCK

The first form of equity financing available to sport organizations is the sale of stock shares. When the shares of stock are sold, the stockholder becomes a part owner of the organization. Each stockholder has specific rights, and these typically include the right to any dividends that are paid by the organization and the right to vote on organizational issues. While the sale of stock is commonly used by corporations to generate funds, there are limitations to a sport organization's ability to issue stocks to fund facility development.

The Green Bay Packers are the only publicly owned team in the four primary North American professional sport leagues (NFL, National Basketball Association [NBA], Major League Baseball [MLB], and National Hockey League [NHL]). The Packers have sold stock to the public at five points in the team's history, with the most recent stock sales in 1997 and 2011. The 1997 stock offering raised $24 million, and the 2011 stock offering raised approximately $67 million for Lambeau Field renovations (Cheffins, 1999; Spofford, 2012). Other North American teams, including the Cleveland Indians, Boston Celtics, and Florida Panthers, have also issued stock during their history, but these stock issues were not directly linked to facility development. The NFL, NBA, MLB, and NHL currently have policies in place that either discourage or prohibit the sale of stock. A public offering of stock requires extensive disclosure of a company's business practices. In order to protect its competitive advantage, a team may be reluctant to pursue a process that would make its business practices public. In addition to reluctance on the part of team owners to pursue this type of equity financing, there is also reluctance on the part of potential shareholders to invest in sport stocks. The North American sport stocks have underperformed the market in each instance. For example, Cleveland Indians stock showed a 50% return on investment for shareholders who bought the stock through the team's initial public offering and sold the stock when the team went private. However, other stocks that were traded on the NASDAQ during this time produced a 123% return on investment for their shareholders (Smith, 2012). The sale of sport team stocks is more likely to be viewed as a souvenir for the die-hard fan than a serious personal financial investment.

The sale of stock is not limited to professional sports, although instances of sale of stock for recreational or amateur sport are less common. At the recreational level, a stockholder system can be used for recreation centers and swimming pools. For example, the Hidenwood Recreation Association in Newport News, Virginia, offers a stockholder membership. This membership includes as $250 stock fee (in addition to the member's annual dues). In return, the stockholder is a voting member, can hold a position on the Association Board of Directors, and is exempt from the fee associated with reserving the swimming pool. The revenue raised through this type of stock issue is commonly, although not necessarily, used for capital projects. Other examples of stockholder programs at local recreation centers include the Shadow Oaks Recreation Association in the Spring Branch neighborhood of Houston, Texas, and the Ken Grill Recreation Center in Berks County, Pennsylvania.

RETAINED EARNINGS

retained earnings
Revenues generated by the sport organization that are reinvested to finance improvements and additions.

Sport organizations may also use retained earnings to fund facility development. Retained earnings are funds that are reinvested in the sport organization. In a for-profit organization, profit can either be distributed to shareholders in the form of dividends, or the profit can be reinvested in the company (i.e., retained earnings). Nonprofit organizations do not distribute earnings through dividend payments. Rather, any excess income is reinvested in the organization in order to expand its capacity to support the organization's mission. The advantage to using retained earnings to finance facility development is that the organization maintains control of how the funds are used (Stewart, 2007).

GIFTS

Another form of equity financing that is available to nonprofit sport organizations is **gifts** or donations. Under the U.S. federal tax code, individuals who make gifts to nonprofit organizations receive a tax deduction equal to their donations. A gift to an eligible nonprofit organization will reduce the donor's adjusted gross income when he or she files his or her federal income tax. Since federal income tax is calculated as a percentage of an individual's adjusted gross income, the tax benefit associated with a donation will reduce the amount of federal income tax that the donor owes the Internal Revenue Service.

gift A donation provided to an organization to finance a project that is tax deductible.

When gifts are solicited specifically for facility development, or "bricks-and-mortar" projects, they are part of the organization's capital campaign. Capital campaigns can support different types of organizations, with different missions, different aims, and different levels of capital needed. The common thread among these capital campaigns is that they are focused on acquisition, development, or renovation of facilities, as illustrated by the following examples. Special Olympics of Massachusetts (SOMA) launched a capital campaign to raise $10.8 million for a new headquarters and training center. The new center will allow SOMA to increase the number of athletes served and provide state-of-the-art facilities to these athletes. The Philadelphia Girls' Rowing Club (PGRC) promotes rowing among women with an interest in amateur rowing, and the organization's house is the oldest structure on Philadelphia's historic Boat House Row. The first phase of the PGRC facility project is the structural stabilization and reconstruction of its piers and docks, requiring $600,000. Duke University launched Duke Forward, a university-wide capital campaign. This initiative is expected to raise $250 million for Duke athletic facilities, in addition to other capital campus improvements.

Debt Finance

As mentioned previously, in order to procure the capital necessary for facility projects, an organization will increase either its liabilities or its equity.

This section will examine what happens when an organization increases its liabilities (i.e., debt financing).

LOANS

Sport organizations commonly borrow money in the form of a loan. The important features of a loan are its interest rate, maturity, and prepayment provisions (Brown et al., 2010). Interest is the amount charged by a lender in exchange for loaning the organization funds. The interest rate, or the percentage of principal charged as interest, reflects the risk inherent in the transaction. The riskier the sport organization is perceived to be, the higher the interest rate it will be charged. Maturity is the date that a loan is paid in full, including both principal and interest. Finally, a prepayment provision establishes what penalties, if any, will be charged should the recipient of the loan funds pay off the amount of the loan earlier than the date of maturity. Any sport organization can pursue loan financing from a financial institution.

Professional sport teams have special loan options available to them through their respective leagues instead of individual banks. In 2011, the NFL reestablished its Stadium Construction Support, or G-4, program, which allows a team to borrow up to $200 million for stadium projects. Teams that have benefitted from the G-4 program include the Green Bay Packers ($58 million) and the San Francisco 49ers ($200 million). As of January 2011, the NBA had a $2.3 billion league-wide credit facility (Lombardo & Kaplan, 2011), with a limit of $125 million allowed per team. MLB also has a $1.5 billion league-wide credit facility. Whereas the funds borrowed through the NFL G-4 program must be used for stadium projects, the NBA and MLB do not specify how the funds borrowed through their credit facilities are to be used. The benefit to the league is that these league-wide loan programs may support franchise stability and improve the fan experience. The benefit to the team (or loan recipient) is access to capital needed for facility projects at a low interest rate. The league's assets (e.g., national media contracts, franchise values, stable underlying league economics) secure the loan, which reduces the risk for the lenders. Remember that the interest rate charged reflects the risk of the investment. In the case of the NFL, teams that borrow through the league's loan pool can secure rates as low as 1.5% (Kaplan, 2012).

BONDS

Bonds are another form of debt financing available to a sport organization. Whereas the loan process depends on a financial institution to provide capital to the sport organization, the funds from a bond issue come from a range of investors active in the bond market. A bond represents a promise to pay back the amount borrowed (principal) plus the interest rate. The investor, or bondholder, holds the bond until the date of maturity, at which time the principal is due.

bonds A debt security in which the issuer owes the bondholder a designated amount; payment, interest, and maturity date details are provided.

Municipal Bonds

Municipal bonds are a special type of bond that may be available for sport organizations that need to raise funds. Municipal bonds can be issued only by state and local government, and they are usually issued for the purpose of financing capital projects. Municipal bonds are an attractive means of debt finance because they are tax exempt. This means that when municipal bonds are issued, the bondholder does not have to pay federal income tax on the interest received. Because of the investor's tax exemption, municipal bond rates are typically offered at a lower interest rate than nonmunicipal bond rates. This lower interest rate reduces the total cost of the project.

municipal bonds Tax-exempt bonds issued by the local or state government to support capital projects.

The rationale for tax exemption of municipal bonds is that the state and local governments issued these bonds for the benefit of the public and the federal government offers an implicit subsidy. Municipal bonds may be issued by state and local governments on their own behalf, as in the case of a local parks and recreation department issuing bonds to finance a new swimming pool. The local parks and recreation department is a division of local government, and it is consistent with the purpose of municipal bonds that they be issued for this type of project.

Municipal bonds are also frequently issued by state and local governments for the purpose of constructing or renovating facilities for professional sport teams. The public benefits from a professional sport stadium are not as immediately obvious. Still, Bloomberg estimates that since 1986, an estimated $17 billion in municipal debt has been issued for professional sport facilities. This represents a total cost to U.S. taxpayers (i.e., federal subsidy) of $4 billion (Kuriloff & Preston, 2012). Presumably, the owners of sport teams have access to well-developed capital markets, including those mentioned previously in this chapter. Still, we see state and local governments embarking on joint ventures with sport teams and issuing municipal bonds on their behalf. From 2003 to 2009, 90.3% of sport facility construction was publicly funded (Brown et al., 2010). In addition to agreeing to provide a specific amount of construction costs (typically funded through the municipal bond process described later in the chapter), state and local governments also provide a variety of noncash support for sport facilities. Governments frequently offer favorable lease terms to professional sport teams that are housed in government-owned facilities. For example, the Dallas Cowboys pay the City of Arlington $2 million per year for the use of the AT&T Stadium complex. According to Ozanian (2012), the Dallas Cowboys were valued at $2.1 billion, making them the most valuable NFL franchise. The Cowboys generate annual revenues of $500 million, which makes the team's lease payment equal to 0.4% of its revenues. In addition to the $2 million per year in lease payments that the city of Arlington receives, it receives a maximum of $500,000 from any future naming rights deals; in turn, it has to cover the debt service on the $325 million in municipal bonds that were issued for stadium construction. Local governments may also provide land and infrastructure improvements, which can double the real cost of a stadium project.

The advantages to the team are clear. When the team enters into a public–private partnership, each party agrees to contribute a specified dollar or percentage of construction costs as well as additional resources. By partnering with a state or local government, the team's share of costs is reduced. Additionally, when the government issues a municipal bond, the total cost of the project is effectively lowered, because (as we have already learned) municipal bonds carry a lower interest rate than bank loans or corporate bonds. Finally, while the costs of facility construction are typically shared, the facility's revenues are not. The sport team is able to maximize new revenue streams in a new facility, and these revenues (e.g., naming rights, premium seating, sponsorship) are captured almost exclusively by the team's owners.

There are also advantages, or perceived advantages, for the local governments of the communities that host professional sport facilities. Common justifications for public subsidies for professional sport facility projects include both economic and noneconomic benefits. The specific economic benefits claimed include job creation, higher wages, and increased tax revenues. These benefits can be realized through (1) the construction and operation of the facility and (2) the economic development that is enabled by the presence of the facility. The construction of a new stadium creates jobs in the construction sector, which benefits the host city if the team hires local residents. The operation of a new stadium also creates jobs, although they are for the most part temporary, seasonal, and low-paying jobs. Sport facilities also attract visitors to the area surrounding the facility. Visitors spend money in hotels, restaurants, bars, and shops, which generates tax revenues through the local sales tax and any special taxes, such as a hotel/motel tax.

Economic benefits are frequently promoted by local leaders and special-interest groups that want to secure public financing for a stadium project. However, there is a general consensus that the economic benefits of sport facilities are often overstated (c.f., Siegfried & Zimbalist, 2000). While local governments are predisposed to accept that sport facilities are "magic bullets" for economic activity and development, the federal government has not accepted these claims. In 2007, the House Committee on Oversight and Government Affairs held separate hearings to examine (1) whether local governments realize the benefits promised by leaders who promote public funding of sport projects and (2) whether public funding of sport projects diverted necessary funding from other government infrastructure projects. Additionally, in 2009, when U.S. Congress was debating the American Recovery and Reinvestment Act (i.e., the stimulus bill), an amendment was offered to prohibit the use of stimulus funds for stadiums. While this amendment was not included in the final passage of the bill, it highlights the skepticism with which some lawmakers treat claims of economic benefits.

In addition to economic claims, public support for professional sport facilities may be justified on social and quality-of-life (i.e., noneconomic) grounds. A facility that allows a city to host a professional team can improve the image of the city. The presence of a professional sport team can confer status as a "major league" city. The image enhancement attributable to a sport team can help to attract tourists as well as potentially attract new businesses. The presence of a professional sport team can also provide residents with a point of connection to or commonality with other residents. Finally, the presence of a sport team can increase community self-esteem, or the symbolic importance of how residents view their community (Eckstein & Delaney, 2002). While these benefits are largely associated with the sport team or event hosted by the community, it is often the facility that allows the attraction or retention of the team or event.

Security for Municipal Bonds

Once the bond is issued, the sport organization must raise sufficient funds to cover the amount owed to the bondholder. While there are numerous municipal bond arrangements, we will focus on three types of municipal bonds commonly used for sport facility projects: (1) general obligation bonds, (2) revenue bonds, and (3) special tax bonds.

general obligation bonds Bonds that are secured by state and local governments' authority to levy income, property, or sales taxes.

General obligation bonds, or GO bonds, are bonds that are secured by state and local governments' authority to levy income, property, or sales taxes. GO bonds are backed by the faith and credit of the government, which means that the revenues from these tax collections will be used to cover the debt service on the bonds. In general, anyone who purchases a taxable good or service in a government's jurisdiction must pay sales tax. Similarly, anyone who earns income within a government's jurisdiction must pay income tax, if a state or local income tax exists. Finally, anyone who owns taxable property within a government's jurisdiction must pay property taxes. Even if an individual rents a property, it is quite likely that the property taxes that the owner owes the government are reflected in the rent that is charged. Because the state and local governments can compel residents to pay these taxes, GO bonds have a very low chance of default and are generally deemed safe investments. However, GO bonds frequently require voter approval of proposed tax increases.

GO bonds are frequently used for public sport and recreation projects. Local recreation and sport capital projects (e.g., swimming pools, marinas, golf courses, parks) are widely believed to enhance the quality of life of a community. Additionally, some recreation projects increase the assessed value of nearby properties, which increases the tax revenues collected by local taxing authorities.

In 2012, voters in Austin, Texas, approved Proposition 14, a $77.7 million bond issue for parks and recreation projects. The bond package included renovation or replacement of swimming pools, playscapes, and basketball courts. The city will issue GO bonds for these projects, and the bond will be repaid with property tax revenue. In addition to the quality of life and property value benefits, supporters of the Austin bond issue insisted in public information campaigns that the project would not increase property taxes. This claim was technically true, as the property tax rate would remain the same. However, if the bond issue had not been approved by voters, the property tax rate in Austin would have *decreased* from 12 cents per $100 of assessed value to 10 cents per $100 of assessed value (Coppola, 2012). The framing provided by supporters was effective in persuading voters that they could have improved sport and recreation assets in the community without an increased tax burden, and the measure passed with 58% of the vote (Travis County Clerk, 2012).

Another option for bond financing is the use of **revenue bonds**. Revenue bonds are issued for a specific project and are secured through the project's revenues. One advantage of revenue bonds is that they do not typically require voter approval. Also, revenue bonds adhere to the benefit principle of taxation. According to the benefit principle, those who derive the benefit from a project should bear the burden of tax payments. A disadvantage to the use of revenue bonds is that it can be difficult to accurately forecast a project's revenue streams. The funded project must be capable of generating sufficient revenue to cover the debt service. If revenue from the project does not meet or exceed estimated revenues, the sport organization could default on its payments to bondholders. Consequently, revenue bonds are riskier than GO bonds and investors demand a higher interest rate.

revenue bonds
Issued for a specific project and are secured through the project's revenues.

Special tax bonds, like GO bonds, are secured by taxes. However, constituents are not legally obligated to engage in the activities or use the services that are taxed in the case of special tax bonds. Common examples of special tax bonds are visitor taxes, such as hotel/motel taxes and rental car taxes, as well as sin taxes, such as taxes on alcohol or cigarettes. The burden for the payment of visitor taxes falls primarily on individuals who are not local residents. This makes visitor taxes popular among residents and voters, but they may have negative effects on a community's tourism industry. In 2004, Dallas was in contention for the new Cowboys stadium. The team's proposal called for a 6% rental car tax and a 3% hotel/motel tax, which would have given Dallas the highest hotel/motel tax rate in the country. One of the most vocal critics of this proposal was Mary Kay, the Dallas-based cosmetics company. Mary Kay officials said that this tax plan would prevent them from holding their annual conference in Dallas. Mary Kay was joined by other companies involved in travel and tourism in lobbying against the proposed tax increase.

special tax bonds
Bonds that are secured by local taxes. Typically in the form of bed, car rental, or sin tax.

Sin taxes, in contrast to visitor taxes, are borne primarily by local residents. In May 2014, by a margin of 56% to 44%, voters in Cuyahoga County,

Ohio, passed a ballot issue to extend the county's sin tax until 2035. The tax extension on alcohol and cigarettes will be used to cover the costs of "constructing, renovating, improving, or repairing sports facilities and reimbursing a county for costs incurred by the county in the construction of sports facilities" (Coalition Against the Sin Tax, n.d.). The extension is estimated to generate $260 million over 20 years, which will be shared among the Cleveland Browns' FirstEnergy Stadium, the Cleveland Indians' Progressive Field, and the Cleveland Cavaliers' Quicken Loans Arena. Cleveland's three major league professional teams spent at least $1.8 million in cash and marketing services in support of the ballot issue, as compared with approximately $131,500 spent by issue opponents. Opponents argued that the sin tax extension would place an unfair burden on Cleveland and Cuyahoga County residents, with a disproportionate negative impact on poor and working-class residents.

Operational Revenues

securitization When sport organizations use contractually obligated income as collateral for debt.

The revenues generated by operations can also be used to finance a facility and cover debt service. This is typically done through **securitization**, where sport organizations use contractually obligated income as collateral for debt. Contractually obligated income includes future revenues that the sport organization is guaranteed to receive, such as revenue from media contracts, naming rights and other sponsorship agreements, and multiyear premium seating contracts. The guaranteed nature of the contractually obligated income makes this method of financing less risky than depending on more volatile operational revenues, such as ticket sales.

Facility Budgeting

The first section of this chapter examined how sport organizations access capital needed to finance a facility project. This section presents the basics of budgeting for a facility.

operating budget Authorizes the funds necessary for the day-to-day operations of the facility or event.

An organization's budget is a key component of its financial management. The **operating budget** refers to "those activities that are ongoing and necessary to maintain the *current capabilities* of the organization to produce, sell, and service its core products and services provided to the customer base" (Lalli, 2012). An operational budget authorizes the funds necessary for the day-to-day operations of the facility or event. The specific categories of expenses vary depending on the type of facility or event.

The financial information included in an operating budget can be formatted in two different ways. The first option is a **line-item budget**. In a line-item budget, revenues and expenses are broken down into specific categories. Revenues are estimated for each category, and expense limits are established for each category. The advantage of a line-item budget is that it is simple to prepare. However, it does not provide information with regard to how spending in the designated categories contributes to the efficient and effective delivery of programs. This makes it difficult for an organization to evaluate the extent to which its budget aligns with its strategic priorities. The second format for an operating budget is a **program budget**. In a program budget, funds are allocated for specific programs or projects. Whereas the operating budget is focused on what the organization buys, the program budget is focused on programs that meet the organization's strategic goals.

Take the operating budget for Qualcomm Stadium, the home of the NFL's San Diego Chargers.[1] Qualcomm Stadium is owned by the city of San Diego, and the Chargers lease the facility from the city. The revenues and expenses included in the facility's operating budget include only revenues and expenses for the stadium, and not for any team or event that leases the facility. Qualcomm's budget includes both a line-item budget and a program budget. When you compare the total expenses in the line-item budget with the total expenditures in the program budget, you find that the totals are the same ($14,534,168 in fiscal year 2009), regardless of budget format. The information from Qualcomm's operating budget can be used to develop a revenue and expense statement for the facility. The **revenue and expense statement** is a financial statement commonly used by governments. For nonprofit and for-profit organizations, the budget can be used to create an income statement.

line-item budget Revenues and expenses are estimated and grouped together into categories.

program budget Funds are allocated for specific programs or projects.

revenue and expense statement Financial statement that presents budgeted and actual revenues and expenses in summary form for a given period of time.

[1]The City of San Diego. (2009). *Fiscal Year 2009 Annual Budget: Qualcomm Stadium.* Retrieved from http://www.sandiego.gov/fm/annual/pdf fy09/19bv2qualcomm.pdf

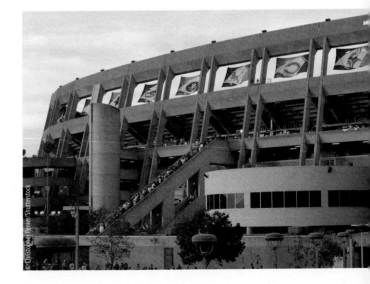
© Christopher Penler/Shutterstock

Budgeting Approaches

An organization's budget should be aligned with the company's strategic plan. Budgeting decisions can be made using a variety of budgeting approaches, of which the most commonly used are incremental budgeting and zero-based budgeting.

INCREMENTAL BUDGETING

incremental budgeting Budgeting system that makes slight changes to the previous period's actual revenues and expenses.

Incremental budgeting is the budgeting approach that has traditionally been used. In incremental budgeting, management makes an allocation decision based on the previous year's allocation. The previous year's budget allocation is treated as a given, and adjustments are made from the status quo. Managers may choose to hold funding constant, increase funding, or decrease funding, but any change is consistent across expense categories and only the proposed incremental change is typically scrutinized. The benefits of incremental budgeting are (1) it has the same impact on programs and projects across the budget, (2) it is quick and easy, and (3) the budget remains stable from year to year. There are also several disadvantages to using incremental budgeting. First, incremental budgeting does not allow for a thorough examination of expenses to determine the extent to which they are in alignment with the organization's strategic goals. Second, if managers know that their future budget will be based on the current year, there is pressure to spend any money that is currently allocated. This practice may result in frivolous spending, especially near the end of the organization's fiscal year. Finally, there is no incentive to cut costs in the current year or to propose alternative ways to accomplish program objectives in the future. Nevertheless, when a facility or event faces budget cutbacks, the default approach is incremental budgeting.

ZERO-BASED BUDGETING

zero-based budgeting (ZBB) Requires each line item from a previous budget be reviewed and approved and starts from a zero amount.

An alternative to incremental budgeting is **zero-based budgeting (ZBB)**. In ZBB, managers must evaluate all spending decisions on a regular basis, with the intent of adapting to a changing business environment and maximizing efficiency. In ZBB, managers start from scratch each year, and the starting budget is zero. Each expenditure is carefully considered and must be justified through cost–benefit analysis. According to Lalli (2011), there are five key elements to ZBB: (1) identification of objectives, (2) evaluation of alternative means of accomplishing each activity, (3) evaluation of alternative funding levels, (4) evaluation of workload and performance measures, and (5) establishment of priorities. The advantages to ZBB are that (1) it forces managers to question every expenditure (which will presumably lead to more effective and efficient budgeting decisions), (2) it prevents budget creep, and (3) it allows managers to link budget expenditures to performance goals. The time required is a major disadvantage and is one of the primary reasons that we rarely see true ZBB implemented. In most cases, it would be impractical for an organization to "zero" out every program and expenditure category. Rather, when practically implemented, ZBB requires strict scrutiny of spending so that all activities are evaluated to determine whether they should be eliminated altogether (i.e., a $0 budget allocation) or whether funding should be increased, decreased, or held constant as compared with the previous fiscal period. In contrast to incremental budgeting, this modified form of ZBB does not require consistent budget increases or cuts for each budgetary unit.

Many sport organizations are classified as nonprofit organizations, and as such, have special budgeting considerations. However, according to Shim, Siegel, and Allison (2011), the estimated revenues for nonprofit organizations differ from for-profit organizations in two important ways. First, the estimated revenues for many nonprofit organizations are not directly related to the provision of services. Second, the objective of a nonprofit is to have equality of revenues and expenses, so any excess revenues from one period should be available in the subsequent period. Whereas for-profit organizations use revenue estimation to establish their budgets, nonprofit organizations may instead estimate program expenditures to determine the budget and raise funds accordingly.

VARIANCE ANALYSIS

An organization's budget is set at the beginning of the fiscal year and is based on estimates of revenues and expenses. An organization may realize unexpected savings or encounter unexpected increases in expenses. Because estimates are likely to deviate from actual revenues and expenses, it is important that organizations periodically compare budgeted figures with actual figures. Variance analysis is an ex-post examination of budgeted and actual figures, and the variance can be either favorable or unfavorable for the organization (Stewart, 2007).

TABLE 4-2   PETCO Park Fund

	Adopted Budget	Year-End Projection	Over Budget (Under Budget)	Variance
Revenues	$18,260,280	$18,059,624	(200,656)	−1.1%
Expenses	$17,361,608	$16,726,289	(635,319)	−3.7%

Data from The City of San Diego Fiscal Year 2013 Adopted Budget Volume II: Department Detail, http://www.sandiego.gov/fm/annual/pdf/fy13/vol2/v2petcopark.pdf.

Variance analysis for PETCO Park is shown in **Table 4-2**. The amount that the organization is over or under budget is calculated by subtracting the year-end projection from the adopted budget. The variance is expressed as a percentage. In this case, revenues failed to meet their budgeted levels. Year-end expenses were less than anticipated, in large part due to lower levels of inflation than expected. According to the adopted budget, the city of San Diego would expect a surplus of $898,672. The real year-end figures showed a surplus of $1,333,335. Variance analysis can act as an early warning system by identifying revenues that fail to meet established goals and expenses that exceed estimates. If revenue and expense variance is minimal, managers may choose to monitor the situation closely. If variance falls outside of an acceptable range, managers should reevaluate the situation and take remedial action as necessary.

Financial Issues in Charity Athletic Events

This section will introduce the financial issues associated with charity athletic events. Charity events that require participants to engage in an athletic event (e.g., running, walking, bicycling) have become increasingly popular since the inaugural CROPWalk—the first walkathon in the United States—in 1969. According to the Run Walk Ride Fundraising Council (2012), events in the 30 largest fundraising series raised $1.6 billion for various causes and included nearly 12 million participants. **Table 4-3** lists the top 10 charity event series and their respective 2011 and 2012 revenues.

The idea behind charity athletic events is that nonprofits outsource fundraising to individuals who either (1) have a personal connection to the nonprofit's mission, (2) have an interest in the athletic activity, or (3) have some combination of the two. The event organizer, which is typically the nonprofit organization, produces the event, and participants raise awareness and money for the nonprofit organizations

TIP

The costs of producing charity athletic events could easily fail to generate enough revenue to cover expenses. One way to reduce costs is to identify, select, and train reliable and competent volunteers. Local schools and businesses can be great sources of large numbers of volunteers.

TABLE 4-3   Run Walk Ride Fundraising Council, Top 10

Organization	2012 Revenues ($ millions)	2011 Revenues ($ millions)	% Change
American Cancer Society Relay for Life	407.5	415.0	−1.81
Komen for the Cure	126.8	131.3	−3.44
March of Dimes	107.0	105.0	1.9
American Heart Association	97.8	99.0	−1.3
National MS Society	82.3	82.4	−0.12
Juvenile Diabetes Research Foundation	81	85.6	−5.43
Leukemia and Lyphoma Society	77.4	87.5	−11.55
American Cancer Society Making Strides Against Breast Cancer	68	61	11.48
American Heart Association Jump Rope for Heart	60.6	61.4	−1.30
Komen for the Cure 3-Day for the Cure	57.5	84.4	−31.87

Modified from 2012 PTPF 30 Results, Peer-to-Peer Professional Forum, a division of Cause Marketing Forum, Inc.

through a combination of their own contribution and peer-to-peer fundraising. The financial commitment required of participants varies depending on the event. For some events, the financial commitment is minimal and takes the form of a nominal registration fee. For example, over the span of one weekend in Austin, Texas, there were four separate athletic events to benefit local nonprofits. These included a 5K to benefit a local pregnancy resource center (registration $25), a 5K to benefit the Rotary Club (registration $20), the Red Poppy Festival 5K and kids' run for a local community festival (registration $25), and the American Heroes 5K to benefit various military charities, including Hope for Heroes and the Texas Military Museum (registration $25).

There are also charity athletic events that require a much more substantial financial investment from participants. Participants in the Leukemia and Lymphoma Society's Team in Training (TNT) program participate in a marathon, half marathon, triathlon, or similar event. Participants receive fundraising support from the organization in addition to sport training that prepares them to complete the endurance event. The fundraising minimum for participants varies based on the event they choose. For example, in 2012, Minnesota TNT members were required to raise anywhere from $1500 to participate in the Minneapolis Marathon and Half Marathon to $5500 to participate in the South Maui Triathlon.

There are also hybrid events, in which a participant is required to pay only the event registration fee but is encouraged to raise additional funds for the selected nonprofit. The early registration fee for individuals who participate in the 2013 LIVESTRONG Challenge (15- to 100-mile bike ride) is $60. However, when individuals register, they are invited to make an individual gift of either $50, $150, $250, or some other amount. Additionally, participants are asked to set an individual fundraising goal. For hybrid events, additional fundraising is encouraged through the use of incentives, which vary based on the organization. An example of the incentives earned by LIVESTRONG Challenge participants is provided in **Table 4-4**.

TABLE 4-4   Breakdown of LIVESTRONG Challenge Incentives

	White Jersey, $10,000	Green Jersey, $15,000	Polka-Dot Jersey, $20,000	Yellow Jersey, $30,000
Ride for the Roses jacket	X	X	X	X
Ride for the Roses jersey	X	X	X	X
Ground transportation to all weekend events	X	X	X	X
Friday RFTR dinner (plus 1 guest)	X	X	X	X
Saturday LIVESTRONG Challenge—Austin dinner (plus 1 guest)	X	X	X	X
Sunday ride entry (plus 1 guest)	X	X	X	X
Sunday ride VIP starting line position (plus 1 guest)	X	X	X	X
Sunday hospitality tent (plus 1 guest)	X	X	X	X
Recognition by jersey level on the LIVESTRONG website for the following year		X	X	
Participant airfare		X	X	X
Three-night hotel stay (Oct. 18, 19, 20)		X	X	X
Saturday "Circuit of the Americas" experience and lunch with celebrity chef			X	X
Invitation to quarterly call with LIVESTRONG CEO, board members, and key stakeholders for the following calendar year				X

Reproduced from http://www.livestrong.org/events/external/116/qualification-levels-and-incentives.

While charity athletic events continue to grow, they have also recently come under attack from nonprofit watchdog groups for being an inefficient use of the dollars raised. The expenses associated with these events vary greatly. While small fun runs may be relatively inexpensive, the costs associated with events that attract large numbers of participants, take place over multiple days, or are heavily incentive-based can be substantial. Consequently, the more expensive the production costs for an event, the less money that is available to support the mission of the selected nonprofit. An athletic charity event can require upwards of 50% of the money raised in order to produce the event. Typical expenses associated with a fun run are provided in **Table 4-5**. For example, The American Institute of Philanthropy estimates that the Avon 3-Day Walk for Breast Cancer (which has an $1800 fundraising minimum) spends 52 cents of every dollar raised on logistics (Kadet, 2011). Still, these events are frequently justified by nonprofit organizations because of the attention from the media and the general public that they attract.

TABLE 4-5   Fun Run Cost Breakdown

Portion of Spending	Expense
2%	Toilets
2%	Online fundraising commissions
3%	Signage
5%	Pre- and postevent furniture (tents, tables, trucks)
6%	Entertainment
6%	Event t-shirts
6%	Water and snacks
7%	Race gear (tracking chip and bib)
7%	Fencing and barricades
8%	Permits and security
48%	Proceeds to charity

Courtesy of Cadence Sports.

SUMMARY

In this chapter, the major financial and budgeting considerations related to facilities and events were presented. First, special financial issues related to capital budgeting were presented with examples of both debt and equity funding used for such projects. Operational budgets were next discussed, including incremental and zero-based approaches to budgeting. Financial issues are also important to events, even if the event does not require funding and operation of a facility by the organization. Thus, the final section of this chapter discussed the popularity and financial success of charity athletic events.

DISCUSSION QUESTIONS

1. Identify a professional sport team near you and research how the team secured funding for its facility. How was the facility financed (i.e., debt or equity financing)? To what extent was the financing method used by the team consistent with the benefit principle?

2. You are the parks and recreation director, and your city council recently announced that all city departments, including the parks and recreation department, will have to implement a mandatory 10% across-the-board cut during the next fiscal year. Do you agree with the incremental approach proposed by the city council? In what ways could zero-based budgeting improve your financial outcomes? You may wish to locate the annual budget for a local parks and recreation department to consider specific impacts and make recommendations.

3. Active City is a local nonprofit that seeks to improve the quality of life for residents in your community. You are on the steering committee for a local nonprofit's annual 10K fundraising event. There have been some concerns raised about the cost of producing the annual 10K, and the steering committee has been asked to consider an alternate proposal: Instead of hosting the 10K, Active City would host a "no-show" fundraiser. Previous supporters, local community leaders, and volunteers would receive a solicitation letter (i.e., invitation to a nonevent) that asks individuals to make a direct donation instead of registering for (and participating in) the race. What are the advantages and disadvantages of the no-show proposal? Would you support canceling this year's 10K for a no-show event?

Case STUDY

The KFC Yum! Center

© Jessicakirsh/Shutterstock

To some extent, the ability of selected funding mechanisms to actually generate the revenues necessary to cover facility costs is speculative. The case of the KFC Yum! Center illustrates what happens when expected revenues for facilities fail to materialize.

In 2005, the Louisville Arena Authority (LAA) was created to oversee the financing and construction of the KFC Yum! Center. The arena opened in 2010, and while it was touted as a $238 million project, the project's total debt service from 2008 to 2042 will total $839,524,341 (which includes principal payments of $349,218,518 and interest payments of $490,305,823). The arena was financed using the following sources for debt repayment: (1) tax-increment financing (i.e., the TIF Revenue Fund), (2) facility revenues (i.e., the Arena Revenue Fund), and (3) a guaranteed contribution of between $6.5 million and $9.8 million from the city of Louisville (i.e., the Metro Revenue Fund).

Using a TIF district to fund sport facilities is a particularly risky strategy. A TIF district is based on the idea that new development (in this case, the arena) will generate additional sales and property tax revenues in the surrounding areas. For example, if the arena is a catalyst for new restaurants and retail shops opening nearby, there would be increased economic activity, which would result in additional sales tax collections for the city. Likewise, if the addition of the arena contributes to area growth and development, the property values in the area would be expected to increase.

The creation of a TIF district allows the incremental increases in sales and property tax revenues to be dedicated to debt service on the project(s) that contributed to these increases. However, in the case of the LAA, the expected development and corresponding tax revenues were not realized. From 2010 to 2013, the expected revenues from the TIF district were over $30 million, but the actual revenues were just above $11.5 million, or 38.4% of the expected amount (Boyd, 2014). Because of this shortfall, the city of Louisville has provided its maximum allowable contribution of $9.8 million each year since 2012.

In addition to the insufficiency of the TIF district, revenues from the facility have also fallen short of expectations. In 2011, the arena showed an operating profit of $1.2 million, but when the debt service is taken into account, the net loss was over $14 million. In 2012, the arena lost over $16 million. The terms of the agreement between the LAA and ULAA (University of Louisville Athletic Association) have negatively impacted the arena's operating revenues. The University of Louisville's basketball teams are the primary tenant of the arena. ULAA pays the following rental rates to the LAA: (1) for men's basketball games, a minimum of $10,000 per game or 10% of gross admission receipts; (2) for women's basketball games and other university-sponsored events, a minimum of $5,000 per game or 5% gross admission receipts. ULAA receives 100% of revenue from programs and program advertisements, 88% of revenues from private suites, and 50% of revenues from concessions, catering, and the gift shop. These favorable lease terms have made the University of Louisville the most valuable college basketball team, worth $36.1 million, according to Forbes. However, these terms have also contributed to the LAA's financial problems.

The revenue shortfalls caused Standard & Poor's to downgrade the LAA's bond twice since 2012. In December 2012, Standard & Poor's downgraded the bonds to BBB–. The downgrade was based on concern over "LAA's continued reliance on potentially volatile tax increment financing (TIF) revenue and uncertainty about stabilized operating costs and direct arena revenue" (S&P revises, 2012). Again, in late 2013, Standard & Poor's downgraded the bonds from BBB– to BB, amid continuing concerns about the ability of the LAA to meet its debt obligations. According to Standard & Poor's, bonds with a BBB– rating are "considered [the] lowest investment grade by market participants," and bonds with a BB rating are "less vulnerable in the near term but [face] major ongoing uncertainties to adverse business, financial, and economic conditions" (Standard and Poor's, n.d.)

The LAA maintains that its financial situation is stable, but it has taken steps to shore up its funding. In October 2013, the University of Louisville agreed to reduce its share of facility sponsorship revenues, which provided an additional $1.5 million over 3 years that the LAA could use for debt service. The LAA also reduced the size of the TIF district, from 6 square miles to 2 square miles. The rationale for this move was that activities farther away from the arena were having a negative effect on tax collections. While these moves will increase the LAA's revenues, its debt service requirements are likely to increase at a faster rate than its revenues, leaving the residents of Louisville on the hook for the cost of the facility.

1. If you were in charge of selecting the financing method for the KFC Yum! Center, which sources of capital funding would you use to reduce financial risk?
2. Identify specific conditions under which TIF would be appropriate and would be expected to generate sufficient revenues?

The information in this case study is drawn from the LAA's public documents, available at http://www.kfcyumcenter.com/arena-information/about-us/louisville-arena-authority.

REFERENCES

Boyd, T. (2014, January 13). After bond downgrades, KFC Yum! Center finances remain opaque. *Insider Louisville*. Retrieved from http://insiderlouisville.com/news/bond-downgrades-kfc-yum-center-finances-remain-opaque/

Brown, M. T., Rascher, D. A., Nagel, M. S., & McEvoy, C. D. (2010). *Financial management in the sport industry*. Scottsdale, AZ: Holcomb Hathaway.

Cheffins, B. R. (1999). Playing the stock market: "Going public" and professional team sports. *Journal of Corporation Law, 24*, 641, 643–646.

Coalition Against the Sin Tax. (n.d.). Issue 7 ballot language. Retrieved from http://www.noclevelandsintax.com/

Coppola, S. (2012, October 19). Austin voters to weigh $78.3 million in bonds for affordable housing. Retrieved from http://www.statesman.com/news/news/local-govt-politics/austin-voters-to-weigh-783-million-in-bonds-for-af/nSg2C/

Eckstein, R., & Delaney, K. (2002). New sports stadiums, community self-esteem, and collective conscience. *Journal of Sport and Social Issues, 26*, 235–247.

Kadet, A. (2011, June 21). Are charity walks and races worth the effort? *Smart Money Magazine*. Retrieved from http://www.smartmoney.com/spend/travel/are-charity-walks-and-races-worth-the-effort-1306536923690/

Kaplan, D. (2012, June 25). NFL seeks to double loan pool by borrowing $600M. *Street & Smith's Sports Business Journal, 15* (11). Retrieved from http://www.sportsbusinessdaily.com/Journal/Issues/2012/06/25/Leagues-and-Governing-Bodies/NFL-finance.aspx?hl=Daniel%20Kaplan&sc=0

Kuriloff, A., & Preston, D. (2012, September 4). In stadium building spree, U.S. taxpayers lose $4 billion. Retrieved from http://www.bloomberg.com/news/2012-09-05/in-stadium-building-spree-u-s-taxpayers-lose-4-billion.html

Lalli, W. R. (2012). *Handbook of budgeting*. Hoboken, NJ: John Wiley & Sons.

Lombardo, J., & Kaplan, D. (2011, January 17). NBA increases league loan pool to $2.3B. *Street & Smith's Sports Business Journal, 13* (37). Retrieved from http://www.sportsbusinessdaily.com/Journal/Issues/2011/01/20110117/Leagues-and-Governing-Bodies/NBA-loan-pool.aspx?hl=nba%20increases%20league%20loan%20pool&sc=0

Ozanian, M. (2012, September 5). Dallas Cowboys lead NFL with $2.1 billion valuation. Retrieved from http://www.forbes.com/sites/mikeozanian/2012/09/05/dallas-cowboys-lead-nfl-with-2-1-billion-valuation/

Run Walk Ride Fundraising Council. (2012). RWRFC fundraising survey. Retrieved from https://www.peertopeerforum.com/run-walk-ride-resources/research/

S&P revises Louisville Arena Authority, Ky. outlook to negative. (2012, December 7). *Reuters*. Retrieved from http://www.reuters.com/article/2012/12/07/idUSWNA072820121207

Shim, J. K., Siegel, J. G., & Allison, I. (2012). *Budgeting basics and beyond*. Hoboken, NJ: Wiley & Sons.

Siegfried, J., & Zimbalist, A. (2000). The economics of sports facilities and their communities. *Journal of Economic Perspectives, 14*, 95–114.

Smith, C. (2012, August 10). Manchester United IPO: History says don't buy. Retrieved from http://www.forbes.com/sites/chrissmith/2012/08/10/manchester-united-ipo-history-says-dont-buy/

Spofford, M. (2012, March 1). Stock sale closes; shares top 268,000. Retrieved from http://www.packers.com/news-and-events/article_spofford/article-1/Stock-sale-closes-shares-top-268000/19d9b0a8-f4ce-497b-b5ae-73f6c72fd973

Standard and Poor's. (n.d.). Credit ratings definitions & FAQs. Retrieved from http://www.standardandpoors.com/ratings/definitions-and-faqs/en/us

Stewart, B. (2007). *Sport funding and finance*. Burlington, MA: Elsevier.

Traiman, S. (2011). US new builds and renovations. *Panstadia 2012 Anniversary Edition, 17*(4), 6–16.

Travis County Clerk. (2012, November 18). Travis County official results: Joint general and special elections. Retrieved from http://www.traviscountyclerk.org/eclerk/content/images/election_results/2012.11.06/20121106tccume.pdf

CHAPTER 5

Bidding and Planning
for Different Events

AMANDA L. PAULE-KOBA

CHAPTER OBJECTIVES

Upon completion of this chapter, the reader will be able to:

1. Write a mission statement that articulates the purpose of an event

2. Define and write SMART goals

3. Assess whether it is feasible to execute an event

4. Explain the event bid process

5. Provide examples of the different types of events

CHAPTER OVERVIEW

This chapter will explain the five main types of events: mega-events, recurring events, traveling events, ancillary events, and community events. When creating an event, the managers need to identify goals and objectives. These will guide all of the forthcoming decisions. When setting goals, the managers should follow the SMART (specific, measurable, attainable, relevant, and time-based) principle. The criteria for the bid process will also be discussed, as many mega-events and traveling events require a bid.

Industry VOICE

Lesley Irvine—Senior Associate Athletic Director and Senior Women Administrator, Bowling Green State University

The mission statement of our athletic department asserts the following: "Bowling Green Athletics is committed to cultivating champions in academics, sport, and life. We target excellence in 18 sports; we achieve it as one team."

I began my tenure on the Bowling Green State University (BGSU) athletic staff in July of 2010. I have been directly responsible for supervising men's basketball, women's basketball, men's soccer, women's soccer, baseball, softball, women's gymnastics, women's swimming, and women's volleyball. I am also in charge of the sports medicine, sport performance, strength and conditioning, and student–athlete academic services areas of the athletic department.

Since arriving at BGSU (which is located in Bowling Green, Ohio), I have gotten to play a key role in bringing two different National Collegiate Athletic Association (NCAA) tournament events to BGSU. I was the tournament director for the first and second rounds of the NCAA Division I women's basketball tournament, which were hosted at BGSU's Stroh Center in 2012. This event was widely regarded as very successful. In addition, I assisted with the NCAA Division I ice hockey regional.

Some of the challenges I have experienced in the field of college athletics relate to the limited staff members and financial resources available to my athletic department, a condition common among athletic departments across the country. I recall that when the BGSU athletic department hosted the first and second rounds of the NCAA

women's basketball tournament, the staff members were all wearing multiple hats. This scenario exemplifies the importance of being flexible as an employee and making yourself available to help out in any way possible, especially if you are an intern or entry-level employee.

To combat resource issues, my organization sets priorities and is strategic. We seek to identify opportunities to raise funds externally and corporate sponsorships. We emphasize the importance of having buy-in from all staff members and university administration so they understand why resources are needed and what they intend to do with those resources.

One of the trends that I see really coming into play, even more than in the past, in terms of facility and event management is the fan experience. What are you offering fans? Having Wi-Fi and a strong Internet connection for fans to check Facebook, send out Tweets, or post to Instagram is essential. It's no longer just about fans coming to watch a collegiate game. It's about creating opportunities through technology and social media to stay connected to fans and to engage those fans prior to and during the game.

In my current position, I am often in charge of hiring a variety of individuals for the athletic department. A lot of individuals look the same on paper. One of the first things I look for when hiring for an entry-level position is evidence that the individual has volunteered and gone above and beyond to start gaining industry experience. When meeting with potential candidates, I am looking for a high energy level, passion, flexibility, willingness to get involved in a lot of different areas, a strong work ethic, and, importantly, eagerness to learn.

I often interact with individuals who are right out of undergraduate or graduate school, and they are misguided about the realities of the industry. They believe they are going to step right into the role of Assistant Athletic Director and make $60,000 a year. This is not the reality for the majority of recent college graduates, so it is important to have realistic expectations. There are many chances to advance once you prove yourself. Once you get your foot in the door, be prepared to work extremely hard.

Introduction

When creating an event, it is essential to identify goals and objectives for the event. It is important to remember that when creating a new event, in addition to your goals for the event, you must assess where it fits in the current marketplace. Being unique is crucial to attracting sponsors, event participants, spectators, and/or media. Further, if you are submitting a **bid** to run a national or international sporting event, you need to follow the bid process provided by the event's rights holder. The criteria of the bid will differ depending on the event, but, in most cases, it is not a solitary process. A multitude of individuals (the organizing committee) will need to come together to gather and present the required information in the most cohesive manner possible.

bid A competitive process in which the objective is to win the right to organize a specific sporting event.

Executing Events

Events by their very nature are not permanent. They occur at different times and in different locations. They also may occur for different reasons. One of the challenges of running events is that there are many types of events, both sport and nonsport related, that event managers and facility managers might have to execute. The variety of events that an event or facility manager may have to deal with is vast and can be challenging if one is not prepared for the realities of the different types of events.

The five main types of events that an event or facility manager may have to deal with are:

- Mega-events
- Recurring events
- Traveling events

- Ancillary events
- Community events

To successfully manage an event, the manager needs to assess the resources the organization has at its disposal, the objectives of the event, and the goals of the event and the event manager. During this assessment, the manager needs to ensure that the organization's resources are sufficient to produce a high-quality event.

Identifying Reasons for Creating, Bidding for, or Hosting an Event

Events are held for a variety of reasons. Some events are created to help a local economy, generate buzz about a new product or sport, or deliver benefits to sponsors/stakeholders. Other events may be designed to raise money for a charity or philanthropic organization. Another possibility is

that an event is created for the purpose of generating revenue for the organization. All of these goals are perfectly acceptable reasons for creating an event. However, the event manager must assess whether the goals for the event are feasible while evaluating multiple factors (e.g., time, resources, staffing, the economy).

Of course, there is the possibility that an event is created with multiple goals in mind. For instance, a company may partner with a professional soccer player to create a youth soccer camp. This youth camp could possibly have the following initial goals:

1. Increase the skills of the young athletes.
2. Raise money for the professional soccer player's foundation or the charity that he or she supports.
3. Generate a profit for the organization running the event or the event owner.

All of these are examples of realistic goals for such an event. Ideally, the youth soccer camp would be able to obtain each of these goals. However, the goals are not as detailed as they could be. How would the director of the event be able to assess whether the goals were achieved or not? When creating goals, an event manager should follow the SMART principle. While there are variations of what each letter stands for, **SMART goals** are **s**pecific, **m**easurable, **a**ttainable, **r**elevant, and **t**ime-based (Doran, 1981; Farrelly, 2010; Meyer, 2006).

Specific refers to the need for goals to be well defined. They should not leave any confusion and they should be clear to everyone involved in the execution of the event. For instance, if you are running the youth soccer camp mentioned earlier, you could change the first goal of the event to, "Increase the shooting accuracy of all participants by 10%." This improvement would be assessed by having a shooting drill on the first day of the camp to measure accuracy and then completing the same drill on the final day of the camp to see if there was a 10% increase in accuracy.

Measurable goals provide enough detail for the event manager to determine if the goal was achieved. For example, the second goal could be adapted to state, "Raise $2500 for the professional soccer player's foundation." This goal could be assessed by tallying the final numbers at the end of the camp. If the camp generated at least $2500 for the professional athlete's charity, then the goal was reached.

Attainable means the goals listed can actually be achieved. An example of a goal that is not attainable would be thinking and stating that the youth soccer camp would raise $1,000,000 for charity. While this is a fantastic goal, it is not very realistic or attainable. The goal stated previously of generating $2500 for the athlete's charity is much more attainable, especially in the first year of an event.

Relevant goals make sense given the event that is being produced and resources available to the organizing team. Further, these goals correlate well with the nature of the particular event. For example, the new first goal of increasing shooting accuracy of all participants by 10% would be a relevant goal for this specific camp. Ideally, each young soccer player's skill development would be enhanced during this camp, so a goal of increasing shooting accuracy is relevant for this event.

Time-based goals have a time limit placed upon them. This limit allows enough time for the goal to be completed but has a specific end time or due date that will identify whether the goal was achieved. An example of a time-based goal would be adding on to the first goal to read, "Increase the shooting accuracy of all participants by 10% by the last day of the camp."

SMART goals An acronym used to describe the goals of an event; stands for specific, measurable, attainable, relevant, and time-based.

TIP

When using the SMART (specific, measurable, attainable, relevant, and time-based) goals principle, it is often helpful to ask another person to review the goals you have set forth for the event. While you may believe that your events meet each of the SMART goal criteria, others may view them as vague. Having a second or third opinion is definitely helpful and will ensure the goals are as thorough and complete as possible.

By tacking the time element of "last day of camp" onto this goal, we have satisfied the time-based component of the SMART goals principle.

It is important to remember that when creating a new event, in addition to your goals for the event, you must assess where it fits in the current marketplace. If you are creating a youth soccer camp for a professional athlete, is this event unique to the area or are there other soccer camps that are held in your region that also feature prominent athletes? Being unique is crucial to attracting sponsors, event participants, spectators, and/or media.

Further, you must assess whether there is a demand for that type of event. In the youth soccer camp example, you need to assess if there are enough young soccer players in the area to fill the camp. The event manager would do this by researching the number of youth soccer teams and leagues within a given geographic area. If soccer were not a popular sport with young athletes in the region, then it would be best to not create this event. Or if you still wanted to create the event to increase awareness and interest in the sport, the goals of the event would need to be altered to be in line with the new purpose of creating the event. The event manager in essence is attempting to assess whether the event is feasible or not.

Event Feasibility

event feasibility
The likelihood that an event can be executed at the desired level given the resources at the event organizer's disposal.

Once you have an idea for an event, it is important to investigate whether this event is feasible. **Event feasibility** examines the likelihood that the event can be executed at the desired level given the available resources (Torkildsen, 1999; Watt, 1998). Examining the feasibility will also help the manager determine a budget for the event. When assessing all of the direct and indirect costs, the manager has a better understanding of exactly what it will take to run this event.

The manager would want to conduct a feasibility study. A feasibility study refers to the analysis of the potential event and assesses the strengths and weaknesses of this event. When conducting a feasibility study, the manager needs to hire the staff necessary to complete the study, plan how the study will be executed, implement the study, write up the results, and distribute the study.

During the feasibility study, some of the questions the manager may ask to decide whether the event can be successfully produced include the following:

- Is there a bid submission?
- Where would we hold the event?
- How many staff members are necessary to execute the event?
- How many volunteers are necessary to execute the event and where would we find the volunteers?
- Is there interest in this geographic region for the event?
- What else is taking place in our region that would compete with the event?
- Where would we find participants for the event?
- Are there sponsors that would be interested in partnering with this event to offset costs?
- What is the best strategy to market this event?
- What are the costs associated with the event?
- What equipment do we already own, what could we borrow, and what do we have to buy?
- What potential barriers might this event face and do we have the resources to overcome those challenges?
- Do we have enough time to produce this event?

The person conducting the feasibility study needs to be unbiased in evaluating whether this event should be produced. If after examining the event the manager decides to proceed, the next step is to go forward with the bid process (if there is one). The general process of determining event feasibility is shown in **Figure 5-1**.

The Bid Process

Each national and international sporting event, run by a national or international governing body, has its own unique bid process. A bid is a competitive process in which the objective is to win the right to organize a specific sporting event. A bid "represents a collection of interests and skills (sports federations, local authorities, economic partners, the media, etc.) that have to be focused on the single objective of winning" (Chappelet, 2005, p. 19).

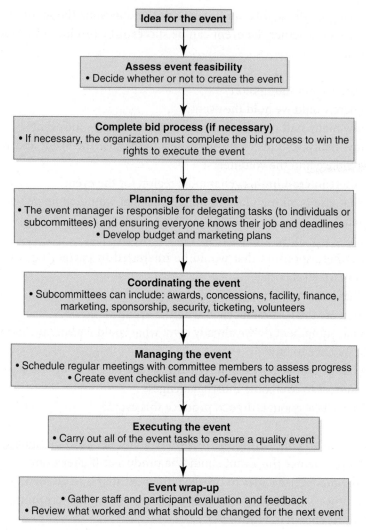

FIGURE 5-1 The Process of Determining Event Feasibility

Event owners, or rights holders, are the individuals or the governing body that controls the event. Sport governance refers to "the exercise of power and authority in sport organizations, including policy making, to determine organization mission, membership, eligibility, and regulatory power, with the organization's appropriate local, nation or international scope" (Hums & McLean, 2008, p. 4). The rights holders are the individuals or groups of people who will ultimately make the decision as to who has successfully won the bid (the right to produce the event). In addition to deciding who has won the event bid, these rights holders are also charged with sanctioning events on a variety of different scales, from youth to professional sports. Examples of governing bodies at all levels include the Amateur Athletic Union (AAU), high school athletic associations (such as the Ohio High School Athletic Association), the National Collegiate Athletic Association (NCAA), the National Football League (NFL), Major League Baseball (MLB), USA Track and Field, and other national governing bodies.

Sport mega-events, such as the Olympic Games or the FIFA (International Federation of Association Football) World Cup, or on a smaller scale NCAA regional events, attract competing bids from nations or cities. Pomfret, Wilson, and Lobmayr (2009) argue that these bids are "mostly made at tax-payers expense and spending is often large and nontransparent" (p. 2). In other words, the city's, state's, and/or nation's residents pay for these events through taxes. The researchers also state that the "benefits from bidding are equal to the net benefits from hosting the event multiplied by the probability of a successful bid, minus the cost of the bidding process. Losing bids incur costs for little if any ex post benefit" (Pomfret et al., 2009, p. 2).

Not all bid processes are the same. The criteria will be different depending on the event; however, there are some similarities that exist across the bid process. Completing a bid process is, in most cases, not a solitary event. A multitude of individuals (the organizing committee) will need to come together in order to gather and present the required information in the most cohesive manner possible.

The organizing committee may be comprised of members of the local convention and visitor's bureaus, sports commissions, and other interested parties (which may include local politicians, media, business leaders, and/or notable athletes). Local convention and visitor's bureaus and sports commissions both exist to attract outside businesses or events to the area. Therefore, the individuals who work at these organizations will be crucial to help the individual in charge of the organizing committee gather facts and figures about the local area, demographics, and key information about area facilities, such as restaurants, hotels, and local attractions, that may be important when completing the bid.

Bid Process to Host the Final Four of the NCAA Women's Basketball Tournament

Putting together a bid to be the Final Four host for the NCAA women's basketball tournament is a complex process. The bid must be perfect because each host city is competing against a wide variety of other equally great cities that want to host this event. The bid should begin with an overview of your infrastructure. You should describe your facility thoroughly, including locker rooms, number of seats, number of suites, etc.

The type of facility alone will not win a city the bid to host. The bid must include a description of the city's demographics, lodging, transportation, and restaurants. The city's visitor's bureau or similar organization should be brought in to help with this portion of the bid. The organizing committee should also include a discussion of their marketing plan, security plan, media, and ticketing plan. The NCAA bid selection committee will want to see the plan of action on how the potential host city will sell out the arena during the two semifinal games and the championship game. This is where showing a history of community support for women's basketball will be crucial.

Ancillary events will add a nice touch to the bid package. Where and when will the fan fest be? What other events will go on in conjunction with the Final Four games? How will the host city engage youth? All of these details need to be thought out and included in the bid. It is important to be creative, be unique, and offer a wide array of different events to make this a celebration and not just a basketball game.

Once the bids are submitted, the NCAA bid selection committee will review each bid. The bids will be narrowed down, and site visits will be made to each finalist city. Members of each city's bid committee will make in-person presentations to the committee. When assessing potential hosts, the NCAA committee will review each city's competition venue, transportation and lodging options, and the region's overall commitment to the event. A huge factor in determining whether a city is a viable candidate to host the Final Four is the venue. Venues must hold a minimum of 18,000 fans, including suite seats.

Economic Impact

economic impact
The amount of new money (financial gain) entering a region that can be attributed to a sporting event or facility.

Economic impact is the amount of new money entering a region that can be attributed to a sporting event or facility (Turco & Kelsey, 1992). The economic impacts of spending are composed of direct, indirect, and induced effects.

Direct effects of economic impact include the need to meet the increased demand of visitors for goods and services through actual dollars spent in the local community. This spending may be generated through concessions, ticket sales, and merchandise sales. *Indirect effects* of economic impact refer to the recirculation of the patrons' dollars that were generated through the direct effects. *Induced effects* refer to the increase in employment, employment opportunities, and household income that result from the economic activity from the direct and indirect effects (Dawson, Blahna, & Keith, 1993; Howard & Crompton, 1995).

Economic impact studies are important in presenting a bid to help convince the public that the event is a good investment. In addition, positive or negative economic results of sport events may be an important method to determine communities' draft budget for the coming year (Lee, 2001).

Calculating the economic impact an event will have on a city or region can be quite difficult. Crompton (1995) discusses 11 misapplications of economic impact analysis. Some of the reasons he lists for the inaccurate analysis include using sales instead of household income multipliers, misrepresenting employment multipliers, omitting opportunity costs, and measuring only benefits while omitting costs.

To combat these misapplications of economic impact analysis, the National Association of Sports Commissions (NASC) proposes two formulas for measuring economic impact (NASC, 2000). The first formula is an estimate of total visitor spending (TVS). In this formula, the number of out of town visitors (OTV) is multiplied by the average spending per day (ASD) and the number of days (ND):

$$TVS = OTV \times ASD \times ND$$

The second formula is much more complex. The first step of this formula is to calculate direct spending (DS). This is done by adding the total administrative operations spending (TAO) to the total visitor spending (TVS):

$$DS = TAO + TVS$$

The next step in this formula is to multiply direct spending (DS) by the regional multiplier (RM), which will produce the total economic impact (TEI) of the event:

$$TEI = DS \times RM$$

The NASC formulas were intended to help standardize how economic impact is calculated. However, not everyone has bought into using either of these two formulas. Thus, it is still important to always examine the methodologies organizations use when stating their economic impact figures.

While events can definitely bring in new money to a region, the bid process can result in cities or regions losing money as well. The failed bids for the

2016 Summer Olympics cost the city of Madrid $42.0 million (Lyon, 2009) and the city of Chicago between $49.3 million and $100 million (Smith, 2009). The costs of bidding for the Winter Olympic tend to be less expensive than the Summer Olympics. For the 2018 Winter Olympics, Annecy, France, had a budget of $26.4 million, which the leaders of the country did not feel was enough to win the bid to host the Olympic Games (Wilson, 2010). In the end, the leaders were correct, as Annecy did not win the 2018 Olympic bid.

mega-event The most complicated type of event to execute because it is often international in nature and requires years of planning to implement.

Types of Events

MEGA-EVENTS

Mega-events are the most complicated type of event to execute. Because they are often international in nature, mega-events often require years of planning to implement and a bid process to gain the rights to host the event. Due to the scope and visibility of mega-events, they are often easily identifiable to the general public. Thus, it is important the planning committee or event manager consider all aspects of the event to prevent damaging the brand.

Due to the nature of mega-events, there is often a bid process involved in securing the rights to present the event. As discussed earlier, bidding for the rights to hold an event involves competing against other potential host cities or sites and presenting the potential city's plan for that event.

Examples of mega-events at the highest level include the Olympic Games or the FIFA World Cup. These events often have full-time staffs devoted to something that occurs once every 4 years. When cities prepare their bid to win the Olympic Games, they must address the following 18 themes:

- National, regional, and candidate city characteristics
- Legal aspects
- Customs and immigration formalities
- Environmental protection and meteorology
- Financial considerations
- Marketing
- General sports concept

- Sports
- Paralympic Games plans
- Olympic Village plans
- Medical and health services
- Security
- Accommodations
- Transportation
- Technology
- Communications and media services
- Olympism and culture
- Guarantees

The Olympics announce which city the Games will be held in years in advance, which ensures that cities' planning committees have a great deal of time to produce a memorable Olympic Games and address each of the 18 themes discussed in their bid.

RECURRING EVENTS

Recurring events happen on a regular basis. They are the "easiest" type of event to execute because they occur consistently. Due to the regularity of these events, the staff is able to understand all of the details of executing the event. The benefit of recurring events is that event managers know how much food to order for the concession stand, the appropriate number of staff and volunteers needed, the amount of security, the timing of the event, and where the signage should be place.

recurring event An event that happens on a regular basis; it is the "easiest" type of event to execute because it occurs consistently.

Examples of recurring events can include Friday night football games at a local high school, a college rivalry game such as the Ohio State versus Michigan football game or the North Carolina versus Duke basketball game, or the New York City Marathon. All of these events may differ in size and the amount of planning that goes into the event, but the one thing they have in common is that they are all recurring events.

TRAVELING EVENTS

Traveling events are events that occur on a regular basis, but in a different location each year. Although they occur on a regular basis, the fact that the location varies from year to year presents a challenge. The individual or

traveling event An event that occurs on a regular basis but in various locations.

group of individuals who are charged with executing the event are rarely the same. This revolving cast presents a challenge for the organizing committee. However, the nice thing is that since the event occurs on a regular basis, the organizers are able to contact the previous host sites to identify what worked well for them, what they would do differently, and what, if any, challenges were present at the event.

An example of a traveling event is any of the NCAA championships. These championships often involve many regional sites in the early rounds and eventually culminate in the top teams arriving in one city to compete for the national championship.

ANCILLARY EVENTS

ancillary event An event that occurs in conjunction with another type of event.

Ancillary events occur in conjunction with another type of event. These events can require as much planning as another type of event, but the major difference is they are paired with a larger event. These events can provide additional revenue for the event organizers through ticket and merchandise sales, additional opportunities to sell or increase the price of sponsorships, and opportunities to involve different target markets.

For example, a fan fest at the NFL Super Bowl would be an ancillary event. The fan fest requires marketing to attract spectators, sponsors to offset the costs, volunteers to help run the games and exhibits, security to keep everyone safe, and so forth. While this event could stand alone, having it in conjunction with the Super Bowl is beneficial because it captures the excitement of many football fans who are in town for the game but may not have a ticket to go to the actual Super Bowl. It allows fans to be part of the Super Bowl experience without having to pay hundreds or thousands of dollars for the game ticket.

COMMUNITY EVENTS

community event A relatively small-scale event that appeals to a specific geographic region.

Community events are smaller in scale and appeal to a specific geographic region. While these types of events may not require the resources that a large traveling event would, they still require planning and forethought before they can be implemented. Local YMCAs or parks and recreation centers are organizations that often hold community sporting events for the people who reside within the town. When planning an event for the community, the event manager sometimes has the freedom to be a little more creative or try different things because it is not occurring on such a large scale.

Examples of community events could be a holiday 5K race, a mini triathlon for young children to expose them to the sport, or a youth swim meet. Even though these events may be considered small to some people, they all still require the planning process.

HOSTING NONSPORTING EVENTS IN A SPORT FACILITY

Between 2008 and 2011, $8.137 billion was invested in new major facility renovation expenses across the NFL, National Basketball Association (NBA), MLB, and National Hockey League (NHL) (Baade & Matheson, 2011). Those figures do not account for the number of new facilities that colleges, universities, or local communities constructed. These facility costs need to be recouped somehow, so organizations often look to bring in outside entities to generate revenue.

When you are in charge of a sport facility, there are times when you may have to host nonsporting events in your facility. These events could vary from a bridal show to a concert to the circus to a business meeting. Since these events are not what the facility manager is generally in charge of executing, it is necessary to ensure there is adequate up-front planning to account for all the details. Some of these details may include properly training the staff, bringing in additional equipment, setting down false floors to cover the basketball court, removing seats, hanging decorations, and so forth.

Timelines for Events

It is crucial that event managers have timelines when running events. These timelines will help keep all of the employees on track and ensure that all tasks are completed in advance. Timelines also help the event manager make sure each area is accounted for and nothing slips through the cracks.

There are different types of timelines that event managers may employ during the event management process. The first is an event timeline. This timeline is useful for all of the planning that is required leading up to the event. It lists who is in charge of each event planning area and the deadlines for when the event must be completed. See **Figure 5-2** for an example of an event timeline.

Event: Youth Soccer Camp
Date: July 15-18, 2014

Days Out	Task	Task Due Date	Responsible Party	Date Completed
−270	Secure soccer fields	10/17/2013		
−120	Create registration forms	3/16/2014		
−120	Secure event sponsors	3/16/2014		
−60	Start airing commercials for camp	5/15/2014		
−45	Finalize coaches for camp	5/30/2014		
−30	Obtain lunch for campers	6/14/2014		
−21	Plan drills for each day of camp	6/23/2014		
−14	Order camp t-shirts	6/30/2014		
−14	Purchase all equipment not obtained through sponsorship	6/30/2014		
−1	Print registration lists	7/14/2014		
5	Process all camp evaluation forms	7/23/2014		

FIGURE 5-2 Event Planning Timeline

The event manager should list the appropriate information at the top of the spreadsheet being used on the event timeline. *Days out* refers to how many days before the event the task must be completed. *Task* indicates what must be finished prior to the event. *Task due date* refers to the exact date the task must be finalized. *Responsible party* is the staff member who is in charge of completing the task. *Date completed* marks the actual date the task was finalized.

The second type of timeline is a day-of-event timeline. This timeline is necessary to guarantee completion of all details that need to be completed on the day of the event. It also indicates who is in charge of executing each of the details listed. **Figure 5-3** provides an example of a day-of-event timeline.

For the day-of-event timeline, *time* refers to when the task is to begin. *Task* indicates what is to be done during the period listed. *Responsible party* is the staff member who is in charge of completing the task. The *notes* section is for anything the event manager needs to highlight or remind the responsible party to do during that task.

Event: Youth Soccer Camp
Date: July 15-18, 2014

Day 1: July 15, 2014

Time	Task	Responsible Party	Notes
6:00 AM	Staff arrives at camp		
6:30 AM	Set up registration/check-in station		
6:30 AM	Check soccer fields for safety		
7:00 AM	Staff meeting		
8:00 AM	Registration open		
9:00 AM	Camp begins		
9:15 AM	Drill #1		
9:55 AM	Water break		
10:00 AM	Drill #2		
10:30 AM	Ensure water coolers are full		
10:55 AM	Water break		
11:00 AM	Drill #3		
11:00 AM	Begin set-up for lunch		
12:00 PM	Lunch		
1:00 PM	Tactics session		
1:30 PM	Drill #4		
2:00 PM	Ensure water coolers are full		
2:25 PM	Water break		
2:30 PM	Scrimmage		
4:00 PM	Camp dismissal		
4:30 PM	Inventory equipment		
5:00 PM	End of day staff meeting		
5:30 PM	Pack up for the day		

FIGURE 5-3 Example Day-of-Event Timeline

SUMMARY

Creating events, whether they are mega-events, recurring events, traveling events, ancillary events, or community events, requires much up-front planning. The event managers must set goals and find a way to differentiate themselves from other events currently in the marketplace. Much of the event's success will be determined in early planning meetings when the key decisions, such as sponsor acquisition, participant recruitment, marketing strategies, and sales, are made. If you are submitting a bid for an event, it is important to work with other stakeholders to ensure that you are putting together the most thorough bid possible for the event's rights holder. Regardless of the type of event and whether a bid is required, it is critical that the manager and his or her team think through each decision in the planning process to maximize their success. Timelines can help the manager stay organized. These tools will keep the whole team on track and ensure that each task is completed by the due date.

DISCUSSION QUESTIONS

1. What is the point of having a mission statement for an event? How does it contribute to the event?
2. What are SMART goals? Why is goal setting important to the overall success of an event?
3. How would you conduct a feasibility study for an event?
4. What types of events require an event bid? How long before an event should you prepare a bid? Who should you include in the process to help you put together the best bid possible?
5. List three examples of each type of event.

Case STUDY

Bidding to Host an NCAA Championship

You are working for a Division I athletic department and are part of the committee working to put together a bid to be a host site for the second and third rounds of the men's NCAA basketball championship. You have been nominated to write the section of the bid that examines and discusses your bid city (including infrastructure, hotels, things to do, restaurants, demographics, and access/proximity to airports).

This bid is a serious and important undertaking for your athletic department. The athletic department has never hosted an event of this size, so you do not have any previous documents to use as a guide.

Further, some previous host cities have had difficulty selling out their arenas. The mistake some previous sites have made was assuming that these tickets would sell themselves because it is an NCAA men's basketball tournament event. You are determined not to let this happen. Therefore, it is important to identify multiple target markets that you can go after to sell tickets.

Your job involves the following tasks:

1. Based on the event requirements just discussed, write up your section of the bid.
2. Explain what makes your host site unique.
3. Identify five target markets that you and your colleagues in the athletic department can target to sell tickets. Explain how you will persuade these target markets to buy tickets.
4. Outline how you will involve the surrounding community in the bid and the event.

REFERENCES

Baade, R., & Matheson, V. (2011). Financing professional sports facilities. In Z. Kotvel & S. White (Eds.), *Financing for local economic development* (2nd ed.). New York, NY: Sharpe Publishers.

Chappelet, J. L. (2005). *From initial idea to success: A guide to bidding for sports events for politicians and administrators.* Chavannes-Lausanne, Switzerland: Sports Event Network for Tourism and Economic Development of the Alpine Space.

Crompton, J. L. (1995). Economic impact analysis of sports facilities and events: Eleven sources of misapplication. *Journal of Sport Management, 9,* 14–35.

Dawson, S. A., Blahna, D. J., & Keith, J. E. (1993). Expected and actual regional economic impacts of Great Basin National Park. *Journal of Park and Recreation Administration, 11*(4), 45–59.

Doran, G. T. (1981). There's a SMART way to write management's goals and objectives. *Management Review, 70*(11), 35.

Farrelly, F. (2010). Not playing the game: Why sport sponsorship relationships break down. *Journal of Sport Management, 24*(3), 319–337.

Howard, D. R., & Crompton, J. L. (1995). *Financing sport.* Morgantown, WV: Fitness Information Technology.

Hums, M. A., & MacLean, J. C. (2008). *Governance and policy in sport organizations.* Phoenix, AZ: Holcomb-Hathaway Publishing.

Lee, S. (2001). A review of economic impact studies on sporting events. *The Sport Journal, 4*(2).

Lyon, S. (2009). Candidates for 2016 Olympics. *BBCSPORT.* Retrieved from http://news.bbc.co.uk/sport2/hi/olympic_games/7884296.stm

Meyer, P. J. (2006). What would you do if you knew you couldn't fail? Creating SMART goals. In *Attitude is everything: If you want to succeed above and beyond*. Merced, CA: Leading Edge Publishing.

National Association of Sports Commissions. (2000). *Economic impact study*. Cincinnati, OH: Author.

Pomfret, R., Wilson, J. K., & Lobmayr, B. (2009). *Bidding for sport mega-events*. Paper presented at the First European Conference in Sports Economics at University Paris 1 (Panthéon Sorbonne) on September 14–15.

Smith, A. (2009). Chicago loses Olympic bid to Rio. *CNN Money*. Retrieved from http://money.cnn.com/2009/10/02/news/economy/chicago_olympics _rejection/index.htm

Torkildsen, G. (1999) Organisation of major events. In *Leisure and recreation management* (4th ed.). New York, NY: Routledge.

Turco, D. M., & Kelsey, C. W. (1992). *Conducting economic impact studies of recreation and special events*. Alexandria, VA: National Recreation and Park Association.

Watt, D. C. (1998). *Event management in leisure and tourism*. Harlow, Essex: Addison Wesley Longman.

Wilson, S. (2010). AP interview: Annecy bid leader quit over budget. *USA Today*. Retrieved from http://www.usatoday.com/sports/olympics/2010-12-13-932394192_x.htm

CHAPTER 6

Designing the Event Experience

BRIANNA L. NEWLAND

CHAPTER OBJECTIVES

Upon completion of this chapter, the reader will be able to:

1. Clearly define the characteristics of the event experience
2. Recognize the importance of designing an event experience that creates meaning
3. Understand how to develop an event experience
4. Appreciate that stakeholders will have varied experiences
5. Identify how the unique elements of an event impact the experience

CHAPTER OVERVIEW

This chapter will outline the elements of designing the event experience, such as understanding experience characteristics, designing the event concept, co-creating event experiences, and attaching meaning. Designing the event involves identifying the unique elements of events; developing a concept, theme, and subsequent experience; and understanding how these elements tie together to create meaning at the event.

Industry VOICE

Rob Runnels—Director of Ballpark Entertainment, Round Rock Express

The Round Rock Express is a Triple-A minor league baseball team in the American Conference of the Pacific Coast League. It is located in Round Rock, Texas, just a few miles north of Austin. Former Major League Baseball pitcher and Hall of Famer Nolan Ryan and his company, Ryan-Sanders Baseball (RSB), acquired the Jackson Generals (a Double-A team) and moved them to Round Rock in 2000. RSB then moved the Generals to Corpus Christi and changed the team name to the Hooks, which were also owned by RSB at the time. While the history is a bit confusing, RSB finally bought the Edmonton Trappers in 2003, and this team became the Round Rock Express as the club moved from Double-A to Triple-A. The Express has been an affiliate of the Texas Rangers since 2011. My role in the organization as Director of Ballpark Experience is to oversee all of the activities during the games from the time the gates open until the last person leaves the stadium. Duties include creating the content for the video boards, writing the game scripts for the announcers, and picking and slotting the songs throughout the game. I oversee the production company, which is the camera crew that covers the game, and I hire and manage the Party Patrol and Street Team. The Party Patrol is a group of college students who dance on the dugouts, throw t-shirts, and interact with the crowd to ensure they have fun. The Street Team is a group of interns whom I mentor throughout the season on creating a game experience through the interaction with fans and spectators.

My career path was quite fortunate and a true testament to the power of networking. I graduated from Oklahoma State University with a degree in marketing. I moved to the Austin area and found a job in the banking industry to make ends meet. One night while playing in a recreational basketball game, I offered to drive an injured player home. We discussed work and future plans, and through that conversation, I learned that the injured player had worked for the Round Rock Express. He suggested I send him my resume, and using his personal network, he facilitated my first interview for an internship in promotions and entertainment. Fortunately, the man hiring for the internship worked the same Christian summer camps that I worked through college. I had incorporated an audiovisual component into the programs at camp, which was the experience the hiring manager was looking for in the internship. That audiovisual experience and the sport camp connection made me a unique candidate and perfect for the job. Following this internship, the Express promoted me to the position I currently hold.

Students interested in working in sport should consider every opportunity as a networking opportunity. I marketed myself, in business and leisure environments, every chance I could, and I asked questions of everyone I met. This tactic not only bettered my own skills and expertise, but I was able to learn the pathways these contacts had followed to get to their current job. It is also important to be well-rounded. I did not realize how well the skills I had developed at the youth summer camp would translate into my current job. Students should be aware of how their skills do transfer to different environments and sell that in an interview. Lastly, a strong customer service background is critical, and a wait staff job can easily help a student develop these skills. The relationships we build at the ballpark are key to our success, so I need employees who can interface and interact well with our customers.

When hiring for entry-level positions, I look for graduates with strong customer service and communication skills. The Express prides itself on our high level of customer service from the front office to the cleaning crew. I hire employees to create a specific atmosphere and build a relationship with our fans, so we have a high expectation for these skills. Graduates also need a strong desire to contribute to the team and should not take opportunities for granted. My biggest pet peeve in new hires is their sense of entitlement and what they are "owed" as they enter the workforce. There is a grave misunderstanding about working in sport; it is not glamorous and it requires deep dedication and hard work. Employees have to start at the bottom, working for very little pay for long hours, and spend a great deal of time working their way up. It is not easy and it requires a lot of discipline. I find that many new hires expect higher-level jobs before they have the experience to fulfill the requirements of the position. I spend a great deal of time managing expectations.

The biggest challenge I face in this position is keeping our fans interested at each game. We have 72 home games, averaging about 9000 attendees per game. If I have the same videos, music, and promotions at multiple games, the experience becomes dull and redundant. I love this challenge because it forces me to be creative and innovative every day to keep the experience fresh and exciting. The Express really supports my ingenuity, and I am successful because they let me experiment, even if I fail—and I have failed! But you know you work for a good organization when Nolan Ryan tells you, "Nice try, but don't do that one again!" and your new ideas are still supported. It is a challenge every day, but it is one that I enjoy taking on.

To work in the "experience" area, employees must really wear a number of hats. It is also vital that new graduates have audiovisual skills. Experience with photo and video editing software is highly suggested. Adobe Photoshop and Premiere skills are highly sought in my area. In addition, a strong command of social media use for promotional and marketing purposes and the etiquette of its use are critical. Students and new graduates should be incredibly aware of their online presence because I will consider that when I am hiring; how you present yourself online speaks volumes to how you might present our organization. The Express has worked hard to create a specific online "voice," so we care very deeply about how our employees and potential employees represent themselves online.

Introduction

When managing a sport event, good planning and implementation are effective only if the event is attractive and compels an audience to attend (Morgan, 2008). When people attend a sport event, it is often for more than just the sport competition itself; they will perceive the competition, the atmosphere, the food, the entertainment, etc., and attach meaning. That meaning then creates an **experience** for the attendee. A central concern of every sport event manager is the experience, both positive and negative, had by the individual. Therefore, to ensure a positive experience, the sport event manager must understand how the design features will influence the

experience In the sport event industry, the meaning attached to the event through the perception of the competition, atmosphere, social interactions, food, and entertainment, among other factors.

experience economy
The consumer's reaction to an event beyond the goods or services of the event alone.

experience and what meaning will be attached to the event by the attendees (Getz, 2012). Since the advent of the **experience economy**, whereby consumers desire occurrences beyond the goods or services alone (Pine & Gilmore, 1999), there has been recognition that the experience is an important foundational element of an event (Berridge, 2012; Getz, 2012; Morgan, 2008; Petterson & Getz, 2009). In the past, experiences were not seen as a distinct core offering; rather, they were combined as an aspect of services (Pine & Gilmore, 1999).

However, there is more to an experience than just the delivery of a service or the purchase of a good. If the design is conceptualized and implemented correctly, the services will set the stage and the goods will become the props to engage and create a memorable event for the individual (Berridge, 2012; Pine & Gilmore, 1999). For example, a guide at a sport museum provides a service as he or she conducts a tour of the History of Baseball section. This tour becomes an experience when the guide is dressed in accordance with a specific era, such as a uniform from the past, with others acting out the scene using props that would have been commonplace for the time. The guide is providing a service, but the tour becomes an experience as the patron is dispatched back in time through the re-creation of the event.

Designing a sport event is a predictive skill; an event manager needs to anticipate what the attendee will want and then how to design around that desire (Berridge, 2012). In the case of sport events, sport itself is the main purpose, but watching or participating in the sport is only a piece of what the attendee expects to experience. To create such a memorable event, one must understand the context in which an event is to take place, beyond the sport itself. Therefore, a sport event manager must have a clear understanding of the event's purpose, the key players (i.e., the stakeholders who are most likely to be affected by the event), the overall event objectives, and the setting and/or environment in which the sport takes place. Once these elements are clearly understood and delineated, the creative elements can be introduced.

Creating the Sport Event Experience

WHAT IS EXPERIENCE?

Above all, experiences are meant to be memorable and to engage in a personal way. However, defining *experience* is challenging because it is highly personal, inherent, and difficult to evaluate (Petterson & Getz, 2009). Experiences are highly **subjective** and **heterogeneous**. Experience is subjective in that two people can have completely different experiences at the same event (Ooi, 2005). For example, consider two marathon runners crossing the finish line at the exact time of 3:59.8. One runner might be ecstatic to finish under 4 hours and has perhaps set a personal record, thereby positively influencing the runner's overall race experience. For the other, this time might be considered disappointing and frustrating, thereby negatively impacting the overall experience. As a race director, you must consider how the elements you have design control over, such as the challenge of the course or how well the aid stations are stocked and spaced, can impact the performance, and therefore, the experience of the participants. If the other design elements are done exceptionally well, one can mitigate the challenge of a poor performance and heighten the impact of a positive one.

Experiences are also heterogeneous in that no two people will have the same experience, even with the same event features. Consider the same two runners from the marathon example attending the prerace exposition to pick up their registration packet. The expo serves as a registration site for the thousands of runners who must attend to pick up their race number and event-related materials and provides a variety of run-related vendors with products to showcase. Perhaps the expo is packed with people, lights, sounds, and vendors, creating an electrified and busy atmosphere. Runner A might love the excitement created by the people and atmosphere, which might positively impact his or her overall experience of the event. Meanwhile, runner B might not be at all interested in what the vendors have to offer and could become annoyed by having to sift through the crowd to get his or her registration packet. Therefore, as an event director, it is important to consider that not all the registered runners will enjoy an expo. As such, traffic flow might be designed to allow for quick pickup of registration packets by those who would prefer to get their information and immediately leave, while enabling other runners to engage with the vendors if they so wish. The director can thereby create an optimal experience for the majority of runners.

subjective A unique and personal venture undertaken by an individual, who attaches his or her own meaning.

heterogeneous Relating to perceptions of an experience that are widely dissimilar.

CONSIDERING STAKEHOLDER EXPERIENCES

stakeholder A person or entity that has a vested interest in the event.

Sport event design is meant for the guests (usually considered to be the fans and other spectators), but a number of other key **stakeholders** whose experiences matter greatly (e.g., volunteers, sponsors, media, residents near the venue, the athlete) are often overlooked (Petterson & Getz, 2009). Most often overlooked is the athlete. Event managers and researchers are often concerned with athletes' event-related motives or satisfaction with participation, but rarely are the athletes' event experiences considered (Petterson & Getz, 2009). For example, sport marketers are quick to research the satisfaction and experience of a spectator at the college football national championship game. And feedback from this key stakeholder group certainly is vital. However, rarely (if ever) are the teams and/or individuals competing ever asked about their participation experience. The participants are the *reason* for the event; it is not staged only for the spectator. The experiences of the athletes are assumed because it is the pinnacle of competition, but the sport event manager should be warned! Disregarding this important stakeholder is risky and can have a negative influence on the experiences of the other stakeholders.

From a fan perspective, the overall experience of the event is closely tied to the performance of the athlete or team. While we know that fans' experiences are often tied to expectations, superior experiences were often the result of positive game outcomes (Petterson & Getz, 2009). For a more casual spectator, perhaps the entertainment or elements beyond the competition impact the experience (Getz, 2012). The volunteers' and officials' experiences are linked to professional development and networking, which are similar to the experiences of the sponsors and vendors, who have interests in the business development experience. Different stakeholders will be directly or indirectly affected depending on their role, so it is important to understand the expectations people bring to sport events (Getz, 2012).

Characteristics of Experiences

As discussed, experiences cannot be designed and delivered like products due to the subjectivity and heterogeneity of the individual (Petterson & Getz, 2009). To make matters even more challenging, the term experience can be used as either a noun or a verb and is often used as such to describe the event. Take, for example, a student describing her experience at the 2012 London Olympic Games: "My experience at the Olympics was amazing! Even though I worked long, exhausting hours, I learned so much about running an event and I got to meet so many people! The networking opportunities were beyond what I expected!" In this one quote, the student touches upon a range of experiences that involve intellectual, physical, emotional, and social dynamics, all of which lead to her overall "amazing experience." Considering how the multifaceted nature of an experience influences the design elements can be quite daunting for a sport event manager. Fortunately, there are characteristics that can be defined and principles that can be followed to support sport event managers in creating the experience.

All events share **generic experiences**. When people attend sport events, they generally expect the opportunity to relax, socialize with others, and have fun. Because generic experiences can occur at any event, they relate more to the individual's state of mind and expectations for the event than the event's theme, concept, or setting (Petterson & Getz, 2009). These generic experiences can be staged to meet the more customary expectations. However, sport event attendees are often there for a *specific* purpose and will have **specific expectations** related to that event. For example, the specific expectations one has for a roller-derby event will be far different than those for a fencing event, although, *generally*, you would perhaps expect to have fun and be entertained at both. Another vital consideration for the sport event design is to note that different stakeholders (e.g., spectators, sponsors, media, volunteers, athletes) will all have varied, but also specific, expectations at the same sport event. Therefore, it is important to consider how the needs of the attendee will affect his or her individual experience. The anatomy of an experience, therefore, can be understood by exploring overall event satisfaction as measured in terms of intensity, duration, memorability, and meaning (Petterson & Getz, 2009) for each stakeholder group.

Intensity is the strength of the experience. For example, the intensity of an experience to which an individual is directly related, such as watching your favorite team at the World Series, would escalate based on those related expectations. **Duration** is the length that experience stays present in the attendee's mind. **Memorability** relates to the ability of the experience to be memorable. The more intense and enduring the experience, the more likely

---

TIP

The event setting and the surrounding environment will shape the visitor's experience (Petterson & Getz, 2009). As such, coordinate the setting and environment into your event design plan!

---

generic experience An experience that is commonly found at every event.

specific expectation An expectation or belief one holds about an event.

intensity (of experience) The strength of the experience.

duration (of experience) The length that the experience stays present for the individual.

memorability The ability of an experience to remain an intense and enduring memory.

meaning The perception and interpretation of the event elements that make the event significant.

one is to remember and cherish the experience. Finally, the experience must hold **meaning** for the attendee. Meaning is shaped by the memories and interests of the individual attending the event and is highly dependent on how that person interprets the event theme (Morgan, 2008).

Experience Dimensions

conative dimension The behavior, or physical responses, of event attendees.

Mannell and Kleiber (1997) posit three dimensions of experience: conative, cognitive, and affective. The **conative dimension** describes experience as actual behavior. This dimension describes the things people physically do; an individual's attitudes are manifested in their behaviors. This behavior can be observed through the purchasing of memorabilia, pictures with athletes or event signage/landmarks, or the framing of artifacts as a reminder of the event. For example, an athlete might frame a photo of herself crossing the finish line with her finisher's certificate and medal as a reminder of completing her first marathon. This experience, and the associated memories, might then drive this person to compete in future marathons or other running events.

cognitive dimension The making sense of an experience through awareness, perception, memory, learning, and judgment.

The **cognitive dimension** relates to making sense of the experience through awareness, perception, memory, learning, and judgment. It is difficult, as sport event managers, to assess what spectators are thinking or imagining

© Natursports/Shutterstock

during a sport event experience, but it can be done. For example, participants of a sport skills event will experience the cognitive dimension when mastering new skills and learning from experts in the sport. Observations or surveys of participants after an event can assist the sport event manager in understanding how the cognitive dimension influenced the experience.

The **affective dimension** concerns the emotions associated with the experience. A sport event can greatly affect emotions or moods. As a spectator, moods can vary along a positive–negative spectrum, depending on how well the team or athlete is performing. Likewise, the teams' and athletes' personal moods can be influenced by the sport event outcome. Due to the spontaneity of sport events, a number of emotions from elation to anxiety or frustration can change from one moment to the next, taking the attendee on a roller-coaster ride of emotion throughout the event. Experiencing the highs and lows of a sport event is not unique to just the spectator; the athlete competing feels dynamics as well. The response from the crowd can help fuel the competition unfolding between the participants, creating a unique affective experience for all involved.

affective dimension
The emotional response to the experience.

In the 1999 article "Welcome to the Experience Economy," Pine and Gilmore discuss two dimensions of experience: *customer participation* and *connection*. One end of the customer participation spectrum is anchored by passive participation, which mainly involves spectating. The participants have no direct interaction with the athletes involved in the competition. Such participants would include cycling spectators attending a road race event and watching from the side of the road. At the other end of the spectrum lies active participation, which allows the participants to play a direct role in creating the event. These participants would include athletes running in a marathon.

The second dimension described by Pine and Gilmore (1999) is the relationship of the experience through connection. *Absorption* anchors one end of the connection spectrum and describes how participants "drink in" the event around them. The participant sitting in the stands watching the basketball game absorbs the action unfolding on the court. At the other end of the spectrum lies *immersion*, which involves a drowning of the senses. The participant is completely immersed in the sights, sounds, and smells infused into the environment. A spectator would be immersed at the same basketball game if he or she were invited onto the court to participate in leading the team into the arena. The fan would experience firsthand the fog that rolls out as lights flash and the music drowns the roar of the crowd.

By incorporating the two dimensions, four broad categories of experiences can be illustrated according to where they fall into the spectra. These broad categories create the four realms of experience—entertainment, educational, escapist, and aesthetic—that can be used to describe different experiences.

The *entertainment realm* tends to include more passive forms of participation that are more likely to absorb the participant than to immerse the participant in the experience. The *educational realm* includes experiences that involve greater immersion and active participation. For example, perhaps an event expo for sport participants includes experts offering short seminars or workshops related to skill mastery or nutritional tips. The athletes participating might have their sport skills and/or diets assessed, allowing an individual to learn from the experts. The *escapist realm* includes experiences that enable the participant to be fully immersed in the active participation. An example of this experience involves an athlete competing in the Olympics. These athletes are fully immersed in the ritual, ceremony, and atmosphere of the Games. Lastly, the *aesthetic realm* includes experiences that are similar to the escapist experiences without the active participation. In this realm, the spectator in the stands watching the Olympic Games would be absorbed in the same ritual, ceremony, and atmosphere but, as a spectator, would be a passive participant.

Designing Experiences

THEMING

theming Alteration of the attendees' sense of time and reality through tangible and memorable cues that leave lasting impressions.

cues A feature or element of the event that is perceived and interpreted by the attendee with the intended outcome of a lasting (hopefully positive) impression or memory.

Once the context and stakeholders of the event are determined, the first design task is to establish the concept and theme of the experience. **Theming** an event involves more than just decorations; it should alter the attendees' sense of time and reality through tangible and memorable **cues** that leave lasting impressions (Getz, 2012). To create impressions that foster meaning, the theme should convey a story using symbolic elements like logos, flags, color schemes, and displays. These elements should be layered throughout the event spaces and places in which the attendees gather.

It is the sport event manager's job to maximize the use of positive cues while minimizing the negative cues (Pine & Gilmore, 1999). Positive cues fulfill the theme through impressions, or takeaways, of the experience,

VIGNETTE 6-1

Noosa Surfing Festival

The Noosa Surfing Festival is held at Noosa Heads on the Sunshine Coast in Queensland, Australia. While the event itself is one of the most popular international longboard surfing events, what is of greatest interest to some visitors is how the area is themed. Although many are not an official part of the event, the businesses in Noosa Heads have chosen to theme their stores to align with the event. Surf-themed elements like longboards, surfing posters, and board shorts are displayed in storefront windows and within the stores, which not only bolsters visitor spending, but also provides further local support and enthusiasm around the event (O'Brien, 2007).

© FlashStudio/Shutterstock

such as exceptional customer service, design elements, entertainment, food and beverage (Getz, 2012), and elements of surprise (Petterson & Getz, 2009). Therefore, incorporating serendipitous moments of surprise for the attendee is a good way to exceed customer expectations and create positive experience outcomes (Chalip, 2006; Getz, 2012; Petterson & Getz, 2009). Positive cues must affirm the nature of the experience by supporting the theme with design elements and memorabilia.

Memorabilia can support cues with the tangible goods available for purchase or free takeaways. For example, the event experience can begin with the event registration process. Consider, as a race director, the positive cues and memorabilia you could incorporate into the registration process for an Ironman triathlon (2.4-mile swim, 112-mile bike ride, and 26.2-mile run that must be completed in under 17 hours). For those brave enough to participate, the event elicits a range of emotions from trepidation to ecstasy, and the experience begins the moment the athlete decides to register. To achieve Ironman status by completing this endurance event is of great importance

memorabilia
Tangible goods that support theme cues and that are available for purchase or as free takeaways.

in the triathlon community, so as an event director, you can facilitate that status with cues in the registration process. Allowing athletes to personalize their bib number can provide a personal cue of the experience (and add a piece of memorabilia). When finalizing the registration, the system could provide written or audio cues saying, "Congratulations! Your registration is complete. Only 102 days until . . . You. Are. An. IRONMAN!" Even the smallest cue and piece of memorabilia, such as in this example, can aid in the creation of a unique event experience.

CREATING LIMINALITY

There's no denying that sporting outcomes will impact the experience. Experiences are tied closely to the expectations sport fans have about their team's performance and competition (Petterson & Getz, 2009). Still, a sport event tends to elicit a sense of something more important that transcends sport itself and creates an energy in the atmosphere that can be shared by all (Chalip, 2006). Attendees feel a sense of community or belonging among the other attendees. This special place where people share very specific commonalities is known as **communitas**. The communitas serves to bring all people together for a shared experience.

communitas A special place where event attendees share a heightened sense of community and belonging.

With roots in anthropology, the sense of community has been discussed in the sport context (Green & Chalip, 1998). At the core of an experience is a zone that creates meaning that transcends the person and creates meaning outside of normal everyday life. For a ritualistic or sacred event, this special, transcended space is known as the **liminal zone**. For an event that is more secular (unsacred) in nature, this special transcended space is known as the **liminoid zone**. In both cases, people experience a phenomenon that takes the individual beyond an average day, creating a feeling that the individual belongs to something bigger. This zone, which is defined by spatial and temporal terms, can be engendered through the event design and programming (Chalip, 2006; Petterson & Getz, 2009).

liminal zone A zone within a sacred, ritualistic event that creates meaning that transcends the person and creates meaning outside of normal everyday life.

Certainly sport events—many of which are steeped with ritual, ceremony, and tradition—have the means to enable liminality to render social value. To many sport event managers, this social value is an important event impact to be leveraged. Liminal events require two key elements: a sense of celebration and social camaraderie (Chalip, 2006). To foster these two elements, the event design must enable points of sociability where people can

liminoid zone A zone within an unsacred, secular event that creates meaning that transcends the person and creates meaning outside of normal everyday life.

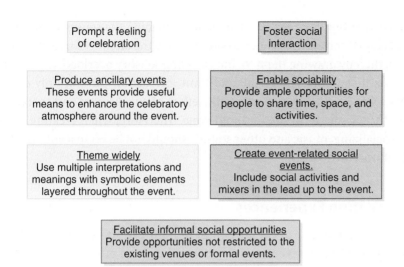

Figure 6-1   Creating the Liminoid Zone.

Data from Chalip, L. (2006). Towards social leverage of sport events. *Journal of Sport & Tourism, 11,* 109–127.

share the experience. Chalip (2006) suggests five strategies to promote celebration and camaraderie (see **Figure 6-1**):

Together, these techniques provide sport event managers with tools that can allow them to use celebration and social interaction to build social capital and enhance a sense of community. Creating a liminoid zone for sport events enables communication and brings together groups that might otherwise not come together (Chalip, 2006). For example, at the Australian Open event in Melbourne, Australia, there is a specific area in the heart of the various staged courts known as Garden Square, which features tennis on the big screen, roving entertainers, and a Fan Zone where sponsors and partners can engage with attendees. The area also has the Heinekin Live Stage featuring a range of music genres and top performers to create a social and entertaining zone for people to come together to share the experience, socialize, and enjoy entertainment beyond tennis.

ENGAGING THE SENSES

In addition to the symbolic elements used to create the liminoid zone, the theme can be enhanced by stimulating the senses. Some of the cues can heighten an experience by just affecting one sense, like the smell of popcorn or hot dogs at a baseball game. Engaging the senses is a balancing act, and the event design should immerse the attendees in the experience, thereby drawing them in, but avoiding sensory overload. Lights and sounds that are overpowering and limit interaction can not only create sensory overload, but also negate the effect of engagement and socialization that is sought in the liminoid zone. Therefore, when creating areas for socializing, music and other sounds should not be set to a volume that disallows conversation.

Co-creating Experiences

There are a number of events competing for the attendees' valued leisure time. On any given weekday or weekend, an attendee can go to a music festival, a performing-arts show, the local shopping center, or a baseball game. Sport events must compete within a very saturated marketplace where people have a multitude of leisure events at which they may spend their valuable time. Co-creation is a design tool that provides additional value to an event by allowing the attendee high-quality interactions with the event (Prahalad & Ramaswamy, 2004; Van Limburg, 2008). Often in sport events, there is a focus on the attendee experience, but it is often a passive one. Further, opportunities for value creation are enhanced when an event provides personalized co-creation as a unique experience (Prahalad & Ramaswamy, 2004). For co-creation to occur, the attendee and event must work jointly. **Table 6-1** describes the concept of co-creation.

VIGNETTE 6-2

Co-creation Using Technology!

There are few examples in the sport event world that enable co-creation, but there are plenty of opportunities for growth in this area. One example is the use of event-specific application technology (or "app"). The creation of an event-specific app that allows users to not only interact with the event but also to interact socially with friends can add to the experience. The ability to set a schedule, check in to various areas of the event, and make and receive updates in real time allows attendees to stay in touch, plan their event experience, and stay up-to-date on the latest information from you, the sport event director, through texts, posts, Tweets, or other social networking technologies.

TABLE 6-1   The Concept of Co-creation

What Co-creation Is Not	What Co-creation Is
Focus on the attendee	Joint creation of experience
Enablement of the "attendee is always right" viewpoint	Creation of a relationship with attendee, not mass market
Pampering of the attendee with lavish customer service	Opportunity for the attendee to co-construct the service
Mass customization of offerings	Creation of an experience with the environment
Transfer of activities from the event to the customer	Shared creation of activities
Attendee as product manager or co-designer	Co-construction of personalized experiences
Product variety	Experience variety
Staging experiences	Innovative experience environments

Reprinted from *Journal of Interactive Marketing 18*(3), C.K. Prahalad, Venkat Ramaswamy, C-creation experiences: The next practice in value creation, pages 5–14, Copyright 2004, with permission from Elsevier.

Interaction is a key driver for the co-creation experience (Van Limburg, 2008). Communitas engendered through the liminoid zone at a sport event is an important tool to create the interaction. The goal of co-creation is to move the attendee from passive–absorbed participant to active–immersed participant within the four realms of experience (Pine & Gilmore, 1999).

Meanings Attached

What is an experience without meaning? In sport, meaning is conveyed through the symbolic elements used to create the liminoid zone: ceremony, ritual, logos, flags, banners, and color schemes (Chalip, 2006; Getz, 2012). Memories and interests of the attendee shape the meaning attached to an experience; it is highly dependent on the interaction between the event theme and the interpretations by the attendee (Morgan, 2008). To be competitive through experience design, sport event managers must address attendees' need for meaning by understanding the role of meaning in their lives and how to evoke meaning through the event (Diller, Shedroff, & Rhea, 2005).

TABLE 6-2   Meanings Attached to Sport Events

Personal	Sociocultural	Political	Economic
Belonging	Sense of community	Community development programs	Increased tourism
Self-esteem	Community pride		New jobs
Mastery	Sharing of customs/ values	Improved infrastructure	New business
Health/well-being	Shared celebration	National identity building	
Accomplishment	Social interaction	International awareness	
Self-discovery			
Nostalgia			

Sport events induce a number of meanings, including personal, social, cultural, economic, political, and nostalgic (see **Table 6-2**). Sport event experiences range from unimportant entertainment to a profoundly transforming experience. Creating the liminoid zone and theming the sport event using symbolism, ritual, and ceremony can deepen the meaning one attaches to the experience, thereby enhancing the memory of the event.

SUMMARY

As this chapter illustrates, creating the event experience involves much more than just offering an event. There are a number of key elements to consider and carefully plan in order to elicit a positive response from event attendees. It is important to remember that the attendees' experiences will be subjective and heterogeneous. Therefore, an event manager cannot control for every specific aspect. Rather, the event manager should consider how theming, creating communities, and allowing for attendees to create their own experience could impact the overall success of the event.

DISCUSSION QUESTIONS

1. Define the *experience economy* and discuss how you could incorporate it into a spectator sport event. How might this differ from a sport participation event?
2. Co-creation is an innovative method for involving your patrons in helping you shape their experiences. Discuss how you might incorporate co-creation elements into a spectator sport event.

3. The liminoid zone is that area that transcends normal space and time. How might you create this for participants *and* spectators at a sport event?
4. Develop a theme for a sport event and discuss how you would engage the senses through this theme.

Case STUDY

Creating an Experience at the UCI World Cup

The Union Cycliste Internationale (UCI) is the international governing body for cycling and sanctions the UCI World Cup, which is a multiround mountain bike race series. The first World Cup series, composed of cross-country events, was held in California in 1989. The Downhill discipline was inaugurated 2 years later, followed by the Dual Slalom in 1998. In 2012, the UCI World Cup Downhill and Cross Country series included 10 staged events in 9 countries across the world, including the United States, Scotland, Italy, South Africa, Belgium, Czech Republic, France, Canada, and Norway. As part of the competition, mountain bikers win points according to their placing in each event, with the reigning series leaders identified by a special jersey. The mountain bike season culminates with the UCI World Trials and Championships staged by the UCI.

As an event director, you have just won a bid to host a UCI World Cup event on Keystone Mountain in Silverthorne, Colorado. In this inaugural multiday event, your main goal is to create an experience your key stakeholders will never forget. You have three main objectives for this event: (1) to create a sense of celebration with multiple points for socialization among the event patrons, (2) to create a memorable experience that encourages customers and mountain bikers to return annually for the event, and (3) to increase the length of stay in Silverthorne. The local government in Silverthorne is interested in offsetting the effects of seasonality during the summer, so they are encouraged by your proposal to extend the amount of time visitors stay in the area.

Using what you have just learned in the chapter about designing events that inspire memorable experiences, develop a design plan for your event. Be sure to consider the following:

1. What is your event concept?
   a. How do you use this concept to theme your event?
   b. How do you create an atmosphere that leaves a meaningful experience?
2. Who are the key stakeholders?
   a. How might their needs differ in a way that could affect their experience?
   b. Will these needs influence your concept/theme as described in question 1?
3. What aspects of the setting and environment could be incorporated into your theme and design concept?

4. How would you create your liminoid zone?
5. When there are multiple races in one event, how do you tie these races together over the multiday event to drive interest, spending, and length of stay among your attendees?

Resources for Case Study: http://www.silverthorne.org; http://www.uci.ch/; and http://www.redbull.com/en/bike/event-series/1326300800262/uci-mountain-bike-world-cup.

Readings for Case Study: Petterson, R., & Getz, D. (2009). Event experiences in time and space: A study of visitors to the 2007 World Alpine Ski Championships in Åre, Sweden. *Scandinavian Journal of Hospitality and Tourism, 9*, 308–326.

REFERENCES

Berridge, G. (2012). *Events design and experience*. Oxford, UK: Taylor and Francis.

Chalip, L. (2006). Towards social leverage of sport events. *Journal of Sport & Tourism, 11*, 109–127.

Diller, S., Shedroff, N., & Rhea, D. (2005). *Making meaning: How successful businesses deliver meaningful customer experiences*. San Francisco, CA: Pearson Education.

Getz, D. (2012). *Event studies. Theory, research and policy for planned events*. New York, NY: Routledge.

Green. B. C., & Chalip, L. (1998). Sport tourism as celebration of subculture. *Annals of Tourism, 25*, 275–291.

Mannell, R. C., & Kleiber, D. A. (1997). *A social psychology of leisure*. State College, PA: Venture Publishing.

Morgan, M. (2008). What makes a good festival? Understanding the event experience. *Event Management, 12*, 81–93.

O'Brien, D. (2007). Points of leverage: Maximizing host community benefit from a regional surfing festival. *European Sport Management Quarterly, 7*(2), 141–165.

Ooi, C. (2005) A theory of tourism experiences. In: T. O'Dell & P. Billing (Eds.), *Experience-scapes: Tourism, culture, and economy* (pp. 51–68). Copenhagen: Copenhagen Business School Press.

Petterson, R., & Getz, D. (2009). Event experiences in time and space: A study of visitors to the 2007 World Alpine Ski Championships in Åre, Sweden. *Scandinavian Journal of Hospitality and Tourism, 9*, 308–326.

Pine, J. B., & Gilmore, J. H. (1999). Welcome to the experience economy. *Harvard Business Review* (Reprint: # 98407) 97–105.

Prahalad, C. K., & Ramaswamy, V. (2004). Co-creation experiences: The next practice in value creation. *Journal of Interactive Marketing, 18*(3), 5–14.

Van Limburg, B. (2008). Innovation in pop festivals by cocreation. *Event Management, 12*(2), 105–117.

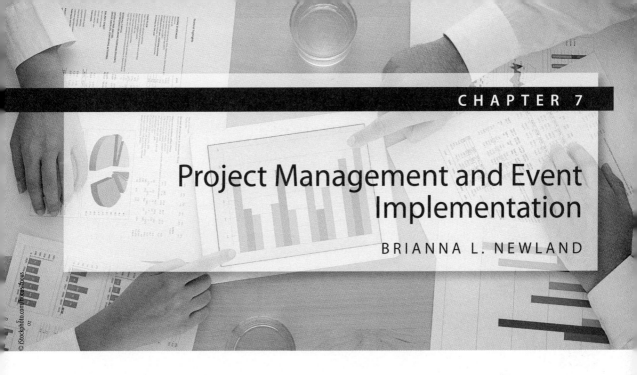

CHAPTER 7

Project Management and Event Implementation

BRIANNA L. NEWLAND

CHAPTER OBJECTIVES

Upon completion of this chapter, the reader will be able to:

1. Describe the necessity of project management in the management of sport events
2. Use project management tools to plan and conduct a successful event
3. Outline the phases of project management

CHAPTER OVERVIEW

This chapter will explore the elements of staging and implementing a sport event. It introduces project management concepts and tools to assist the sport event manger in planning and implementing the event. Concepts such as the work breakdown structure, Gantt charts, and other project management tools will be introduced.

Industry VOICE

Michael Gilason—Vice President, Main Line Expo and Events

Courtesy of Michael Gilason

Main Line Expo and Events, located just outside of Philadelphia in King of Prussia, Pennsylvania, is an organization that specializes in trade show and special event decoration. Our organization's mission is to provide exceptional service by transforming venues beyond expectations, while our vision is to be a leader in the event industry by continuing to grow and prosper in a competitive marketplace. My role in the organization is to oversee all aspects of sales, operations, and logistics to ensure continued success.

My career path has been interesting and unexpected. I graduated from Northern Arizona University with a bachelor of science degree in parks and recreation management and had planned to work in leisure management in some capacity. But, like many, my journey did not follow the path I had originally set for myself. I started in sales, working in insurance and ancillary benefits for larger corporations. From there, I moved into management consulting before joining Main Line Expo and working in the special events industry. The skills I developed in sales and management consulting have honed the expertise necessary to run a small business and take on this challenging role.

Working in the special events industry can be very exciting and fast paced. For those interested in this area, I would recommend that you *network, network, network* and gain as much hands-on experience as possible. The events industry is filled with incredible talent to learn from, so take advantage. The cliché, *it's who you know*, is true. I am more likely to interview someone based on an industry contact's reference than simply a name from a pile of papers. It is critical that you not only meet industry contacts, but also build relationships with them so they can adequately speak to your skills and expertise.

When hiring for entry-level positions, I look for eagerness and adaptability along with hands-on experience through volunteering or internships. It is also helpful if the candidate has worked for other event management companies, even on a part-time basis in a serving role (such as a waiter or cleanup crew). If students are interested in this area, I recommend volunteering for as many events as possible and/or creating your own events. There is no better way to learn how to adapt to this fast-paced environment and build industry contacts than through hands-on experience.

There are a number of opportunities in this field, but it is not without its challenges. The state of the economy is one of the biggest challenges I face, as companies tend to spend less on events during slow economic times. To manage this challenge specifically, we focus on strengthening the long-standing relationships with our current customers to ensure no business is lost during these slower periods. Another challenge that smaller companies like mine face is competing with larger national event-decorating suppliers, who often secure exclusive partnerships with venues. Not only do such partnerships eliminate customers' choices, but they also cut out the competition. These arrangements are excellent if you win the exclusive bid, but unfortunately smaller organizations are unlikely to do so. To combat this competitive disadvantage, we consistently exceed our customers' expectations so they will advocate to the venues on our behalf and demand to work with their own decorators. Depending on the exclusivity contracts, our organization has benefitted from this approach.

The special events industry involves numerous moving parts in a highly unpredictable environment. There are a number of vendors (e.g., audiovisual, lighting, decorating, equipment) that require clear expectations and coordination of tasks. Project management tools allow event managers to properly coordinate the vendors to not only ensure success of the event, but to facilitate and develop relationships properly and efficiently. Event managers will come to rely very heavily on these vendors, so it is vital that you find suppliers that are trustworthy and dependable. Doing so will ensure that event implementation is manageable and relatively stress-free!

Introduction

"The devil is in the details" expresses the idea that whatever one does, he or she should do it thoroughly—meaning, the details are important. This is an important idiom to remember when planning and staging events because there is high pressure and often only one opportunity to "get it right." Therefore, sport event managers must incorporate techniques that offer advantages and support for managing events. Project management techniques offer the sport event manager this advantage by integrating the various objectives from the event units (i.e., marketing, sponsorship, operations, and logistics) into one workable plan for the entire project—the sport event. This chapter examines how project management tools can assist the manager in the planning, staging, and implementation of a sporting event.

Project Management

WHAT IS PROJECT MANAGEMENT?

Project management is the dynamic process of organizing and managing appropriate resources in a controlled and structured manner to deliver the clearly defined work required to complete a project within the given scope, time, and, often, cost constraints (Patel, 2008; Young, 2007). Sport events, whether they are one-off, annual, or weekly, are projects. A **project** is a temporary and one-time venture undertaken to create a unique product with specific outcomes and benefits (Patel, 2008)—in this case, the sport event. An important aspect to keep in mind is that the event is a deliverable of the project management process (Allen, O'Toole, Harris, & McDonnell, 2011). The event itself might occur over a few hours, days, or even weeks, but the

project management The dynamic process of organizing and managing appropriate resources in a controlled and structured manner to deliver the clearly defined work required to complete a project within the given scope, time, and, often, cost constraints.

project A temporary and one-time venture undertaken to create a unique product with specific outcomes and benefits.

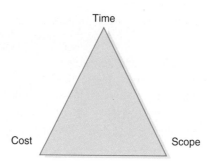

FIGURE 7-1　The Project Management Triangle

project management process may take place over many months, or, as in the case of the Olympic Games, many years. Project management integrates all the management tasks necessary to oversee the work before, during, and after the event has occurred.

There are two main challenges of project management. The first challenge is to ensure the event can be delivered within the defined constraints (i.e., time, cost, and scope). Known as the **project management triangle** (Allen et al., 2011), each constraint cannot be altered without impacting the other sides of the triangle and, in the process, the *quality* of the event (see **Figure 7-1**).

The *time* constraint refers to the amount of time allotted to complete the project. Since sport events are bound by a specific date, when the project runs behind schedule, cost and scope are (often negatively) impacted.

The *cost* constraint refers to the amount of money budgeted to complete the project. If a sport event manager does not want to affect the event quality in any way, then costs will go up considerably when behind schedule. Most sport events are greatly bound by costs, especially in the initial planning stages.

Take, for example, a softball tournament. Much of the planning and coordination begins before the team registration fees begin trickling in. Therefore, sport event managers must carefully forecast a budget that takes into consideration not only the event elements, but also *when* the money will be accessible. Marketing expenses are frequently required early in the implementation stage. By building

---

project management triangle The cost, time, and scope constraints that impact the final quality of an event.

TIP

First-year and one-off event budgets are very difficult to forecast. Do your research early! Call multiple vendors and suppliers of your event equipment and ask for detailed bids. Not only will this provide you with a picture of your expenses, it will also give you an opportunity to negotiate better prices.

relationships with key vendors, event managers can defer payment to after the event in order to avoid up-front expenses. The ability to delay payment is key when the money is not immediately accessible.

Changes to the other two sides of the triangle could be very detrimental to the costs associated with the event. If an event falls behind schedule and containing costs is a concern, then scope—and the quality—will be compromised. The final constraint, *scope*, refers to what must be done to produce the event. It involves the planning, coordination, and implementation of the sport event. Project management tools help to prevent delays that can be costly and impact the quality of the event. Let us return to our softball tournament example. Perhaps in the planning stage the event manager had planned to hire a DJ to entertain the spectators and players in the common area between games. However, the event planning has fallen behind schedule and costs have gone up. The event manager can no longer pay the $1500 to have the professional DJ perform the weekend of the tournament. However, with a little creativity, the event manager is able to secure a university student and amateur DJ for a fraction of the price, $600. This quick thinking allows the event to still provide entertainment, but the quality will be compromised, if we assume that the amateur does not have the skills and expertise of the professional DJ.

The second (and perhaps more ambitious) challenge is the proper allocation and assimilation of the inputs (e.g., people, money, time) needed to meet the objectives of the event (Patel, 2008). Project management tools help the event manager systematically define the tasks necessary to meet overall objectives, delegate those tasks to the right people, allocate financial resources appropriately, and coordinate when the tasks must be completed. Project management accounts for elements that are not usually found in ongoing management of typical organizations. Events have a specific end date, budget, and deliverable (the event itself) that cannot be improved upon (Allen et al., 2011). While conventional products are continuously updated and improved based on consumer feedback, events do not have that same luxury. An event must produce its best product the first time, especially if it's a one-off sport event.

© iStockphoto.com/hocus-focus

VIGNETTE 7-1

The 2010 New Delhi Commonwealth Games

The 2010 Commonwealth Games were beset with a number of expensive obstacles throughout the planning and staging phases that nearly compromised the event to the point of cancellation. Besieged by severe construction delays, financial corruption of the Games' officials and contractors, withdrawal of high-profile athletes (such as Usain Bolt) from the competition, terrorist threats, violent storms damaging poorly constructed event venues, poor venue conditions (including the athlete village), an outbreak of dengue fever, and a collapsed bridge, it is a wonder that the Games occurred at all. These delays and complications did come at a price, impacting the quality of the venue structures and escalating the costs from 6.5 billion rupee ($1.2 million USD) to 11.5 billion rupee ($2.1 million USD).

domain As used by the International Event Management Body of Knowledge, a division of the labor required at an event.

administration domain The event management domain that includes the finance, human resources, information, procurement, stakeholders, systems, and time elements of an event.

design domain The event management domain that contains the event's content, theme, program, environment, and production, entertainment, and catering needs.

Phases of Project Management

A main aim of project management is to control risk and potential failure by providing a clear direction that aligns with the strategic goals and objectives for the event. The management of the sport event will pass through a number of phases, each of which will include a number of tasks that yield a deliverable that sparks the next phase. The number of phases varies by industry, but most disciplines that utilize project management tools agree on five core phases: initiation, planning, implementation, monitoring, and shutdown (Patel, 2008; Young, 2007). Further to that, the International Event Management Body of Knowledge (EMBOK) has conceptualized a three-dimensional depiction of the phases, domains, and processes necessary to create and deliver sport events. This conceptualization is adapted in **Figure 7-2**.

According to EMBOK (2006), the **domains** can be further divided to provide greater detail for the management of the event. For example, the **administration domain** contains the following elements: finance, human resources, information, procurement, stakeholders, systems, and time. The **design domain** contains the event's content, theme, program, environment, and production, entertainment, and catering needs. The **marketing domain** is composed of the event marketing plan, marketing materials, merchandise, promotion, public relations, sales, and sponsorship. The **operations domain** consists of communications, event infrastructure, logistics, the venue, technical needs, participants, and attendees. Finally, the **risk domain** involves compliance issues, emergency plans, health and safety plans, insurance needs,

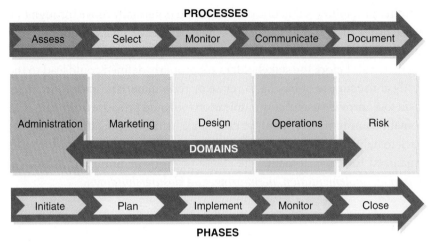

PROCESSES

Assess → Select → Monitor → Communicate → Document

| Administration | Marketing | Design | Operations | Risk |

DOMAINS

Initiate → Plan → Implement → Monitor → Close

PHASES

FIGURE 7-2   EMBOK Model for Event Management

Adapted from International EMBOK Executive (www.embok.org), 2006.

marketing domain
The event management domain comprised of the event's marketing plan, marketing materials, merchandize, promotions, public relations, sales, and sponsorship.

operations domain
The event management domain that consists of communications, event infrastructure, logistics, the venue, technical needs, participants, and attendees.

legal concerns, security needs, and any risk-related decisions. These domains could easily represent the departments that are developed to manage the sport event and provide an organizational structure. However, because smaller events do not have the financial or human resources to cordon off these domains into departments, typically a small number of staff members must work within all of these domains. Therefore, it is important to organize the work by domain to ensure that the tasks necessary to complete the project and deliver the event are completed.

Each domain will have tasks specifically associated with the particular phase at hand. Some domains may depend on the other domain in order to begin or complete work. For example, it is important that the event stakeholders are clearly defined by the administration domain prior to the marketing domain developing the materials directed to stakeholders.

© Yuri Arcurs/ShutterStock

risk domain The event management domain that consists of compliance issues, emergency plans, health and safety plans, insurance needs, legal concerns, security needs, and any risk-related decisions.

Another possibility is that one domain could potentially move through one phase faster than another domain, which can create chaos if not properly managed. Going back to the stakeholder example, developing the marketing materials before the stakeholders are properly defined could lead to the costly consequence of having to revise or redo materials. Project management tools provide useful communication tools and processes to ensure each domain communicates openly at each stage, while keeping the domains on track to deliver a successful event. Planning by stage will also keep the tasks organized for each domain. The stages of event planning are *initiation*, *planning*, *implementation*, *monitoring*, and *closure/shutdown*.

INITIATION

initiation phase The stage in event planning that allows sport event organizers to define the event, set objectives, and determine the sport event's feasibility.

First and foremost, the sport event requires direction. The **initiation phase** allows sport event organizers to define the event, set objectives, and determine the sport event's feasibility. Many events are unsuccessful because inadequate information collection in the initiation phase leads to unclear goals and objectives, unrealistic resource and time estimates, and changes to objectives mid-project (Zarndt, 2011). Further, if you are seeking financial assistance for the sport event with a bank loan, for example, a bank will most likely require a detailed feasibility study before granting funds (Lock, 2013). In the initiation stage, a feasibility study will detail the viability of a sport event and the managerial requirements necessary to deliver it. This report may also detail date and venue suggestions, an assessment of competing events operating within the host location, potential sponsors, market research identifying potential customers and sponsors, a draft budget, identification of key stakeholders, and, in some cases, the potential social, political, and environmental impacts (Allen et al., 2011). A thorough feasibility study will include alternative configurations of the sport event to enable a variety of options prior to the planning phase. The end of the initiation phase is often marked by a red or green light to continue to the planning stages. **Table 7-1** identifies the areas by domain to explore feasibility of a sport event.

One very important area on which to focus the feasibility study is the financial concerns, under the risk domain. A good event manager should know whether an event is financially feasible prior to green lighting the event. To determine what financial risk exists, a breakeven analysis should be conducted using the breakeven equation, EBIT = revenues – variable costs – fixed

TABLE 7-1   Feasibility Areas by Domain

Administration	Design	Marketing	Operations	Risk
• Expertise of staff • Resource viability: draft budget, staff requirements • Identification of key stakeholders • Timeline for project completion	• Event date and venue • Location accessibility • Program and production viability • Environment capability	• Competing events • Market research • Customer identification • Sponsor identification • Promotion, public relations, sponsor capability	• Managerial requirements • Venue/infrastructure capability • Social, environmental, political impacts • Technical capability	• Social, environmental, political impacts • Financial concerns • Operational concerns • Legal concerns, insurance • Security

costs of production $(PQ - VQ - F = 0)$. This equation is an incredibly useful way to examine the number of attendees (or registered participants, if you are running a tournament, for example) required for the event to break even. The key to a strong analysis is to accurately predict all of the operational expenses involved, both variable and fixed. This can be very difficult for a first-time event that does not have a financial history. In this case, strong budget forecasting and obtaining accurate bids for the event expenses are critical. When considering event revenue streams, an event manager should not only consider direct event revenues (such as participation registrations), but also the supplemental revenue-generating options such as concessions, auxiliary event ticket sales, sponsorship, memorabilia, etc. The revenues will be projected based on a per unit average.

PLANNING

In the **planning phase**, the various options suggested in the initiation stage are reviewed to determine the best ones, and the planning begins. Planning is straightforward and can be considered a process of asking questions (Young, 2007), such as:

- What actions need to be taken?
- When will these actions occur?
- Who is going to take on these actions?
- What resources (including human, financial, and supplies/equipment) are required for these actions?

planning phase
The proactive and dynamic stage in event planning in which the various options suggestion in the initiation phase are reviewed for the best course of action and preparation of the event.

The answers to these questions can be used to develop a project form that is completed in order to reduce risks and uncertainty, establish standards of performance, provide a structure and procedures for executing work, and serve as a means to obtain required outcomes (Young, 2007). **Figure 7-3** is an example work plan form that can be used in the planning and implementation stages. A different form can be used for various stages throughout the preparation process.

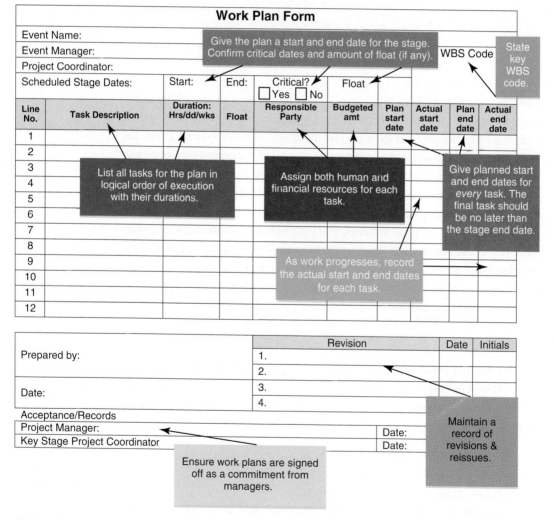

FIGURE 7-3   Example Work Plan

The planning stage is dynamic and continuous, and sport event managers must remain proactive and diligent. It is wise not to plan all the details at the outset to avoid reworking the plan and wasting valuable time. Further, it is important to identify the key workers who will be involved in the planning process. The planning team should cover all of the previously mentioned domains to ensure well-balanced skills and expertise. Additionally, there are a number of factors, both internal and external, that can have a massive impact on the outcome of the project.

External factors lie outside of the organization's and sport event manager's control but can have a profound impact on the event—including cancellation. *Acts of God* include extreme weather (e.g., hurricanes, devastating storms, heavy snow/blizzards), and earthquakes. *Fiscal policy* can impact an event when the national government modifies or enacts policy changes on taxation and other financial measures, such as choosing to abandon a government-funded event. An event can be impacted by *statutory regulations* when national or local government imposes new legislation. Such regulations can be particularly important for events that occur in foreign countries, which can be impacted by international, foreign, and local law.

The internal factors are within the sport event manager's scope of control and are likely to affect the staff and project day to day (Lock, 2013). While these factors are internal, at times, the sport event manager might not have authority or power to control them. In this case, the effect on the outcomes can be more detrimental. Proper planning should promote efficient work and maintain the project management triangle elements (time, scope, and costs), thereby saving the staff from the frustration of overcoming crises caused by poor planning (Lock, 2013).

IMPLEMENTATION

The third phase is the execution, or **implementation phase**, of the event plans. Each domain will have a specific plan that contributes to the overall event plan that must detail how and when the work will be completed (Young, 2007). For example, to attract attendees to the sport event, the marketing plan is executed in the early stages of implementation and most likely long before other plans, such as the event execution plan. One positive outcome of a successful marketing plan is a high number of event attendees, which will affect the logistics plan and the resources necessary to execute it.

implementation phase The execution of the event plans.

Thus, all domains must remain in close communication, as decisions are based on the comparison of plans and reality. One way to ensure that everyone stays on the same page is to use the work plan form (review Figure 7-3). Once the work plan is complete, managers can confirm that all tasks meet the following conditions (Young, 2007):

- Are assigned to someone who will take appropriate action
- Have financial resources allocated to them (if necessary), which allows for monitoring control over budget and spending
- Are realistic and achievable given the time constraints

This stage is marked by high activity and requires strong, effective communication among the event team members. There is the possibility that managers will need to revisit the planning stage in light of major problems or changes to the event program (Allen et al., 2011). Poor communication during this stage can lead to a major source of conflict and work slippages.

MONITORING/CONTROL

monitoring and control system The controls that are implemented to ensure that performance standards are achieved as the sport event is executed.

Monitoring and control systems are implemented to ensure that performance standards are achieved as the sport event is executed. According to Young (2007, 2013), there are three operating modes:

- Measuring, which determines progress through formal and informal reporting
- Evaluating, which determines the cause of deviations from the plan and how to react
- Correcting, which involves taking actions to correct the deviations from the plan

The overall event plan and schedule will dictate how and what objectives are to be met. The job of the sport event manager, then, is to regulate the activities and resources to achieve the results defined by the plan (Young, 2007). Because the event environment is dynamic, a great deal of flexibility is necessary in the planning stages, but the execution and monitoring of the event should be systematic in order to achieve goals (Van der Wagen & White, 2010). There are a number of reasons why events fail, including failure to plan, external factors, incompetent staff, poor control of costs or lack of income, and lack of leadership. Monitoring and controls can help safeguard the organization and assist in achieving a successful event.

The best controls are simple and provide risk prevention and feedback on progress (Van der Wagen & White, 2010; Young, 2013). Preventive controls are established in the planning stages and continue into execution. For example, requiring that only key staff be authorized to sign purchase orders or requiring that all purchase orders be signed by a superior prior to purchase can help to curtail unauthorized spending. Also designing a checklist for event setup would serve as a preventive control *and* a feedback control. As the checklist is completed on event day, it can serve as a way to document missing activities and/or other information. Feedback controls can assist with decision making during an event by allowing an event worker to evaluate a situation and make a decision. For example, perhaps during a warm-up session, the athletes relay an issue with the equipment. The event staff can implement a preventive measure to alleviate the problem prior to competition starting.

closure/shutdown
The final stage of event planning to ensure nothing is lost, equipment is returned properly, and the flow of those involved occurs seamlessly.

CLOSURE/SHUTDOWN

The last stage of the project is the **closure or shutdown** of the event, and it, too, must be carefully planned. Management of attendees' departure, removal of equipment, and event cleanup can take a great deal of time and effort. Shutdown requires proper planning and execution to ensure nothing is lost, equipment is returned properly, and the flow of those involved occurs seamlessly. Shutdown is the most forgotten element of the project (Allen et al., 2011). Like the planning and execution stages, shutdown should include a work breakdown structure, task and responsibility checklists, and a schedule, which is subject to risk analysis (Allen et al., 2011). Items and equipment should be inventoried as they are packed up (especially small items like walkie-talkies) both to ensure that nothing is lost and in preparation for the next event. Proper coding and organization of equipment will not only ensure the details are organized for the next event, but also can help with the close-out of contracts and bills to vendors and suppliers.

© Brian McEntire/Shutterstock

Tools of Project Management

SOFTWARE

Make good use of technology. There are a number of project management programs that offer free online software. Further, there are a number of computer software programs that provide a link to a mobile phone application so the sport event manager can easily navigate from computer to tablet to smartphone, depending on location and accessibility. Much of the current software and web/mobile applications are excellent for planning a sport event, but due to the dynamic nature of an event, some programs are limited in their usefulness. A few examples of project management web applications include Copper Project, Viewpath, and eTask-it. Of the software systems, Microsoft Project and OpenProj are easy to obtain and readily configured. All of these examples can easily produce Gantt charts, assign resources to tasks, and follow progress.

WORK BREAKDOWN STRUCTURE

work breakdown structure (WBS) Project tasks broken down into manageable parts.

The **work breakdown structure (WBS)** is simply the project tasks broken down into manageable parts. Once the scope of the event has been defined, the WBS allows the work required to deliver the event to be visually categorized and communicated to the staff (Allen et al., 2011). The WBS allows the numerous tasks to be aggregated under specific categories in order to better manage the large scope of work. For example, the tasks related specifically to the marketing plan would be grouped and presented on the WBS as "Marketing." Once completed, the WBS resembles a hierarchical chart, with the event itself at the top and the major activity flowing down the chart (Shone & Parry, 2010).

GANTT CHART

Gantt chart A bar chart that illustrates the various tasks that must be completed for the event in a time-sequence order.

A **Gantt chart** is a bar chart that illustrates the various tasks that must be completed in a time-sequence order (Shone & Parry, 2010). The Gantt chart displays the details of the work to be completed for the WBS and can be created using the following components (Allen et al., 2011):

- *Tasks* break down the work involved into manageable activities.
- *Timelines* set the time scale for each task. Factors to consider are the start and end time and the availability of the assigned resources (both human and financial).

- *Priorities* set the priority and identify what tasks must be completed prior to the current task starting.
- *Milestones* assist in monitoring the event. Tasks that are of particular importance are designated as milestones.

The benefit of this chart is that the tasks are displayed interdependently. One can easily see when a task is to start and end, the progress to date, and what tasks are dependent on one finishing prior to another beginning. A limitation is the inability to visually track resource (staff) workload. While some software programs do allow the event manager to assign resources to tasks, these resources do not appear on the Gantt chart. Therefore, it is difficult to gauge the workload of each resource visually. More sophisticated programs will have a means for monitoring workload, but they will not appear in this chart.

PROGRAM EVALUATION AND REVIEW TECHNIQUE CHART AND CRITICAL PATH

The **program evaluation and review technique (PERT) chart** illustrates the tasks, duration, and dependency information, which can be useful in defining the **critical path** for the project (Van der Wagen & White, 2010). The PERT chart allows for a series of subtasks to be analyzed to find the most efficient scheduling, or the critical path (Allen et al., 2011).

RUN SHEETS

The **run sheet** is vital for the execution of the event, as it is the program, or schedule, of events (Van der Wagen & White, 2010). The run sheet will detail the timing for each element of the event schedule and provides correct sequencing and timing of those elements. Sequencing in the run sheet will specify the order of actions, while timing will identify when the action will commence (Van der Wagen & White, 2010).

CHECKLISTS

The **checklist** is an indispensable control tool that the sport event manager uses to ensure that each individual is performing all tasks essential for the success of the event. Checklists serve as a preventive control during the

program evaluation and review technique (PERT) chart An illustration of the tasks, duration, and dependency information, which can be useful in defining the critical path for the project.

critical path An analysis of the most efficient scheduling of tasks and subtasks.

run sheet A detailed schedule of the sequencing and timing for each element of the event.

checklist A preventive control tool that ensures each individual is performing all tasks essential for the success of the event.

planning process to account for the specific tasks prior to the event. Additionally, they are a feedback control during the event as a record-keeping process as a means to prevent problems and serve as a means for reducing risk, should plans go awry (Van der Wagen & White, 2010).

FLOOR PLANS AND FLOW DIAGRAMS

floor plan An illustration of where equipment or items are to be placed within the event venue.

Floor plans illustrate where equipment or items are to be placed within the event venue. These plans are integral in the proper ordering of equipment based on attendee numbers and in determining whether the venue has the space to accommodate the event design and occupants. **Flow diagrams** are a graphical representation of how attendees will move through your event and venue. These diagrams ensure queues are held to a minimum, thereby avoiding line backups; display how attendees will enter and exit the venue or event areas; and can determine and mitigate potential areas of risk due to an emergency or other problem. Flow diagrams are especially important for high-traffic areas, such as routes from the parking locations, areas where high numbers will congregate (such as registration or ticket queues), and regions where space is limited or dense.

flow diagram A graphical representation as to how attendees will move through the event and venue.

SUMMARY

Because the sport event contains the characteristics of a project, the traditional tools of project management prove incredibly useful to the sport event manager. Project management can offer structure to the sport event and allow for detailed planning, monitoring, and evaluation. Event managers can benefit by using tools such as the WBS and Gantt charts to analyze, categorize, assign, and implement the sport event plan.

DISCUSSION QUESTIONS

1. Discuss why project management is vital for a successful event. What tools might best support a sport event manager and why?
2. Discuss the stages of event planning and describe how resources might be assigned for the development of a 3-day three-on-three basketball tournament.
3. Describe the domains of event management and the main duties of each area. Why is it important that each domain be designated for an event?

Case STUDY

Staging Events with Multiple Venues

The logistics of planning and staging a multivenue sport event is no easy task. There will be a number of elements that are compounded by the additional venues, including, but not limited to, scheduling, human resources, equipment resources, communication between venues, security within and between venues, and additional traffic/parking challenges (especially if athletes/patrons require shuttling between venues). The following case introduces the challenges faced when staging a multivenue sport event.

You are the new event director for the inaugural State Games in [the city and state of your choice]. As the newly appointed director, you are tasked with organizing the venues and equipment as well as the schedule for the weeklong event. As the schedule is developed, consider the following.

- A total of 25 sports have been included in the program. These include:

Archery	Diving	Softball	Track and field
Badminton	Fencing	Sport skydiving	Triathlon
Baseball	Flag football	Swimming:	Volleyball
Basketball	Golf	indoor	Weightlifting
BMX racing	Racquetball	Swimming:	Wheelchair
Bowling	Rowing	open water	basketball
CrossFit	Skateboarding	Tennis	Wrestling

Note: These listed sports do not include all of the available events. For example, swimming offers a number of sprint- and long-distance as well as relay events. Take this into consideration when developing your schedule and staging plan.

- The games are inclusive of all ages and ability. You must decide the age divisions as part of the scheduling process. The games allow any athletes 12 to 100 years of age to compete.
- The games offer three competitive levels: novice, intermediate, and advanced.

You may find it helpful to review the Cornhusker State Games website as a resource as you work through this case: www.cornhuskerstategames.com. Using what you have just learned in the chapter about staging and implementing events, develop a plan and schedule for the State Games. Be sure to include the following:

1. The city and state chosen to host the games.
2. A list of venues and the sports they each will host. This list must be realistic and based on the venues available in the city you chose in question 1. The venues should also be illustrated on a map, along with parking availability and shuttle transport pickup/drop-off points (if relevant).

3. The complete schedule for each venue over the weeklong event, detailing the following specifically:
   a. The type of competition for each sport (e.g., tournament vs. head-to-head) (All sports will have different competition needs.)
   b. The schedule breakdown by age group and level
   c. The resources needed at each venue (e.g., numbers of officials, volunteers, staff)
4. Your overall plan for the staging implementation of the event:
   a. Operations and logistics
   b. Equipment needs
   c. Human resources
   d. Financial resources
   e. Other

REFERENCES

Allen, J., O'Toole, W., Harris, R., & McDonnell, I. (2011). *Festival and special event management* (5th ed.). Brisbane, Australia: John Wiley & Sons.

International Event Management Body of Knowledge. (2006). *Event management body of knowledge: An introduction.* Retrieved from http://www.embok.org.

Lock, D. (2013). *Project management* (10th ed.). Burlington, VT: Gower Publishing.

Patel, V. (2008). *Project management.* Jaipur, India: Oxford Book Company.

Shone, A., & Parry, B. (2010). *Successful event management: A practical handbook* (3rd ed.). Hampshire, UK: Cengage Learning.

Van der Wagen, L., & White, L. (2010). *Events management: For tourism, cultural, business, and sporting events* (4th ed.). New South Wales, Australia: Pearson Publishing.

Young, T. (2007). *The handbook of project management: A practical guide to effective policies, techniques, and processes.* London, UK: Kogan Page.

Young, T. (2013). *Successful project management.* London, UK: Kogan Page.

Zarndt, F. (2011). Project management 101: Plan well, communicate a lot, and don't forget acceptance criteria. *OCLC Systems and Services, 27*(3), 170–174.

CHAPTER 8

Marketing the Facility and Events

BRIANNA L. NEWLAND

CHAPTER OBJECTIVES

Upon completion of this chapter, the reader will be able to:

1. Clearly understand the elements of a marketing plan
2. Recognize the importance of a well-developed marketing strategy and plan
3. Develop an integrated marketing communications plan
4. Realize the importance of knowing and building a relationship with the consumer
5. Identify how the unique marketing elements can influence an event

CHAPTER OVERVIEW

This chapter will discuss the importance of properly marketing the facility and/or event. It will discuss marketing elements, such as understanding the consumers, building the relationship, and communicating the message. This chapter will highlight the use of social networking and other digital methods within the marketing plan.

IndustryVOICE

Melissa Schaaf—Director of Marketing, Wells Fargo Center, Comcast-Spectacor

Courtesy of Melissa Schaaf

The Wells Fargo Center is a multipurpose sports and entertainment venue owned by Comcast-Spectacor. As home to the Philadelphia Flyers (National Hockey League), the Philadelphia 76ers (National Basketball Association), and the Philadelphia Soul (Arena Football League), the Wells Fargo Center attracts more than 250 annual events, drawing nearly three million customers annually. Comcast-Spectacor's vision for the Wells Fargo Center is to be the premier sports and entertainment venue in the United States, attracting national prestigious events such as National Collegiate Athletic Association (NCAA) championships, Olympic trials, and more.

As Director of Marketing, my job is to oversee the marketing for all the events that occur at the Wells Fargo Center on the entertainment side. While I support the sports teams that play at the venue, those teams have their own marketing and public relations staffs.

My career path was directly related to the internships and volunteer opportunities that I sought while in college. I graduated from the University of Delaware (UD) with a degree in sport management. While a student at UD, I was fortunate to secure an internship with the Philadelphia Eagles in the Premium Seating department. Through networking and relationships that were made while in this position, I was able to attain a position with the Wells Fargo Center as a hospitality coordinator after graduating from UD. In this role, I was responsible for planning ancillary events, including pre-event block parties that accompanied larger events at the venue. I was in the hospitality department for

about 8 months before I accepted a position in the marketing department as an assistant marketing manager. Shortly thereafter, I was promoted to marketing manager. After a few seasons in the marketing department, I accepted an opportunity to relocate to another venue that our company manages in Orlando, Florida, to serve as the Director of Marketing for the venue located on the campus of the University of Central Florida. Two and a half years later, I was offered the opportunity to relocate back to Philadelphia for my current position as the Director of Marketing at the Wells Fargo Center.

For me, the opportunities that emerged were largely due to the internships I was able to secure in college and the networking relationships I built once in those positions. Students interested in working for a facility, like the Wells Fargo Center, really need to take advantage of practical field experiences that are available to them. Whether you are volunteering for events on campus or taking a leadership role in other organizations that you are a part of, it is important to put yourself out there and make connections. Positions in the sport and entertainment industry are limited and highly competitive; therefore I highly suggest that students take advantage of every opportunity that presents itself in order to gain experience and meet key people who will be integral to their future career goals.

In regard to securing an entry-level position in our industry, graduates with the ability to multitask are highly sought after. At any given time, we can have anywhere from 3 to 20 events on sale, so a graduate who can manage time well, prioritize, and handle a number of different projects at once will stand out in the marketing field. A student who has held a part-time job and volunteered for events while still attending class full time will rise to the top because, for me, this demonstrates that the student can juggle a number of responsibilities successfully, which is a quality that I look for when hiring. Versatility, adaptability, and creativity are also important skills to possess. Given the fast-paced and dynamic environment we work in, a person with the ability to think outside the box and have fresh new ideas is highly desired. Working in facility management is not a 9 to 5 job, and working nights, weekends, and holidays is part of the business. As such, I feel that it is crucial that graduates who enter the sport industry be passionate about the work and really love what they do. Those who are team players, hardworking, and dedicated to their job will be successful. Lastly, to stand out in a job interview, research the organization and have a strong understanding of the position requirements and expectations. A thorough background of industry trends and creative solutions to common challenges will put a candidate ahead of others in the hiring process.

The marketing environment is dynamic and continually changing, and this can be both a challenge and an opportunity. How we reach people with our marketing message continues to change, and keeping up with current trends can prove difficult. In the past, we could place a TV or radio ad about an upcoming event and reach our intended market well, but the social media–driven world we currently live in has highlighted new trends in how people get their information. A strength of the Comcast-Spectacor family is the communication among the 130-plus facilities that we operate. The open communication and information sharing among our venues really help us to capitalize on new tactics or promotions that have proved successful, which enables us to adapt successfully in an ever-changing climate.

A current trend in facility and event marketing is this shift toward digital marketing. Not only do we see a shift to the use of social media for information and communication by event attendees, but entertainers are also changing how they interact with fans and sell their events. For example, some artists will do a presale only through Facebook or Twitter and avoid the more traditional formats for reaching consumers, which can take longer to generate sales. The use of social media can be cost-effective for venues in some of our smaller markets. Shows that come through those smaller venues may have lesser budgets based on the area and demand, and social media allows these arenas to do more with less. However, many times digital marketing can come at a higher cost, which is often above their means. Being at the company headquarters in Philadelphia allows us to test new digital marketing campaigns, and when they are successful, we can find ways to execute these in an effective way for our smaller markets.

One challenge that we face in our industry is that students might not be aware of the variety of opportunities in facility management. Within Comcast-Spectacor, we have hospitality, food services, finance and accounting, ticketing, event management, sales, sponsorship sales, and marketing—all of which fall within the scope of event and facility management. There are numerous job opportunities that students can take advantage of to get a foot in the door in this industry if they are aware that the positions exist. Understanding what opportunities exist just slightly outside of sports within facility and event management can really broaden the job options available to students.

Introduction

Marketing a product involves knowing the customer well and communicating how a product meets needs. But, it's much more than that. Organizations, including sport events and facilities, need customers to survive.

To attract and retain those customers while building demand for a brand, an organization must do the following:

- Develop a brand that will stick in the mind of the consumer.
- Create awareness about the products and/or services offered.
- Generate a perception in the mind of the consumer that leads to brand equity and loyalty.
- Differentiate the organization and products/services from the competitor.

These are not easy tasks and require coordination of a well thought-out strategy and plan.

Sport is even more unique than other business fields and industries for a number of reasons, as demarcated by Mullin, Hardy, and Sutton (2007):

- *Sport is consumed as it is produced.* Unfortunately, sport cannot be created and shelved to purchase when the moment suits us. While it is possible to watch the event again, if it is recorded and/or rebroadcasted, it will never inspire the same effect as the live event.
- *Sport is intangible.* While we would all enjoy bringing LeBron James home and placing him on our mantle or playing a pickup game with him in our backyard, this is not possible. To make sport more tangible, organizations sell merchandise related to the game or event. However, this is not the same as taking the athlete home as you would a new pair of shoes.
- *Sport is emotional, subjective, and* **heterogeneous**. Fans and sport participants experience sport very differently. For some, the experience can elicit myriad emotions that ebb and flow throughout the sport event. Many can be deeply affected by the team's performance, which can influence their everyday life. Others might enjoy the game but feel no further effect. Further, no two people will have similar sport experiences. While one might be drawn to the strategy of play, another may enjoy the fanfare and atmosphere, and a still another may be completely bored and wish he had gone to the movies. Sport is deeply personal, which is challenging for sport marketers.
- *Sport is inconsistent and unpredictable.* It is much easier to sell tickets to sporting events when the team is winning. But when the team is in

heterogeneous
Relating to perceptions of an experience that are widely dissimilar.

a multiseason slump, even the most loyal of fans can get discouraged. Further, weather can threaten performance, lineups can change, and momentum and injuries can be game changers.

- *The core product is uncontrollable.* Adding to the unpredictability and inconsistency, this game itself is out of the control of the sport marketer. Marketers cannot set rosters, acquire players, or make decisions that can influence the outcome of the game. To counter this, marketers sell merchandize and mementos and develop **product extensions** that create an experience and atmosphere around the event.
- *Sport organizations cooperate and compete simultaneously.* The sport industry is unique in that it requires other organizations in order to be competitive. Those teams must have strong talent in order to create an atmosphere that is both competitive and entertaining. If one team consistently dominates, this would impact interest in the sport. Therefore, teams agree to cooperate on certain levels to preserve the competitive environment.

product extension
An additional event component that creates an atmosphere and experience for an event.

As one can see, sport is a unique enterprise and marketers must promote products and services that are inconsistent and unpredictable, intangible, perishable, subjective, and open to interpretation (Mullin et al., 2007). Further, the environment is highly competitive and requires strong research on the consumer and environment before a viable strategy and plan can be developed.

Feasibility

To develop a strong marketing strategy and formulate a plan, a facility and/or event must determine what is feasible. For events, a **feasibility study** is typically conducted in the initiation stage of planning and provides information for event directors to do the following:

feasibility study An assessment that is conducted to determine key market characteristics.

1. Provide quality information to support decision making.
2. Identify reasons *not* to proceed (such as risk, cost, lack of resources, etc.).
3. Develop a strong marketing strategy and plan, if the event is a "go."
4. Help establish a vision, mission, and concept for the event.
5. Assist in securing funding or other support.

This study should also be completed by facilities, although the focus is slightly different. The marketing director for a facility must determine the feasibility and capacity to host events, what events to attract, and any reasons to not proceed. While the focus is slightly different for the event marketer than for the facility marketer, both use feasibility results to devise the best course of action.

A feasibility study should consider three key elements. First, one must determine the market characteristics. What is the demand for such an event? Or, in the case of the facility, what is the demand for events to use this location? Is the market currently saturated with similar events or other facilities that could potentially host? Is the barrier to entry difficult? That is, to host such an event, will it require substantial human, financial, and operational resources? A good event marketer will determine if such an event can not only be implemented, but also sustained over a specific period while remaining competitive. Second, one must consider the geographic factors that could potentially influence viability of the event. Is the venue difficult to access? What are the amenities near the venue? Can the community support the influx of people? Will the environment be easily damaged by the event? What infrastructure does the location provide? That is, will the event require additional equipment and/or structures? And finally, one must carefully analyze all financial aspects, including projected revenue and operating costs. It is wise to develop a pro forma (as discussed in the "Facility Design and Construction" chapter) and conduct a breakeven analysis (as discussed in the "Project Management" chapter) very early in the process. A **breakeven analysis** is used to determine at what point the event can cover all the expenses and begin to make a profit. It is important to be as accurate as possible when determining the startup costs, as these numbers will help determine the sales revenue needed to pay ongoing operational expenses.

While all types of feasibility are important to the event manager in deciding to move forward with event implementation, the climate is of utmost importance to the marketer. In addition to determining whether the event can move forward, the marketer will also consider the internal and external strengths of the event through a **SWOT analysis**. The acronym SWOT stands for strengths, weaknesses, opportunities, and threats. A SWOT analysis allows a marketer to capitalize on strengths and opportunities while mitigating the potentially negative effects of weaknesses and threats. Take, for example, a

breakeven analysis An assessment used to determine at what point the event can cover all the expenses and begin to make a profit.

SWOT analysis A tool used to assess the internal and external strengths and weaknesses of an event; SWOT stands for strengths, weaknesses, opportunities, and threats.

TABLE 8-1   SWOT of a Youth Triathlon Event

Internal	External
Strengths	**Opportunities**
✓ Event staff has over 5 years of experience hosting triathlons. ✓ The facility is financially stable and capable of an event addition. ✓ Current events have grown consistently.	✓ Outreach to a local organization that promotes physical activity and health could enable access to children. ✓ A strong relationship with governing officials could lead to potential funding sources.
Weaknesses	**Threats**
– The staff has never done a youth-specific event. – The event location is a high-traffic area, so additional support will be necessary.	– Weather could cancel the event unexpectedly. – The environment is very saturated for youth sport in general and triathlon specifically.

SWOT conducted on a potential youth triathlon event. As you review the table, notice how the strengths and weaknesses focus on the internal environment of the organization while the opportunities and threats target the external climate (**Table 8-1**).

Once a feasibility study and SWOT analysis have been conducted and the decision makers have decided to implement the event, the next step for the marketer is to determine the strategy and lay out the plan.

Developing the Marketing Strategy and Plan

Before a strong marketing plan and campaign can be developed, a marketer must determine the purpose of the event and the main goals. To begin, the mission and vision of the event must be determined. A **mission statement** defines the purpose of the organization (or event). It identifies why the organization exists for the consumer and allows for the development of organizational goals. The **vision statement** is what the organization would like to accomplish. This statement describes what the organization aspires to be and/or do as it grows and evolves.

As described previously, sport marketing is unique, which creates a number of marketing challenges. To add to these challenges, consider that the sport product itself is complex and dynamic. From a sport event perspective,

mission statement
A statement defining the purpose of the organization (or event).

vision statement
A statement of what the organization would like to achieve or accomplish.

© TK Kurikawa/Shutterstock

the core product is the competition itself, which includes the type of sport played, the participants (athletes, coaches, and officials), and the environment (e.g., the challenge of a triathlon race course or the weather conditions at a golf tournament) (Pedersen et al., 2014). Additionally, sport events typically include product extensions that create an atmosphere around the event. These extensions can include a festival with music that accompanies the sport event, half-time shows, games for children and families, and other non-competition-related activities. For example, the X Games in Austin, Texas, in June 2014 featured nine festival areas meant to entertain day and night. The areas included X Music, featuring Kanye West, The Pretty Lights, and Slightly Stupid, among others. The Galleria was a retail hub that included a fashion event, graffiti walls, an X Games museum, and a movie theater. The Playground came complete with hydra-tag, obstacle courses, and other games and activities for children and adults alike. Ride the Track allowed attendees to rent a board and have a chance to "shred a world-class race course." The ESPN Clubhouse featured a pop-up sports bar with food, drinks, and access to sports via large high-definition TVs. The Gaming Shack included a competition among the best gamers, battling for X Games gold in a national gaming showdown. The Garage introduced kart racing, remote-controlled cars, and racing simulators, while the Texas Ranch was a big stop for all things Texas, including a saloon, mechanical bull, and local Austin grub and artists (X Games Austin, 2014).

Segmentation

Once an organization has defined its purpose and identified future aspirations, marketers must consider which consumers would be most interested in the products or services offered by the organization. Because consumers are so heterogeneous, considering incredibly large consumer bases can be a daunting task. Therefore, marketers break consumers into smaller clusters or groups identified by certain characteristics rather than attempting to sell to everyone. This process is known as **segmentation**. Typically, these categorizations are determined through demographic, psychographic, media preference and use, and purchasing behavior characteristics. **Demographics** categorize consumers based on age, gender, ethnicity, education, income, socioeconomic status, profession, geographic location, religion, type of sport played, and other such identifiers. **Psychographics** categorize based on the consumers' interests, beliefs, and attitudes. Also, the motives that drive consumers to participate and watch sport would be considered here. Greater detail and discussion on this topic can be found in the "Consumer Behavior" chapter.

Considering the increased adoption and use of technology, it is important for marketers to know consumers' **media preference and use**. Not only is it important to understand how they consume sport (e.g., TV, Internet, radio), but also what they use to access information (e.g., smartphones, computers, newspaper, TV, radio) and the preference for various mediums (e.g., organization applications, Twitter, Facebook, email, print). Knowledge of this information can help marketers better streamline communication in ways that best suit the audience. For example, if 20- to 29-year-old men get their information through social media, then putting an ad in a newspaper is not a wise marketing decision. Tweeting information would target this group better.

Finally, **purchasing behavior** describes the frequency and use of products and services. Knowing what individuals buy and when/how they buy it can help you understand purchasing trends better. For example, perhaps you notice that Bob Smith purchases baseball tickets on family promotional nights and only on these nights. A marketer could target Bob with family-themed offerings to attract him to additional events. Armed with such information, marketers can target those most likely to consume the product or service. The **target market** is the consumer most likely to purchase the product. An example of segmenting a sport event is provided in **Table 8-2**.

segmentation The breaking of consumers into smaller clusters or groups identified by certain characteristics rather than attempting to sell to everyone.

demographics The categorization of consumers based on age, gender, ethnicity, education, income, socioeconomic status, profession, geographic location, religion, type of sport played, and other such identifiers.

psychographics The categorization of consumers based on the consumers' interests, beliefs, and attitudes.

TIP

Take the time to understand your consumers. It is a waste of money to create advertisements through the newspaper if your target market does not read it. Knowing media preferences and usage can help you better communicate your message using the correct medium.

TABLE 8-2   Segmentation Elements: Local Youth Triathlon

Demographics	Psychographics	Media Preferences	Purchasing Habits
Boys and girls 7 to 12 years old, middle- to upper-middle class families, located in the central Texas area	Active families with swimming, biking, or running backgrounds, interested in new sports, adventurous, look for family-oriented activities	Consumption methods: social networks (Facebook, Twitter), moderate to heavy Internet, TV, and smartphone use	Frequently purchase/ use fitness and sport goods/services, active gym or sport recreation memberships

Building the Relationship

media preference and use The categorization of consumers based on the type of media consumed and how it is consumed.

purchasing behavior The frequency with which individuals consume a product and the manner in which they use the products and services.

target market The consumer most likely to purchase the product or service.

customer profile A description of the customer or set of customers based on their demographics, psychographics, media preferences, and purchasing behavior.

Once the customer characteristics have been identified, a customer profile can be developed. A **customer profile** is a description of the customer or set of customers based on their demographic, psychographic, media preferences, and purchasing behavior. The profile gives you the information you need to further develop relationships and increase spending with existing customers, while using information gathered from them to attract new customers. This process is known as **relationship marketing**, which is "the marketing activities directed toward establishing, developing, and maintaining relational exchanges" with customers (Morgan & Hunt, 1994, p. 22). The strategy of relationship marketing is to invest in the development of long-term relationships with customers and other key stakeholders in order to garner a better understanding of one another's expectations and concerns (Pressy & Tzokas, 2006). Competitive advantage is gained when the organization properly aligns its products and services with customer demand, allowing for stronger bonds to develop between organization and consumer—yet another competitive advantage (Pressy & Tzokas, 2006). Customers are likely to see direct benefits from products and services that better align with their individual wants and needs (Morgan & Hunt, 1994).

To build a relationship, organizations require a means to maintain vital information about customers. **Data-based marketing (DBM)** software is a comprehensive system that captures critical demographic, psychographic, media use, and purchasing behavior information on customers and potential customers in order to enable direct marketing strategies (Mullin et al., 2007). However, when organizations are trying to build a relationship with a customer, more information is required. Customer relationship management

(CRM) systems expand on the information gathered in the DBM to include information such as the following (Mullin et al., 2007):

- Purchase transactions, including what was purchased, amount purchased, and frequency of purchase
- Key relationships, such as family, friends, and coworkers
- Frequency of attendance, key dates attended, popular reasons for attending (e.g., birthday celebrations, work incentives)
- Brief notes on any interactions with the customer (e.g., unsatisfactory experience)
- Personal information such as favorite teams or sports, birthday, anniversary, the company they work for and their business contact information
- Results of customer surveys, feedback about services or products, and email preferences
- Information on direct mail, email blasts, wellness calls, or other marketing campaign touches

While appealing, a CRM system can be difficult to implement. Organizations must integrate the DBM and CRM into every facet of the organization to ensure the optimum level of information is collected. Every opportunity to capture and properly code and categorize information must be capitalized upon. According to Gordon, Perrey, and Spellecke (2013), organizations that use data at the foci of marketing decisions (through the use of DBM and CRM) can improve their marketing return on investment by 15% to 20%. However, the data in and of themselves are not the reason for success. According to Gordon et al. (2013), organizations that successfully use DBM and CRM can identify valuable opportunities and use the data-derived information to communicate specific and relevant messages.

Positioning

Understanding customer needs and delivering a product that is perceived as more valuable than *and* distinctly different from other products is the key to winning and keeping customers (Moore & Pareek, 2010). Sport organizations position their products in ways that make them stand out from the competitors. **Differentiation** entails **positioning** the product in the minds of the consumer by highlighting the important attributes and benefits.

relationship marketing A marketing strategy that seeks to develop and maintain relationships with customers, while using information gathered from them to attract new customers; the client–consumer relationship is emphasized over a more purely transactional behavior.

data-based marketing (DBM) A comprehensive system that captures critical demographics, psychographics, media use, and purchasing behavior information on customers and potential customers in order to enable direct marketing strategies.

differentiation The positioning of a product in the minds of the consumer by highlighting the important attributes and benefits.

positioning Developing and delivering a product that is perceived as more valuable than and distinctly different from other products.

For example, Nike and Under Armour sell similar products. When you think about the two brands, however, they are different. Think about the attributes you assign to each. What makes them different in your mind? To stand out in a highly cluttered sport marketplace, organizations use a number of strategies to stand out, including the following (Moore & Pareek, 2010):

- *Contrasting their product* or service's key features and benefits against the shortcomings of the competition.
- *Grabbing the unoccupied* by filling a gap that the competition has not yet secured. For example, Tough Mudder roared into the running marketplace by offering a unique alternative to the "boredom of marathoning." "Why run miles on pavement," Tough Mudder asks, "when you can do this?" (Tough Mudder, 2014).
- *Repositioning* the product. While repositioning can require a large investment, doing so can change or enhance the perception of a product and produce positive financial rewards for the organization. Consider the Tampa Bay Buccaneers of the National Football League. In the late 1990s, under new ownership, the Buccaneers repositioned themselves with a new logo, stadium, coaching staff, and team philosophy. While this was an incredibly hefty investment, the changes paid off with a Super Bowl win in 2002.
- *Creating exclusivity* is another strategy to position a product. This can be difficult to do. Finding ways to include elements in your event that do not exist in other products can make your event more exclusive and unique.

All organizations seek a competitive advantage over the scarce resources in a marketplace. By identifying potential sources of competitive advantage, marketers can determine which will be promoted as a means to differentiate their product from the competition (Moore & Pareek, 2010).

Price

Determining how to price a product or service is no easy task. There are a number of philosophies on what constitutes a fair price, but all agree that price must cover the cost of the product and the return to the producer to compensate for the risk incurred (Moore & Pareek, 2010). Where the debate lies is in determining how high the realized profit should be in regard to said risk. It is clear

TABLE 8-3   Pricing Factors—The Four Cs

Factor	Description
Customer	Analyze the customer profile characteristics to determine how characteristics would impact certain pricing strategies and/or how specific segments will respond to pricing.
Competitor	Analyze how the consumer perceives the value of the product as compared with competing products. Also analyze the competitors' pricing schemes.
Company	Analyze the production costs and the minimum price necessary to cover these costs.
Climate	Analyze the external factors that can impact cost of production and consumers' ability to spend.

that consumers can be very **price sensitive**, so marketers should be cautious when setting a pricing strategy. Customers equate price to value and quality. **Table 8-3** illustrates the four Cs (customer, competitor, company, and climate) that should be considered when setting a pricing strategy.

price sensitivity
Susceptibility to variations in price.

As price relates to sport events and the facility, consumers will consider much more than just the price of entry. The cost to the consumer includes travel to the venue, parking, concessions, and other costs related to the event. Thus, the consumer must feel that the overall value of the sport event experience exceeds (not matches) the price of admission.

Place

As discussed earlier, sport is unique from other industries because it is simultaneously consumed and produced. Therefore, how the sport product is distributed is also unique. In sport, **place** refers to the location of the sport product (e.g., stadium, park), where the product is distributed (e.g., online event registration, event admission sales at the venue), the geographic dynamics of the target market (e.g., international, national, local), and other channels that might be relevant to the sport product (e.g., media distribution, availability of the product by season, broadcast). Further, the accessibility of

place The location of the sport product where the product is distributed; the geographic location of the target market and other channels that might be relevant to the sport product.

the facility can impact the sport product greatly. Easy access to the venue from major roadways, the flow of traffic in and out of the venue space, and the environment at the venue can all impact on the perception of the facility and the event hosted there.

Promotion

Promotion is the most visible aspect of the marketing plan, and, in fact, many confuse the two terms. *Marketing* is the overall, broad strategy for a sport product, whereas *promotion* is a specific tactic used as part of the marketing plan to attain goals. These two terms should not be interchanged. **Promotion** is the communication of the marketing message. It is used to not only communicate the overall message of the organization, but also to further position the sport product in the mind of the consumer. The **promotion mix** is the varied use of a number of promotional methods, such as advertising (print, TV, radio, electronic); personal selling; public, community, and media relations; direct and online marketing; public service announcements; publicity; and sponsorship. The promotional mix is used to communicate the desired message and image about the product, create awareness and educate the consumer about the product, and persuade the consumer to buy the product (Moore & Pareek, 2010).

promotion The communication of the marketing message.

promotion mix The varied use of a number of promotional methods to create a message.

Communicating the Message

As the most visible aspect of the marketing plan, promotion involves the dissemination of information about the organization and product in ways that build strong equity with the brand and ensure good publicity for the firm (Moore & Pareek, 2010). Understanding how marketing decisions are made and how they impact the long-term strategy of the event or facility is important. In the case of a sport event, a strong marketing communications plan must be developed to create awareness and promote the event, but it should be remembered that the event itself is a strategic marketing tool. Therefore, marketing communications, or the promotional mix, must be designed not only to present the event and/or facility in the most appropriate manner, but also capitalize on the event itself as a way to interact with customers. An emerging way to harness the synergy across various marketing tactics to achieve marketing outcomes is known as

integrated marketing communication (IMC). IMC uses a consistent delivery strategy through which brand positioning, personality, and key messaging are delivered synergistically across every element of communication (Smith, Berry, & Pulford, 1999). With IMC, all sources of contact a stakeholder has with the event are potential delivery channels (Shimp, 2003). Because opinions are formed based on marketing messages and interaction with the business (Belch & Belch, 2004), it is important to coordinate all messages and points of contact between the marketer and consumer. IMC consists of various tactics that work best when they are integrated to achieve the overall marketing goals (Raj, Walters, & Rashid, 2009).

Traditional marketing has its place, but it can be costly and might not help marketers reach their target markets. Integrating the message into a number of tactics ensures greater opportunity to achieve marketing goals (Raj et al., 2009). With the average consumer exposed to over 3000 advertisements daily (Kimmel, 2005), consumers are worn out by familiar/repeated messages. Marketers aggressively promote messages that can stand out and grab the attention of the consumer in a cluttered marketplace (Hutter & Hoffman, 2011). However, there is a cost. These additional activities produce a higher marketing budget and prompt even stronger avoidance and worn-out behavior from consumers. There has been a trend in recent years toward more digital marketing tactics and use of social media. This can be a very cost-effective tactic if the target market's media preferences align.

Guerrilla and viral marketing tactics have grown in an effort to creatively capture new audiences through innovation and surprise (Hutter & Hoffman, 2011). The objective of **guerrilla marketing** is to gain large effects at low expenses (Baltes & Leibing, 2008), while **viral marketing** uses social networks to increase brand awareness through self-replicating processes (Raj et al., 2009). Guerrilla marketing certainly has viral tendencies, but it does not necessarily depend on social networks to increase awareness. While past efforts of guerrilla marketing were considered "below the line," as the focus was to weaken competitors and level the playing field (Levinson, 1984), recent efforts are customer focused, specifically to win customers (Solomon et al., 2009). Rather than sabotaging a brand, which could have a potential negative effect on the saboteur, organizations are using guerrilla tactics to surprise their target markets. For example, Adidas set up a giant shoebox at an event and as customers walked by, a secret door would open

integrated marketing communication (IMC) A delivery strategy that ensures brand positioning, personality, and key messages are delivered synergistically across every element of communication.

guerrilla marketing A marketing strategy that uses unique methods to gain large effects at low expenses.

viral marketing The use of social networks to increase brand awareness through self-replicating processes.

and free shoes would be given to the passerby. This tactic introduced the audience to a new product line in a surprising and innovative way, thereby creating a buzz around the new shoe offering.

The objective of both of these approaches is to create a buzz around a product to inspire word-of-mouth advertising at a low cost. The advent of social networking has facilitated further word-of-mouth through viral marketing and has become a crucial strategy for marketers. Social networking sites have enabled organizations to connect with consumers on an individual level that traditional methods have been unable to do. Information can spread more readily by word-of-mouth among social networks, which organizations can capitalize upon to generate a significant increase in sales while reducing promotion costs (Li, Lai, & Chen, 2010).

SUMMARY

Marketing for facility and sport events requires a very complex plan actualized through a clear and well-developed overall strategy. Successful execution of the plan will occur through careful research of internal and external factors that influence the sport product, the consumer and competitors, the ability to capitalize on opportunities this information provides, the execution of the plan, and careful assessment of the results. Considering ways in which several marketing tactics can be integrated into the promotional mix to ensure multiple opportunities to engage with customers is critical.

DISCUSSION QUESTIONS

1. Describe why feasibility studies are necessary. How is a SWOT analysis used to develop a marketing plan?
2. Explain why it is necessary to segment. What are the elements that make up segmentation? How might this information be used to create a consumer profile?
3. What is relationship marketing? Describe how this might be implemented for a sport event.
4. Discuss the importance of a pricing strategy. Explain the four Cs and describe how they impact pricing.
5. What is integrated marketing communication? Describe the various tactics and how you might incorporate them into a promotional mix for a sport facility.

Case **STUDY**

If You Build It, Will They Come?

Contrary to popular belief, "they" do not come simply because you've built a facility and/or created a new event. It takes a strong feasibility study, informative market research, and a well-developed marketing strategy and plan to get "them" to the facility and/or event. One area of potential growth is in the youth sport tourism sector. The Sports Facilities Advisory (SFA) observed that sport recreation centers can serve as a destination for competitive amateur and youth sport events but fail to meet their potential because of poor planning and management (PRWeb.com, 2014). The Vadnais Sports Center in the Twin Cities, Minnesota, area is a classic example of the *if we build it, they will come* mentality that utterly failed. The facility was built in 2010 through the support of $26 million in revenue bonds issued by Vadnais Heights on behalf of the nonprofit group Community Facility Partners (Anderson, 2014). After poor revenue projections and growth through rentals, the city found itself covering shortfalls of hundreds of thousands of dollars (PRWeb.com, 2014). In 2013, the facility was put up for sale after Community Facility Partners defaulted on the bonds when the city stopped financial support (Anderson, 2014). In the spring of 2014, Ramsay County signed a letter of intent to buy the facility for $10.5 million.

Suppose Ramsay County has decided to outsource management of the facility to your private sport management firm. The first order of business for your firm is to develop a strong marketing strategy and plan to make this facility profitable in the next 3 years. Before you can do this, however, you need information in order to develop the strongest plan possible. Answer the following questions:

1. What are the new mission and vision for this facility? How do they differ from in the past and how will they influence positive change in the future?
2. The facility has been purchased and the county expects results. Even though the wheels are in motion, you still need to conduct some research. What information would you need to collect for a feasibility study? What might you still need to know in order to make this facility profitable?
3. What goals and objectives would you set for years 1, 2, and 3, respectively?
4. What is your overall strategy for the facility?
5. Develop a marketing plan based on the information you have collected in questions 1–4.

Resources for Case Study: Information on the Vadnais Sports Center purchase: http://www.startribune.com/local/east/253303441.html; Vadnais Sports Center website: http://www.vadnaissportscenter.net.

REFERENCES

Allen, J., O'Toole, W., McDonnel, I., & Harris, R. (2011). *Festival and special event management* (5th ed.). Milton, Queensland: Wiley.

Anderson, J. (2014, April). Ramsey County signs on to buy Vadnais Sports Center for $10.5 million. *Star Tribune, East Metro*. Retrieved from http://www.startribune.com/local/east/253303441.html

Baltes, G., & Leibing, I. (2008). Guerrilla marketing for information services. *New Library World, 109*, 46–55.

Belch, G. E., & Belch, M. A. (2004). *Introduction to advertising and promotion* (5th ed.). New York, NY: McGraw-Hill.

Gordon, J. W., Perrey, J., & Spellecke, D. (2013, July). Big data, analytics and the future of marketing and sales. *Forbes.com*. Retrieved from http://www.forbes.com/sites/mckinsey/2013/07/22/big-data-analytics-and-the-future-of-marketing-sales/

Hutter, K., & Hoffman, S. (2011). Guerilla marketing: The nature of the concept and proposition for further research. *Asian Journal of Marketing, 5*(2), 39–54.

Kimmel, A. J. (2005). Introduction: Marketing communication in the new millennium. In A. J. Kimmel (Ed.), *Marketing communication: New approaches, technologies and styles* (pp. 1–6). Oxford, United Kingdom: Oxford University Press.

Levinson, J. C. (1984). *Guerrilla marketing: Secrets of making big profit form your small business*. Boston, MA: Houghton Mifflin.

Li, Y-M., Lai, C-Y., & Chen, C-W. (2011). Discovering influencers for marketing in the blogosphere. *Information Sciences, 181*, 5143–5157.

Moore, K., & Pareek, N. (2010). *Marketing: The basics* (2nd ed.). New York, NY: Routledge.

Morgan, R. M., & Hunt, S. D. (1994). The commitment-trust theory of relationship marketing. *Journal of Marketing, 58*, 20–38.

Mullin, B. J., Hardy, S., & Sutton, W. A. (2007). *Sport marketing* (3rd ed.). Champaign, IL: Human Kinetics.

Pedersen, P. M., & Thibault, L. (Eds.). (2014). *Contemporary sport management* (5th ed.). Champaign, IL: Human Kinetics.

Pressey, A., & Tzokas, N. (2006). Relationship marketing: Theory, applications and future research directions. *Journal of Marketing Management, 22*(1), 1–4.

PRWeb.com. (2014, June). Underperforming sports complexes: The Sports Facilities Advisory says poor planning and management to blame. *prweb.com*. Retrieved from http://www.prweb.com/releases/2014/02/prweb11552781.htm

Raj, R., Walters, P., & Rashid, T. (2009). *Event management: An integrated and practical approach*. London, United Kingdom: Sage.

Shimp, T. A. (2003). *Advertising, promotion, and supplemental aspects of integrated marketing communications* (6th ed.). Mason, OH: South-Western Publishing.

Smith, P. R., Berry, C., & Pulford, A. (1999). *Strategic marketing management*. London, United Kingdom: Kogan Page.

Solomon, M. R., Marshall, G. W., Stuart, E. W., Barnes, B., & Mitchell, V. W. (2009). *Marketing: Real people, real decisions* (5th ed.). England: Pearson Education, Ltd.

Tough Mudder. (2014). About the events. *toughmudder.com*. Retrieved from https://toughmudder.com/events/what-is-tough-mudder

X Games Austin. (2014). Festival: Come for the sports, stay for the party. *xgamesaustin.com*. Retrieved from http://xgamesaustin.com/festival/

CHAPTER 9

Consumer Behavior

BRIANNA L. NEWLAND AND THOMAS J. AICHER

CHAPTER OBJECTIVES

Upon completion of this chapter, the reader will be able to:

1. Describe the concepts of socialization, involvement, and commitment
2. Define motivation and apply it to sport participation and spectating
3. Explain the different motivation factors
4. Outline the decision-making process in the purchasing decision by sport participants and spectators

CHAPTER OVERVIEW

This chapter will discuss the motivations to participate in and spectate sport events. It will discuss communication and persuasion and decision making by the consumer.

Industry VOICE

Jennifer Berger—General Manager, Pacific Sports

Courtesy of William Gieser.

Pacific Sports is an endurance sport event management company headquartered in California that specializes in event production, management, and corporate sport marketing development. Our mission is to "bring life to your lifestyle" by providing participants with a fun, safe, and competitive environment to satisfy their endurance needs. We want to give people the opportunity to live an active, healthy, happy life. As General Manager, my role is to assist with the planning, development, and management of our participant-driven events.

Prior to my position, I spent the majority of my career working with Major League Baseball teams such as the Baltimore Orioles, Atlanta Braves, and Cincinnati Reds. During this time, I served in a variety of roles, such as marketing, entertainment and event production, and special projects. It was not until recently that I realized my love for the endurance sport industry and began working for various event organizations. During this time, I was able to assist with the production of the L.A. Triathlon and the Rose Bowl Half Marathon, among others.

No matter what the role—whether event producer, race director, general staff, you name it—there are a few key steps to becoming involved in the sport event industry. The very first step is to care about and have actively participated in that sport so that you can produce a quality event experience for your participants based on your own experiences. The next step is to volunteer for as many local or regional sport events as possible to develop a better understanding of what it takes to manage those types of events. Finally, attempt to get a certification or complete continuing education opportunities that are provided by

the governing bodies of the specific sport. Each of these efforts will improve your knowledge of the specific sport and the skills, knowledge, and strategies to be able to host a quality, safe, and fun event.

When evaluating individuals for entry-level positions, I look at their ability to communicate clearly and follow directions. These skills are critical for both entry-level employees and day-of-the-event volunteers because they are likely to work directly with the event's participants and spectators. Applicants who demonstrate these skills during the interview process show me that they can be successful in these types of roles. Personal communication skills and negotiation skills are extremely valuable in the event industry but are often lacking. I also place value on those who have a love for the sport. Individuals who work in this industry need to have a high level of knowledge about and a strong appreciation for the sport to endure the long hours associated with managing events.

Within the participatory sport event production industry, the biggest challenge we have faced is working with the local municipalities to use their streets, parks, and other facilities for our events. In our industry, we do not own our facilities because of the temporary nature of our events. Therefore, we depend on the government agencies or private organizations that own or manage the property we would like to utilize to host our events. Managing this challenge involves two key components: developing a course the participants like and developing strong relationships with those organizations that own the facilities. Once we have developed the course, we build on our relationships with the various organizations to ensure long-term success.

One of the current trends in the participatory sport event industry is the increased focus on creating unique challenges or experiences to enhance participants' experiences. The current trend is to move away from the standard 5K race into developing events based on a theme or providing participants with a challenge in addition to the run. One issue with this mentality is we see events designed, implemented, and succeeding for a couple of years and then disappearing once the trend passes. Therefore, it is important for event producers to develop a strong understanding of the marketplace so they can be innovative in designing the event to match the desires of the participants in the marketplace. Technology is another mechanism that event producers can use to enhance the event experience for the participant. For example, the event could incorporate innovative ways to time participants, to engage or interact with participants, or to provide more cost-effective ways to do something.

Understanding consumers', and potential consumers', motivations and behaviors is integral in developing an event. Knowledge of why individuals participate in different kinds of events, and how long they participate in their selected events, helps event producers meet consumers' needs. Gaining this knowledge involves researching the marketplace. Research will also reveal where consumers find their information, which enables the event producer to market the event to them. One thing I have found is that individuals are intrinsically motivated to participate in events for the fun, challenge, or health benefits they can gain from their participation. Our business is to produce events that tie into those motivations.

Introduction

In sport, there are a number of key consumers to consider. Understanding how and why these key consumers behave as they do is critical for the success of a sport facility and/or event. But, more importantly, how an individual is introduced to sport can have a long-term impact on how involved and committed the person becomes as a consumer. For example, perhaps your parents took you to baseball games at Wrigley Field as a child. In all

likelihood, the meaning you attached to the experience of watching the Cubs play baseball and the overall experience and atmosphere that the event staff created at the stadium deeply influenced how you consume baseball to this day.

Understanding how and why an individual or group comes to consume sport is integral for future success. Building on the motivations and factors that drive consumer decision-making processes prompts more effective marketing strategies, streamlined communications, and, as a result,

© Chad McDermott/Shutterstock

more loyal consumers. This deeper understanding of the consumer can also help facility and event managers design event experiences that better meet the needs of their patrons. In other words, if you don't know what the consumer wants, how can you be sure you are delivering it through your sport events? Within this chapter, the concepts of socialization, involvement, and commitment and the motivating factors that drive consumer behavior will be explored. Having established this foundation, the decision-making processes that individuals utilize to make their selections will be outlined.

Consumption Factors

SOCIALIZATION

socialization The process whereby individuals learn skills, traits, values, attitudes, norms, and knowledge associated with the performance of present or anticipated social roles.

Socialization has been defined as "the process whereby individuals learn skills, traits, values, attitudes, norms, and knowledge associated with the performance of present or anticipated social roles" (McPherson & Brown, 1988, p. 267). How an individual is introduced to sport can influence his or her future involvement in and commitment to sport and sport events. There are three components to how an individual can be socialized into sport (Brustad, 1992): socialization *into* sport, socialization *via* sport, and socialization *out of* sport (see **Table 9-1**).

INVOLVEMENT

consumer involvement A blend of the individual's interest in sport and the degree of importance sport has in his or her life.

Socialization into sport assumes some type of involvement. **Consumer involvement** is a blend of the individual's interest in sport and the degree of importance sport has in his or her life (Wakefield, 2007). Many sport spectators and participants become highly involved with their sports, so much so that it consumes their lives. For example, a highly involved baseball fan will purchase season tickets (or attend as many games as possible), will spend

TABLE 9-1   Sport Socialization

	Socialization *into* Sport	Socialization *via* Sport	Socialization *out of* Sport
Description	The social and psychological influences that shape an individual's initial attraction to sport	The acquisition of attitudes, values, and knowledge as a consequence of sport involvement	The influences that contribute to an individual discontinuing his or her sport participation
Source of Influence	The prevalent attitudes and values within the family or peer group	The prevalent attitudes and values of teams, coaches, clubs	The prevalent attitudes and values of family, peers, sport

money on merchandise, and will travel to sporting events specifically for the team. Typically, individuals can be involved in sport in one of three ways: *cognitively*, *emotionally*, or *behaviorally*. **Cognitive involvement** is the acquisition of information/knowledge about a sport. Seeking information through print, electronic, and digital media as well as attending seminars and trade shows would be considered cognitive involvement. **Emotional involvement** is the individual's affective response to the sport. It includes the attitudes, feelings, and emotions the individual associates with sport. Finally, **behavioral involvement** is the action one takes in sport, through participating and/or spectating. Individuals who are highly involved tend to feel more deeply about sport and are more likely to devote more time and money to sport.

cognitive involvement The acquisition of information/knowledge about a sport.

emotional involvement The affect that a sport event produces in the individual.

behavioral involvement The action one takes in sport, whether as a participant or a spectator.

COMMITMENT

The more an individual becomes involved in sport, the greater the individual's **commitment** and, thus, the intensity of his or her attachment. Willingness to expend money, time, and energy increases as the sport becomes more ingrained in a person's identity (Wakefield, 2007). The more highly identified the person (as a participant or fan), the more central that identity becomes to the individual (Shamir, 1992). An individual who closely identifies with a sport typically makes statements like "I am a triathlete" (sport identification) and "I am a Broncos fan" (team identification). Consumers who are highly involved in and committed to their sport or team are less price sensitive and are likely to remain loyal to the sport product.

commitment The frequency, duration, and intensity of attachment to sport.

VIGNETTE 9-1

"Tri-ing" Triathlon

In 2009, the TribeGroup released the results of a study on triathlon demographics and spending habits. The Mind of the Triathlete study collected data on over 15,000 triathletes, revealing an average participant age of 38 years, with 65% between the ages of 30 and 49. Of the participants, 59.6% were male, and 88% were Caucasian. Participants had a high socioeconomic status, with median household incomes of $126,000. Most triathletes spent 50% of discretionary income on bikes and bike equipment, with 17% going toward race entry fees. Triathlon has grown tremendously since its inclusion in the 2000 Sydney Olympic Games. USA Triathlon observed double-digit growth through 2007 and continues to grow steadily every year. Understanding demand for the sport and the consumer profile of triathlon participants has enabled growth over the last decade (USA Triathlon, 2014).

Motivating Factors

ORGANIZATIONAL FACTORS

organizational factor
An element that differentiates one event from another and influences a participant's motivation to attend an event.

There are a number of **organizational factors** that differentiate one event from another and influence a participant's motivation to attend an event. How the organizational factors are perceived by the attendee, such as how well the organization is prepared to stage the event, can influence participation choices. The organizational components of the facility and/or the infrastructure and interstructure of the event can also impact these perceptions. Hallmann, Kaplanidou, and Breur (2010) outlined several organizational components that event managers should include in the production (e.g., marketing, logistics, security, and sponsorship) to enhance the event's image. Failure in any one of these production elements may impact how or why consumers are attracted to an event and/or how the event's customer service is perceived. These factors can negatively impact future attendance as well as word-of-mouth marketing and advertising for the event.

Several studies have researched event participants' evaluation of organizational factors and the impact on the event's image. For example, Getz and McConnell (2011) found that sport participants' desire for events to be well organized, to provide a challenging course or scenic route, and to offer a user-friendly website factored more heavily into their opinion of the event than

VIGNETTE 9-2

Krispy Kreme Challenge

Most runners would not find the prospect of consuming 2400 calories and running 5 miles in under an hour appealing. However, what started as a dare between a few North Carolina State University (NC State) sophomores has turned into what Runner's World listed as one of its favorite crazy races. To complete the event, runners start at the local Krispy Kreme store and run 2.5 miles to the famous bell tower on NC State's campus. Participants then eat a dozen glazed donuts before running back to the Krispy Kreme store. The event benefits the North Carolina Children's Hospital and has raised more than $750,000 in the 9 years of its existence. In the 2014 edition of the race, more than 3000 runners completed the event, and through participation fees, donations, and sponsorships, the event owners were able to donate $200,000 to the North Carolina Children's Hospital. The uniqueness of the event is its biggest attraction. Individuals are drawn in because of the challenge it provides, as it is the only race of its kind. In addition, the race draws on social factors through the camaraderie it generates in both the fundraising and the running competitions.

more common factors such as cost, prizes, or exclusivity. Furthermore, sport event managers should pay particular attention to signage, competent officiating, and efficiency throughout the entire event (Ryan & Lockyer, 2002). Participants have also reported they want to be treated as serious athletes who expect accuracy in timing, measurement, and performance recording by the event officials regardless of the event's competitive level (Trauer, Ryan, & Lockyer, 2003).

Similar organizational factors may impact individuals who attend sport fantasy camps or events. For instance, Gammons (2002) outlined five motivational factors to attend a sport fantasy camp, three of which relate directly to organizational factors: (1) desire to be associated with a famous event, (2) opportunity to train in a famous or meaningful facility, (3) increased identification with the organizing group (e.g., club or team), (4) enhanced association with sport heroes, and (5) development of personal skills. Similar elements may play a part in other types of events. For instance, both the Boston Marathon and the Ironman World Championships in Kona, Hawaii, require individuals to qualify or to be chosen through a lottery process in order to register. The prestige and pride that participants associate with these events is highly motivational. Many of the individuals who participate in such highly touted marathon or triathlon events tend to discuss them as career goals or events they *have* to finish.

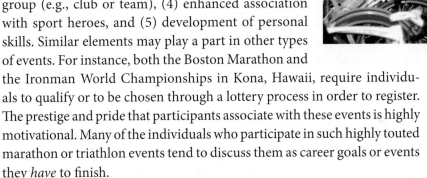

ENVIRONMENTAL/DESTINATION FACTORS

The attractiveness of a destination or the environment in which an event is hosted may impact the individual's motivation to attend or participate in an event. Kaplanidou and Vogt (2010) define these **environmental/destination factors** as beautiful scenery, new and/or exotic places, new or unique cultural experiences, locale prestige, and other factors directly related to the host destination. The destination's attractiveness may enhance individuals' motivation to travel to a destination and selection of the events in which

environmental/ destination factor The attractiveness of a destination or the environment in which an event is hosted that can impact individuals' motivations to attend or participate in an event.

individuals participate (Snelgrove & Wood, 2010). The location of sites and itineraries are often contingent upon the diverse natural conditions, which do not readily lend themselves to the satisfaction (accessibility), demographic, or economic needs of the traveler (Bourdeau, Corneloup, & Mao, 2002).

Further environmental/destination factors may impact individuals' decisions to travel to a location or facility. First, accessibility, or the ease with which an individual can reach the location through standard transportation, is important. Take, for example, rock climbers. These individuals are motivated by the physical and mental requirements of the route, the outdoor setting, and the remoteness of the site provided by the destination (Attarian, 2002; Bordeau et al., 2002). However, in order for these athletes to enjoy the challenge of their sport, they need access to the environment they intend to climb (both natural and artificial). The creation and improvement of rock climbing walls have led to an increase in participation rates within the sport by enhancing accessibility for more people (Mittelstaedt, 1997). On a much larger scale, spectators at the Lillehammer Olympic Games reported that the availability and ease of transportation to the event impacted their purchase decisions (Teigland, 1999). Finally, accommodation and entertainment quality, perceived value, friendliness of the host community, and the physical environment can affect the motivation levels to participate in a sport event (Shonk & Chelladurai, 2008).

The topography of the location or the challenge created by the destination may also provide a source of motivation. For example, snow skiers are drawn to the technical difficulty of the various courses, which depends largely on the destination's topography (Richards, 1996). Individuals who participate in sport fishing and scuba diving are drawn to locations based on the quality of the sporting experience (Roehl, Ditton, Holland, & Perdue, 1993; Tabata, 1992). Similarly, marathon runners may select a specific event based on whether the topography provides for a challenging or easy course (Shipway & Jones, 2007).

Research suggests that timing impacts the influence of destination factors. For instance, Snelgrove and Wood (2010) suggest that destination motivations may be limited to first-time visitors, while repeat visitors may be motivated by other factors. This finding is further supported by several other research studies demonstrating the role of novelty in event choices (Bello & Etzel, 1985; Kaplanidou & Gibson, 2010; Lee & Crompton, 1992;

Wahlers & Etzel, 1985). Walker, Hinch, and Higham (2010) have found that some participants had a moderate place motivation while others did not indicate the same motivation, further supporting the mixed results of destination as a source of motivation.

SOCIAL/GROUP FACTORS

Social identities provide individuals with a sense of belongingness or membership to a wider social group, a place within that environment, and the subsequent opportunity to use membership of that group (Green & Jones, 2005). Traditionally, individuals identify with specific social groups such gender, race, religion, and work; however, as previously noted, as a person becomes more involved and committed to sport, leisure, and recreation, these contexts may form stronger, more valued social identities for the individuals (Green & Jones, 2005).

social identity
A sense of belongingness or membership to a wider social group.

Several researchers support social identity as a potential source of motivation to select certain events. Most participants and spectators in large sporting events engage in their sport with someone else rather than alone so they may share intense or unique moments. For example, Cassidy and Pegg (2008) have found that individuals who participated in the Australian University Games did so primarily because they could "go with friends." Ko, Park, and Claussen (2008) suggest that event managers capitalize on this behavior by creating a fun environment in which individuals can socialize with others rather than focusing too much on the competition itself.

COMPETITIVE FACTORS

Competitive factors can be described as the factors that motivate a person to enter into a rivalry or event in order to measure ability in relation to another person or a standard (McDonald, Milne, & Hong, 2002). This motivation is linked to individuals' ability to challenge themselves (Getz & McConnell, 2011). The challenge may come in the form of competing against other athletes (Cassidy & Pegg, 2008; Kurtzman & Zauhar, 2005) or against the course or event (Gillet & Kelly, 2006). In either case, a successful outcome can enhance self-esteem (Ogles & Masters, 2003). Selecting events based on the level of competition is a consistent motivating factor for individuals.

competitive factor
A rivalry or event meant to measure ability in relation to another.

Due to the importance of competitive factors, the tourism industry has begun to provide more sport and physical activities as additional marketing dimensions for travelers (Gibson, 1998). In doing so, these organizations have developed new and intriguing opportunities for individuals to challenge themselves while on vacation. One example is the Caribbean Running Cruise, an event in which runners cruise the islands of the Caribbean and run the islands when the boat docks. For more information, visit www.cimcruise.com.

mastery factor A factor relating to the skill, learning, and personal challenge of participating in sport.

emotional factor The excitement, enjoyment, and self-fulfillment individuals gain from participating in sport.

These factors have led to numerous changes in the sport facility and event industries. For instance, Richards (1996) outlined how facility owners have enhanced their golf courses, ski slopes, and tennis courts to provide consumers with the same quality and challenge enjoyed by their professional idols.

MASTERY FACTORS

Mastery factors are tied to, and even enhanced by, competitive factors and refer to an individual's autonomous motivation to gain mastery of skills. Individuals who are driven by skill development, learning, and personal challenge are more interested in the intrinsic factors associated with sport participation. Certainly those driven by competition factors cannot win without strong mastery of skills, but the individual driven by mastery is typically interested in self-competition, not winning. The final outcome is about the personal challenge and accomplishment, not the external rewards.

EMOTIONAL FACTORS

Kaplanidou and Vogt (2010) define **emotional factors**, as they relate to motivation, as the excitement, enjoyment, and self-fulfillment individuals gain from participating in sport tourism. They explain that individuals find it important to have fun when participating at an event. Emotional factors can be further subdivided into escapism, nostalgia, and enjoyment.

Escapism has long been considered a source of motivation for travel (Crompton, 1979) and is defined as participating in an event or traveling to a facility to get away from the routines and stresses of everyday life, but not necessarily away from people (Yfantidou, Costa, & Michalopoulos, 2008). Individuals who travel to compete in or spectate events do so to escape from their home lives. Fans travel to support their teams to enjoy a release from everyday life, camaraderie, and a sense of belonging (Stewart, 2001). Likewise, event participants believe events are pleasurable and integral to their lifestyle; they engage in them as an opportunity to have fun and for the thrill of it (Getz & McConnell, 2011).

Traveling for sport can spark feelings of nostalgia and yearning to relive previous life experiences, thereby providing spectators and participants with a different type of reality (Fairly, 2003). Nostalgia can range from an attachment to physical places, such as museums, stadiums, or halls of fame, to actual experiences of participating or watching a sport in which an individual once participated. For instance, one may choose to attend a Chicago Cubs game just for the opportunity to attend a game at historic Wrigley Field, or a lover of bicycle racing may attend a ride-along at the Tour de France.

People will select to attend or participate in events because of the excitement or enjoyment that being a part of the event provides. People who are considered thrill seekers desire novel and adventurous experiences associated with events (Wahlers & Etzel, 1985). For example, younger golfers tend to rate thrill, boredom alleviation, and surprise as important factors for the golf events they attend (Petrick, 2002). Regardless of age, gender, or class rank, students tend to participate in intramural sports out of interest in the activity or for the enjoyment derived from simply engaging in play (Cooper, Scheutt, & Phillips, 2012).

LEARNING FACTORS

Learning factors refer to the individual's desire to learn about or explore the facility or destination. These factors may enhance an individual's motivation to select an event (Ryan & Glendon, 1998; Snelgrove, Taks, Chalip, & Green, 2008). Individuals who attended the 2002 Federation of Association Football (FIFA) World Cup in South Korea did so because they wanted to take the opportunity to learn more about the local culture (Kim & Chalip, 2004). International sport tourists, including the event participants, typically want to learn about the culture of the host country when they attend these megaevents (Funk & Bruun, 2007). Participants in the Gold Coast Marathon held in Queensland, Australia, selected the event specifically because they wanted to learn more about the Australian culture (Funk, Toohey, & Bruun, 2007).

learning factor
The desire to learn about or explore the facility or destination of a sport event.

Individuals who participate in charity sport events may also be driven by a desire to acquire knowledge and information about the charity organization. For instance, participants in some local charity events (e.g., 5K fun runs) selected these events because they want to learn more about the cause associated with the event (Filo, Funk, & O'Brien, 2008; Wharf Higgins, & Lauzon, 2003). It is important to note that having a charity does not guarantee an increase in participation. For example, Snelgrove and Wood (2010) found that cyclists participating in events to raise money for the National Multiple Sclerosis Society were not particularly concerned about learning more about the organization. In fact, they found some of the other factors (e.g., socialization, cycling identity) to be much stronger reasons for selection.

The Decision-Making Process

The decision-making process can be as complex or as simple as the product, good, or service the person is purchasing (Blythe, 2013). The amount of time it takes an individual to complete the decision-making process will fluctuate depending on the complexity of factors. For example, it may take an event director several months or even a year to select the perfect venue for a sporting event, while it may take only moments for a person to decide to participate in that same event. In the example of venue selection, the event director may put out a request for proposals and receive several bids to host the events at certain venues. It may take weeks or months to narrow down the pool of potential locations and to conduct site visits. Once completed, the event director will continue to evaluate alternatives and ultimately make a decision. In contrast, a person intending to play in a basketball tournament may simply research a few events online, discuss the options with his or her teammates, and make a selection. Despite the complexity of the first example and the simplicity of the second, both people have followed similar steps to reach the decision.

Blackwell, Mianiard, and Engel (2005) outline seven stages in the consumer decision process (CDP) model: need recognition, search for information, prepurchase evaluation of alternatives, purchase, consumption, postconsumption evaluation, and divestment. While described as stages, the process is not strictly linear; individuals may return to or skip various stages based on the information they receive during the process.

need A state of perceived deprivation.

want The form taken by human needs as they are shaped by culture and individual personality.

NEED RECOGNITION

The first stage of the CDP model is need recognition. Kotler, Brown, Adam, and Armstrong (2004) define **needs** as "states of felt deprivation" and **wants** as "the form taken by human needs as they are shaped by culture and individual personality" (p. 4). To explain this further, people *need* to live a healthy lifestyle and *want* to participate in a sport event to do so. In terms of the decision-making process, a need recognition occurs when individuals perceive that something is missing from their lives. In the case of sport facilities and events, the two earlier examples highlight this stage: The event owner recognizes that he or she needs a facility to host the event, and the participant feels a need to reconnect with his or her friends and believes that playing in a basketball tournament is the perfect way to do so.

SEARCH FOR INFORMATION

The information search can be one of the most time-consuming stages of the CDP. Individuals can search for information from a variety of sources, which may be broadly categorized as internal (from memory) and external (from outside sources). Internal searches occur when individuals reflect on their past experiences with the sport product and information they already know about it. The amount of this experience or information may be limited. Therefore, the bulk of the information evaluated is collected from outside sources, which may be broken down into formal and informal communication (Middleton, Fyall, & Morgan, 2009).

Informal communication is the information we receive from our friends, family, or groups of people we interact with socially. Word-of-mouth communication is the most common form of informal communication. For example, you may be in the process of planning a softball tournament in your community and mention the event to a friend. Your friend may suggest that the facility where she played her last softball tournament could be the perfect location. With this information, you would likely seek out more specific information about the facility. Social media platforms may also be a source of informal communication, as you may get more information about events you commonly participate in through Facebook groups, Twitter feeds, message boards, or blogs you frequent because of their discussion of the sport.

Formal communication is any information generated by the facility or event owner. Although this is not an exhaustive list of potential sources of information, formal communication is found in the form of brochures, advertisements, product placements, sales people, retail displays, and so forth. In addition, it is a common practice for facility owners to participate in conventions and conferences associated with various sports. On a much larger scale, the National Association of Sport Commissions (NASC) hosts the annual NASC Sports Event Symposium for its membership base, which include visitor's bureaus,

informal communication The information we receive from our friends, family, or groups of people we interact with socially.

formal communication Information generated by the facility or sport event owner.

sport commissions, chambers of commerce, and individual members (www.nascsymposium.com). During this conference, nearly 800 individuals from these organizations attend, and several event owners and facility owners meet to discuss how they can partner with one another for future events.

PREPURCHASE EVALUATION AND PURCHASE

During this stage, the individual considers the different alternatives and makes a selection. As outlined previously, the individual's selection will depend on the motivational factors for hosting, spectating, or participating in the event. Using the event owner example from before, event owners may want to host their events in a unique destination to attract individuals who may not normally participate; thus, they will consider destination or environmental factors to select their event. In the participant example, the player is hoping to reconnect with friends by playing in this basketball tournament. Therefore, the athlete is drawn to an event that meets the social factors she is seeking. During this stage, the consumer will develop a set of alternatives and evaluate all of the information gathered during the information search.

Individuals at this stage establish a set of criteria or rules by which they can judge the alternatives so they know which selection will meet their needs. Blythe (2013) suggests there are three broad categories of decision rules. Noncompensatory decision rules are absolute and will not be deviated from. They are of greater importance than other factors. For example, someone searching for a softball league to participate in may not want to drive more than 20 minutes to games or practices. This person would be willing to select only softball leagues within that driving radius. Alternatively, compensatory rules allow for concessions and negotiations. Using the same example, the person may wish to pay only a certain amount for the season but will concede to a higher amount because of the convenience of the drive time. Finally, conjunctive rules are the rules by which individuals judge the final alternatives in the consideration set. These rules are similar to noncompensatory rules in that they must be met for the alternative to be selected. Ultimately, these are the rules by which the final decision is made. This act of making a final selection is known as **purchase**.

purchase The act of making a final selection.

CONSUMPTION AND POSTCONSUMPTION EVALUATION

consumption The active use of a product or service.

Once individuals have purchased the product, they transition into the **consumption** phase, in which they use the product, good, or service. Once the event is over, event owners or consumers evaluate their experience with the facility or event. To do so, they evaluate the various experiences they had to determine whether using that facility or attending that event satisfied their needs. They may also evaluate any issues, challenges, or problems that occurred during consumption that led to dissatisfaction. The major difference between an event owner and a consumer at this stage is the event owner should evaluate the event and facility far more formally to ensure that the goals and objectives for hosting the event were reached and that the facility provided the proper service, amenities, and location. In contrast, participants or spectators would evaluate their experience informally based on the enjoyment of the event, or how well the event met their expectations. For example, after participating in a half marathon, runners may evaluate the exposition, crowd support, volunteer support, and other event structures to determine how much they enjoyed the event and whether they would consider participating in the event a second time.

DIVESTMENT

The are two major components of **divestment**. First is the disposal or removal of remaining items associated with consuming the product that have little to no value to the consumer (Blythe, 2013). Second is the termination of the relationship and the return of postevent evaluations and other information. For instance, after hosting a beach volleyball tournament at a resort in Florida, the facility owner may ask for feedback of their performance. The event owner would provide this evaluation and return any items they may have used while implementing the event (e.g., keys, tables, chairs). The goal of the facility owner will likely be to maintain this relationship if the event was successful for their organization; even if this was not the case, they could use the event owner's feedback to improve the quality of their services and amenities to host future events.

divestment The disposal/removal of the items associated with consuming a product or service and/or the ceasing of the relationship with the organization altogether.

SUMMARY

Within this chapter we outlined the decision-making process that an event owner uses when selecting a host facility and that a participant or spectator uses when selecting an event. The consumption factors help define participants' and consumers' association with a sport and can be utilized to develop strong customer relationships. Motivational factors of participants and spectators were also outlined and may impact the design of your event or facility. Depending on your consumers' motivations, you may change your event's design.

DISCUSSION QUESTIONS

1. Define and provide examples of the three consumption factors.
2. Utilizing an event in which you have participated in the past, describe why you attended the event. Use one of the motivational factors outlined to explain your motivation for participating.
3. You would like to host a small community event of your choosing. Using the seven steps in the decision-making process, provide an example of how you would select a facility to host your event.

Case STUDY

Creating a Consumer Profile

In 1996, athletes in the sports of triathlon and mountain biking set out to determine which athlete was the "fittest on the island" of Maui in the beautiful, but geographically challenging, Hawaii. The race—originally titled AquaTerra and now known as XTERRA—consisted of an open-ocean swim, a mountain bike race, and a trail run. The new off-road format was attractive not only to triathletes and mountain bikers, but also to other outdoor enthusiasts. The first event has spawned more than 70 challenging off-road triathlons and running events in the United States in addition to the XTERRA World Tour. What is interesting about this event is that it combines two very different types of consumers. Mountain bikers tend to be more laid back, whereas triathletes are known for their hard-core training and avid dedication; however, neither consumer can resist the challenge and thrill of this racing format.

As the new marketing director for XTERRA, you have been tasked with developing a consumer profile for your supervisor. He has asked you to research and document the demographics and psychographics for the general triathlete, general mountain biker, and XTERRA athlete and to then answer the following questions:

1. Based on the profiles you have developed for each of these athlete types, how do these sport consumers differ? How are they similar?
2. How might you attract an athlete who identifies with and is highly involved in triathlon to try an XTERRA event? How might you do this for mountain bikers?
3. Triathletes do not own mountain bikes, making it impossible to ride their bikes off-course. How might you overcome this equipment barrier?
4. Develop a brief plan that details the data you collected and recommendations to attract new athletes to the sport.

Case resource: XTERRA website: http://www.xterraplanet.com/.

REFERENCES

Attarian, A. (2002). Rock climbers' self-perceptions of first aid, safety and rescue skills. *Wilderness and Environmental Medicine, 13*(4), 238–244.

Bello, D., & Etzel, M. (1985). The role of novelty in the pleasure travel experience. *Journal of Travel Research, 24*, 20–26.

Blackwell, R. D., Mianiard, P. W., & Engel J. F. (2005). *Consumer behaviors* (10th ed.). Mason, OH: Thomson Southwest.

Blythe, J. (2013). *Consumer behavior.* Thousand Oaks, CA: Sage Publishers.

Bourdeau, P., Corneloup, J., & Mao, P. (2002). Adventure sports and tourism in the French mountains: Dynamics of change and challenges for sustainable development. *Current Issues in Tourism, 5*(11), 22–32.

Brustad, R. J. (1992). Integrating socialization influences into the study of children's motivation in sport. *Journal of Sport & Exercise Psychology, 14*, 59–77.

Cassidy, F., & Pegg, S. (2008). Exploring the motivations for engagement in sport tourism. Retrieved from http://eprints.usq.edu.au/4211/1/Cassidy_Pegg .pdf?origin=publication_detail

Cooper, N., Schuett, P. A., & Phillips, H. M. (2012). Examining intrinsic motivations in campus intramural sports. *Recreational Sports Journal, 36*(1), 25–36.

Crompton, H. (1979). Motivations for pleasure vacation. *Annals of Tourism, 6,* 408–424.

Fairly, S. (2003). In search of re-lived social experience: Group-based nostalgia sport tourism. *Journal of Sport Management, 17*(3), 284–304.

Filo, K. R., Funk, D. C., & O' Brien, D. (2008). It's really not about the bike: Exploring attraction and attachment to the events of the Lance Armstrong Foundation. *Journal of Sport Management, 22*(5), 501–525.

Funk, D. C., & Bruun, T. (2007). The role of socio-psychological and culture-education motives in marketing international sport tourism: A cross-cultural perspective. *Tourism Management, 28,* 806–819.

Funk, D. C., Toohey, K., & Bruun, T. (2007). International sport event participation: Prior sport involvement; destination image; and travel motives. *European Sport Management Quarterly, 7*(3), 227–248.

Gammons, S. (2002). Fantasy, nostalgia and the pursuit of what never was. In S. Gammon & J. Kurtzman (Eds.), *Sport tourism principles and practice* (pp. 61–72). Eastbourne, UK: Leisure Studies Association Publications.

Getz, D., & McConnell, A. (2011). Serious sport tourism and event travel careers. *Journal of Sport Management, 25*(4), 326–338.

Gibson, H. J. (1998). Active sport tourism: Who participates? *Leisure Studies, 17*(2), 155–170.

Gillett, P., & Kelly, S. (2006). "Non-local" masters games participants: An investigation of competitive active sport tourist motives. *Journal of Sport Tourism, 11*(3–4), 239–257.

Green, B., & Jones, I. (2005). Serious leisure, social identity and sport tourism. *Sport in Society, 8*(2), 164–181.

Hallmann, K., Kaplanidou, K., & Breur, C. (2010). Event image perceptions among active and passive sport tourists at marathon races. *International Journal of Sport Marketing & Sponsorship, 12*(1), 37–52.

Kaplanidou, K., & Gibson, H. J. (2010). Predicting behavioral intentions of active event sport tourists: The case of a small-scale recurring sports event. *Journal of Sport & Tourism, 15*(2), 163–179.

Kaplanidou, K., & Vogt, C. (2010). The meaning and measurement of a sport event experience among active sport tourists. *Journal of Sport Management, 24*(5), 544–566.

Kim, N., & Chalip, L. (2004). Why travel to the FIFA World Cup? Effects of motives, background, interest, and constraints. *Tourism Management, 25,* 695–707.

Ko, Y. J., Park, H., & Claussen, C. L. (2008). Action sports participation: Consumer motivation. *International Journal of Sports Marketing and Sponsorship, 9*(1), 111–124.

Kotler, P., Brown, L., Adam, S., & Armstrong, G. (2004). *Marketing* (5th ed.). Sydney, Australia: Prentice Hall.

Kurtzman, J., & Zauhar, J. (2005). Sports tourism consumer motivation. *Journal of Sport & Tourism, 10*(1), 21–31.

Lee, T., & Crompton, J. (1992). Measuring novelty seeking in tourism. *Annals of Tourism Research, 19,* 732–751.

McDonald, M., Milne, G., & Hong, J. (2002). Motivational factors for evaluating sport spectator and participant markets. *Sport Marketing Quarterly, 11*(2), 100–111.

McPherson, B. D., & Brown, B. A. (1988). The structure, processes, and consequences of sport for children. *Children in Sport, 3,* 265–286.

Middleton, V. T. C., Fyall, A., & Morgan, M. (2009). *Marketing in travel and tourism.* London, UK: Routledge.

Mittelstaedt, R. (1997). Indoor climbing wall: The sport of the nineties. *Journal of Physical Education, Recreation, & Dance, 68*(8), 43–47.

Ogles, B. M., & Masters, K. S. (2003). A typology of marathon runners based on cluster analysis of motivations. *Journal of Sport Behavior, 26*(1), 69.

Petrick, J. (2002). An examination of golf vacationers' novelty. *Annals of Tourism Research, 29,* 384–400.

Richards, G. (1996). Skilled consumption and UK ski holidays. *Tourism Management, 17,* 25–34.

Roehl, W., Ditton, R., Holland, S., & Perdue, R. (1993). Developing new tourism products: Sport fishing in the south-east United States. *Tourism Management, 14,* 279–288.

Ryan, C., & Glendon, I. (1998). Applications in leisure motivation scale to tourism. *Annals of Tourism Research, 24,* 301–323.

Ryan, C., & Lockyer, T. (2002). Masters' games involvement: The nature of competitor's involvement and requirements. *Event Management, 7,* 259–270.

Shamir, B. (1992). Some correlates of leisure identity salience: Three exploratory studies. *Journal of Leisure Research, 24,* 301–323.

Shipway, R., & Jones, I. (2007). Running away from home: Understanding visitor experiences and behaviour at sport tourism events. *International Journal of Tourism Research, 9*(5), 373–383.

Shonk, D. J., & Chelladurai, P. (2008). Service quality, satisfaction, and intent to return in event sport tourism. *Journal of Sport Management, 22*(5), 587–602.

Snelgrove, R., Taks, M., Chalip, L., & Green, B. C. (2008). How visitors and locals at a sport event differ in their motives and identity. *Journal of Sport & Tourism, 13,* 165–180.

Snelgrove, R., & Wood, L. (2010). Attracting and leveraging visitors at a charity cycling event. *Journal of Sport & Tourism, 15*(4), 269–285.

Stewart, B. (2001). Fan club. *Australia Leisure Management,* (Oct/Nov), 16–19.

Tabata, R. (1992). Scuba diving holidays. In B. Weiler & C. M. Hall (Eds.), *Special interest tourism* (pp. 171–184). London, UK: Bellhaven Press.

Teigland, J. (1999). Mega-events and impacts on tourism: The predictions and realities of the Lillehammer Olympics. *Impact Assessment and Project Appraisal, 17*(4), 305–317.

Trauer, B. B., Ryan, C. C., & Lockyer, T. T. (2003). The South Pacific Masters' Games: Competitor involvement and games development—implications for management and tourism. *Journal of Sport & Tourism, 8*(4), 270–283.

USA Triathlon. (2014). Demographics. Retrieved from http://www.usatriathlon .org/about-multisport/demographics.aspx

Wahlers, R. G., & Etzel, M. J. (1985). Vacation preference as a manifestation of optimal simulation and lifestyle experience. *Journal of Leisure Research, 17,* 283–295.

Wakefield, K. (2007). *Team sports marketing.* Burlington, MA: Butterworth-Heinemann.

Walker, G. J., Hinch, T., & Higham, J. (2010). Athletes as tourists: The roles of mode of experience and achievement orientation. *Journal of Sport & Tourism, 15*(4), 287–305.

Wharf Higgins, J., & Lauzon, L. (2003). Finding the funds in fun runs: Exploring physical activity events as fundraising tools in the nonprofit sector. *International Journal of Nonprofit and Voluntary Sector Marketing, 8,* 363–377.

Yfantidou, G., Costa, G., & Michalopoulos, M. (2008). Tourist roles, gender and age: A study of tourists in Greece. *International Journal of Sport Management, Recreation, and Tourism, 1,* 14–30.

CHAPTER 10

Sponsorship

LYDIA M. DUBUISSON

CHAPTER OBJECTIVES

Upon completion of this chapter, the reader will be able to:

1. Define and distinguish between different levels of sponsorship in the United States
2. Uncover possible sponsors and determine who is responsible for making the decisions
3. Identify a good sponsorship fit
4. Identify trends regarding sponsor–property relationships
5. Outline the importance of objectives, activation, and evaluation
6. Explain the components of sponsorship agreements

CHAPTER OVERVIEW

This chapter will outline the main components of sport sponsorship and will help future sport facility and event managers generate ideas for forming successful relationships between sport properties and their sponsors. A definition of sponsorship will be provided, followed by a discussion of the various levels of events (from international to small local) and the various sponsorship opportunities possible at each level. The common sponsorship inventories available to both facilities and sport events will then be outlined. Finally, acquisition of sponsors, activation of the sponsorship, and relationship marketing will be reviewed.

Industry VOICE

Lindsay Laurent—Director of Licensing and Strategic Revenue, Bowling Green State University

As Director of Licensing and Strategic Revenue for the Bowling Green State University athletic department, I manage all branding and licensing efforts for the athletic department and monitor the use of all university marks. In addition, I am responsible for creating external revenue streams for the basketball arena. The two areas I oversee bring in over $500,000 of revenue to the athletic department annually.

Like so many in the licensing industry, you could say I "fell into" my current role. To arrive at my current position, I have taken an extremely unconventional path, which has included taking nearly any job in athletics that was open. I believe it is important to be willing to take unpaid positions if that is all that exists in order to gain experience. My diverse unpaid experiences helped get me where I am today. In 10 years of working in college athletics, I have held positions in the following areas: coaching, athletic operations, sports information, stadium hospitality, external relations, and licensing. Each experience was invaluable and provided perspectives on how different areas of the department coexist and create a cohesive message. I draw upon these perspectives as licensing director for the department. Having a solid understanding of how the various branches of the department work helps me to brand the university teams, products, and messages.

The areas of sponsorship and licensing are always evolving, and a trend that continues on most campuses is finding new ways to protect your mark. Many factors influence the need to find new ways to protect marks; most important are publicity and popularity. For larger, more notable institutions, licensing can be tricky because everyone is trying to capitalize on the school's success. Licensing directors have to be on the pulse of what is happening around their campus. For example, sites like Etsy, Pinterest, and other social boards have bred a new type of licensee. Crafters use these sites to create handmade or low-production items to sell to fans. Many do this without a proper license.

To capitalize on the current trends, I am constantly on social media looking for new ways people try to use our marks. Whether it is in song lyrics, photography, or fan websites, all could be classified as infringers if they improperly use a mark or likeness of the university. I have developed a crafter's license for the homemade products. This license is minimal and does not require royalties to be paid if annual sales do not exceed $2000.

When hiring a new employee or intern, I look for energy and excitement from the candidate. In my opinion, the best candidate isn't always the most qualified on paper. I am looking for a certain personality and someone who brings a skill set that complements my existing team. I also look for individuals who have displayed resiliency somewhere in their educational or professional career and who can overcome obstacles.

My advice to new graduates is that not everyone will get their dream job straight out of college. Most will have to take a job they don't necessarily find glamorous in order to gain experience. However, these opportunities can be the most beneficial. Even if the work environment isn't ideal, there are always ways to learn from a situation. And some of the most negative situations can be the most impactful to your career.

Once you've broken into this field, my advice is to learn to take criticism with poise and move on.

Not every proposal or idea you pitch will be met with enthusiasm. It is in your best interest to develop productive ways to cope with criticism. Make sure you can identify what is constructive and apply that feedback in your next project. Doing so ensures you will never make the same mistake twice and shows your supervisor you are listening. Making the most of criticism is key as you move forward with your career. The more responsibility you receive, the more criticism you will also receive.

Introduction

The importance of sponsorship in producing successful events and providing revenue for a facility cannot be ignored. How does one find potential sponsors? What is the process for creating a sponsorship agreement? What are the different parts of a sponsorship agreement? All of these questions will be answered in this chapter.

Sponsorship Defined

As defined by Mowen and Graefe (2002), a **sponsorship** is a contract negotiated "between a corporation and another event, organization, or property, whereby the sponsor pays cash or provides in-kind services for rights to the commercial and marketable benefits associated with that property" (p. 32). A company or **sponsor** pays for the right to be associated with the sport organization or **property**, whether through a direct cash payment or by exchanging some service for these rights (i.e., **in-kind payment**). For example, a local media outlet may run television advertisements in exchange for tickets to games. These relationships have become an increasingly valuable revenue stream for sport organizations. In 2011, total sponsorships in North America totaled $18.11 billion, a 5.5% increase from 2010. IEG, an industry-leading sponsorship consulting agency, reports that sport organizations accounted for $12.38 billion in 2011, up from $11.66 billion in 2010, making the sport industry the strongest of all categories, including entertainment, causes, arts, festivals, fairs, and annual events, as well as association and member organizations (Andrews & Wheaton, 2011).

Defining Each Level

Shani and Sandler (1996) created what they referred to as the "sports pyramid," which places sport events and organizations in one of five categories

sponsorship A legal contract between a sport property and another entity exchanging something of value, whether cash or an in-kind service/product, wherein the sport property allows the sponsoring organization the rights to commercialization of its brand and the resulting benefits derived from these actions.

sponsor The organization purchasing rights from the sport organization. This company may be a sport-oriented organization itself (e.g., sporting goods company) or may not be (e.g., financial entity).

property In reference to sport sponsorship, the sport organization or entity being sponsored.

in-kind payment
An exchange of something of value other than cash currency for the purpose of entering a business relationship between a sports property and a sponsoring company

according to geographic reach and level of interest. Though there are also global and international scale categories, this chapter will focus on three categories: national, regional, and local (Shani & Sandler, 1996, p. 6). This system will be expanded by an additional component—the area in which a sponsor wishes to buy—to help categorize sponsor levels. Currently, levels are determined mainly by how far a sport organization or event reaches in terms of geography and the distance fans will travel or the location of the majority of the sport organization's fan base. In the current sports environment, more categories are needed to determine the sponsors' perspective and why companies might consider a property in its purchase decision.

National-level sport events involve interest from one or possibly two countries, such as the Super Bowl or the World Series (Shani & Sandler, 1996). These events are nationally televised. Spectators generally travel from around the country, and interest is not localized within the host city. Regional organizations or events are more geographically limited (Shani & Sandler, 1996). They may include individual professional teams such as the Atlanta Falcons of the National Football League (NFL) or college athletic programs such as the University of Minnesota's basketball team.

Local levels "have the narrowest geographic focus, usually a city or community, and usually appeal to a specific segment in the area" (Shani & Sandler, 1996, p. 6). Examples include a high school track program or a minor league baseball team. Media coverage, if any, is confined to local sources, and fan interest does not expand very far outside the local region. In the suggested new model, a large local-level sport like high school football may be covered regularly in the local media and draw large crowds. Little League baseball games or softball tournaments, on the other hand, do not. A sponsor may wish to invest in the high school sport to make a more visible local impact—hence the need to further distinguish large local from small local.

Recreational and leisure activities may be considered local depending on the size and scope. Some well-organized and popular events reach much farther.

An additional dimension—participation versus spectator orientation—must be included to more clearly delineate this local category. The previously mentioned events tend to have a spectator turnout that far exceeds participant numbers. For an event that exists primarily for the sake of participation (not spectating), the emphasis of marketing shifts from increasing spectatorship to driving up numbers of active participants. Participation-oriented events are gaining regional and national status. This category is for people who are playing the sport largely for pleasure and not simply watching. Obstacle races, such as Muddy Buddy and Warrior Dash, are excellent examples of a growing trend toward participation-oriented sports for fun.

Included in this local category are sports for which people will travel to participate. Golf, water sports, and hiking are but a few examples that fit well here. These types of activities can help generate tourism. Sports at these levels often take place at publically funded venues and property such as city parks. Demands and expectations placed on publically funded community property and their sponsors can be very different from those placed on privately held businesses. Some of these considerations will be noted throughout the chapter.

Interconnectivity of Levels

Part of the difficulty in clearly differentiating the levels of sponsorship is due to the marketing **activation** process. A company buying at a national level will still want to create platforms for activation down to even specific local areas. Simply running a national television advertisement is not enough to engage consumers with the products or to develop more personal relationships with the consumers. Sports can be useful for these levels of activation. It is much more engaging when people can sample a product and interact with a sponsoring company's employees rather than just watching a television commercial telling them about the product. This is why it is not uncommon to see product samples of major brands being promoted at even relatively small local events. The model in **Figure 10-1** illustrates interconnectivity of numerous levels a sponsor may consider. The arrows

activation A specific action taken toward leveraging the sport–sponsorship relationship.

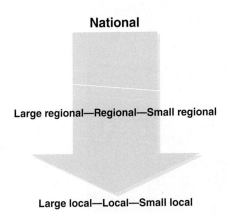

National

Large regional—Regional—Small regional

Large local—Local—Small local

FIGURE 10-1   Model of sponsorship interconnectivity

indicate activation direction. National companies with strategic marketing plans will potentially activate through the regional categories down to even a small local recreational or leisure level. Regional companies may also activate through a variety of local sports platforms.

Sponsorship Inventory

FACILITY NAMING RIGHTS

naming rights The nonsport entity's (sponsor's) exclusive ownership of the name of the venue where sport events occur (i.e., the stadium, arena, or ballpark); used interchangeably with "title sponsorship."

When trying to categorize the level at which to place facility **naming rights**, it may seem difficult at times to find a clear fit. The level and consistency of coverage may seem much larger than the scope of just that one city. Brands often garner national media mentions and are shown on television nationally when a home game is played, which translates into powerful impression value. Visibility of the sponsoring entity as well as media mentions and brand association with teams and their conferences or leagues are powerful drivers for sponsors' investments.

Financial institutions are trending toward the practice of facility naming rights, with "nearly 20% of the teams in four major sports leagues [having] the name of a financial services company affixed to their home building" (Bhasin, 2011, para. 1). This trend may be a testament to the fit between institutions that specialize in how to handle large sums of money and properties with expenses and revenues in the multimillion-dollar range. However, naming rights are not just for the national-level sponsors and properties. This potential revenue source is actually an area on which local-level sports, such as high school venues, can now capitalize. For those responsible for revenue generation at a local level, putting together a plan to indicate to prospective sponsors the amount of exposure and media mentions they could receive could go far toward convincing a business that this is a worthy investment and not simply a philanthropic endeavor.

© Richard Cavalleri/Shutterstock.

VIGNETTE 10-1

Banks Go Local

In Evans City, Pennsylvania, NexTier Bank partnered with Seneca Valley School District to invest in the naming rights to the Raiders Stadium used for football, track and field, and soccer, as well as graduations. Middle school through high school holds events at the stadium, amounting to potentially thousands of people from the home and visiting teams at each event. The cost of the partnership amounted to $50,000 across 10 years plus signage expenses. Assistant Vice President, Marketing Communications Manager, Lauren Way explained that "no other media can provide as many viewers for the cost" (Albro, 2010, p. 42). In contrast to the occasional advertisement in a newspaper that would also cost thousands of dollars, a stadium name is visible all year and the NexTier name is mentioned each time a story is written about sport events occurring there. Include the concept that the bank is supporting the local community youth and educational system with its sponsorship contribution and no traditional advertising can compare (Albro, 2010, p. 42).

Local sport, recreational, and leisure activities should consider sponsorship as a means of generating revenue through venue naming rights. The scenario in the vignette sounds ideal, but sponsorship at these levels needs to be exercised with caution and an awareness of the reaction local citizenry may have toward sponsorship in certain areas. In the case of park agencies, Mowen and Graefe (2002) suggest that citizens' attitudes toward sponsored facilities within the parks and recreation purview depend on the circumstances. Citizens do not have favorable attitudes toward corporate sponsorship purchasing "naming rights of specific park facilities and settings" (p. 45). Mowen and Graefe (2002) speculate that this might have to do with permanency of visual noise in a setting considered to be "environmentally sensitive" (p. 45). It would appear properties may wish to maintain the outdoor natural setting to the best of their ability in order to better ensure public favor and to protect the environment. It may be wise to determine whether there will be a negative reaction to sponsorship in cases involving schools and parks. These public-sector areas are of particular concern to the community in regard to whether sponsorship would be appropriate (Mowen, Kyle, & Jackowski, 2007).

sponsorship inventory Any place or location, whether physical or digital, that can be exchanged for something of value (cash or in-kind service/product) with the purpose of a sponsoring organization being able to achieve its sponsorship objectives.

OTHER FACILITY INVENTORY

The types of **sponsorship inventory** within and around sport facilities are numerous. Traditional on-site forms of inventory include perimeter advertising and logo placement around and throughout the facility and handout materials (Wishart, Seung, & Cornwell, 2012). Facility signage is certainly a significant and very visual sponsorship inventory, but there are many other ways to generate revenues within facilities. Parts of the facility can be sponsored such as concourses or even the field itself as a separate buy. One study uncovered a possible new sponsorship space—the in-stadium game personnel. The facility or event staff impact fan experience and thus can be powerful brand ambassadors for sponsors (Park & Choi, 2011).

New opportunities continue to present themselves as technology improves. The ever-more-advanced Jumbotrons and digital signage, such as ribbon boards, within stadiums and arenas now offer new space to sell. Also, they can be changed frequently, allowing for reselling or multiple selling of the same space to different sponsors. Such signage reduces visual clutter and enables completely new concepts, such as sponsored in-game promotions, to emerge. The flexibility trend does not end with digital technology. The physical setting has been developing toward this goal as well with further implications for emphasis on activation and on-site product sales. Jim Renne, Principal Architect with the Rossetti firm, explains the concept of sponsor activation spaces (as opposed to simple signage). These are strategically placed spaces with transition in mind. Similar to a movie set, sponsor sets can be easily changed for fresh, new appearances even at the same venue (personal communication, April 16, 2013).

While more ways and places to sponsor are becoming available, it is important to understand the value of the inventory. Research supports some commonly accepted ideas but continues to uncover less obvious insights. For instance, Park and Choi (2011) note that signs and banners located around the perimeter of the playing field and on center field, in the case of Major League Baseball, continue to be the most visible to fans. Further, larger signs with strong contrasting colors tend to garner more attention. However, the televisions located near the restrooms in the hallways are also attention grabbers, as people do not want to miss the game and thus notice attached sponsors (Park & Choi, 2011). Note that visibility alone does not necessarily translate into results for the sponsoring company. Activation plans should be developed to engage with the consumer on a more personal basis.

Unlike naming rights, facility signage can generate cash flow for the property without much repercussion to the sponsoring corporation, even among the local levels of public-sector entities. Attitudes of community members in one study were found to be more favorable toward indoor facility signage within facilities as opposed to outside in the natural setting (Mowen & Graefe, 2002). Mowen and Graefe (2002) suggest that the partnership take care to "maintain the integrity and aesthetic quality of natural environments" (p. 45). Potential partnerships should be evaluated to determine which properties possess the best fit for the community, environment, and organization.

Event Sponsorship Inventory

Though substantial sums by a few corporations go into purchasing the naming rights of facilities and even more sponsors buy into in-stadium signage, ever-more-popular strategies include event sponsorship. IEG states that sport events receive 69% of corporate sponsorships (Association sponsorships grow, 2012). A significant deciphering factor is the mobility of the sponsoring name, logos, and activation potential. As opposed to a fixed location, **title sponsors** are mobile and can travel with the sport to its different locations, or markets, and may become synonymous with the event itself (e.g., PGA's FedEx Cup and NASCAR's Sprint Cup Series). Media exposure may be more consistent as well. Title sponsors for these sport events are continually associated throughout the length of the agreement as opposed to the naming rights to a facility, which is mainly featured only when the team that plays there is discussed. Sport events or tours can claim further advantage as they have potential to expand nationally and internationally. For instance, the only global-sized sport sponsorship platforms available are events such as the Federation of Association Football (FIFA) World Cup and the Olympic Games. This could explain the immense value placed on these relationships. In one example, AT&T partnered with the Byron Nelson Championship for 2015 and 2016 and is valued between $6 million and $8 million because the event is covered by CBS or NBC (Smith, 2013).

There are other inventory spaces available, as with facilities for events. Temporary or mobile signage can be placed throughout and around the location. Event naming and signage may be more readily accepted sponsorship behavior at the local levels. It would appear that when signage is temporary, citizens may be less prone to feel that it is damaging the environment or creating an eyesore in public use places. Unlike the fixed signage on facilities, the less intrusive, less commercialized approach by the sponsors at community levels, such as events taking place at parks, may be a more beneficial approach (Mowen & Graefe, 2002).

title sponsor See *naming rights.*

Local levels of sport, recreation, and leisure have an opportunity to increase sponsorship levels. Consider, for example, a high school event, local 5K run, or charity golf tournament offering anything other than a simple plan of primarily tangible visual focus for the sponsoring company. Featured logos on promotional items, signage at events, and some level of hospitality are the commonly listed inventories, varying in amount according to price. Regardless of event size, media coverage is highly desirable and can impact sponsorship price. On-site communications previously discussed is an area that can be of focus to enhance value for corporate sponsors, particularly if it can "relate in some nature and extent of media coverage" (Wishart et al., 2012, p. 347). These aspects may prove to be even more important than the actual attendance numbers, particularly in the case of charity causes. Due to the philanthropic association with many local-level sports and recreational and leisure events, this conclusion may be extended to these events as well, though they may not necessarily be nonprofit status. Community-based endeavors are likely to encourage goodwill support. Thus, with these types of events, sport marketers should be especially vigilant to pay close attention to ways to provide better on-site communications and prioritize resources for stronger media presence.

Though discussed separately with a focus on their differences, the two categories of facility and event sponsorship can merge if a sporting event with its own sponsors takes place within a stadium containing its own separate sponsors. For savvy sport business managers, this scenario provides unique new revenue-building opportunities. As sport organizations look to increase use of these large buildings and surrounding parking areas, it is possible not only to bring in externally managed events, but to create events that can be held at the sport venue.

Finding and Acquiring Sponsors

With the definitions outlined, the process of seeking out and acquiring can begin. While there are commonalities among all the levels and platforms, there will be some unique considerations for each. It is important to realize that this is a rapidly changing area in the sport environment. It will be critical for sport marketers to stay aware of and be proactive regarding the future of these important relationships between properties and sponsors.

VIGNETTE 10-2

Getting Creative: When Titled Sponsored Events Meet Sports Venues to Achieve Multiple Objectives

Uri Geva, owner of the Brazos Valley Bombers, a summer collegiate baseball team in Bryan, Texas, explains that creating events to be held within the Bombers' field has been useful in generating revenues and drawing people to the ballpark, thus increasing awareness of the team. One nonsport event known locally as BOO Fest has been created by the Bombers organization. It has become an annual event that reaches out to families within the team's community, allowing children to safely experience Halloween. The sport team is named as the host and holds the event at its ballpark. Free candy and activities are provided, complete with costume contests. The children can do their trick-or-treating at different booths sponsored by area businesses. Further, the Bombers organization offers transportation from a location with more parking. In 2012, the Bombers could include at least three major sponsors in their press release for the event. That is in addition to all the booths sponsored by businesses. In all, numerous objectives are achieved. The Bombers entice people to experience family fun at the ballpark, driving awareness of the team, and new sponsorship opportunities are created, not to mention excellent public relations. Events like this are worthy of a press release and warrant news coverage by providing safe family fun on a popular day.

Before doing anything else, it is important to "know yourself first," explains Tim Zulawski, Vice President of Sponsorship Sales and Services with the NFL's Atlanta Falcons (personal communication, December 17, 2012). Understanding one's own sport organization is critical to establishing the best sponsorship fit. Then it is possible to identify companies that match in a way that positively impacts the property's business model. Zulawski advises asking, "Who values your market?" Conceptually, these considerations are a good start toward helping guide the process to filter through many of the possible businesses and narrow down possibilities based on potential for optimizing success in a partnership.

© PensiveDragon/Shutterstock

matchup hypothesis
In reference to prop-
erty and sponsor-
ship, the belief that
the more congru-
ent the relationship,
the more effectively
the brands will con-
nect in the minds
of the consumers
(e.g., a tire company
sponsoring a race-
car series).

Whether the potential sponsors have approached the property or the property is in search of new partnerships, the sport organization and potential sponsor need to examine the goodness of fit. The overview concept can be explained by the **matchup hypothesis**, which emphasizes that a congruency between the sporting event and the sponsor results in better connection of images in the minds of the fans. A local shoe store and pet store would be good matches for the New York City 5K Run/1 Mile Walk and Dog Walk fundraiser. It makes sense to have shoes associated with the run/walk and pet products for the twist of getting to bring one's dog along for the fun. The closeness of the sponsor and sport organization or event can make for a smooth brand transfer in the mind of the fans and consumers because there is already similarity.

Who ultimately makes the decision to buy the sponsorship? The process of finding and contacting potential sponsor decision makers is likely to vary among the different levels. At a national and regional level, there will more often be high-level experts involved with these purchases and evaluations. Media buyers and companies specialize in planning and buying media- or promotion-oriented outlets. Media Brokers International (MBI) claims sports marketing as one of the six categories, alongside print, television, radio, out of home, and the Internet (www.media-brokers.com). Large companies may involve marketing agencies like these to handle this complex area of advertising under which sport sponsorship often falls.

At local levels, when working with the larger potential sponsor companies, some of the challenges encountered are similar to those seen with the regional- or national-level sport organizations. For instance, if Belmont University's Master of Sport Administration (MSA) program were to approach Aaron's Rentals regarding a title sponsorship of its annual "Belmont MSA Golf Scramble" benefiting Special Olympics Tennessee, the sports sales representative would be directed to the regional office, where marketing decisions are made. It is also possible that there is a media-buying company contracting for the large-chain furniture rental store that would need to receive the bid. This prospect is in regard to more significant spending such as a title sponsorship of $10,000 rather than a one-time donation of $100. It is very important to provide at least 6 months, possibly a year, in advance to arrange agreements in these formal manners. The sponsoring companies will need time to plan this expense into their fiscal budgets for larger investment-oriented buys. However, there may be a smaller pot of money available that local managers of large chains can spend in their community for causes such as this that.

Once the potential candidates and decision makers have been identified, a budget discussion should ensue to be sure there is an understanding of what a sponsor should be prepared to invest. At any level, it is very important to be aware that potential sponsors need to have plans and a budget not just for the **rights fees** but also for **leveraging**, activating, and evaluating the sponsorship relationship. A commonly accepted amount is two to three times the investment in the sponsorship cost for the rights (Shank, 2009). Simply stated, the relationship is less effective, or will fail, if an organization does not promote the fact that the relationship even exists in the first place.

Not only is it beneficial for screening purposes, but a sponsor's willingness to invest in marketing can be revealing. A sport organization may want to uncover this intention for several reasons. First, plans for solid marketing practices can indicate to the sport organization that this company may be a good business partner. Companies with strong marketing plans will probably be healthier and have a better chance of succeeding. Secondly, the sport organization is the beneficiary of additional advertising when the sponsor advertises for its own purposes. A local car dealership promoting a local nonprofit event in every commercial it runs not only promotes goodwill to the community for the car dealer because it supports a worthy cause, but it greatly increases awareness for the local event. Thirdly, a property should uncover sponsor intent to properly invest in a healthy business relationship that has a better chance at longevity. This concept is key to the most successful sport–sponsor relationships. Longer relationships allow for time to build the connection between sponsor and property in the mind of the fans. In other words, the factor of time allows for more effective image transfer, which is, according to the research, consistently "one of the most important benefits of sponsorships" (Coppetti, Wentzel, Tomczak, & Henkel, 2009, p. 31). Thus, it is important to consider which business partnerships will be the strongest in this regard and would be important to discuss and plan before entering into a contract.

Determining Objectives

Once the sponsors have been screened and commitment to budget established, the partnership can move forward. There are two main categories under which an array of objectives can be housed: direct and indirect. **Direct objectives** are intended to drive immediate sales. These objectives may provide an opportunity to quantify revenues. **Indirect objectives** are the larger

rights fees The amount charged by the property to the sponsor for the sponsor's legal commercial use of the sports organization's protected copyrights, trademarks, logos, and the like.

leveraging The process of ensuring the sponsorship relationship is known to the target markets through strategic marketing and business actions occurring after the rights fees have been exchanged.

direct objective A business and marketing action specifically crafted toward increasing sales.

indirect objective An outcome other than achieving immediate sales or gains such as increasing awareness to new market segments or a campaign to reposition a brand.

group of ways to utilize sport sponsorship to achieve desired results, including influencing brand awareness, brand attitudes, and brand image (Shank, 2009; Coppetti et al., 2009). Objectives of this nature will take time to execute, and it can be difficult to establish clear returns with standard measurement tools. In facilities and sporting events, one can readily find large and colorful company logos displayed in prominent places such as scoreboards or along the outfield, which point to indirect objectives.

Whether direct or indirect, a good way to uncover and define what these objectives should be can be found in the widely accepted SMART formula (specific, measurable, attainable, relevant, and time-based), which is outlined elsewhere in this text (Doran, 1981). Taking the time to meet with sponsors regarding this simple formula could amount to much better communication with the goal of increased success. Staying coordinated will help to identify and prepare for the continually changing objectives as market opportunities allow (Farrelly, 2010). Seiferheld (2010) recommends meetings monthly or at least quarterly to stay on top of any inevitable changes. Working more closely together is the future direction of sport sponsorship. As stated by Farrelly (2010), "Sponsorship has shifted from a marketing tool to a business platform where the need for strategic collaboration and mutually beneficial outcomes for both the sponsor and sports entity is seemingly more vital" (p. 320). Due to its importance, relationship marketing warrants a section all its own.

Relationship Marketing

The concept of uniquely multifaceted relationships helps to encompass the ultimate uniqueness behind this particular business arrangement. As Zulawski points out, "What sports does better than anyone else is create an opportunity to build relationship" (personal communication, December 20, 2012). In reference to the property sponsor relationship, this component is a strong enough outcome to encourage continued investments for some companies. For example, suppose a CEO utilizes a luxury suite to entertain clients and deepen informal friendships, ultimately resulting in a lucrative contract. Zulawski asks, "How can you put a value on that?" In fact, quantifying such outcomes is becoming an area of focus, and the results are staggering. Brazil revealed close to $1 billion in exports that their trade and investment promotion agency, Apex-Brasil, credits directly to the hospitality programs available through a IndyCar sponsorship deal (Mickle, 2011).

The hospitality relationship aspect itself can be viewed as its own category. Owner Uri Geva suggests a format of "marketing objectives and hospitality objectives" when trying to determine what a potential sponsor desires from its agreement with the Brazos Valley Bombers (personal communication, December 21, 2012). Sport events lend themselves nicely to a business-to-business type of relationship. Understanding this will enable sport marketers to be proactive and innovative toward assisting their sponsorship partners to make the most of these scenarios.

Providing a space for these relationships to flourish, such as suites, is a common practice, but more attention should be paid to what the sport property could do to make this experience even better. It would appear that deeper connections with the sport and time spent together might be a key. In the Brazil example, Silvia Pierson, Operations Manager in the United States for the Apex-Brasil agency, explains the choice of IndyCar over arguably more popular sports such as football. Her points include the level of interaction with the sports property, such as meeting the drivers, and the fact that "it's not a three-hour event. It's a whole weekend" (Mickle, 2011, p. 6). People are able to connect to a team, or drivers in this case, and they have time to get to know each other. The literature suggests sponsors should focus on "enhancing enthusiasm for the team" as a powerful way to positively influence purchase intentions (Smith, Graetz, & Westerbeek, 2008, p. 401). It stands to reason that heightening connection toward the teams or drivers and fostering a fun, social environment would produce extremely desirable outcomes, as can be seen with Brazilian business. It could be argued that this is a recipe for a good relationship environment for business people to network.

Relationships in sport are multidimensional in ways other businesses or advertising alone simply cannot reproduce. The two examples outlined above are important, but many other relationships may be formed. Sponsor to fans, property to fans, property to sponsor's consumers, and fans to fans are more relational aspects present at every sporting event. Finding out how to truly deepen these many relationships should be at the center of a sport marketer's focus. One could argue that relationship should be ground zero for objectives and all other objectives should revolve around how to achieve this first one. Dr. Richard Luker, in his book *Simple Community*, suggests a new way to sell by shifting focus from traditional ways to one that sees "people, not consumers," tells "stories, not messages," and focuses on the peoples' stories not the brand's (Luker, 2009, p. 30). Alexandris and Tsiotsou (2012) contend that "marketers in professional sports leagues should . . . avoid linking sponsorship with commercialization" (p. 374). These same authors note a current trend for companies to "include sponsorship under their corporate social responsibility policies" (p. 375), including activities such as supporting community youth sports and partnering properties' charitable events. Current and future sport marketers should be aware of this increasingly important trend shift and its implications.

Evaluation

There are many reasons companies choose sport sponsorship as a marketing strategy. This section identifies the basic categories of direct and indirect objectives, with an emphasis on relationship marketing. Ultimately, most sponsoring companies would like to see a positive impact in sales. An employee of Anheuser-Busch stated the following in explaining its sponsorship of the Ladies Professional Golf Association (LPGA): "Bottom line at the end of the day is selling more beer" (Choi, 2010, p. 54). The implications are that there is a growing necessity to create plans around measurable outcomes or a more deliberate strategy of building sponsors' brand image rather than simply generating exposure (Farrelly, 2010, p. 331). According to Farrelly (2010), the trend can be seen with major sponsors like Coca-Cola, Nike, and IBM, who are putting less emphasis on logo presence at sporting events and facilities (p. 331).

What defines success? How can a sponsorship finally get to the point of increased sales? The definition for determining whether a sponsorship campaign "worked" will vary from business to business based on purposes of the agreement. It is useful to review the differing ideas by experts in both the academic setting and the practitioner setting. Some will argue a growing necessity for identifying resulting revenue increases, and others will contend that the benefits cannot be easily quantified in hard dollars but, based on the numbers of sponsors in sport, are nonetheless being achieved in sport like nowhere else. These relationships are extremely costly, as outlined in previous examples; properties need to justify these costs and sponsors need to experience positive outcomes. By better identifying objectives from the start, measurements can be developed to better ensure these desires are being met. Yet ambiguity regarding these objectives is commonplace among all levels in the current environment. Starting with regular SMART meetings would be a step in the right direction.

Return on investment (ROI) may be more obtainable with direct objectives. Direct objectives do not contain many variables and are thus fairly easy to assess. For instance, if a sponsor runs a special promotion at a particular event, the number or sales can be tracked by how many coupons were redeemed. This is certainly a simplification of the situation, but determining how much revenue is resulting from any given spending is the desired result. More sponsors are becoming increasingly demanding in this regard. With the amount of spending that occurs in these relationships, it is no wonder. Unfortunately, ROI is notoriously difficult to measure with sport sponsorship, which contains so many variables. Direct connection to any particular campaign can be hard to establish in hard dollars. Moving forward, there is a call for more measurement focus on return on objectives (ROO), which involves driving traffic to stores and websites and media measurements for a better overall understanding of effectiveness (O'Keefe, Titlebaum, & Hill, 2009). This approach may account for the vast nature of sport to offer better assessment of indirect objectives.

There is a definite need to redefine what determines effectiveness. The direction is headed toward one of a more developed partnership that puts "less value on exposure and more emphasis on brand image" (Farrelly, 2010, p. 331). This trend indicates a shift toward needing to work together and integrating both businesses' objectives for a mutual good. Farrelly uncovered properties in one study that terminated contracts in part due to lack of collaboration from a "culture built on securing rather than managing sponsorships" (2010, p. 329). Relationship has its fingerprints everywhere; thus measurements should begin to reflect when relationships are breaking down.

In efforts to track changes based on sport sponsorships in ROI and/or ROO, evaluation should be considered throughout the process of a sponsorship. The following should be specifically developed around the objectives set out in the planning process. Fan surveys should be conducted before, during, and after strategic plans take place. Before-and-after sales analysis, periodic financial analysis, media mentions and news coverage, traffic changes in the store and on the website, improvement to distribution channels, and product placement are are all considerations in determining sponsorship success.

VIGNETTE 10-3

Question the Model: Grassroots Change at the Local, Recreational, and Leisure Levels

With such costs associated with rights fees and leveraging and activation expenses, one may question whether it is even reasonable for smaller companies to be sponsors. Maybe it's too much trouble or will take too much time to help potential sponsors get the most out of their investments. And how can a small sports property land worthwhile sponsorships? This all sounds very complicated, and often the personnel and resources are not available to see to all these steps and ensure sponsorship success. Before reverting back to the traditional style of gold, silver, and bronze packages, consider calling the current sport sponsorship model into question. Maybe there is a new model that offers a "win" for all the relationships involved with the sport.

Instead of trying to create a list of inventory to sell, think partnership and participation based on engagement and fun! Generate lists of in-event games or fun activities that can be offered to local sponsors. The agreement is based on the sponsor's company and its employees taking full responsibility for and ownership of planning and setting up the activity, helping run on-site operations during the event, and cleaning up after the event. Further, they would be encouraged to promote the event through their own media channels and on their store sites. They are welcomed and encouraged to use products as prizes or even offer on-site sales opportunities. The freedom is theirs, but the property simply requires commitment to on-site engagement.

The downside is obviously based on the current model of measurement. If determining success based on how many sponsors provided money for the event, there would be an immediate problem of sponsors signed up who have not provided hard cash.

Now think of the upside: a fairly easy sell that was fun for the people involved in the "selling," so these spots probably filled up quite fast, and by local community-connected businesses no less. The businesses are happy because they can afford the commitment and it is a rallying point for their own internal environment. The businesses begin promoting the event on their own sites and through their marketing channels—social media, advertisements, and word of mouth by involved employees and customers. When the event occurs, there are numerous additional fun activities that the sport property does not have to organize or man. The atmosphere is much better because of the sponsors' direct involvement bringing fun to the fans—which, by the way, there are probably far more of because of all the collective advertising. So at the end of the day, the event can enjoy more awareness, more fans, more fun for all, and less property commitment of time and resources from start to finish. How much money would need to be raised based on the current model to support what just happened, in essence, for free?

These are the kinds of outcomes that may happen when viewing sponsorship through the lens of relationship. Reexamining the current transactional model may reveal even better ways to achieve objectives.

In the modern technological age, social media chains should be intentionally activated and methods predetermined to assess success. Considering that these channels are in essence word of mouth by nature, there should be considerable chatter and trackable referrals and mentions, or depending on the trend of the day, "likes," "Tweets," "Retweets," and so forth.

Activation

The best-laid plans mean absolutely nothing without proper execution. Activation is the portion of the sponsorship that engages with the fan, ideally with some sort of close interaction that enhances the fan's experience. Mayo and Bishop state clearly that "it is now known that the activation drives the greatest gains in ROI as it drives demonstrable purchase consideration increases" (Mayo & Bishop, 2010, p. 11). What a sponsor does with and at the sport event or facility is vital to the entire relationship. However, a valid question to ask would be "Who sets the objectives and implements the plans of action?" The answer is not so simple. There appears to be ongoing debate not only as to who is responsible for setting objectives, as previously discussed, but also as to who should finance and execute them—the sponsor or the property? The best answer, in an increasingly relationship-oriented environment, is that both are responsible.

First and foremost, communication between organizations and education appears to be very important to setting the stage for success. One of the reasons many sponsors place responsibility with the sports team is because they may not understand the inventory being purchased and how it can be leveraged. Rob Hoffmann, Corporate Sales Manager of the National Hockey League's Pittsburgh Penguins, reveals that several companies have official and exclusivity status to the Penguins' marks and logos "and they don't do anything with them" (O'Keefe et al., 2009, p. 50). O'Keefe et al. (2009) call for better planning between the property and sponsor as well as efforts by the sports property to better educate the sponsor. It is important for sponsors to know what their own inventory is and how to use it.

It has been said previously that the sponsors must know their own objectives and what they want from the property. It is sport event managers' responsibility to lead the corporate sponsors to this knowledge. It is not enough to just provide a list of inventory but to help them understand the how and why for activation. The companies must also be educated up front about additional expenses and personnel that will need to be provided for these plans and their execution.

When making recommendations for successful activation, the sport property should pay careful attention to involvement of the sponsor organization on site as well as the types of activities offered. Standard sample giveaways are not the most desirable, or successful, way to activate. Coppetti et al. (2009)

note that when fans are "provided the opportunity to participate in attractive sponsor activities, to interact with some of the sponsor's employees and to meet other consumers, they are likely to evaluate the sponsorship more favorably due to these positive experiences" (p. 30). A fun social experience during an engaging activity that allows the fan to interact with sponsor employees directly is a good goal for on-site activations. Take, for example, the Muddy Zombie Mud Run and Carnival in College Station, Texas, which offers sponsors a chance to host game booths, blending these objectives nicely. This sponsorship opportunity makes sense for several reasons. People will have an affinity toward those with whom they have fun and toward those who created the experience. Sponsors' employees are not only brand ambassadors who know the company and products, but they are also a human extension of the company with whom fans can connect and develop a relationship. Sports fans may be more likely to want to purchase from a person than a faceless company.

The Agreement

After a sponsor and a property have determined they will be a good fit, the documentation and legal agreement must be created. Agreements will vary largely across event levels, from international to small local. Regardless of the number of specifics included or the length of the document, there are certain areas that should be addressed at each level:

- Determine and clearly define the length of the contract—for example, January 1 to December 31.
- Outline the benefits to the sponsor. This may be challenging and may focus mainly on the inventory being purchased, such as signage placement, and media inclusion.

- Define the payment obligations of the sponsor, including the agreed-upon price, method of payment, and repercussions for late payments. Type of capital exchanged (e.g., monetary and/or in-kind) should be considered and outlined as well (Mowen & Graefe, 2002, p. 37).
- State any contingency plans resulting in termination of the partnership or event. There are two main categories of contingencies:
  - Indemnification. Legal action that can occur when a party is at fault, resulting in possible financial losses.
  - Force majeure. Termination of agreement upon event cancellation when neither party is considered at fault due to causes beyond either party's control. Reed, Bhargava, and Kjaer explain that actions falling under this category are those rendering the event impossible, such as a labor strike. The authors note that since September 11, 2001, most contracts within the United States will include clauses for "act or threat of terrorism" (Reed, Bhargava, & Kjaer, 2010, p. 87). Weather at outdoor events is considered foreseeable (i.e., it is understood that bad weather could result in event cancellation), in which case both parties should secure cancellation insurance. Responsibility for this can be included in the contract (Reed et al., 2010, pp. 87–88).

Inventory is the more tangible benefits part that a sponsor is purchasing, but there are some additional important concepts that influence the price for a sponsorship deal. Wishart et al. explain that beyond just the visual logo placement, sponsors also value media coverage, hospitality, customer interactions, access to property offerings (e.g., sport celebrities and consumer databases), and technological sophistication (2012, pp. 337–339). These are all part of the on-site communication components but may fall within the negotiable territory.

One of the important price factors pertains to the target market offered by the sport property. If the property can deliver concentrated numbers of people highly desired by a sponsoring company, the price will potentially remain in the property's favor. Having access to a desired target audience may be even more important to a sponsor than the total number of people reached (Wishart et al., 2012). Thus, sport managers should take note—know one's self first—and then approach sponsors who seek what the property has to offer.

SUMMARY

This chapter has defined sponsorship, its components, and trends within the industry that have important implications for sponsorship opportunities. Strategies for finding good property/sponsor fits and forming relationships that will result in success for every party involved should be followed, as doing so will help both the sponsor and the facility or event owner achieve their goals and objectives. The underlying theme is that creating a win–win relationship is accomplished by developing creative solutions to meet those goals and objectives. Remaining aware of this quickly evolving aspect of sport business will enable sport managers to proactively ensure continued relationships with an ever-vital partner.

DISCUSSION QUESTIONS

1. Identify some new or unique ideas for sponsorship activation that fit the criteria of maximizing success. How can a sport organization, the fans, and the sponsors all benefit from these ideas?

2. Consider activation spaces in sport facilities or at sport events. Where would good locations be and why? Remember to consider the fans' experience from arrival at the location until they leave.

3. Select a local sport organization for this question. Evaluate its current sponsorships to determine which relationships are good examples of the matchup hypothesis. Which relationships are bad examples?

4. Using the same sport organization and sponsors, evaluate one of the relationships from both the sponsor's and sport property's perspective. First, establish what these two organizations should expect from the relationship. Next, determine which of these items should be included in the sponsorship agreement. Finally, determine who should be responsible for leveraging and activating these items.

Case STUDY

Sponsorship and the Brazos Valley Senior Games

The Brazos Valley Senior Games (BVSG) were launched locally in 2006 in College Station, Texas, with several goals in mind. The competition was intended to provide individuals age 50 years and older with an opportunity to compete in various sports, socialize with other seniors, and have fun. The games were created under the auspices of the National Senior Games Association, which is the overall governing body and highest level of competition for these athletes. Communitywise, it made sense to utilize this sport event as a way to generate potential tourism. Thus, the

Bryan–College Station Convention and Visitors Bureau (CVB) was a good fit to assist with starting and helping to support the competition. The CVB provided a meeting place and individuals to serve on the board of directors. This cooperation was vital toward the success and sustainability of the event over the next several years.

The initial leadership direction was more that of recreational competition in nature. In 2008, new leadership in the president position provided a vision of more intense competition with high-quality events and an ultimate goal to grow the games into a large annual community event. The new president was careful to build a strategic board of directors that included people connected to the major business facets around town. The aggressive plans began to work in relatively short order. From inception, the numbers of athletes grew substantially from less than 200 athletes to over 400. Close to 20 different types of events were offered in efforts to become the best local senior games in Texas.

The president was passionate about and highly committed to the growth of the BVSG, taking on many of the functions, such as sponsorship, himself. Growth continued and athlete feedback was quite good. Then the next step in the vision came to pass when the state level granted the BVSG the bid to host the Texas State Games for 2010 and 2011. This opportunity should have been a good thing, but it proved to be the demise of the organization. As with many businesses (and non-profits in particular), budgetary problems were pervasive.

The way revenue was generated was limited and did not readily produce enough income to support high-quality competition, venues, and prizes. Registration fees were collected but were often less than $30 per person. Thus, sponsorship was vital but was also sparse. The highly energetic president devoted most of his time and much of his own resources toward providing high-quality events, several of which he organized and oversaw himself. It was ideal and encouraged that each event coordinator would generate his or her own sponsors for each event. Staffing events with unpaid volunteers, most of whom would be full-time employees elsewhere, would not be successful since their time and energies would be limited. Hence, the president did most of the searching for sponsors for the entire event himself, as he was retired and more fully focused on his vision for the games. While the occasional cash sponsor was signed, many of the partner sponsors were in the form of in-kind trade, which meant fewer hard dollars available to spend as needed. Some of the board members also contributed in this fashion, but it just wasn't enough.

In the first year hosting the State Games, overestimates and some very large bills for medals, t-shirts, and venues became problematic. Further, due to the timing of the event, the athlete turnout was far lower than expected and the numbers estimated much higher than was usual for a standard local senior games event. Other parts of the BVSG also began to fall apart. With the massive growth also came increased time demands for nonpaid volunteers, who played crucial parts in the execution of successful events. The CVB had to move to an advisory role, and several other board members had to do the same. The BVSG simply could not recover. The second year was relinquished to a larger Games that had much better funding and was in a position to take on the demands of such an event. These damages were too great, and the local BVSG reached its breaking point and dissolved on the horizon of achieving its greatest success to date.

Though the nonprofit organization was officially dissolved, the good news was that the City of College Station Parks and Recreation Department saw the importance of the event and elected to take it on. Back to the original goals of recreational competition, the local senior games would at least be available as one of very few left in the state of Texas. Having even a simple event is far more desirable than having none, which has been the trend in recent years. There are goals of being consistent with this event and growing the brand with time; however, simplicity and cost-effectiveness are at the root of each decision.

A systematic analysis of the area for sponsors with matching target markets and objectives would be the first step. Secondly, prospective large investment sponsors should have been approached a year in advance. These should have been the primary focus for the president and others on the board specializing in revenue generation. Ideally, each sport organizer should have been presented with the training and strategy to generate sponsors for his or her own events. But there are also many other viable plans and solutions that could have saved the BVSG. Taking concepts learned in this chapter and applied to this case study will assist the reader in preparing for this very real-world scenario. This would be a good time to reflect upon and develop some creative and innovative plans and techniques for sponsorship to ensure success for sport businesses and worthy endeavors such as the Brazos Valley Senior Games.

1. Consider some sponsors who may have been a good fit for this particular organization. Why were these selected? Feel free to utilize your local community as though these games were taking place there.
2. Given the specifics for this event, what might have been some strategies for the sponsors identified in Question 1 to leverage and activate this investment? Hint: Consider every party involved, not just the property and the sponsor.
3. Pretend to be the Senior Games president and restructure the organizational strategy so that a more organized or strategic approach could have been taken to increase sponsorship of this event. What could have or should have been done differently, by whom, and why?

REFERENCES

2012 sports business timeline. (2012). *SportsBusiness Journal, 15*(35).

Albro, W. (2010, Jan–Feb). Not every naming-rights deal needs to be with a high-profile facility. *ABA Bank Marketing,* 42–44.

Alexandris, K., & Tsiotsou, R. H. (2012). Testing a hierarchy of effects model of sponsorship effectiveness. *Journal of Sport Management, 26*(5), 363–378.

Andrews, J., & Wheaton, K. (2011). The most important rule of sponsorships: Invest rather than buy. *Advertising Age, 82*(38), 14.

Association sponsorships grow, but at a below-average rate. (2012). *Association Meetings, 24*(1), 7.

Bhasin, K. (2011). Why do so many banks put their names on stadiums? Retrieved from http://www.businessinsider.com/banks-stadium-naming-rights-2011-2?op=1

Choi, J. A. (2010). The impact of ethnic diversity on the ladies professional golf association: A case study of Anheuser-Busch and its sponsorship objectives and strategies. *Sport Marketing Quarterly, 19*(1), 51–57.

Coppetti, C., Wentzel, D., Tomczak, T., & Henkel, S. (2009). Improving incongruent sponsorships through articulation of the sponsorship and audience participation. *Journal of Marketing Communications, 15*(1), 17–34.

Doran, G. T. (1981). There's a S.M.A.R.T. way to write management's goals and objectives. *Management Review, 70*(11), 35.

Farrelly, F. (2010). Not playing the game: Why sport sponsorship relationships break down. *Journal of Sport Management, 24*(3), 319–337.

Luker, R. (2009). *Simple community.* St. Petersburg, FL: Tangeness Press.

Mayo, D., & Bishop, T. (2010). Fixed rights to activation ratios can harm sponsorship ROI. *Journal of Sponsorship, 4*(1), 9–14.

Mickle, T. (2011). Agency finds success promoting Brazil through IndyCar deal. *Street and Smith's SportsBusiness Journal, 14*(21), 6.

Mowen, A. J., & Graefe, A. R. (2002). Public attitudes toward the corporate sponsorship of park agencies: The role of promotional activities and contractual conditions. *Journal of Park and Recreation Administration, 20*(2), 31–48.

Mowen, A. J., Kyle, G. T., & Jackowski, M. (2007). Citizen preferences for the corporate sponsorship of public-sector park and recreation organizations. *Journal of Nonprofit and Public Sector Marketing, 18*(2), 93–118.

Muret, D. (2012). With flying colors. *Street and Smith's SportsBusiness Journal, 14*(49), 1–25.

O'Keefe, R., Titlebaum, P., & Hill, C. (2009). Sponsorship activation: Turning money spent into money earned. *Journal of Sponsorship, 3*(1), 43–53.

Park, S. R., & Choi, A. J. (2011). Visual signs/logo-identity in the major league baseball facility: Case study of Tropicana Field. *International Journal of Applied Sports Sciences, 23*(1), 251–270.

Reed, M. H., Bhargava, M. N., & Kjaer, J. G. M. (2010). Terminating a sponsorship relationship: Conditions and clauses. *Journal of Sponsorship, 4*(1), 79–92.

Seiferheld, S. (2010). Try a S.M.A.R.T. way to turn sponsorships into partnerships. *Street and Smith's SportsBusiness Journal, 13*(31), 14.

Shani, D., & Sandler, D. (1996). Climbing the sports event pyramid. *Marketing News, 30*(18), 6.

Shank, M. D. (2009). *Sports marketing: A strategic perspective* (4th ed.). Upper Saddle River, NJ: Pearson Prentice Hall.

Smith, A., Graetz, B., & Westerbeek, H. (2008). Sport sponsorship, team support and purchase intentions. *Journal of Marketing Communications, 14*(5), 387–404.

Smith, M. (2013). Title sponsors in hand, PGA tour eyes digital, international growth. *Street and Smith's SportsBusiness Journal, 15*(36), 1–26.

Wishart, T., Seung, P. L., & Cornwell, T. B. (2012). Exploring the relationship between sponsorship characteristics and sponsorship asking price. *Journal of Sport Management, 26*(4), 335–349.

CHAPTER 11

Traditional Revenue Generation in Sport and Recreation

BRIAN MENAKER

CHAPTER OBJECTIVES

Upon completion of this chapter, the reader will be able to:

1. Identify the types of revenues available in spectator sport, participation events, and recreation facilities

2. Differentiate between methods of revenue generation in a variety of facilities and venues

3. Consider how to utilize different facilities for revenue-producing events

4. Articulate the strengths and weaknesses of the various revenue production strategies

5. Identify multiple revenue opportunities for facilities

CHAPTER OVERVIEW

This chapter will review the various techniques used to generate revenue through sport and recreation organizations and facilities. Techniques and principles of revenue generation from sport, participatory, and recreation facilities and events are categorized and summarized. The difference between direct revenues from events and ancillary revenue will be explained. Categories of sources of revenue include venue-related revenue such as ticket sales, concessions, merchandise, event fees, and participatory event monies such as exposition-related income and registration fees.

Industry VOICE

Hank Zemola—Chief Executive Officer, Chicago Special Events Management

Courtesy of Special Events Management.

Chicago Special Events Management is a live producer of outdoor events. Our mission is to use special events, in any form, as a way to raise awareness and as fundraising endeavors for not-for-profit organizations. We host a large variety of events, including sport, art, and entertainment events. Based in Chicago, Illinois, we are the largest special event company in the Midwest, employing 22 managers and more than 150 seasonal workers. My role as the CEO is to manage the entire organization and assist the employees with the various roles within the organization, such as public relations, sponsorship sales, and media and marketing for each of the events we host.

I started my career with the United Parcel Service and climbed the ranks, serving in various capacities within the organization. During my time there, I was formally trained to work with corporate lobbyists to develop their support on House bills. Secondary to this role was the planning and implementation of special events to engage the community with the organization and demonstrate that the organization is a good community partner. This experience led to my desire to continue to work in special events, and I began working with the Chicago Area Runners Association as the executive director. After a few years in that role, I transitioned into my current role with Chicago Special Events Management.

The best path for students who would like to work in the sport event industry is to work in numerous capacities, such as volunteering, interning, and freelancing, to be able to explore the different positions and facets of the industry. The more exposure they get with the event industry, the more familiar they will become with themselves, their capabilities, and their general interests. In addition, this experience will help them understand where they may fit within the industry.

There are two main things I look for when hiring: good oral and written communication skills and the desire to work in the event industry. In our industry, we are constantly communicating with individuals involved with the event. Whether it is the local government, the sponsors, the vendors, or the participants, it is important for our employees to be able to communicate well and represent our organization the right way. Secondly, anyone can work in the special events industry; however, it takes a lot of commitment and desire to succeed. There is a tremendous amount of work in the planning and implementation of an event, and this may mean very long hours and working on the weekends. Without a high level of desire to make sure your customers are entertained or satisfied with your event, you likely will not have long-term success in this industry.

Oversaturation is a major challenge we face in the event industry. This has led to increased costs to manage events and a decreasing amount of sponsorship dollars to support the event and the number of participants who enter the event. Secondary to the issue of oversaturation is the overwhelming of the municipalities and community agencies that assist with the events as their budgets and staffs are reduced. From a funding standpoint, we attempt to manage the sponsorship relationships and establish more efficient ways for companies to interact directly with their consumers. Special events offer sponsoring organizations the unique ability to engage in two-way communication with their consumers that other methods of advertising cannot generate. As such, we are always researching new ways and ideas to create events that fit well with both the organizations and the consumers. Developing an understanding of the marketplace is very important to creating successful events.

As you think about revenue generation, one thing to remember is that the consumer is looking for a specific product or service at a specific value. People, no matter their economic standing, are looking for a good value. For example, from a concessions perspective, if I can maintain a lower cost than the market for concession items, this will add value to the event overall. Many facilities and events overprice these items because they know they have a captive audience. By maintaining a below-market rate, consumers at our events leave with a better experience, knowing they participated in a great event with tremendous value.

Introduction

Sport facilities and associated events provide owners, operators, managers, and other connected stakeholders the opportunity to generate revenue through a number of forms of creative planning. All of the numerous types of sport facilities and venues can be profitable by providing the right services. Arenas, stadiums, convention centers, multipurpose facilities, event-specific venues, and other public assembly facilities can provide locations for sporting events, concerts, and other public assembly events. These facilities may also be used for participatory events. Public parks, fields, and roads can be used for road races, urban challenges, obstacle course races, and other revenue-producing physical activity events. This chapter highlights the revenues that can be accumulated through the use of sport, recreational, and public facilities and other sport and physical fitness events.

Why Is It Important to Identify Sources of Revenue?

Sport and fitness venues are diverse and flexible spaces that have numerous uses. Large venues such as arenas, stadiums, field houses, and gymnasiums are used for only a finite time in hosting their primary tenants' contests. Unlike a typical commercial retail store, which may be open every day of the year, large-scale facilities are not used every day for sporting events. An empty venue does not produce revenue. Therefore, it is important to consider the multiple ways to utilize an arena, stadium, or other public assembly building beyond the primary intended use, whether that be football, baseball, soccer, basketball, hockey, you name it. There are alternatives for raising

revenues beyond sporting events, including using the facilities to supplement other events hosted outside or near the venue. This chapter will discuss all of the ways that sport- and fitness-related facilities can be used to produce revenue.

Ticket Sales

Selling tickets for events is the most common and direct way for host facilities to ensure revenue from visitors. A ticket gives the visitor the right to a seat, or an area to stand if the ticket is general admission or standing room only, for the purpose of watching a game, concert, or other event. The **gate receipt** refers to the total amount of money received for tickets at a certain game. A venue can increase its gate receipt by offering visitors options when it comes to ticket sales. The venue can offer single-game tickets, season tickets, miniseason ticket plans, and group ticket sales.

gate receipt The sum of money received from ticket sales for a particular event.

The price of tickets is a considerable investment, as illustrated by an overview of the price offerings by the major North American sports leagues (see **Table 11-1**). According 2013 Fan Cost Experience reports, the average ticket in a Major League Baseball (MLB) stadium was $27.48, with the highest team average being $53.38 for the Boston Red Sox and the lowest being $15.99 for the San Diego Padres (Greenberg, 2013a). The average National Football League (NFL) ticket price was $81.54, with the New England Patriots offering

TABLE 11-1   Average Ticket Prices

League	Average Ticket Cost	Average Premium Ticket
NFL	$81.54	$247.85
MLB	$27.48	$90.48
NHL	$61.62	$148.90
NBA	$50.99	N/A

the most expensive ticket at $117.84 and the Cleveland Browns offering the lowest at $54.20 (Greenberg, 2013b). For the 2013–14 National Hockey League (NHL) season, seats averaged $61.62 across the league, with the Toronto Maple Leafs' average ticket price being $122.20 and the Dallas Stars' tickets averaging $37.28 (Greenberg, 2013c). The average National Basketball Association (NBA) seat for the 2012–13 season (excluding club seats, suite prices, and floor seats) was $50.99, with the New York Knicks having the highest average ticket cost of $124.22 and the Charlotte Bobcats offering the cheapest average ticket of $29.27.

While the average ticket price comes at a considerable cost to the consumer, there is clearly a large discrepancy of ticket prices among teams. Offering season ticket plans can serve as a way to discount the single-game face value of a seat to loyal fans and ensure that a large portion of seats are sold before the season. However, there are many other strategies beyond full-season ticket packages to increase revenue through ticket sales.

>
>
> **TIP**
>
> The NBA requires teams to offer 500 tickets at $10 or less for every game; however, they are not required to be part of season ticket plans or single-game tickets. During the 2012–13 season, the NBA reported one million tickets offered for $10 or less (Greenberg, 2012).

Ticket Sales Strategies

Teams and venues have identified a number of different ways to improve ticket sales, including differential pricing, flexible season ticket pricing, money-back guarantees, web-based tickets, and secondary ticket exchanges (Howard & Crompton, 2005).

DIFFERENTIAL PRICING

Differential pricing is based on three variables: quality, time, and place. Quality refers to the reputation, strength, and draw of the opponent. Time corresponds to the day of the week, time of day, or part of the season. Teams may raise prices based on which day of the week the game is played. For example, MLB teams charge higher ticket prices when traditional powers or rivals come to visit, such as when the Boston Red Sox visit the New York Yankees. For baseball teams, games in the months of April, May, and September are often discounted because children are in school and have less ability to attend games. Place is determined by location of seat (Howard & Crompton, 2005). Seats closer to the playing surface or those with special amenities, such as club

differential pricing Differences in pricing of a seat based on quality, time, and place. Quality refers to reputation, strength, and draw of the opponent. Time corresponds to the day of the week, time of day, or part of the season. Place is determined by location of seat.

seating, may be pricier than the seats up near the ceiling rafters. Using club and other luxury seating to raise revenue will be discussed later in the chapter.

FLEXIBLE TICKET PRICING

Many teams use a scheme that offers flexible season ticket plans. For example, the NBA's Cleveland Cavaliers offer a partial season ticket plan that gives fans the opportunity to purchase tickets to 10 games that are determined by the team before the season. Included in the Cavaliers packages are the ability to use the Cavaliers Ticket Exchange to sell unwanted tickets, a 15% discount off of team shop purchases, priority to purchase tickets for the playoffs, and the ability to spread out payment over time. Often tickets to the most desirable and popular games are included in the package along with games against teams that may not draw as well. This strategy is a way to entice fans to purchase tickets to less attractive games while offering discounts to popular games that are likely to sell out.

Flexibility can also come in the form of voucher programs. In addition to offering seats through the team box office or web-based systems, teams may sell tickets through cooperate partners at their stores. An example of such a program in the Clevcland, Ohio, area is Discount Drug Mart's promotion of selling tickets to local sporting events in their stores. The program, known as the Indians "Perfect 10" Voucher Pack, offers flexibility to fans. Individuals can buy single tickets to 10 games, 2 tickets to 5 games, 10 tickets to 1 game, or any combination of tickets (Cleveland Indians, 2013). This type of promotion and partnership can help increase attendance and ticket revenue at games while encouraging fans to shop at the sponsor's stores. Additional ticket packages include family ticket plans. A typical family package could include four tickets, four hot dogs, four soft drinks, and a program for a discounted price.

money-back guarantee
An agreement between the ticket seller and buyer that the buyer will receive a full refund if the event does not meet a standard of satisfaction for the patron.

MONEY-BACK GUARANTEES

A number of teams have included **money-back guarantee** conditions in their ticket packages or single-game tickets. The Jacksonville Sharks of the Arena Football League, after a successful season winning their division, announced a money-back guarantee to all new season ticket holders. In the team's press release regarding the money-back guarantee, the Vice President of Ticketing, Steve Curran, gave the following reasoning for engaging in the program: "Like any business, we believe in our product. After three-plus years of positive feedback and helpful criticism, we guarantee that you will have a great time at Sea Best Field if you give us a try" (Jacksonville Sharks, 2013). Other teams have picked one game to offer the guarantee. For one game in December of 2012, the NBA's Phoenix Suns guaranteed a good time for all guests or a complete refund of the ticket price. Following the game, they received 365 refund requests but drew 17,517 fans, which was over 2700 more than the team averaged the previous season and their highest attended game of the year to date (Soshnick, 2013). The team anticipated a higher rate of refund requests, so the promotion ended up being more successful than originally predicted. The money-back guarantee seems to be a good way to market to prospective new season ticket holders. The trade-off of having to refund the ticket price to the customer versus adding ticket revenue works out in the venue's favor because it has been shown that fans are unlikely to ask for a refund.

WEB-BASED TICKETS

Traditionally, customers would buy tickets from a team box office, over the phone, at retail stores, by mail order, or through Ticketmaster outlets. Now, the Internet has become a primary tool to purchase tickets. Preventing brokers or scalpers from selling and reselling tickets on the secondary ticket market has become a challenge for teams and venue owners and operators, especially with the development of relaxed secondary ticket market laws and websites such as StubHub. The question for teams is how to make revenue off of the secondary ticket market when a patron resells tickets. In 2000, the MLB's San Francisco Giants decreased no-shows by reselling tickets through their ticket exchange at a 50% reduction and generated half a million dollars in additional revenue (Dickey, 2000). Ticket exchanges offering season ticket holders an opportunity to resell tickets in a safe and legal environment have been offered.

ELECTRONIC TICKET DELIVERY

Many venues and teams are using electronic and paperless ticket delivery as a more convenient way to deliver tickets to fans. The traditional ticket is also becoming a thing of the past with the emergence of new technologies, including smart phones. FanPass is the electronic ticketing delivery system developed and used by Major League Baseball. Flash Seats, owned by Veritix, a company based in Cleveland, Ohio, is a ticketing system used by many college arenas (including those operated by Boise State and Texas A&M), professional venues such as Ford Field and Quicken Loans Arena, and the 2014 NCAA Basketball Final Four held in Arlington, Texas (Flash Seats, nd). The benefits of the electronic ticketing systems include fast entry into the venue, no tickets to forget, and a reduction in counterfeit tickets. Visitors can choose a credit card, driver's license, or other form of electronic identification, or they can use a Quick Response (QR) code or a mobile device application. The card is swiped or the code read by a handheld device operated by a representative at the entry gate. Seat holders are given a seat locator identifying their seats within the venue (Flash Seats, 2013).

Electronic ticket delivery can help limit lines into the venue and reduce the staffing required at ticket windows on game day. This ticketing capability can help raise revenue by making ticket purchases easier, offering the potential ability to deduct service charges from paper tickets, and allowing teams to add a service charge to paper tickets. Electronic ticket delivery is an innovative way to use technology to increase ticket revenue while minimizing the barriers to obtaining tickets from a team and reducing loss of revenue to the secondary ticket market.

LUXURY SUITES AND CLUB SEATS

Beyond the general seats in a large public assembly facility, luxury suites and club seating are often available. The highest priced seats are often club and

©Ken Durden/Shutterstock

luxury suites. A primary reason for the stadium boom of the 1990s and 2000s was the lack of luxury seats in the older venues. The first venue to utilize luxury suites was the Houston Astrodome, which opened in 1965. The arena considered to be at the forefront of using suites was the Palace of Auburn Hills (home to the Detroit Pistons). Club seats and luxury suites are often cited as the primary reason for building new arenas or stadiums.

Luxury suites are similar to a hotel room with seating areas to watch the action in the venue. Areas to serve food and beverages and to socialize are a benefit of these spaces. Food and beverages are often included with the price of the suite or are charged to the account holder. These suites are often leased for a season or multiple years to corporate entities who are team sponsors, who use the tickets for client development, or who use the space for game-day events or other purposes. Suite holders may be able to use the suite for functions during a game or on a nongame day.

Club seats are premium seats in a venue that have prime views of the game while providing extra amenities not available to other patrons. The club seats at Progressive Field (home of MLB's Cleveland Indians) are located on the first-base line, enabling outdoor viewing of the game (suites are often behind windows, which can be lowered or raised depending on weather). According to the Indians' website, these seats offer access to "the climate-controlled Club Lounge, situated directly behind their seats. All tickets to Club Seats include all-inclusive food and non-alcoholic beverages within the Club Lounge" (Cleveland Indians, 2013). Alcohol may be purchased but is not included with the price of club seat tickets.

LOADED TICKETS

Stored-value tickets have become commonplace at MLB stadiums. Patrons pay one price for a seat. The tickets include ballpark admission and an additional value that is programmed into the ticket, which can be used to purchase food, beverage, and merchandise. The stored value is accessible via a barcode scanned at the venues. MLB's Philadelphia Phillies call their package Power Tickets and sell and promote their stored-value tickets heavily on their ticket webpage. They estimate that patrons with Power Tickets spend 70% more on concessions and merchandise (Muret, 2009).

PERSONAL SEAT LICENSES

The personal seat license system traces back to the debenture system first employed by Royal Albert Hall in London. When the hall was built in 1871, the builders offered 999-year leases for 1200 of the 5500 seats to help finance construction. Leases may be resold by the owners and have been sold for as much as £1.2 million. The concert hall receives £960 for administrative fees from box holders. The box holder is able to attend most of the concerts. This system is also used for seats at the All England Lawn Tennis and Croquet

personal seat license (PSL) A paid license that affords the buyer the right to buy season tickets for a specific seat in a stadium. The license is transferable and seat rights may be sold to another person once the owner decides not to purchase season tickets.

Club in Wimbledon and Twickenham Stadium for Rugby Union Football (Daily Mail Reporter, 2008).

In the United States, the **personal seat license (PSL)** gives the holder the ability to purchase a specific seat in a stadium as long as the individual holds those seat rights. The idea of the first PSL is credited to Stanford University's tennis coach Dick Gould, who was trying to raise funds for a new tennis stadium for the school. Colleges used this strategy in years before by exchanging better seats in their stadium for donations to the university. The strategy is also used at professional sports venues. For example, Churchill Downs, the famous horse racing track in Louisville, Kentucky, offers PSLs for the Kentucky Oaks and Kentucky Derby for a 3- or 5-year period. PSL license fees range for this racetrack from $3600 to $135,000, and $290 to $1400 for each ticket. The license fee must be paid in November, the year prior to the next year's racing season (Churchill Downs, 2013).

PSLs are most popularly used with NFL teams, who are limited to the amount of events they can sell tickets to due to a shorter season than that of most other professional leagues (10 home games, including preseason exhibition games). PSLs often are called by a promotional name unique to the particular team. For example, the Seattle Seahawks' PSLs are called Charter Seat Licenses, the Cincinnati Bengals' PSLs are called Charter Ownership Agreements, the San Francisco 49ers' and the Pittsburgh Steelers' PSLs are called Stadium Builder's Licenses, and the Dallas Cowboys' PSLs are called Seat Options (PSL Source, 2013).

PSLs can account for a significant amount of revenue to pay for stadium construction costs. The two NFL teams of New York, the Jets and the Giants, expect to make $325 million and $400 million, respectively, from PSLs to put toward the $1.7-billion construction costs for MetLife Stadium. The highest costing PSL under an agreement with the Jets costs $30,000, while the Dallas Cowboys have a PSL worth $150,000 (Nelson, 2012). Some argue that utilizing PSLs can price out fans who may be able to afford tickets but not the fee for the license. However, this has not seemed to be a deterrent to attendance, and attendances at NFL stadiums with PSLs remain steady. PSLs may be exchanged by the holder via the PSL source online exchange.

Promotions

Venues will often have special promotions or events in conjunction with a game day to help increase attendance. Many of these events are linked to a sponsor as a promotional opportunity. The concept of sport promotion is often associated with Bill Veeck, past owner of MLB's Cleveland Indians, St. Louis Browns, and Chicago White Sox from the 1940s through the 1970s. Veeck is regarded as one of the most innovative promoters in sport history. Some of his more famous promotions included "lucky chair" giveaways (with such prizes as 36 live lobsters), orchid giveaways on Mother's Day, and free admission days for cab drivers and bartenders. His efforts in 1959 yielded the best attendance for the White Sox since the 1929 season. Many of Veeck's concepts of promotions can be used to help improve attendance and gate receipts (Corbett, n.d.).

Free product or souvenir giveaways are some of the most common forms of promotions used by venue and team owners. Popular promotions include hat day, jersey day, dollar hot dog day, and soft drink day. Combining events can help create interest and improve attendance. Many college basketball teams have a local elementary school or community youth team play a shortened game at halftime. It is a way to entertain crowds at halftime and introduce parents and families to a form of inexpensive entertainment in the hopes of turning the halftime entertainment participants into future ticket buyers. Promotional days that honor or recognize certain groups can also be excellent forms of promotion. These groups may include youth sports leagues, camp groups, service industry professionals, Boy Scouts, Girl Scouts, and members of the military.

Ancillary Revenue

Ancillary revenue refers to the income generated from goods and services that enhance the primary product or service. Concessions, parking, and merchandise are some of the most common forms of ancillary revenue available at sporting events (see **Table 11-2**). While none of these services are necessary components to the sport spectating experiences, they are often expected by ticket holders and patrons.

ancillary revenue
Income generated from goods and services that enhance the primary product or service; examples include concessions, parking, and merchandise.

TABLE 11-2   Average Prices for Ancillary Items at Major League Venues

League	Beer	Soft Drink	Hot Dog	Parking	Program	Cap
NFL	$7.05	$4.48	$5.07	$30.57	$3.71	$21.60
MLB	$6.09	$3.67	$4.14	$14.06	$2.99	$15.99
NHL	$7.34	$4.39	$4.74	$16.63	$2.54	$19.88
NBA	$7.08	$4.17	$4.82	$15.21	$3.10	$20.06

CONCESSIONS AND FOOD OPERATIONS

An integral part of the fan experience at spectator venues often revolves around food. Concession stands are small kiosks or locations in a venue that serve snacks or food. They are known as concessions because they are often operated by a third party independent from the venue. Venues may sell their own food or operate a concession company. Centerplate, Levy Restaurants, and Aramark are well-known food and hospitality concessionaires that run food operations in professional and college sporting facilities and venues.

Traditional food offerings in venues include hot dogs, soft drinks, popcorn, and candy. However, gone are the days when hamburgers, hotdogs, candy, popcorn, pretzels, and soda made up the totality of food and beverage options. In contemporary professional stadiums, sushi and other gourmet items (such as lobster rolls) are often offered—and, frankly, expected—as stadium fare. The stadium experience has become another form of food court by offering multiple restaurant choices. Often the food of local restaurants and delis is featured. This partnership can provide revenue for a local business while offering fans food options they enjoy consuming outside the venue. If individuals know they can purchase their favorite food inside the stadium, it may prove to be a positive revenue producer for the facility. Many new venues have added chain restaurants or fine dining to make their locations year-round destinations. For example, Miller Park in Milwaukee, Wisconsin, operates a TGI Friday's franchise, while Yankee Stadium in Bronx, New York, has a Hard Rock Cafe open year round, game or no game. Including famous restaurants as part of the venue can help increase the gate receipt. The projected gross food and beverage revenue for one NFL stadium is over $5 million (AECOM, 2013).

One issue that stadiums and arenas face is alcohol sales. There has been debate about whether alcohol sales contribute to fan misconduct. Many stadiums around the world prohibit alcohol sales within the seating areas or in the stadium, period. In the United States, alcohol is a ubiquitous part of the concession offerings in professional venues. The potential for revenue production is significant for many venues. Nonetheless, the majority of facilities that reside on college campuses refuse to sell alcohol for any events. Some college football stadiums (e.g., University of West Virginia's Milan Puskar Stadium) have introduced alcohol sales in their stadium as a way to increase attendance and add ticket revenue. Professional stadiums have increased the selections of beer and even include hard liquor for sale.

When serving alcohol, it is important to be aware of a state's dram shop laws. The server, concessionaire, and team are liable if an individual whom the patron knows to be intoxicated is overserved on the premises and commits a crime or injures someone else in a traffic accident. Further, all guests, regardless of age, must provide valid photo identification (Zullo, Bi, Xiaohan, & Siddiqui, 2013). Dram shop laws make the venue and servers liable for alcohol-related negligence. Also, venue operators should consider the type of event being played in the facility. If a venue has a liquor license and allows alcohol sales at many events, there may be event-specific restrictions on sale. It may not be appropriate to allow alcohol consumption at high school events, and many college conferences do not allow sales at their events. For example, the Southeastern Conference (SEC) prohibits alcohol at all conference-sponsored events.

VIGNETTE 11-1

Raising Revenue for a Venue While Fundraising for Student Groups

College athletics departments are always looking for supplemental revenue from events held in their venues. Many college stadiums utilize benches for their seating. At one Midwestern university, fans often complained about the discomfort they experienced while sitting on the benches but were prohibited from bringing outside items into the stadium for security reasons. The venue operators decided to make an effort to appease their fans while creatively cashing in on their discomforted posteriors. The athletic department began to give season ticket holders the opportunity to purchase a chairback with the team's logo on the back for the season for $50. There is the option to pay an additional charge to keep the personalized chairback at the end of the season as a souvenir or return it to be reused in subsequent seasons. In addition, many student groups at the university sought to raise money for the groups. Because the chairbacks need to be installed before the season and removed at the end of the season, the department hired sport clubs or service organizations affiliated with the university to aid in installation and removal. They paid 15 groups $1000 each for their efforts during each installation and removal effort, which cost the department $30,000. At the end of the year, 30,000 chairbacks were installed, which raised $1.5 million in additional revenue. Thus, using revenue strategies such as chairbacks is a way to raise revenue for a venue while producing goodwill and providing revenue for student groups.

PARKING

concessionaire An entity given the rights to operate and sell goods or services on premises that belong to another. Venues often enter into agreements to sell parking and food concessions on their premises.

Depending on location, venues may operate their own parking facilities, contract to outside companies or **concessionaires**, or rely on surrounding areas and have no control over event parking. An example of a parking concessionaire is Central Parking, one of the world's largest parking facility operators. The company operates city, airport, and stadium parking lots. There are a number of advantages to operating facility-owned and -controlled lots. In addition to adding to overall profit of an event, it may serve as a way to lure patrons to the venue earlier in the day prior to a game to take part in pregame fan festivals, tailgating parties, or other events that complement the game. Including ample parking in the facility plan gives more flexibility and ability to raise revenue surrounding game day. However, it may be more cost-effective to have an outside dedicated concessionaire operate parking lots and not dedicate other facility personnel and energy to parking-related issues.

MERCHANDISE

Merchandise sales are another form of ancillary revenue. Whether it is a sporting event of the primary tenant, a special tournament event, or an outside group renting a facility, patrons often want to buy souvenirs to commemorate their experience. Teams may operate their own merchandise tables, booths, or stores or may contract to a concessionaire to manage and sell their merchandise. Many stadiums and arenas are home to club stores where patrons may purchase products they cannot get anywhere else. These stores are open on game day and are often open all year long.

Alternative Uses for Sport-Specific Stadiums

What uses are there for a baseball stadium when the team is on the road? How about in the winter months? An outdoor stadium with capacity for 80,000 people may not be appropriate for many types of outdoor events. Baseball stadiums have unique shapes that make them difficult to use for other events. Also, in what ways can an outdoor venue be rendered useful in cold and harsh climates? An indoor venue, in contrast, may be used every day of the year. In the offseason, indoor stadiums may still be used for sporting events even in climates where weather limits outdoor activities.

Regardless the type, large stadiums often present challenges for use outside their intended sport or season.

Many venues have embarked on the strategy of hosting special events or events that are not traditionally hosted in that type of venue. Baseball stadiums have hosted international friendly soccer matches when their primary tenant is on the road or in the off season. During college bowl season, Yankee Stadium and AT&T Park (home to the San Francisco Giants) have been used for football games, even though they are oriented for baseball. Baseball stadiums have also become the hosts of college football games. Yankee Stadium in New York has sought to host a college football game once a year. Many baseball stadiums have started to host or plan to host college football postseason bowl games. The Marlins Stadium in Miami will hold the Miami Beach Bowl postseason game beginning in 2014, hosted and administered by the American Athletic Conference (American Athletic Conference, n.d.). Tropicana Field, home of MLB's Tampa Bay Rays, hosts the Beef 'O' Brady's St. Petersburg Bowl every December. An additional scheduling and revenue-producing opportunity is hosting concerts for national and international touring musical performers. Acts that draw crowds beyond the capacity of an indoor arena are often options for further facility use. Visits by major religious figures, such as the pope, have graced outdoor sport venues in years past, including Pimlico Race Course (in Baltimore, Maryland), Yankee Stadium, and Giants Stadium (former home to the NFL's New York Giants), among others (United States Conference of Catholic Bishops, n.d).

In frigid winter months, large venues often transform their stadiums into public ice rinks or host ice hockey competitions for the NHL and college teams. Since these games are thought of as novelties and played in stadiums with larger capacities, they are able to draw a considerable number of fans over the average crowd for a typical regular season game. The NHL has had much success with their Winter Classic game held on or around New Year's Day in a football or baseball stadium. This event began in 2008 and

was expanded in the 2013–14 season as the NHL Stadium Series, with a series of games in New York and Los Angeles. Television ratings for the outdoor games have yielded five of the six highest-rated regular season games. The 2011 version played at Pittsburgh's Heinz Field drew 68,111 fans (El-Bashir, 2011). Additionally, when the game is played in a baseball stadium, which is guaranteed not to be used by its primary tenant in January, college, high school, and alumni games can be held in the venue and yield additional ticket revenue.

Tennis venues have also sought to bring in visitors and revenue through scheduling concerts and other untraditional events. The U.S. Tennis Association's (USTA) Billie Jean King National Tennis Center in Flushing Meadows, New York, hosts the qualifying and main draws of the U.S. Open tennis tournament for 3 weeks each year. The other 11 months of the year the operators seek out other events to fill the tennis center. While the facility hosts USTA, NCAA, and high school tournaments throughout the year, Arthur Ashe Stadium (which is the main stadium of the tennis center) is often too large to be a useful venue for youth tournaments, and team matches require six courts at a time. In 2008, Arthur Ashe Stadium was host to a Women's National Basketball Association (WNBA) game between the New York Liberty and the Indiana Fever for the first-ever regular season basketball game played outdoors (Brill, 2008).

HOSTING CHAMPIONSHIPS

Numerous effective uses of available space exist for venues of all shapes and sizes, ranging from alternative competitive events on open dates to hospitality events. Renting a facility to high school or college teams for tournaments or games is a great option for professional, municipal, college, and high school venues. Professional and college sports facilities are used to host high school championships. These stadiums are often the largest venues the athletes will play in during the year and give them the chance to feel like they are playing in a big-time atmosphere. The University of Northern Iowa's UNI-Dome and Syracuse University's Carrier Dome (in New York) host the state championship football games for their respective states because they are large-capacity facilities and protect players and fans from inclement weather that is likely in those states in late November when the championship games are played.

HOSPITALITY EVENTS

Hospitality events are also a great option for venues, whether during an event, on a day without a scheduled event, or in the off season. For example, Citi Field, home baseball stadium of the New York Mets, offers many hospitality and event options when the stadium is not in use for games, during the 6 months when MLB is not in session. Citi Field lists 19 locations within their stadium that can be used for hospitality purposes during games or completely independent of game day or in the offseason. These events can include academic conferences, business meetings, trade shows, birthday parties, bar/bat mitzvahs, fundraisers, corporate events, or other family events. For these events, venues offer a number of potential event services, including appearances by former players, audiovisual displays, coat check, custom team apparel, gifts, furniture rentals, floral arrangements, décor options, lighting, menu selections, mascot appearances, personal event coordination, rentals, and parking packages. Providing each of these services can be included in different pricing packages for events. Utilizing these spaces, offering multiple party and event opportunities, and providing the resources to carry out these events can ensure facilities are being used when the house is dark and brings in additional revenue to the organization. However, it is important to require that groups renting or using facilities have their own insurance policies and furnish proof of the policy (New York Mets, 2013). When serving alcohol in spaces rented in an event for hospitality or party events, venues will permit sales and consumption provided that their concessionaire is in control of the serving of alcoholic beverages.

In summary, stadium managers should seek to schedule or plan novel events such as bowl games or nontraditional sporting events for their sport-specific stadiums as a way to make use of the venue on an otherwise dark day. In addition to adding revenue, using these facilities can show that the organization is innovative and will likely lure other potential clients to rent or utilize the facility.

Multipurpose Sport Facilities

Spectator sport venues make up a large share of sport facilities, but multipurpose facilities may be used for spectator sports, participatory events, and physical fitness. Many municipalities or private entities have built indoor multipurpose facilities that can be used for fitness, recreation, and competitive sports. In addition, indoor and outdoor sports practice facilities built by private entities have been developed. These facilities can be focused on one sport or can address the needs of multiple sports. Types include ice hockey rinks, indoor turf fields, sport court buildings, swimming pools, weight rooms, and training centers. SPIRE Institute in Geneva, Ohio, and Birmingham CrossPlex in Birmingham, Alabama, are two examples of large sports training and competition facilities that seek to draw local, regional, and national competitions. The types of events offered in these facilities include team practices, swimming meets, track and field meets, youth and Amateur Athletic Union (AAU) basketball competitions, and road races.

SPIRE and CrossPlex collect membership fees, facility use fees for practice usage, and entry fees for tournaments and invitational events. CrossPlex houses a 4000-seat indoor track facility with a hydraulic banked track, an Olympic-size swimming pool with seating for 1600, nine volleyball courts, a 5000-seat basketball arena, and the ability to host other sports (Birmingham CrossPlex, 2013). SPIRE operates a training academy for postsecondary school athletes wishing to improve their skills and grades before enrolling in college (SPIRE, n.d.). The facility is comparable to the CrossPlex facility and hosts collegiate conference championships in swimming, volleyball, and track and field. It is the yearly host of the National Association of Intercollegiate Athletics (NAIA) national championship in track and field. The venue produces income from entry fees, spectator admission, and concessions. Additionally, the public may use the indoor track, swimming pool, and fitness and weight facilities through membership programs or pay-by-use arrangements. Thus, these facilities operate as recreational and spectator sport venues.

Participatory Events

While spectator events in arenas or stadiums and recreational events in multipurpose complexes are lucrative revenue producers, participatory events are another part of the sport industry that is worth considering. These events, which are often defined by their novelty and/or physical difficulty, may appeal to endurance athletes and individuals who are motivated by health consciousness, fundraising, or a chance to try a new, fun fitness activity.

Many of these events include professional, elite, and competitive components, but the vast majority of participants are not looking to win money; they simply wish to push themselves to complete the event. Road running races, triathlons, and other themed noncompetitive races are options for raising money for charity or for-profit endeavors. This section will focus primarily on running races held on public streets.

ROAD RUNNING RACES

Running races come in many sizes. Local 5K races may draw 100 runners, while a World Marathon Major event may draw 45,000 participants and 2 million spectators. Races of all size rely on registration fees. A **dynamic pricing** strategy is employed in many races. The earlier an individual registers, the lower the price. The New York City Marathon charges a registration fee depending on membership in the New York Road Runners (NYRR) and citizenship. NYRR members pay $216, while U.S. citizens pay $255 and International competitors (including citizens of Puerto Rico and other U.S. territories) are charged $347. In 2013, 50,266 people finished the New York City Marathon.

Revenue is not always made simply through the individuals who compete. In addition to the race, major marathons host expositions, or expos, which charge exhibitors fees to display and sell their products. Expos are open to the public, and races sell race-related merchandise to competitors and other visitors. Runners are required to attend the expos to pick up their numbers and other complimentary items included in the race registration fees. Fees paid for these races are nonrefundable and are often due months ahead of time. For instance, the Boston Marathon, held the third Monday in April, has a registration deadline in September. Since marathon training often lasts 6 months, runners may have no idea what injuries or other issues will keep them from racing. Race organizers usually expect that 10% of the registered runners will not show up. No-shows can bring in over $1 million in revenue to a major marathon. Smaller races can learn a lesson from this strategy, as requiring preregistration for an event can boost revenue.

Other participatory events have become lucrative business ventures. Mud runs such as Tough Mudder, obstacle course races such as the Spartan

dynamic pricing A process of pricing that is similar to differential pricing but concerned with the fluctuation of the price of a seat for an event based on demand. Determinants of dynamic pricing may include weather, quality of opponent, promotional offerings, or day of the week.

Race, and adventure races such as the Urban Dare allow individuals to combine running skills with physical agility. These events can use parks, private property, local streets, or even professional venues such as stadiums and arenas. The CrossFit Games are often held in convention centers and arenas, with finals held at the StubHub Center in Carson, California. While these events are participatory events and raise the bulk of their funds from entry fees, spectator admission and ancillary income are also used to increase revenue. These events typically charge over $100 per entry as a result of the liability and intricacies of setting up obstacles.

VIGNETTE 11-2

Using Technology to Increase Registration Revenue

A sub-elite running club from northern Florida was interested in raising money for their upcoming trip to the National Club Cross Country Championships. As experienced runners and event organizers, they decided to put on a 5K cross-country meet in their hometown in an effort to defray the cost of travel to the national championship race. The event was held on Halloween and was called the Pumpkin Run. Their question was, how could the club maximize their revenue by putting on a race that would draw 100 participants while potentially drawing repeat participants in future years? They decided entry fees and concessions would be the best way to raise income. The members of the club used advertising in local running stores along with web-based registration technologies. An online race entry website was used to advertise and collect registration information and fees. In addition, the race director put the race on the Running in the USA calendar, a free service that compiles race information all around the country. As a result, individuals from other states entered the race, since there was a market for trail and cross-country races but a limited selection of them in the region on that weekend. The organizers purchased 200 water bottles at $1 per bottle as an alternative to T-shirts as the race-day handout and bought pumpkins as awards, instead of the traditional medals or plaques. A club member who worked at a bakery was able to get baked goods at no charge to sell at the event.

Overall, the race drew 80 runners. Concession sales were lackluster and raised $20. The organizers were hoping to have 100 participants, which would defray their complete costs to the national meet. However, in the subsequent weeks, they received fees for 30 no-shows, which was a quarter of all registration revenue and resulted in a total of $1500 in revenue. This event illustrates how collecting entry fees ahead of the race along with putting the race online can increase revenue. Through cooperation with community organizations, creative thinking with regard to awards and concessions, and web-based registration processes, a small group can put on a sporting event to support their endeavors.

SUMMARY

There are multiple ways that facility and event operators can raise revenue from their events. These methods range from ticket sales, which may involve running promotions, to ancillary revenue from concessions, to merchandise sales, to parking fees. Primary tenants are not the only ones who can bring revenue to a facility; concerts, high school games, college games, and championship events are also potential revenue sources. Utilizing suites, club seating, and other spaces within a venue during the season and out of season can add flexibility and ways to produce more revenue. Multipurpose venues and city streets can provide areas for participatory events, including road running events. Overall, the possibilities for producing revenue from sport facilities and events are endless. A little creativity and innovation can go a long way in helping venue and event operators produce income.

DISCUSSION QUESTIONS

1. List the multiple types of sport facilities, and describe how sport managers and event planners can produce revenue for each. Consider the versatility of each facility.
2. Does the type of facility impact the type of revenue that can be raised?
3. What are some ethical considerations with regard to serving alcohol at sporting events? Does the type of event impact whether alcohol sales are appropriate?
4. What is ancillary revenue, and what strategies can be used to increase it?
5. In what ways can revenue be raised at road races from participants and spectators?

Case STUDY

The 50/50 Raffle Goes Digital

The electronic raffle has become ubiquitous in professional sporting events lately as a driver of ancillary revenue, as a visitor to the Quicken Loans Arena in Cleveland, Ohio, can likely attest. In 2013, Cleveland sport fans saw a new feature unveiled at major sporting events. The Cleveland Cavaliers offer fans the ability to enter a 50/50 raffle, where half of the pot goes to the winner and the other half to Cleveland Foundation charities. Other arena tenants, the Lake Erie Monsters hockey team and the Cleveland Gladiators arena football team, partake in these raffles to support charities as well.

The ability to offer these raffles nightly is made possible due to technological advances. Pointstreak 5050, a Canadian company, has pioneered digital raffle capabilities, developing many advantages over traditional ticket raffles. This company has teamed with many professional teams, including those in the Cleveland area. Tickets are sold by employees who have handheld devices with ticket printers attached. This give sellers the ability to walk throughout the arena to distribute tickets, while automatically entering patrons into the drawing. This system has increased the amount of revenue that can be taken in during a raffle. It allows fans and ticket sellers to know how much the pot is worth at all times through integration with scoreboard displays, provides possibility for unlimited tickets to be sold, and produces instant sales and reconciliation reports. In addition, a title sponsor of the raffle may represent another form of revenue for the team.

Following the popularity and success of the 50/50 raffles at Quicken Loans Arena, MLB's Cleveland Indians has adopted the same technology to provide raffles for the 2014 season. On opening day, the winner took home $6335, while the charity raised the same amount. Other teams across North America are utilizing this raffling technology. For example, at an NHL playoff game between the Pittsburgh Penguins and New York Rangers, the winning pot was $48,700. Many teams have seen their contributions to their charities increase significantly, especially the Phoenix Coyotes, who saw a 723% increase compared to using paper tickets in previous years. Overall, this type of raffle offers excitement for fans, creates more awareness about team charities and title sponsors, provides more sponsorship opportunities, and supports charitable foundations.

Pretend you are the manager of a multipurpose indoor sport facility and wish to capitalize on the revenue-generating possibilities offered by technological advances, such as those employed at Quicken Loans Arena. Consider the following:

1. In what ways can technology increase your ability to enhance revenue production and fundraising for your organization?
2. What revenue-producing opportunities might an electronic raffle provide?
3. How might the nonprofit versus for-profit status of your organization affect how you distribute the proceeds of your 50/50 raffle?
4. Detail the benefits and potential outcomes of using your chosen technology to enhance ancillary revenue.

REFERENCES

AECOM Technical Services. (2013). Coliseum city football stadium revenue study. Chicago. Retrieved from http://newballpark.org/2013/07/16/coliseum-city-football-stadium-revenue-study/

American Athletic Conference. (n.d.) American Athletic Conference introduces Miami Beach Bowl. Retrieved from http://theamerican.org/news/2013/10/24/FB_1024135758.aspx

Birmingham CrossPlex. (2013). Retrieved from http://www.birminghamcrossplex.com

Brill, L. (2008). Liberty players excited for Outdoor Classic. Retrieved from http://www.wnba.com/outdoor_080711.html

Churchill Downs. (2013). Personal seat licenses. Retrieved from http://www.churchilldowns.com/tickets/seat-licenses

Cleveland Indians. (2013). Indians Introduce Perfect 10 Flex Pack ticket option for 2013 season. Retrieved from http://m.indians.mlb.com/news/article/40415526/indians-introduce-perfect-10-flex-pack-ticket-option-for-2013-season

Corbett, W. (n.d.). Bill Veeck. Retrieved from http://sabr.org/bioproj/person/7b0b5f10

Daily Mail Reporter. (2008). For sale: The Albert Hall with a £1.2 million view. Retrieved from http://www.dailymail.co.uk/news/article-1023841/For-sale-The-Albert-Hall-box-1-2m-view.html

Dickey, G. (2000). Giants new tickets plan a winner. Retrieved from http://www.sfgate.com/sports/article/Giants-New-Ticket-Plan-a-Winner-2755154.php

El-Bashir, T. (2011). 2011 Winter Classic: Capitals star Alex Ovechkin works on ending offensive slump. *Washington Post*. Retrieved from http://www.washingtonpost.com/wp-dyn/content/article/2011/01/02/AR2011010202375.html

Flash Seats (2013). Flash Seats is the future of ticketing today. Retrieved from http://www.flashseats.com/

Greenberg, J. (2012). Jump ball: NBA tix going up post-lockout. Retrieved from http://www.fancostexperience.com/pages/fcx/blog_pdfs/entry0000019_pdf000.pdf

Greenberg, J. (2013a). 2013 MLB fan index. Retrieved from http://www.fancostexperience.com/pages/fcx/blog_pdfs/entry0000021_pdf005.pdf

Greenberg, J. (2013b). Are you ready for some FCI: Rising prices in NFL. Retrieved from http://www.fancostexperience.com/pages/fcx/blog_pdfs/entry0000025_pdf002.pdf

Greenberg, J. (2013c). Lockout costs: NHL prices increase in 2013. Retrieved from http://www.fancostexperience.com/pages/fcx/blog_pdfs/entry0000020_pdf001.pdf

Howard, D. R., & Crompton, J. L. (2005). *Financing sport* (2nd ed.). Morgantown, WV: Fitness Information Technology.

Jacksonville Sharks. (2013). Sharks offer season ticket money-back guarantee. Retrieved from http://www.arenafootball.com/sports/a-footbl/spec-rel/032513aaa.html

Muret, D. (2009). Royals, Indians will join MLB clubs selling stored-value tickets. *Street & Smith's Sport Business Daily*. Retrieved from http://www.sportsbusinessdaily.com/Journal/Issues/2009/01/20090119/This-Weeks-News/Royals-Indians-Will-Join-MLB-Clubs-Selling-Stored-Value-Tickets.aspx

Nelson, T. (2012). NFL stadium personal seat licenses compared. *MPR News.* Retrieved from http://minnesota.publicradio.org/display/web/2012/11/15/ sports/nfl-personal-seat-licenses-compared

New York Mets. (2013). Metropolitan hospitality. Retrieved from http://mets.mlb .com/nym/metropolitanhospitality/index.jsp

PSL Source. (2013). Frequently asked questions. Retrieved from http://www.psl-source.com/faq/psl_source

Soshnick, S. (2013). Money-back offer from NBA's Suns yields 365 refund requests. *Bloomberg.* Retrieved from http://www.bloomberg.com/news/2013-01-07/ money-back-offer-from-nba-s-suns-yields-365-refund-requests.html

SPIRE Institute. (n.d.). Retrieved from http://www.spireinstitute.com

United States Conference of Catholic Bishops. (n.d.). Pope Benedict XVI's itinerary. Retrieved from http://www.uspapalvisit.org/itinerary_en.htm

Zullo, R., Bi, X., Xiaohan, Y., & Siddiqui, Y. (2013). *The fiscal and social effects of state alcohol control systems.* Ann Arbor, MI: Institute for Research on Labor, Employment, and the Economy.

Customer service is more about the big picture than the small, unique moments that most of us tend to dwell on. Working in this field, you need to be able to see how everything that happens in your event impacts peoples' perception of the event. It is important to concentrate on the overall satisfaction levels of participants, volunteers, and spectators rather than the outliers who are either extremely unhappy or extremely pleased with the event. With that level of focus, you can determine strategies and methods to raise the bar on the level of service you provide to your constituents.

Introduction

The spectator sport industry is a multibillion-dollar-a-year business that sees millions of fans attend events, spend their hard-earned money, and look to spend a few hours with family and friends away from their daily realities (Wysong, Rothschild, & Beldona, 2011). In the major spectator sport industry, competition has increased with the addition of rival leagues of same and/ or different sports and the ongoing expansion of playing seasons. Many sport organizations also face resistance from their customers as a result of increased cost and heightened expectations for better performance and event quality (Howard & Crompton, 2004). As traditional revenue streams begin to stagnate and new sources of income are more difficult to come by, sport managers must look inward to understand how to maintain their standing in the marketplace while attempting to grow despite the glaring issues ahead of them. Because even the best teams in each league can no longer rest on their accumulated brand equity and identity, the notion of customer service is becoming more and more important in today's sport organizational landscape. Turban, Lee, King, and Chung (2002) define customer service as "a series of activities designed to enhance the level of customer satisfaction—that is, the feeling that a product or service has met the customer expectation." These organizational activities are designed to create and maintain relationships with your customers—relationships that should lead to many of the desired outcomes inherent to the organization–customer interaction: satisfaction, loyalty, positive word of mouth, and repatronage.

Marketing literature suggests that the provision of high-quality services

©dotshock/Shutterstock

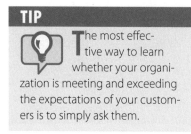

TIP

The most effective way to learn whether your organization is meeting and exceeding the expectations of your customers is to simply ask them.

is critical to increase customer satisfaction and loyalty, which in turn increases the profitability of an organization (Anderson, Fornell, & Lehmann, 1994; Anderson & Sullivan, 1993; Dagger & Sweeney, 2007; Fornell, 1992). According to the work of Ko, Zhang, Cattani, and Pastore (2011), service quality has received attention from numerous scholars and is considered one of the most important issues in the sport and recreation landscape. They cite three main reasons for its perceived importance: (1) It is a measure of management performance, (2) it is related to the positioning of the organization, and (3) it is a key determinant of ultimate consumer behavior variables such as customer loyalty.

As we delve deeper into our discussion of customer service, it is of utmost importance to first understand those qualities that sport managers should either look for when recruiting organizational personnel or work to train into current staff members. In no particular order, **Table 12-1** presents the

TABLE 12-1   Fifteen Qualities of Effective Customer Service

Customer Service Skill	What It Is	Why It Is Important
Patience	Quiet, steady perseverance; even-tempered care	Customers will require help of all kinds, and we must attend to each situation in a calm manner.
Attentiveness	Mindfulness and consideration of others; courteousness; politeness	It is imperative that we treat each concern as our own. A thoughtful approach will communicate genuine care and concern.
Effective Communication Skills	Sound written and oral skills replete with proper grammar and knowledge of situational communication	Dealing with agitation and frustration calls for an ability to communicate in a manner that will mitigate anxiety and solve issues.
Product Knowledge	A thorough understanding of the inner workings of your team, organization, and product	Every employee should know basic answers to common FAQs in the event of being stopped by customers during an event. This basic knowledge will communicate passion and excitement for your product.
Use of "Positive Language"	The ability to frame your response in an optimistic and customer-centered way	Small changes that utilize "positive language" have a significant effect on how your customers *hear* your response and create a perception of your organization.
Acting Skills	Skills necessary to maintain a cheerful and helpful persona in spite of customer frustration	While many concerns have simple responses, the more complicated ones require calm under pressure—either genuine or "created" through simple acting skills.

TABLE 12-1   Fifteen Qualities of Effective Customer Service (Continued)

Customer Service Skill	What It Is	Why It Is Important
Time Management Skills	An understanding of the time demands necessary to effectively handle customer concerns	Not *every* customer concern has an answer, no matter how much time we spend with the customer. Do your best with each customer, but know when to move on to the next one.
Ability to Read Customers	The skills (both in-person and electronic) necessary to understanding the mood of your customer	Both in-person and electronic customer service have subtle clues that tip off a customer's mood state. It is imperative that we pick up on those clues in order to solve the issue in the best possible manner.
A Calming Presence	An external display of peace and composure	Many times, customers just want to have their complaints heard. The ability to remain calm and steady will alleviate many problems before they get out of hand.
Goal-Oriented Focus	The ability to direct the customer service issue toward one of several different organizational goals	While each customer service issue is different, the ability to understand the main idea of the issue and direct it toward an organizational goal increases the likelihood of a mutually beneficial conclusion.
Ability to Handle Surprises	The ability to think on one's feet when the customer service interaction takes an unexpected turn	While a customer service employee is expected to handle many different problems, one cannot prepare for and anticipate every issue. One must understand his or her support structure in order to send the issue to the right person.
Persuasion Skills	The ability to direct customers to your products and services and away from competitors	In some customer service situations, customers are merely curious of what you have to offer. Being able to direct these customers to your products and services will help your organization capture unplanned business in the face of a competitive marketplace.
Tenacity	Sound work ethic combined with a willingness to do what must be done—every time	Being able to put yourself into the customer's shoes will allow you to exhaust all angles so that, in the event that a direct solution is not possible, an amenable solution is possible.
Closing Ability	The ability to conclude a customer service interaction with confirmed satisfaction of all presented issues (not to be confused with the sales term "closing")	Taking the time necessary to ensure that all customer issues have been attended to is vital to continued patronage and customer loyalty. Do not take shortcuts when concluding a customer service interaction.
Willingness to Learn	The desire to use available feedback to make necessary changes that will improve service levels	Mistakes will happen when dealing with customers. Taking those mistakes in stride and learning from them will ensure that similar situations will be dealt with more appropriately next time.

15 qualities that are necessary in making sure the needs and wants of an organization's fan base are attended to.

Combining the skills outlined in Table 12-1 with the personalities of organizational employees is the starting point toward fostering relationships with all of your current and potential customers. According to the work of Gronroos (1990), relationship marketing endeavors "to establish, maintain, enhance, and commercialize customer relationships so that the objectives of the parties involved are met" and is accomplished through "a mutual exchange and fulfillment of promises" (p. 5). No matter the context (e.g., sport spectating, parks and recreation), the sport organization seeks the patronage of its customers and, in return, should provide products and services worthy of that patronage. The important notion to remember here is that relationship building is an ongoing process that goes beyond short-term gain and extends to repeated usage (along with additional potential uses from friends and colleagues) through the continued commitment to understanding the needs and wants of your customers and demonstrating an advancement of those needs and wants.

To establish a relationship with our customers, we must first understand why customers attend our events, facilities, and programs. While many researchers have investigated this issue, Trail and James (2002) identified nine motives that most appropriately encompass why individuals consume sport products and services:

- *Achievement*—A feeling akin to vicarious living whereby the individual feels a sense of accomplishment when his or her team performs well
- *Acquisition of knowledge*—The desire to learn more about the rules, statistics, and players in a particular sport
- *Aesthetics*—The grace and beauty inherent in sports and activities
- *Drama*—An attraction to an event whose outcome is in question until the very end of the contest
- *Escape*—A desire to get away from the normal daily routine and experience something different
- *Family*—A desire to enjoy sport and activity events with loved ones

- *Physical attraction*—The enjoyment derived from watching players who are physically fit and carry some manner of sex appeal
- *Physical skills*—An appreciation for the time and effort necessary to execute high levels of play on a regular basis
- *Social interaction*—The desire to interact with other fans at a sporting event or program

While not an exhaustive list, these nine motives provide sport and recreation managers with a great starting point to begin establishing sound relationships with each of their patrons. It should go without saying that many consumers may embody only one of these motives, while others may be driven to action by several of the motives from the list. Moreover, these nine motives have various levels of spillover into the sport and recreation fields, and it is of utmost importance to get an accurate and up-to-date understanding of where each of your customers stands in order to provide the highest level of service to each of them.

Marketing expert Mari Smith (www.marismith.com) has generated a list of best practices as a measuring stick for organizations of all kinds to gain a better understanding of how in touch they are with their customers and the relationships they have with their customers:

- Conduct regular surveys with your customer database to ensure that you understand the current challenges and needs of your market.
- Integrate customer feedback as much as possible in order to improve your products and services.
- Understand the power of social media (yes, even park and recreation departments should have a social media presence), and maintain active profiles on the major social networking sites.
- Have effective feedback systems in place.
- Use a reliable customer relationship management strategy.

TIP

Use your own sport-spectator experience as a foundation when analyzing your customers.

- Conduct regular training sessions for all members of your staff to ensure that proper customer service practices are being used in every customer encounter.
- Stay on the cutting edge of new technologies in your field.
- Embrace high tech, but *always* maintain "high touch" by personally (not via email, text, or social media message) reaching out to your partners, vendors, and customers.
- Strive for a high customer satisfaction rate.
- Consistently go out of your way to let your customers know how much your organization values them (beyond their financial contributions).

As an organization, the more of these best practices you regularly and effectively integrate, the more likely you will enjoy long-term success in your industry. For purposes of comparison, companies that are very well known for their exceptional customer service are Zappos, Starbucks, Southwest Airlines, and Ford Motor Company. Taking the above information into consideration, it should be more clear that customer service should not be an afterthought, but a proactive strategic management policy to make each customer feel special, accommodated, and taken care of.

Ways to Measure Customer Service and Service Quality

Having an understanding of what customer service is, why fostering relationships with our relevant constituents is important, and which items should

be considered when attending to the needs and wants of your customers, you may be asking yourself how you can assess your organization's level of customer service. Harkening back to the best practices recommended previously, having a realistic and up-to-date assessment of where your organization stands in terms of its customer service is an effective tool toward maintaining your success in the marketplace.

To date, many attempts have been made to explore the concept of service quality in various segments of the sport and leisure industry. Researchers employed one of two tactics: They either modified SERVQUAL to tailor it to the services of the sport industry (Crompton, MacKay, & Fesenmaier, 1991; Howat, Absher, Crilley, & Milne, 1996; Wright, Duray, & Goodale, 1992), or they developed scales based on unique characteristics of specific segments of the sport industry.

There have also been several attempts to measure service quality in the spectator sport setting (Kelly & Turley, 2001; Ko & Pastore, 2005; Theodorakis, Kambitsis, Laios, & Koustelios, 2001). For example, by modifying the five dimensions of SERVQUAL (reliability, assurance, tangibles, empathy, and responsiveness), McDonald, Sutton, and Milne (1995) developed the TEAMQUAL concept. McDonald and colleagues measured the performance of ticket takers, ticket ushers, merchandisers, concessionaires, and customer representatives by assessing both the expectations and perceptions of professional basketball fans. The researchers suggested that overall service quality could be measured by averaging the scores of the five dimensions.

Theodorakis et al. (2001) developed the SPORTSERV scale to assess perceptions of service quality among sport spectators. This scale is composed of the five dimensions of SERVQUAL: tangibles (i.e., cleanliness of the facility), responsiveness (i.e., personnel's willingness to help), access (i.e., accessibility of the stadium), security (i.e., team provides high standards of security during games), and reliability (i.e., team delivers its services as promised). Additionally, Kelley and Turley (2001) developed a nine-factor structure that includes employees, facility access, concessions, fan comfort, game experience, showtime, convenience, price, and smoking.

A more recent scale that measures both core and peripheral product elements is the Scale of Event Quality in Spectator Sports (SEQSS) (Ko, Zhang, Cattani, & Pastore, 2011). Remember that elements of the **core product** are those directly related to the event occurring on/in the field, court, track, or recreation center. These elements, unfortunately, are mostly out of our control. Elements of the **peripheral product**, in contrast, are those that occur in and around the stadium, arena, or recreation center. They are mostly under our control. The following description of this scale includes the scale-specific concepts. Elements that are central are labeled C, and those that are peripheral are labeled P. These elements are of chief importance no matter the sport or leisure context:

- *Game quality* (C) refers to fan perceptions of game performance (e.g., excitement, drama), particularly in regard to the athletes/participants.

core product The main product that is made by the company for the customer (i.e., the sport event or contest).

peripheral product An element of the core product that complements its existence (e.g., concessions, merchandise, dance teams).

- *Augmented service quality* (P) refers to the quality perceptions of the secondary products offered in conjunction with the event (e.g., in-game entertainment, music, concessions).
- *Interaction quality* (P) focuses on how the product or service is delivered. It considers two dynamics:
  - Employee–customer—Perception of how the service is delivered during the service encounter in which the attitude, behavior, and expertise of service personnel are highlighted.
  - Interclient—Perception of how the service is delivered during the service encounter in which the attitude and behavior of other clients are highlighted.
- *Outcome quality* (P) refers to what the consumer receives as a result of this interaction with a sport or leisure organization (e.g., socialization; overall evaluation of experience, which may be tied to the event's outcome; enjoyment).
- *Physical environment quality* (P) refers to perceptions of facility ambience, design features, and quality and use of signage/symbols.

An obvious observation from reviewing these elements of sport and leisure service quality is that there are more peripheral (P) elements in this measurement tool than core (C) elements. Recall that sport and leisure organizations have significantly more control over the peripheral elements than the core elements. While many fans and spectators attend events for the core product, it should be overwhelmingly evident that much of their decision to come to another event is determined by elements well within our control as a sport organization. To reiterate a previous point, this new information should reinforce the necessity to both hire and train your staff (everyone from the general manager or facility owner to the maintenance staff) in a manner that will help your organization stand out from your competition. To quote Booker T. Washington, "Excellence is to do a common thing in an uncommon way." While sport and leisure professionals can do little to help their teams and participants be successful on the field/court/rink, they can certainly go the extra mile for each and every one of their customers in order to make them feel welcome and valued.

TIP

Remember that it is easy to bring fans to your events when your core product is performing well, but attention to detail and sound customer service will manifest themselves when your core product is underperforming.

These varied attempts to accurately measure service quality benefit sport and leisure professionals in that there are many scales available that can help organizations gauge their effectiveness in providing high levels of customer service. It is important to remember that no perfect instrument exists that fully encompasses all of the inherent concepts of service quality. Rather, each organization should attempt to utilize the method most appropriate for the questions it wants to answer.

Outcomes of Service Encounters

Now that there is an understanding of what customer service is, why service quality is of vital importance to sport and leisure organizations, and how to measure service quality encounters, one must understand the outcomes of service quality to have a more complete picture of organizational success. While it can be argued that there are many outcomes in service encounters, this chapter will focus on satisfaction and loyalty. The thrust of this discussion is to use the attendance motivators described previously to elicit productive customer outcomes that will ensure an organization's long-term success. Throughout this section, overlap of concepts will be evident, as many of the same elements that motivate us to attend sport and leisure activities manifest themselves as potential outputs after the service encounter has concluded.

Satisfaction

Beard and Ragheb (1980) define sport and leisure satisfaction as "the positive perceptions or feelings an individual forms, elicits, or gains as a result of engaging in activities of their choosing." Years ago, satisfaction was the primary outcome sought by many sport and leisure organizations as the measuring stick of overall performance. Berry and Parasuraman (1991) suggested that customers evaluate their personal satisfaction in a service encounter by assessing the following five elements (as you read the following elements, compare them to information presented earlier):

- *Reliability*—The ability to perform the promised service dependably and accurately
- *Tangibles*—The appearance of physical facilities, equipment, personnel, and communications materials

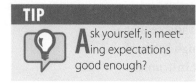

- *Responsiveness*—The willingness to help customers and to provide prompt service
- *Assurance*—The knowledge and courtesy of employees and their ability to convey trust and confidence
- *Empathy*—The provision of caring, individualized attention to customers

While these elements are still relevant in today's service setting, one can see that attending only to these concepts in every service encounter is merely the starting point in striving for viability (where it was the endpoint in prior research). As researchers studied this issue more intently, it was determined that while a general contentment with products and services is important, simply meeting the needs and wants of customers did not necessarily lead to additional uses. While many authors still argue that satisfaction should be a chief goal for a product or service, 60% of consumers who switched to a competitor in the same product category said they were satisfied with the prior product or service (Chitturi, Raghunathan, & Mahajan, 2008). As a result, sport and leisure organizations have looked to grow customer satisfaction into customer loyalty.

Loyalty and Repatronage

In a follow-up study to previous work on the subject, Oliver (1997) suggests that loyalty consists of four stages. The first stage is a cognitive stage, during which information about the product or service is evaluated and may be primarily cost-based. This first stage, while typically low in the spectrum, is vital to moving customers toward deeper levels of loyalty. Efficient informational channels, effective use of social media, and well-trained customer service personnel adept at answering questions will help attract customers to add a product or service to their consideration set. Initial awareness is paramount.

Oliver (1997) describes the next stage of loyalty as an affective stage, a combination of liking the service and experiencing satisfaction. Once adequate information about the product or service is gathered, a trial use typically follows and is used as the basis of comparison between a previously used product or service and this current one. While trial lessons, sample products, and free consultations can mean short-term loss of profits, the time and resources invested to move customers to this stage should go a long way toward establishing a solid relationship with that customer. At this point in the loyalty process, comfortability and familiarity are necessary for a second use (and third and fourth, for that matter).

As loyalty continues to increase, the individual progresses to the third stage, which is conative loyalty (Oliver, 1997). Oliver suggests that this is a behavioral intention stage. Individuals indicate an intention to purchase the product or use the service in the future. Once customers reach this stage, they have a positive level of satisfaction with the product or service, so much so that they are now willing to spend their resources with the organization. Referring back to the skills necessary to thrive in a customer service encounter, the ability to close is one of the more important abilities. Many customers respond to questionnaires that they are willing to purchase a given product or service, but beyond that response, organizations have few ways to know if that intention ever comes to fruition. Knowing that your customers have intent to purchase your product or service combined with a suggested sound customer relations management system and effective trained or inherent closing skills should equate to converting more "intentions" to actual behavior.

According to Oliver (1997), the final and highest stage of loyalty is the action stage. This is where the individual's behavior toward the product is a consistent occurrence or habit. This sequence of quality to satisfaction to loyalty elicits consumption behavior by the individual. The important takeaway from this final stage (as mentioned earlier) is that as more and more outlets compete for the **discretionary income** of today's consumers, converting customers from satisfied to loyal must be an ongoing and evolving process. Sport and leisure professionals must heed the suggestions proposed earlier in this chapter to stay current on what their customers need and want. Once we think we know what our customers need more than they do, we *will* be surpassed by a competitor who better attends to their actual needs and wants. Staying profitable and relevant in today's sport and leisure marketplace takes the diligent work of an entire organization, and once the focus shifts from customer-oriented to outcome-oriented, success will be hard to come by.

discretionary income
Monies left over once all financial obligations have been attended to by an individual or family.

TIP

Remember that it takes hard work to provide excellent customer service, but the work doesn't stop once you've cultivated a good relationship with the customer. You must work to maintain it or another organization will take your customer.

SUMMARY

This chapter has provided insight into the concept of customer service. Customer service is attending to the needs and wants of your customers in a manner that works to solve each issue effectively while preserving the relationship created between the service provider and the individual. A large section of this chapter was dedicated to understanding helpful skills and abilities that current and potential customer service professionals should either possess or develop in order to be effective service providers. Additionally, knowing why our customers attend events gives us an advantage in tailoring aspects of the core and peripheral product to best suit the needs and wants of our customers. Being familiar with alternative ways of measuring service quality will not only set your organization apart from competition, but will also save your organization valuable resources in targeting external firms to provide those services for you. Lastly, understanding primary outcomes of high-quality customer service will help you to go above and beyond with every service encounter so that you keep your current customers coming back (in addition to bringing a friend or two along). While many organizations have turned a blind eye to this vital component of long-term success, more and more sport and leisure companies are beginning to realize that exceptional service quality must be built into the organizational mission and practiced from the top down.

DISCUSSION QUESTIONS

1. Choose a favorite sport or leisure organization. Identify and describe the core and peripheral elements of this organization. Highlight several ways that you can optimize the customer service of each element.
2. Many of the potential measures of service quality were not discussed in detail. Find a measurement tool mentioned in the chapter. Compare and contrast that measurement tool to the SEQSS. Which tool do you think is better for the sport or leisure organization you chose in Question 1?
3. Interview a staff member for a sport or leisure organization in your town. Provide the list of skills mentioned in the chapter to your interviewee. Ask that person to name three of those skills that he or she currently possesses and three that he or she has had to work to develop.
4. Refer to the list of motivators described in the chapter. Which of those motivators is most important to you and why? Ask a couple classmates the same question. Were your responses similar to your classmates' or different? Why do you think that is?
5. Think about a sport or leisure event you have recently attended. Using the elements of the SEQSS, assess that event and evaluate your level of satisfaction and loyalty. Would you go back? Why or why not?

Case **STUDY**

Analyzing Sport Organization Websites as Extensions of Customer Service

As a way to extend themselves to their fans, sport organizations have embraced the Internet and its wide-ranging power to deliver information and interactive content to those who follow them. Sport organization websites are often their window to the public. These websites contain information about the team, its schedule, various team and league initiatives, and fan-specific information such as promotions and giveaways, among other items. A poorly designed website can sometimes be the difference between patronage and spending one's money elsewhere—in the same way that a poor interaction with a customer service representative can turn an individual away from a company. Because many sport fans cannot directly interact with their favorite sports team and their personnel, these websites are typically the best way to gather important information in a one-stop-shop setting. What basic information do you think should be included within an organizational website in order to satisfy a customer looking for information?

Before you begin, take some time to analyze the websites of the St. Louis Cardinals of Major League Baseball and the Gateway Grizzlies of the independent Frontier League. While exploring these websites, take special note of elements attributable to the core product and the peripheral product. What are the pros and cons of each website? Does one seem better prepared than the other, or are they relatively equal? Assuming the website is your only way to engage with the team, what are some elements contained within the websites to give you a realistic understanding of what you will encounter once you arrive at the respective stadiums? Do the websites offer the ability to communicate with a customer service representative? If so, what platform(s) do they offer?

Once you have taken some time to arrange your notes, refer to the information regarding the SEQSS (game quality, augmented services, interaction quality, outcome quality, and physical environment quality). How well do the two highlighted websites measure up to the SEQSS? Are any elements of the measurement tool difficult to assess based on the remote nature of the organizational website? Does there need to be a web-specific tool to help measure the customer service efforts of sport organizations? How would you revise the SEQSS to better assess sport websites for their customer service qualities?

Once you have analyzed the websites with the SEQSS, answer the following questions:

1. What recommendations would you deliver to the Cardinals and Grizzlies to help improve their website customer service?
2. Should teams even worry about how complete (or incomplete) their websites are?
3. Upon making your recommendations, how would you convince these teams (the "so-what?!" factor) that website customer service is integral to their business operations?

REFERENCES

Anderson, E. W., Fornell, C., & Lehmann, D. R. (1994). Customer satisfaction, market share, and profitability: Findings from Sweden. *Journal of Marketing*, *58*(3), 53–66.

Anderson, E. W., & Sullivan, M. (1993). The antecedents and consequences of customer satisfaction for firms. *Marketing Science*, *12*, 125–143.

Beard, J., & Ragheb, M. (1980). Measuring leisure satisfaction. *Journal of Leisure Research*, *12*(1), 20–33.

Berry, L., & Parasuraman, A. (1991). *Marketing services: Competing through quality*. New York, NY: Free Press.

Chitturi, R., Raghunathan, R., & Mahajan, V. (2008). Delight by design: The role of hedonic versus utilitarian benefits. *Journal of Marketing*, *72*, 48–63.

Crompton, J. L., MacKay, K. J., & Fesenmaier, D. R. (1991). Identifying dimensions of service quality in public recreation. *Journal of Park and Recreation Administration*, *9*, 15–27.

Dagger, T. S., & Sweeney, J. C. (2007). Service quality attribute weights: How do novice and longer-term customers construct service quality performance? *Journal of Service Research*, *10*(1), 22–42.

Fornell, C. (1992). A national customer satisfaction barometer: The Swedish experience. *Journal of Marketing*, *56*(1), 6–21.

Gronroos, C. (1990). Relationship approach to marketing in service contexts: The marketing and organizational behavior interface. *Journal of Business Research*, *20*(1), 3–11.

Howard, D. R., & Crompton, J. L. (2004). *Financing sport* (2nd ed.). Morgantown, WV: Fitness Information Technology.

Howat, G., Absher, J., Crilley, G., & Milne, I. (1996). Measuring customer service quality in sports and leisure centers. *Managing Leisure*, *1*, 77–89.

Kelly, S. W., & Turley, L. W. (2001). Consumer perceptions of service quality attributes at sporting events. *Journal of Business Research*, *54*, 161–166.

Ko, Y. J., & Pastore, D. L. (2005). A hierarchical model of service quality for the recreational sport industry. *Sport Marketing Quarterly*, *14*(2), 84–97.

Ko, Y. J., Zhang, J., Cattani, K. P., & Pastore, D. (2011). Assessment of event quality in major spectator sports. *Managing Service Quality*, *21*(3), 304–322.

McDonald, M., Sutton, W., & Milne, G. (1995). Measuring service quality in professional team sports. *Sport Marketing Quarterly*, *4*(2), 9–16.

Oliver, R. L (1997). *Satisfaction: A behavioral perspective on the consumer*. New York, NY: McGraw-Hill Companies.

Theodorakis, N., Kambitsis, C., Laios, A., & Koustelios, A. (2001). Relationship between measures of service quality and satisfaction of spectators in professional sport. *Managing Service Quality*, *11*(6), 431–438.

Trail, G., & James, J. (2002). The motivation scale for sport consumption: Assessment of the scale's psychometric properties. *Journal of Sport Behavior*, *24*(1), 108.

Turban, E., Lee, J. K., King, D., & Chung, H. M. (2002). *Electronic commerce: A managerial perspective*. Upper Saddle River, NJ: Prentice Hall.

Wright, B., Duray, N., & Goodale, T. (1992). Assessing perceptions of recreation center service quality: An application of recent advancements in service quality research. *Journal of Park and Recreation Administration, 10*(3), 33–47.

Wysong, S., Rothschild, P., & Beldona, S. (2011). Receiving a standing ovation for the event: A comprehensive model for measuring fan satisfaction with sports and entertainment events. *International Journal of Event Management Research, 6*(1), 1–9.

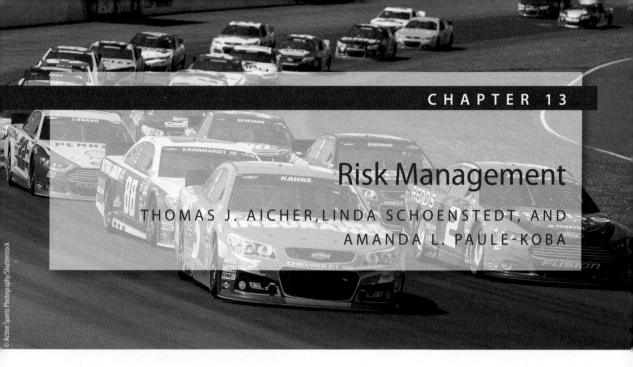

CHAPTER 13

Risk Management

THOMAS J. AICHER, LINDA SCHOENSTEDT, AND
AMANDA L. PAULE-KOBA

CHAPTER OBJECTIVES

Upon completion of this chapter, the reader will be able to:

1. Define risk and risk management
2. Outline key risk issues and types of risk
3. Identify concrete methods for minimizing risk
4. Apply risk reduction techniques elucidated in this chapter

CHAPTER OVERVIEW

Implementing a comprehensive risk management plan is vital to a facility and/or event. In today's litigious society, understanding how to mitigate financial loss and negligence should be front and center in minimizing risk and potential lawsuits. The growth of new and renovated sport facilities and the creation of diverse events has made this area of the industry much more difficult for managers.

Industry VOICE

Michael Muñoz—President, Muñoz Agency

After earning my bachelor's degree from the University of Tennessee, while playing collegiate football for the Volunteers, I earned by master of business administration degree from Miami University. I went on to work for Proctor and Gamble's healthcare and female beauty divisions, eventually taking what I learned there to create my own agency.

The Muñoz Agency, based in Cincinnati, Ohio, is a full-service marketing agency. As our website says, we are "driven to inspire organizations to pursue the hearts of their consumers. In close partnership with our clients, our team will utilize our idea process to empower organizations to truly capture the loyalty of their consumers in a meaningful way" (www.munozagency.com/index.html).

Along my path from student to Proctor and Gamble employee (where I served in multiple roles) to president of my own agency, I tried to be very strategic in each position I took. Each different area I worked in allowed me to develop a different skill, including public speaking, marketing, leadership, and business analytical skills. This variety made me more well rounded and prepared for the work I currently do at the Muñoz Agency.

One of the biggest initiatives that the Muñoz Agency is currently working on is our NFL PLAY 60 Character Camps. The National Football League's (NFL) youth campaign, PLAY 60, encourages children to get outside and be active for 60 minutes a day in order to reverse childhood obesity. The problem is that while the PLAY 60 program has been successful, it has not reached the Hispanic consumer. We are using our knowledge in developing events and have joined with the NFL to create PLAY 60

Character Camps in handpicked NFL cities. These camps are 2-day events in which the Muñoz Agency team works along with the NFL teams to reach the Hispanic youth in their market. The character camps initially took place in 6 cities in 2012 and increased to 14 cities in 2013.

During these PLAY 60 Character Camps, the Muñoz Agency goes into the team's facility to execute the camp. We do not have extensive knowledge of the facility layout, security, and so forth. However, we are still responsible for keeping the children who are attending the camp safe. Thus, the Muñoz Agency team works with the NFL team to make sure there is a solid risk management plan in place. We communicate what we expect from each NFL team and let them know that what we are asking of them is being asked of each team that is holding one of the Character Camps. This helps each team buy in to what is needed and work to ensure a safe environment for all.

To execute these camps, we have a very large intern program. When looking for an intern, we look for someone who is proactive, can embrace change, has experience making unique contributions in the workplace, and is a natural leader. One of the most important things a potential intern can have is good verbal and written interpersonal communication skills. Being able to express oneself both verbally and in writing is essential and can quickly eliminate individuals from moving further in their internship interview process. The Muñoz Agency does a lot of work on the phone, so potential interns must be able to represent themselves and the agency well over the phone.

In terms of risk management at the camps, we acknowledge that every camp will have its own barriers and risks that have to be dealt with. This is why when the Muñoz Agency staff looks for interns, we look for individuals who are able to embrace change and can handle conflict. Having good people in place can help mitigate risk. It is also necessary to convey clear expectations to the interns so they understand their role and what is required of them in order to help ensure a safe event.

Although there is only so much time for undergraduate students to develop their resume while in college, it is crucial that students start gaining industry experience. This will give potential employers confidence that the student is ready to jump right into work and there will not be a ramp-up period. Again, there is no substitute for experience, so students must be willing to take advantage of the opportunities in front of them and also work to create their own opportunities.

Introduction

Facility and event managers must be mindful of the need to mitigate negligence insofar that spectators and participants are protected under the law. They have a duty to act reasonably and prudently in situations involving their spectators and participants. Having knowledge and training in what constitutes duty, breach of duty, proximate causes of injuries, and the injury itself is critical in determining the liability for a facility or event. Since the enactment of the Tort Claims Act, persons engaging in activities involving personal risk have had increasingly greater expectations concerning their safety and are litigating in increasing numbers (Pyles & Pyles, 1992).

Litigation resulting from personal injury or financial loss is at an all-time high. Lawsuits have risen, especially since 2008, when the U.S. recession began. In a struggling economy, sport managers should expect that even the smallest incident may result in a lawsuit (Cunningham, 2010). Facility and event managers should have a heightened sense of responsibility and employ the appropriate checks and balances to help ensure a safe and successful result for their respective organizations. Consequently, it is important to develop a strong understanding of the different types of risk and the best strategies for minimizing the impact of the risk. One thing is certain and important to realize, eliminating risk completely is extremely difficult even under the best circumstance. Reduction of the likelihood of an occurrence, however, can be achieved with proper training, supervision, and action plans.

What Is Risk?

The challenge of defining **risk** is that individuals subjectively categorize different behaviors and actions as risk. For example, one cyclist in a riding group

risk The probability that a hazard will lead to a loss.

may see a descent as an opportunity to increase her speed above 40 miles per hour, while another cyclist may proceed with great caution because he is worried about the potential of potholes, animals, or other road debris that may cause him to crash. For facility and event managers, the same differences in perception are at work; thus we have evaluated broader definitions to capture the different levels of risk. Van der Smissen (1990) defines risk as an uncertainty or chance of loss, usually accidental loss, which is sudden, unusual, or unforeseen. Giddens (1988) defines risk as "dangers that we seek to actively identify, confront, and control" (p. 23). Finally, Griffith (2011) states that risk is "the probability that a hazard will lead to a loss" (p. 1), which is the definition we consider most applicable to sport facility and event management. The broadness of the term allows it to apply to any component of the facility or event that could engender a loss or negative outcome for the managers. Moreover, the term implies there are varying degrees to both hazards and losses, which in the subsequent sections of this chapter should become clear.

Types of Risk

Given the various types of facilities and events, it is nearly impossible to generate a complete list of the types of risks facility and event managers may face. Rushing and Miller (2009) outline four broad categories of risk: public liability caused by negligence, public liability excluding negligence, business operations, and property exposures. Public liability caused by negligence occurs when the facility or event manager fails to provide a reasonably safe environment for individuals to work, spectate, or participate in the sporting activity. Ensuring a safe environment may include providing proper warning signs, supervision, security, equipment, facilities, medical/emergency care, and travel/transportation (Rushing & Miller, 2009). Public liability excluding negligence occurs when individuals are affected by the practices of the personnel within the facility. For example, claims may include discrimination, sexual harassment, wrongful termination, invasion of privacy, or false imprisonment (Rushing & Miller, 2009). Risk associated with business operations includes business interruptions, property loss, contractual issues, or employee health. Finally, natural disasters, fire, vandalism/terrorism, and theft comprise property exposure risks.

Facility and event managers tend to primarily focus on the risk associated with bodily injury to the spectators and/or participants. These risks can include slips and falls, injuries during participation, or altercations between spectators. However, risk may also include inadequate waivers of responsibility forms, lack of appropriate insurance, incomplete training or supervision of employees and participants, weather-related risks, and others, as outlined in **Table 13-1**.

Terrorism and Sport

A more recent risk development in sport event and facility management has been the threat or the occurrence of terrorist activity. The attacks on the World Trade Center in 2001 impacted the sport industry in terms of how facility and event managers perceived terrorist threats on their facilities and events. Most individuals recognize only the 1972 Munich Olympic Games terrorist attack and the 1996 Centennial Olympic Park bombing in Atlanta, Georgia, as occurrences of terrorist activity at sporting events. However, as Toohey (2008) points out, there were 168 sport-related terrorist attacks in

TABLE 13-1 Broad Categories of Risk

Human Risks	Facility Risks	Environmental Risks
• Sport participation	• Accreditation	• Legal issues
• Spectators	• Facility/equipment/ property	• Economic circumstances
• Terrorism	• Employment/training	• Political circumstances
• Athlete protection	• Storage	• Management activities/ controls
• Loss prevention	• Transportation	
	• Safety/security	

TIP

For those unfamiliar with the attack that occurred during the 1972 Munich Olympic Games, the documentary *One Day in September* is a highly acclaimed depiction of those tragic events.

the world between 1972 and 2004, with no signs of abatement. To underline the growing concerns for risk at various venues, Toohey (2008) also notes that sport is a platform where many spectators and participants are aggregated in one place with numerous opportunities and methods of potential attack. The bombing during the Boston Marathon in 2013 highlighted the challenge of policing such large areas, especially when crowds enter and exit from a variety of points.

Following the bombings in Boston, other marathons changed their security procedures. For instance, the Chicago Marathon now limits runners to entering through four distinct checkpoints. Additionally, each runner must collect his or her own bib and timing chip at the exposition. Previously, friends or family members were allowed to pick up these items for others. Runners are also restricted to using a race-issued clear plastic bag for gear check. One of the final changes involves family members and/or friends congregating at the start and finish lines. For the first time, spectators who want to meet their friends or family members who participated in the marathon are required to go through one of two security checkpoints.

Similarly, venues and closed events (i.e., confined areas with few points of entry) have made several adjustments over the years to deal

VIGNETTE 13-1

Boston Marathon Tragedy Changes Risk Management Strategies

On April 15, 2013, the bombings at the Boston Marathon, which killed 3 individuals and wounded 264 others, brought the need for risk management and security to the forefront of event managers' minds. This was the largest mass-casualty attack on U.S. soil since September 11, 2001.

This attack marked changes to security at the Boston Marathon and marathons across the country. The Boston Athletic Association has decided that runners cannot have backpacks or bags at or near the start or finish lines or along the course. Bags are also not allowed on the buses that run between the start and finish lines. Runners are allowed to bring a change of clothing and shoes in designated clear plastic bags and leave them in Boston Common, which is approximately a half mile from the finish area, prior to the race.

Additional security measures for the Boston Marathon include an increase in uniformed and plain-clothes police officers and additional bomb-sniffing dogs. There are additional security procedures in place that the marathon director and security personnel are reluctant to disclose.

with the potential threat of terrorist activity. For instance, it is commonplace for facility and event managers to search backpacks and purses upon entry to the facility, ask spectators to walk through metal detectors or use the metal detecting wands to ensure no weapons are being brought onto the site, and disallow hazards such as bottles or solid trash that can be thrown and cause injury or potentially contain explosive material. The National Football League has implemented a policy stating that only clear or see-through bags are allowed into the stadium in order to ensure safety and expedite fan entry into the stadium.

© Julien_N/Shutterstock

Facilities have also invested millions of dollars in surveillance equipment to increase the security of their stadiums (Carey, 2011). For instance, they have installed security cameras that can zoom in on any seat in the stadium, as well as video equipment to record for later review. The two serve both as a method of monitoring spectator activity and as a deterrent for much lower forms of crime. Some major events have utilized dirty bomb detectors, while others sample the air quality to identify any potential contaminants in the air designed for a terrorist attack. In the case of Super Bowl XLV, hosted in Dallas, Texas, a drone was used to patrol the airfield above the facility to ensure it was safe from attack and could retaliate if needed. These strategies to reduce the likelihood of a terrorist attack begin to highlight how organizations may manage their risk.

What Is Risk Management?

To overcome the potential problems associated with risks, sport facilities and events should establish a sound framework to minimize the potential and severity of the risk, a process known as **risk management**. Risk management has been defined as "systematically identifying threats (risks) to your organization and developing ways to minimize them from

risk management A sound framework to minimize the potential and severity of the risk.

occurring" (Office of Sport and Recreation, 2009, p. 2-1). Taylor and Booty (2006) state that risk management strategy "provides a framework for determining an individual company's response to risk, including who would undertake the work involved at a tactical level" (p. 232). This means facility and event managers should develop a standard set of policies, procedures, and processes so that employees, volunteers, and other stakeholders know how to best minimize the various risks associated with hosting the event.

To create a strong risk management plan, facility and event managers should include what may be "foreseeable." The broad range of concerns requires one to be a forward thinker, crisis manager, and problem solver in order to provide the protections and enjoyment fans, spectators, and participants have come to expect.

What Are the Benefits of Good Risk Management?

The value of a good risk management plan cannot be understated as it brings considerable value to facility or event owners. Proper risk management can reduce the likelihood of undesirable and costly impacts, increase the safety of the patrons, and improve financial issues more generally (Sawyer & Smith, 1999). For example, a softball tournament organizer would want to ensure that the backstop, which prevents foul balls from flying into the stands, is in proper condition. If not, a foul ball that travels through the backstop could potentially injure one of the spectators and lead to an expensive lawsuit and healthcare claim, resulting in a major loss for the facility manager/owner.

A quality risk management program may also reduce costs associated with insurance premiums (Viney, 1999). Similar to driver's insurance, the longer a facility or event demonstrates a quality safety record, the less the insurance premium costs. Risk management may also improve the quality of the sporting experience the event offers (Viney, 1999). In the era of the mud, obstacle, and beer runs, these organizers go to considerable lengths to ensure the safety of their participants, which leads to greater levels of satisfaction. The measures facility and event managers take to ensure the safety of the participants and spectators will likely enhance the visibility and image of the organization as individuals learn about the quality of service that the organization provides. Finally, risk management will enhance the managers', employees', and volunteers' level of confidence in their abilities, which will lead to better strategic outcomes for the organization (Viney, 1999).

Steps in the Risk Management Process

The idea of managing risk is imperative both for hallmark and mega-events and for small-scale events on either a global or local level. Many of the elements to consider are similar but will differ when considering the size and scope of an organization's objective. As previously highlighted, the numerous types of events inherently create a limitless number of risks because they vary in size, structure, operation, sport, and countless other aspects.

RISK IDENTIFICATION

Properly identifying risks associated with the facility or event requires a mix of knowledge, experience, and critical thinking. At this stage, facility and event managers should evaluate the environment, structures, and marketplace to determine the sources of risk associated with the previously described areas. When managers lack experience or knowledge, there are several resources they can use to assist with **risk identification**. First, the local, state, or national sporting organization may be able to provide them with the typical risks associated with the event they are planning to host. For example, if an event manager is working with the local sports commission to host her first weight-lifting competition, it would be important to meet with the local- and state-level clubs to determine the various risks associated with participation. Additionally, the event manager may seek counsel from event organizations that have hosted similar events. Their knowledge and expertise in the area will likely be invaluable to identifying areas of risk that are not as obvious. Finally, some national governing organizations provide audits or checklists associated with hosting sport events. An audit is a systematic critical examination of the facility or event to identify key risk (related to organizational risks) or safety issues (related to injury risks).

risk identification
Evaluation of the environment, structures, and marketplace to determine the sources of risk associated with the sport facility or event.

VIGNETTE 13-2

Tragedy Without a Plan: Pocono Raceway

In the case of the Pocono Raceway tragedy in August of 2012, NASCAR (National Association for Stock Car Auto Racing) was holding a Sprint Cup race at the 2.5-mile track in Long Pond, Pennsylvania, when a lightning storm hit the area. Reportedly, NASCAR and track officials did not heed the warnings they received from a local meteorologist to suspend the race because of a severe storm moving into the area. This lack of response led to fans scrambling for shelter as the storm was upon them. During the storm, a 41-year-old man was killed and nine other people were injured from lightning strikes, which likely could have been prevented. NASCAR might have avoided this tragedy by having a set policy or standard operating procedure for handling severe weather during a race, complete with a timeline of when to cancel/suspend the race and let spectators know to retreat to safety. Another precaution would have been setting a radius for when lightning is too close, similar to the policies developed for National Collegiate Athletic Association events.

RISK ANALYSIS

risk analysis Categorization of the levels of risks based on the severity and likelihood of occurrence.

Once facility and event managers identify the sources of risk that can impact either the facility or event, the next step in the process is to categorize the levels of risks, a process known as **risk analysis**. Most facility and event managers categorize risk using two questions: How likely is the risk to occur, and what are the consequences associated with the risk? **Figure 13-1** provides a matrix to assist with the categorization process.

Simple Risk Matrix

Likelihood	Consequences		
	Minor	Moderate	Major
Likely			
Possible			
Unlikely			

Risk Treatment Key

Intolerable Risk Level Immediate action required.
Tolerable Risk Level Risks must be reduced so far as is practicable.
Broadly Acceptable Risk Level Monitor and further reduce where practicable.

FIGURE 13-1   Risk assessment matrix

	Consequences		
Likelihood	Minor	Moderate	Major/Catastrophic
Likely	**Kids sneak in without paying**	Injury from unruly fans throwing debris	None
Possible	Slip and fall on wet bleachers or ice	**Hypo- or hyperthermia from severe weather temperatures**	Player suffers severe life-threatening injury from tackle
Unlikely	Food poisoning from concession stand due to improper refrigeration	Camera and speakers are stolen after game	**Spectator has fatal cardiac arrest** **Bomb threat**

FIGURE 13-2   Example of a risk matrix chart for a high school football game. Orange text indicates intolerable risk level, purple text indicates tolerable risk level, and green text indicates broadly acceptable risk level.

The risk matrix gives a visual representation of what could happen, how serious the incident could be, and the frequency of a potential occurrence. The likelihood of an occurrence is shown in relation to the consequences of the occurrence. Analyzing the risks developed in the first stage enables facility and event managers to begin to determine which risks need further evaluation. **Figure 13-2** provides an example of a completed matrix. While the list of risks is not exhaustive for a high school football game, it does illustrate the types of risks associated with events and the level of frequency and impact associated with them.

RISK EVALUATION

Once the risk analysis is completed, the next step is to determine whether the risk is acceptable or not, a process known as **risk evaluation**. To answer this

risk evaluation A process of determining the acceptability of the risk through a cost–benefit analysis.

question, the organization should evaluate the mission and vision of the organization and the risk matrix to indicate whether the risk is worth the costs associated with minimizing it. Using a financial term, facility and event owners would evaluate the risk using a cost–benefit analysis. For instance, the addition of alcohol to an event may improve overall sales and possibly atmosphere; however, it will also increase the level of insurance required and additional security and permits to be able to sell alcohol. In this event, the increase in sales volume may not be worth the additional expenses incurred, and therefore, the event or facility manager may choose not to have alcohol at the event.

RISK TREATMENT

risk treatment A method of managing risk that involves minimizing the impact and/or occurrence of the risk.

Once the risks for a particular event are identified and the risk matrix considered, facility and event managers must decide how they should handle the potential risks or which method of **risk treatment** they will use. Within the sport event context, there are five common strategies facility and event owners use to minimize the impact of risk: avoidance, acceptance and financing, reduction through proactive measures, transfer, and retention.

risk avoidance A method of managing risk that involves discontinuing the component of the activity considered to be a risk.

Risk avoidance occurs when managers establish the risk as both a major risk and nonessential to the mission of the organization and, therefore, discontinue the component of the activity considered to be a risk (Rushing & Miller, 2009). The avoidance strategy is used when the likelihood of injury is high and happens fairly frequently. For example, Florida has the highest incidence of lightning strikes and frequent storms. School administrators and managers should postpone, reschedule, or cancel outdoor games and events for the safety of everyone involved when the threat of severe weather has moved into the area. At times, risks associated with sport event participants and spectators are unavoidable. As a result, facility and event managers must implement one of the following strategies.

risk acceptance A method of managing risk that involves preparing for the risk through budgeting, deductibles, or self-insurance.

Preparing for the risk through budgeting or establishing deductibles or self-insurance is considered acceptance and financing, or **risk acceptance**. In this scenario, the facility or event managers absorb all of the liability and financial responsibility for anything that might happen regarding the participants, stakeholders, and facility. The operating budget of the event and venue should include provisions for possible injuries and damage in the unlikely event of an occurrence. When accepting the risk, the sport manager is assuming the risk and potential need to pay small settlements, as in the case of injury or repairs if fans or participants damage equipment. The manager may also be absorbing the expense of small medical bills, emergency personnel, and sports medicine clinicians because the calculations for risk frequency and severity are low.

When the risk is unavoidable and greater than an acceptable level, facility and event owners may employ **risk reduction through proactive measures** by establishing a series of controls to reduce either the likelihood of occurrence or the consequences associated with the risk. One method of control is to establish a set of standardized practices for employees and volunteers to follow, or a standard operating procedure (SOP) manual. The importance of practicing the protocols in the SOP manual, as well as continued training and updates for employees and volunteers as new potential risks are identified, cannot be underestimated. Clearly, one cannot predict everything that could possible happen during an event, and thus the SOP manual provides employees a series of guidelines to use as a method to deal with various issues. Employee manuals may also be helpful for delineating some specific guidelines that have been identified as critical, such as weather-related emergency protocols, communication procedures, and injury or illness strategies. Training and practice scenarios should be required of all staff and conducted on a regular basis. First aid, cardiopulmonary resuscitation (CPR), and automated external defibrillator (AED) training and certification should be provided and encouraged in light of new legislation in many states requiring these safety measures to be in place at facilities and venues.

Risk transfer consists of moving the risk to another entity. There are two commonly used methods to transfer risk: insurance and waiver of liability. The use of insurance or an insurance policy covers the potential monetary or financial losses considered too large for the facility or event managers to handle independently. By taking out insurance, facility and event managers opt to pay a premium or dollar amount to have these losses covered in the event of a lawsuit due to injury, a financial loss due to unexpected low attendance, a contract violation, and other developments. Similar to personal auto coverage, amounts may depend upon the inherent or obvious risks identified, the level of the liability limits, the amount of the deductible, and the safety record. Limited-liability coverage is the total amount of coverage

risk reduction through proactive measures A method of managing risk that involves establishing a series of controls to reduce either the likelihood of occurrence or the consequences associated with the risk.

risk transfer A method of managing risk that involves moving the risk to another entity.

available to the facility or event for general claims against the organization. Amounts vary based on the event as well as the location of the event. The laws vary from state to state in terms of the minimum liability coverage that facility and events owners should possess. Deductibles are the amount of money paid when a claim is made. Typically, the larger the deductible, the smaller the premium. A high deductible may be a wise decision for the organization in terms of the upfront costs to host the event; however, the deductible costs should be built into the operating budget. See **Table 13-2** for commonly used insurance coverages.

The second common form of transferring risk is the waiver of liability. Many facility and event managers will require participants, and potentially spectators, to sign a waiver that limits or eliminates liability in the event of

TABLE 13-2   Common Types of Insurance Coverage for Events

Insurance	Description
Accidental medical	Covers medical expenses incurred as a result of an injury while participating in an insured activity
Accidental death and dismemberment	Covers accidental death or the loss of limb or limbs as a result of participation
Blanket coverage	Insures property under a single amount applying to several different pieces of property
Business income/ interruption	Covers loss of income in case the insured's business is shut down by a covered loss
Causality/liability insurance	Is primarily concerned with the legal liability for losses caused by injury to persons or damage to property of others
Event cancellation insurance	Protects against loss due to rain, hail, snow, or sleet, which causes cancellation or reduced earnings of an outdoor event
General liability insurance	Covers professional and commercial risks; broad term meaning liability insurance other than automobile liability or employer's liability
Liquor liability	Provides coverage for bodily injury or property damage for which you may be held liable by reason of alcohol consumption
Umbrella coverage	Provides coverage over a single underlying policy, or several different underlying policies

In consideration of being allowed to participate in any way in the [Organization Name] athletic sports program, related events, and activities, the undersigned acknowledges, appreciates, and agrees that:

1. The risk of injury from the activities involved in this program is significant, including the potential for permanent paralysis and death, and while particular rules, equipment, and personal discipline may reduce this risk, the risk of serious injury does exist; and,
2. I KNOWINGLY AND FREELY ASSUME ALL SUCH RISKS, both known and unknown, EVEN IF ARISING FROM THE NEGLIGENCE OF THE RELEASEES or others, and assume full responsibility for my participation; and,
3. I willingly agree to comply with the stated and customary terms and conditions for participation. If, however, I observe any unusual significant hazard during my presence or participation, I will remove myself from participation and bring such to the attention of the nearest official immediately; and,
4. I, for myself and on behalf of my heirs, assignees, personal representatives, and next of kin, HEREBY RELEASE AND HOLD HARMLESS [Organization Name], their officers, officials, agents, and/or employees, other participants, sponsoring agencies, sponsors, advertisers, and if applicable, owners and lessors of premises used to conduct the event ("RELEASEES"), WITH RESPECT TO ANY AND ALL INJURY, DISABILITY, DEATH, or loss or damage to person or property, WHETHER ARISING FROM THE NEGLIGENCE OF THE RELEASEES OR OTHERWISE, to the fullest extent permitted by law.

I HAVE READ THIS RELEASE OF LIABILITY AND ASSUMPTION OF RISK AGREEMENT, FULLY UNDERSTAND ITS TERMS, UNDERSTAND THAT I HAVE GIVEN UP SUBSTANTIAL RIGHTS BY SIGNING IT, AND SIGN IT FREELY AND VOLUNTARILY WITHOUT ANY INDUCEMENT.

_____DATE

SIGNED:_____ (participant's signature)

FIGURE 13-3   Example of a waiver release form

an injury (see **Figure 13-3**). These waivers of liability typically require participants to comply with the rules and behaviors expected in order to participate. For example, a waiver may indicate that the event is not responsible for injuries that occur if the participant violates a written rule set forth by the event or facility. Many spectator events have disclaimers written on the backs of tickets they purchase, as well as posted signs of warnings or rules for behaviors.

As with insurance, the laws vary from state to state; thus, it is important to understand the laws within your facility's or event's state. In most cases, if the event or facility provides the participant with a safe environment with proper medical personnel present, then the waiver will hold up. All events and facilities are required to provide a standard of reasonable care to their participants and spectators, but accidents do happen. In an incident in 2011 at a Texas Rangers baseball game, a 39-year-old fan fell over a railing 20 feet to his death while trying to catch a ball thrown by Josh Hamilton for his son. Even though Rangers Ballpark in Arlington (now called Globe Life Park) exceeded the building code for railing height at the park, management has decided to raise the rails in front of the seating areas; to post new signs reminding fans not to lean on, sit on, or stand by the rails; and to make a verbal warning through a public address announcement at the beginning of all games.

risk retention A method of managing risk in which the organization does not employ any risk management strategies.

The final method for managing risk occurs when the organization does not employ any of the preceding strategies. Rather, the facility or event manager has adopted **risk retention** because the likelihood of occurrence is extremely low and/or one of the treatment strategies would compromise the objectives of the event. For example, an event organizer hosting a tennis tournament at one of the local parks may list a tornado as a possible risk; however, because the likelihood of severe weather is minimal that time of year, the event owner would decide not to take out various forms of insurance or include management strategies in the SOP manual. Frequently, it is not the case that treating the risk impacts the objectives of the event, and therefore, some form of planning to manage the risk should occur.

RISK MONITORING

risk monitoring The continuous assessment of the risk associated with facilities and events, as well as the management strategies to reduce those risks.

The last step in the risk management process should not be viewed as a final step, but rather as a continuous assessment of the risk associated with hosting the event, as well as the management strategies to reduce the risks (Westerbeek et al., 2006). **Risk monitoring** occurs throughout the entire planning, implementation, and evaluation stages of the event process; however, most view it as a component of the evaluation stage. It is important to review the procedures and policies set in place during each stage of the event to ensure they are well designed to minimize the level of risk associated with hosting the various events.

During the event implementation stage, for instance, facility and event managers would monitor the activities associated with the various risks they have identified, such as the communication of risk, the occurrence of risk, and the overall response to the risks that occur. Monitoring the risk at the implementation stage may allow for facility and event managers to make adjustments to the policies and procedures designed during the planning stage. For example, a local facility is hosting an upcoming soccer tournament featuring children 12 to 18 years old. Initially, the field surface was sound, so they planned for the minimal amount of injury risk associated with typical soccer play. However, the night before the tournament, a heavy rainstorm moved through the area, which caused significant wear to the field. The additional stress on the fields may increase the chance of risk because of the unevenness created from use on the wet surface. Therefore, the tournament director and facility manager determine a method to rotate the fields throughout the day so that the facility manager may level the field surface after each use.

Tracking the performance of and evaluating your risk management plan will allow for better training of employees, identification of gaps within your SOP manual, and further development of proper reporting systems. Common monitoring strategies at the evaluation stage of the event include the following:

- Documenting occurrences and updating the risk management plan as necessary
- Reviewing the occurrences of incidents and the consequences associated with them
- Reviewing unexpected occurrences and developing a plan to mitigate or manage them in the future
- Gathering information from managers, employees, and volunteers to determine any other risk management issues (Sport New Zealand, 2014)

In addition to these activities, it is important to gather information from other stakeholders associated with the event. For instance, participants and spectators may have identified areas of risk associated with their own or others' behavior on the field of play or in the audience. Other stakeholders with information pertaining to the facility or event may include city officials, media, sponsors, and contractors, all of whom may have perceived differing levels of risk associated with the facility or event.

A final strategy to monitor risk would be to employ a risk manager. This is a very important hiring decision because the risk manager should possess excellent organizational and follow-up skills. The risk manager will develop and maintain the facility and employee policy manual, provide training and practice for any certifications, educate in the areas of communication and procedures, and, ultimately, be responsible for running a first-rate facility and/or event. It may also be necessary for the risk manager to develop a facility maintenance schedule, update insurance requirements, communicate with all stakeholders current status reports, and retain legal counsel to review contracts, potential lawsuits or settlements, and changes in negligence and premises liability laws.

SUMMARY

As competition for additional participants and spectators increases, so does the responsibility for running facilities and events that everyone takes pride in. Employees should be invested as much as possible in the desire to produce the best events in safe, well-maintained facilities that are managed by a strong and motivated sport manager.

While not every risk or accident can be predicted, evaluating the risk management plan in view of occurrences at other facilities as well as one's own can help prevent liability and negligence from happening. A good rule of thumb is to critically think about worst-case scenarios and what can be done to prevent them. The sport manager is responsible for identifying potential risks and then eliminating or reducing these risks.

DISCUSSION QUESTIONS

1. Define risk and risk management, and explain the importance of a good risk management program for a facility or event.
2. What role have terrorism and other attacks had on risk management and sport events?
3. Define and differentiate the strategies associated with treating risk.
4. Outline and explain the strategies a facility or event manager can use to monitor risk management policies and procedures.
5. Identify a sport event or facility and use the steps in the risk management process to explain how this event/facility manages risk.

Case **STUDY**

Tough Mudder Death

The Tough Mudder describes itself as "a 10–12 mile (18–20 km) obstacle course designed to test all-around strength, stamina, teamwork, and mental grit. Tough Mudder is Probably the Toughest Event on the Planet. Probably" (Tough Mudder, n.d., para. 1). According to their website, "for a Tough Mudder, life is about pushing boundaries and overcoming all obstacles through teamwork—and having fun along the way" (Tough Mudder, n.d., para. 7).

The events that occur at a Tough Mudder event vary, but each one is uniquely challenging, and, some may say, painful. Each obstacle requires strength, agility, grit, and camaraderie. The Leap of Faith requires participants to jump for a dangling cargo net to pull them to safety. If they don't make it, the participants fall into the water and must swim. In Balls to the Wall, participants climb a 3.5-meter wall with only a muddy rope. Once on top, they must descend on the other side. This is especially taxing at the end of the course. Electroshock Therapy entails participants running through a field of live wires. There are hay bales and sinkholes throughout the field, which can cause a participant to fall into the electrified mud.

In Walk the Plank, participants jump from 12 feet in the air into a deep, muddy pit of water below. Once in the muddy water, participants must swim 40 feet to the other side. Tough Mudder urges participants to skip this obstacle if they are unable to swim. The Walk the Plank obstacle was the site of the first death at a Tough Mudder event.

In April 2003, 28-year-old Avishek Sengupta drowned while participating in a Tough Mudder in West Virginia. Sengupta jumped in the water of the Walk the Plank obstacle but never resurfaced. Tough Mudder staff and emergency personnel removed Sengupta from the water and performed CPR on him. The staff and emergency medical technicians resuscitated him so that his heart was beating and he was breathing, but his brain was "compromised" due to the length of time he was submerged in the water.

One spectator, Antoinette DiVittorio, recounts the incident in an article written by Andrew Metcalf (2013). "I was waiting on the side where the water was, watching people jump in," says DiVittorio. "His teammates were waiting on the side of the water when one guy said to a staff member 'my teammate jumped into the water and didn't come out yet.'" According to DiVittorio, the staff member didn't take action for a few minutes after being told Sengupta was still in the water. It wasn't until she and one of Sengupta's teammates asked the staff member, "Why aren't you doing anything?" that the staff member took action.

"At that point in time they made everyone stop jumping," DiVittorio recalls. According to DiVittorio, one staff member in a wetsuit began searching the top of the water and continued to do so for a couple of minutes until another staff member ran down to the site, asked what was going on, and, finding out, ordered the other staff member to put on a scuba tank and goggles to search underwater.

"It seemed like an extensive period of time went by before anyone went under," recalls DiVittorio. "Within one minute of trolling the bottom, they pulled him out."

DiVittorio estimated that an ambulance didn't arrive until about 30 minutes after Sengupta was pulled from the water, despite her seeing multiple ambulances located across the course. During that time, she said rescuers attempted to resuscitate Sengupta.

Pretend you are the manager for a Tough Mudder event, and consider the following:

1. Research the risk management procedures for Tough Mudder and other extreme sport events. What protocols are in place in the event of an emergency?
2. How would you have handled the situation?
3. Create a risk management plan for the Tough Mudder to ensure that another death does not occur. Be thorough in this plan. You must discuss how you would deal with the event overall, giving five specific obstacles.

CASE REFERENCES

Metcalf, A. (2013). Witnesses describe scene at fatal tough mudder jump. *Elkridge Patch*. Retrieved from http://elkridge.patch.com/groups/sports/p/witnesses-describe-scene-at-fatal-tough-mudder-jump

Tough Mudder. (n.d.). What is Tough Mudder? Retrieved from https://toughmudder.com/events/what-is-tough-mudder

REFERENCES

Carey, B. (2011). Stadium security continues to evolve ten years after 9/11. *Sports Illustrated*. Retrieved from http://www.si.com/more-sports/2011/09/09/stadium-securitychangessince911

Cunningham, G. (2010). Sports centers, recreational facilities facing more risks in tough economy. Retrieved from http://www.propertycasualty360.com/2010/04/12/sports-centers-recreational-facilities-facing-more-risks-in-tough-economy

Giddens, A. (1988). Risk society: The context of British politics. In J. Franklin (Ed.), *The politics of risk society* (pp. 23–24). Cambridge, UK: Polity Press.

Griffith, M. (2011). The uncertainty of risk management: Kneejerk reactions do more harm than good. Retrieved from http://www.sportrisk.com/2011/11/the-uncertainty-factor-in-risk-management/

Office of Sport and Recreation. (2009). *Risk management resource for recreation and sport organisations*. Retrieved from https://secure.ausport.gov.au/__data/assets/pdf_file/0009/435951/Risk_Management_June09.pdf

Pyles, C. D., & Pyles, R. B. (1992). Risk management of sports facilities. *Journal of Legal Aspects of Sport, 2*(1), 53–64.

Rushing, G., & Miller, J. J. (2009). Facility and event risk management. In T. H. Sawyer (Ed.), *Facility management for physical activity and sport.* Champaign, IL: Sagamore Publishing.

Sawyer, T. H. & Smith, O. (1999). *The management of clubs, recreation, and sport.* Champaign, IL: Sagamore Publishing.

Sport New Zealand. (2014). Risk management for event organizers. Retrieved from http://www.sportnz.org.nz/

Taylor, C., & Booty, F. (2006). Risk management. In F. Booty (Ed.), *Facilities management handbook* (2nd ed.). Burlington, MA: Elsevier/Butterworth-Heinemann.

Toohey, K. (2008). Terrorism, sport and public policy in the risk society. *Sport in Society Journal, 11*(4), 429–442.

van der Smissen, B. (1990). *Legal liability and risk management for public and private entities, volume 2.* Cincinnati: W. H. Anderson.

Viney, C. (1999). *A sporting chance: A risk management framework for the sport and recreation industry*, Tasmania, Australia: Office Sport & Recreation.

Westerbeek, H., Smith, A., Turner, P., Emery, P., Green, C., & van Leeuwen, L. (2005). *Managing sport facilities and major events.* New York, NY: Routledge.

CHAPTER 14

Measurement and Evaluation

THOMAS J. AICHER

CHAPTER OBJECTIVES

Upon the completion of this chapter, the reader will be able to:

1. Explain the importance of continuous measurement and evaluation of facility and event organizations

2. Identify stakeholders who may provide valuable information for organizations to understand their performance

3. Differentiate measurement and evaluation techniques and the impact each measure has on the organization's various internal and external stakeholders

4. Define and articulate the strengths and weaknesses of the various internal and external measurement techniques

CHAPTER OVERVIEW

This chapter will review the various techniques to measure the performance of the event or facility from a multi-stakeholder perspective. First, it will establish the importance of continuous evaluation of the organization and its performance from preevent to postevent to ensure all stakeholders' expectations are met. It will outline the major components of SERVQUAL—economic, environmental, and social—along with other methods of evaluating the organization's performance.

Industry VOICE

Martin Robertson—Senior Lecturer, Event Management, School of Tourism, Bournemouth University

Evaluation and measurement are immensely important to the field of event and facility management. They are core functions in two key areas of my work: (1) in my role as an academic researcher within the higher-education/university environment at Victoria University in Melbourne, Australia, and (2) in my role within the event industry as part of a research team working on behalf of an event owner. For a wide range of reasons, event evaluation is significant both for the organizers and for the event industry. Evaluation is—and has been—vital in furthering the knowledge of the event manager, with findings sometimes affecting immediate plans (i.e., those occurring within 2 years) and sometimes affecting midrange plans (i.e., those occurring within 3 to 5 years). What is of increasing importance, however, are those types of research that can be ongoing and responsive to the needs of a rapidly changing market and to a far greater range of stakeholders and stakeholder needs.

I have chosen to be involved in event research because I enjoy it so much. The areas of research analysis for events are extending each and every day, and while the maintenance of exacting process and quality control is of paramount importance, it does, nonetheless, offer so many opportunities to contribute usefully. I began my event research career in the public sector collecting and evaluating data from event visitors, destination attractions, and venues. Thereafter, I was employed by a university to carry out a range of research activities related entirely to events and the teaching/learning environment for event management. The list of activities relating to this research is very long but includes the following

areas: large-scale visitor analyses (exit polls), assessment of sociocultural impacts, policy analyses, media analyses, and analyses of festival leadership perspectives of sustainability.

There are a number of challenges a researcher can face. First, it is important that event research develops in a way that ensures a balance of high-quality, progressive, and imaginative forward-looking work. Second, the maintenance of research applications should serve both current and less long-term research outcomes. Both are necessary. Accordingly, the biggest challenge is to involve industry and funding agencies. As a relatively recent area of research that lacks a strong academic pedigree and security, funding is another challenge. To facilitate these challenges, active workshops and partnerships are required. In my opinion, there needs to be a realization that evaluation will increasingly have to embrace a number of methodological techniques for a rapidly changing environment. Accordingly, more publications, both academic and industry focused, need to be made available and promoted to support this evolution.

As for trends, I have found that event research has been slow to progress. It is clear that this will change, and research within both facility and event management will grow in importance. However, the recognition of the importance of evaluation seems to lag with industry. One dynamic trend is research that seeks to look into the future and attempts to include numerous community stakeholders. Workshops run by councils and by universities continue to grow. Similarly, publications produced by national agencies as well as academic institutes help to bridge the gap between academic environments and practitioners.

For those interested in evaluation and measurement of events, a good grounding in both quantitative and qualitative methods is necessary. While it is not imperative that candidates be remarkable in the use of these methods, it is important that they have an understanding of both (and some of the opportunities they offer). The ability to ask strong questions and properly design a research study is also highly important. No matter the evaluation design and the methods of data collection employed, humility and patience are required. Not only the research objective and, where appropriate, the research participant, but also to the inquiring mind. Attention to detail and quality is critical. And, have fun! Inquiry can be very fulfilling and can bring great pride and enjoyment.

Bridging academic and industry research activity provides incredible value to the whole area of event provision and can impact future events. There is also great crossover potential with various other areas of inquiry (i.e., corporate, public, entertainment, academic). Students need to think more about to whom or what their research can contribute.

Lastly, it is important that each research area be seen as a single project, with findings that can contribute to the greater industry. Very often it may not be the whole project but elements of that project that will have immense value for another project—present or future. So record everything you do!

Introduction

The facility and event industry faces many challenges and serves a variety of stakeholders who each play a significant role in the success of the organization. It is therefore very important that facility and event organizations measure their organizations' operations based on the objectives that serve as a guide for the facility or event. For instance, Hall (1992) suggests that evaluation is not an afterthought for event management; rather it is a strategic necessity for the organization to be able to evolve and be successful in the future. As we detailed previously with planning, measurement and evaluation are integral to the organization's success.

Why Are Measurement and Evaluation Important?

Getz (2007) articulates seven reasons why facility and event organizations should incorporate measurement and evaluation into their procedures. These include the following:

1. To identify and solve problems
2. To find ways to improve management
3. To determine the value of the facility or event

4. To measure success or failure
5. To identify and measure impacts
6. To satisfy sponsors and other stakeholders
7. To gain acceptance, credibility, and support

Each of these items assists the organization in measuring its performance compared to the objectives it has set forth. For instance, if a local recreational facility were attempting to expand its revenue source through sponsorship, it would be very important for the facility to measure the success of its current sponsors. In doing so, it would be able to potentially expand its current relationships and use the information to attract new partners. Each measurement should be developed to evaluate the organization's success or process of attaining its overall objectives. In the following sections of this chapter, I will outline various methods to measure organizational performance toward these types of objectives.

What Are Performance Measurements Used For?

performance measurement An outcome that describes how well the organization is using its internal and external inputs to produce the desired output.

Performance measurements can serve to evaluate numerous functions within facility and event organizations. Behn (2003) suggests there are eight common purposes for performance management: evaluation, control, budgeting, motivation, promotion, celebration, learning, and improvement. These measurements describe how well the organization is using its internal and external inputs to produce the desired output. While these objectives may appear to be too employee specific, they may also be used to determine how well the facility or event is performing and allow the organization to evolve as it moves forward. For instance, a sport complex may celebrate a successful soccer season in which they increased participation rates, reduced their expenses, and enhanced their relationships with their various partners. Another example would be the sport complex using these measurements to improve the event in the future or potentially utilizing the success of this event to attract other events to their facility.

How and When to Measure Performance?

When measuring organizational performance, most facilities fall into the trap of measuring performance only annually and utilizing a single measurement to determine their overall performance. Typically, events will perform only a **postevent analysis** to measure performance and will focus on a single outcome of the event (e.g., participant satisfaction). When conducting performance studies, the impact of time on the memory may be detrimental to measuring the organization's performance accurately. Over time, stakeholders will likely remember only the very good (i.e., halo effect) or the very bad (i.e., horn effect), which will bias any information collected from these individuals. In addition, financial measurements may not be as accurate over time. For instance, if a recreational ski resort runs a special in November for the upcoming season, their level of sales may be increased for the month of November; however, because they are selling these items at a lower rate than normal, this promotion could impact their annual sales performance. In either case, it would be more effective for facilities and events to measure performance using a continuous and multifaceted approach.

postevent analysis
Measurement of a specific variable of interest after the event has occurred.

To ensure they are accurately measuring performance, organizations should first vary from whom they collect data. Concentrating on one group of stakeholders will paint only a part of the picture from the event. The best way to understand this concept is through a brief illustration. A local community bid on, was selected, and hosted a national slow-pitch softball tournament. At the end of the event, the facility managers met to discuss the notes they took during the event, and overall they found there were numerous issues with logistics and timing to consider for future events. Upon conclusion of their review, they sent summative reports to both the sponsors and the organizing committee of the event (in this case the United States Specialty Sports Association) per their original agreement and made suggestions for future improvement. After receiving the feedback from the management team, both groups, sponsors and event owner, were quite surprised, as both groups were pleased with the event and thought it was a resounding success. For instance, what the management team saw as a logistical issue, the sponsors of the event thought was a great plan because it ensured all of the participants and spectators flowed through the sponsors' area, which allowed them to successfully market their products. The event organizing committee felt the timing of the games was consistent and even more efficient than the events they had hosted in the past, and were also pleased. This brief example demonstrates the importance of measuring various individuals' opinions of the event to ensure all groups

© alexskopje/ShutterStock

are satisfied with how it was managed. If the facility management team had not elicited feedback from these groups, they may have made changes to future events that would have had an adverse impact on sponsor and event owner satisfaction.

Organizations will also want to vary the techniques they use to collect data. Broadly, data are collected in two distinct forms: **qualitative** and **quantitative**. Each form brings value and understanding to the facility's or event's overall performance. Some of the most common sources for quantitative data include attendee statistics, sales figures, financial reports and accounts, economic impact analyses, environmental impact analyses, and social impact analyses. Quantitative data develop a numerical analysis of the organization's performance, while qualitative data offer a deeper understanding of the stakeholders' perceptions, attitudes, and other information. For instance, qualitative data come in the form of attendee perceptions, interviews with attendees and staff, management notes and commentary, and interviews with external stakeholders (e.g., sponsors, community members), among other forms. The two broad techniques allow the organization to develop a broader understanding of how well the organization is achieving or progressing toward its objectives. In the following sections, I will outline more specific methods of data collection that organizations may employ to measure performance.

qualitative Research methodology used to develop more in-depth description of behaviors and experiences.

quantitative Research methodology used to provide a numeric analysis of the organization's performance.

What to Measure?

When measuring organizational performance, the default for most organizations is to measure financial performance. This may be an effective approach for the organization to determine how well it is performing financially, but it does little to measure other variables that should be considered equally important (e.g., customers/participants, sponsors, external stakeholders). Therefore, rather than using a single measurement approach, facility and event organizations should employ the **triple bottom-line approach**, in which they measure the impact the event has on (1) its consumers, (2) internal business operations, and (3) external business operations. Each prong should be evaluated with the overall business objectives as a framework to indicate success. Additionally, rather than using a single measurement, facility and event managers should maintain a continuous evaluation approach and measure the three prongs of the triple bottom line. An outline of each prong follows, including a strategy of how to measure each performance indicator.

triple bottom-line approach A method of measuring organizational performance focused on the impact the event has on its consumers, internal business operations, and external business operations.

CUSTOMERS/PARTICIPANTS

Facility and event organizations cease to exist if they do not have customers or participants using their facility or partaking in the events they host. There are several key variables organizations should concentrate on when evaluating customers' perceptions of the organization. Some of the most common variables include service perceptions, overall satisfaction, attitudinal changes, and lifestyle change.

Ko and Pastore (2005) developed a conceptual framework for sport and recreation organizations to better understand service quality in recreational facilities. Using Bitner and Hubbert's (1994) definition, service quality refers to "the consumer's overall impression of the relative inferiority/superiority of the organization and its services" (p. 77), Ko and Pastore developed the Scale of Service Quality in Recreational Sports (SSQRS). This measurement approach focuses on four main categories: (1) program quality (i.e., range of programs, operating times, and program information, (2) interaction quality (i.e., employee–client and client–client interactions), (3) outcome quality (i.e., physical and social benefits), and (4) physical environment (i.e., ambience, design, and equipment). Lastly, they include a measurement of overall customer satisfaction with the facility.

Each item of the SSQRS can be operationalized (i.e., defined in the context of the study) and measured to determine if the facility can improve in the SSQRS dimensions. For example, a local park could survey individuals who frequently use the park to determine their level of satisfaction with the facility. The SSQRS would measure attributes about the park (e.g., cleanliness, safety, benefits sought) to determine if areas exist in which the park is considered deficient. Further, they may want to measure how well the park users were treated by the employees and other park goers, as well as how pleased they are with the array of equipment provided by the park among other variables. In doing so, the recreational facility managers may find that individuals are very pleased with the staff and range of activities but feel that lighting and other facilities need improvement. This knowledge would allow the managers to improve these areas, which would lead to higher customer satisfaction and potentially increased usage.

Facility and event managers may use the SSQRS findings from their evaluations to develop stronger customer segmentation strategies. Facility and event organizations typically segment their customer or participant bases into three categories: goods or services sought, customer relationship, and image and reputation. The first category, goods or services sought, differentiates the customers or participants based on the attributes the individuals value the most about the facility or event. These attributes may be price, quality, options available, and benefits sought from participation, among many others. For example, cycling events may differentiate according to the distance that individuals must complete, and in doing so, they may vary the cost to participate. This strategy will allow individuals who are not well conditioned to participate in a shorter event, while others have the opportunity to challenge themselves with a longer distance. The price of each event should be directly related to the distance and level of support associated with the participants' expectations so they will feel satisfied with their purchase.

The second way organizations may use SSQRS findings is to differentiate themselves through the relationships they have with their customers. This strategy involves evaluating the relationship or interaction between the customer and the staff in the facility. For instance, suppose parents take their child to participate in the local recreational baseball league. While there, they encounter a rather unpleasant person working at the concession stand. While the parents' child really enjoys the team and playing the game of baseball, the parents may consider an alternative recreational league to participate in because of this encounter. Additionally, these relationships may impact the longevity or continued participation in an organization's events.

The longer individuals participate in an organization's events, the more accustomed they become to the organization's processes, and the expectations of organizational performance may be increased. Each time individuals receive a certain level of treatment, they expect the same or better each time they return, which may take a toll on an organization if they do not continually assess and train their employees to perform at a high level. If facility and event organizations fail to do so, they may suffer from a negative event, as in the preceding example.

The last way in which organizations may use the SSQRS is to inform their strategies in managing the image and reputation of the facility. Similar to word-of-mouth advertising, the image and reputation of a facility and event may have either a positive or negative impact on the customer segmentation strategies. For example, a ski resort may define itself as a wealthy, challenging, and exclusive retreat. This would minimize the number of consumers who may be able to afford to ski at the resort; however, it would provide the level of exclusivity individuals may seek. Another example could be a small 5K fun run. This short running event could take on a reputation of being a lively, fun, family-friendly event, in which everyone is welcome to participate, or it may be billed as a competitive race that individuals use to test their abilities against other elite runners. In either case, the strategies used to develop and maintain the image and reputation should be consistent with the organizational objectives.

INTERNAL OPERATIONS

Facility and event organizations employ **financial measurement** approaches to determine how well the organization is contributing to the bottom line. If not directly tied to the organization's overall business objectives, using these measurements may potentially have a negative effect on the long-term health and viability of the facility or event. Organizations commonly use traditional financial measurements (e.g., return on investment, debt versus equity, gross profit) developed from the financial statements to outline the financial standing of the organization. While these measurement approaches do help the organization understand how it is performing, other aproaches may provide greater insight into the organization's financial performance and the impact on organizational objectives.

financial measurement An outcome used to determine how well the organization is contributing to the bottom line.

revenue growth and mix measurement An outcome used to denote how well the organization is performing toward organizational objectives such as market share, increased markets, or expanding its revenue sources.

Revenue growth and mix measurements denote how well the organization is performing toward organizational objectives such as increasing market share, increasing markets, or expanding its revenue sources. For example, a golf course may measure its overall gross profit and find that it is doing well as an organization. However, if the organization's stated objective is to increase the number of members or broaden its sources of revenue, this measurement would not afford it the information it needs to correctly determine how well it is performing toward this objective. Rather, the organization would want to break down its sales and sources of revenue to determine how much it is generating from each business category (e.g., pro shop, concessions, green's fees, memberships), and it may notice that it has undervalued certain categories in which it may enhance the revenue streams.

Instead of evaluating and improving revenue streams, facilities and events may turn to cost reduction or efficiency measurements to determine if they may enhance the organization's performance. For instance, a recreational facility may evaluate its marketing strategy to bring in new customers. With the various media it uses to reach potential clients, it could measure which methods are generating the greatest number of new or interested members. This approach would provide the organization with the information to determine which platforms are most effective and then eliminate or reduce spending on the underperforming methods. Other options may include using technological advancements (e.g., online ticket sales for events), which would eliminate the need for certain staff, though an unpopular choice.

Lastly, organizations may evaluate how well they manage their assets to generate a return on the resources they currently possess. Management of assets may come in a variety of forms—capacity management, space utilization, event performance, to name a few. These types of measurements allow organizations to develop an understanding of how much return they are getting for the use of the space or other assets. A fitness center, for instance, may evaluate the current setup of the gym. With the focus on developing new workout trends and an alternative desire for individual- and group-based training, they may want to eliminate certain sections that are underutilized. Doing so would allow the gym to maximize its use of space, eliminate some of the equipment in the facility, and reduce the cost of maintenance. Additionally, it may schedule classes that have demonstrated greater popularity than others, which would lead to great profitability.

The second major component of internal operations is **human resources measurements**. This element can be very challenging for facilities and events to measure because of the dependence on volunteer staff to manage events. Common measurement approaches organizations may use to measure their full-time staff members would be employee retention through the frequency of turnover, or people leaving the organization. They may also find value in measuring employees' job satisfaction, organizational commitment, motivation, productivity, and other factors. These measurements would allow the organization to better develop an understanding of its employees' perception of the organization and assist with the human resource management component. Ultimately, and to use a cliché, our organizations are only as strong as our weakest link. Similar to financial measurement approaches, these approaches should be consistent with the organizational objectives and provide support and guidance to the employees so they may help the organization reach those objectives.

human resource measuresment An outcome that allows the organization to better develop an understanding of an employee's perception of the organization.

EXTERNAL OPERATIONS

Facility and event operations impact the host community in three common ways: economically, environmentally, and socially. The United Nations World Tourism Organization suggests that organizations monitor these three impacts to ensure a sustainable tourism destination by ensuring each impact has been brought to a level consistent with the local residents, visitors, and business interests. The most commonly discussed measurement approach of the three is the economic impact analysis; however, the latter two are gaining momentum as economic impact studies are called into question quite often. Facility and event management organizations use these studies to gain public support or recognition for what they bring to, or do not take from, the community. For instance, if managers of a parks and recreation

©iStockphoto/Thinkstock

department are attempting to pass a public referendum to use tax dollars to build a new swimming facility, then they would want to use the economic impact study to demonstrate the positive growth the facility will generate for the local community. The environmental impact study will outline how the department will minimize the impact the construction may have on the local environment, as well as how they will minimize the impact of the harsh chemicals they use to regulate the pools' pH levels. Lastly, they may want to report how the new facility will create a more health-conscious community and help the people within it become more active. A further discussion of each technique follows.

Economic Impact Analysis

Economic impacts are used to measure the effect of a facility or an event on the local community. An economic impact study measures the organization's ability to generate new revenue for the host community, increase impact on individual-level income within the host community, or produce new jobs within the host community. Each of these measurements will generate a continuous impact, which has led to the use of multipliers to estimate the overarching impact of a single dollar spent at a facility or an event. The multipliers measure both direct impacts (e.g., spending on hotels, restaurants, event participation) and indirect impacts (e.g., event suppliers, employees, local government taxes). For instance, an individual traveling to Boston, Massachusetts, for the sole purpose of participating in the Boston Marathon generates new spending in the local community, which would not have existed without the event. The money the individual spends during the trip on hotels, restaurants, and shopping then turns over through the local community as it is used by the businesses to pay their employees and replenish their supplies and as it becomes tax revenue for the local government, for example. The revenue will continue to travel through the local economy, with some money being lost at each stage.

To estimate this relationship, organizations use three common multipliers: sales, income, and employment. The use of these multipliers should be carefully interpreted to ensure that a more accurate estimate of the event's or facility's impact has been calculated. Howard and Crompton (2005) outline the details and how to properly employ the multipliers, and more importantly the five inviolable principles of economic impact analyses. Failure to follow these principles will lead to an over-estimation of the event's or facility's impact. The principles also shed light on the various economic impact analyses provided by organizations when attempting to attain government support mentioned previously. These inviolable principles are list in **Table 14-1** with examples of how they may affect the estimated impact.

TABLE 14-1   Five Inviolable Principles of an Economic Impact Analysis

No.	Principle	Reasoning
1	Exclusion of local residents and deflectors	These two groups do not generate new money. Locals would have spent money elsewhere within the community. Deflectors are local residents who would have spent money outside of the community but remained local because of the event. While considered new money, the amount is negligible.
2	Exclusion of "time switchers" and "casuals"	Time switchers are nonlocal spectators who were planning a visit to the community but changed the timing of their visit to coincide with the sport event. Casuals are visitors already in the community, attracted by other features, who elected to go to the sport event instead of doing something else.
3	Use of income rather than sales output measurements of economic impact	Sales multipliers inflate the numbers but do not tell the local public how much they will truly benefit; sales do not guarantee more jobs.
4	Use of multiplier coefficients rather than multipliers	Coefficients attribute an increase to the injected change created by visitors. Multipliers attribute an increase to income generated.
5	Careful interpretation of employment measurements	Are the positions full- and part-time jobs? Are the "new" jobs really new or just a transfer of time between workers? Are the positions seasonal?

Umstead Trail Marathon

Visitor Survey

AT Consulting Services is requesting your support in determining the economic impact of the Umstead Trail Marathon. The information provided will allow us to assist the Umstead Trail Marathon organizer with the information needed to ensure quality future events, as well as assist with future negotiations for the development of trails. We greatly appreciate your support!

What is your home zip code?   _____

How many people are traveling in your party? Be sure to include yourself.   _____

Approximately how much will your traveling party spend IN TOTAL during your entire stay in the Raleigh Area for the following categories:

Lodging: _____   Marathon Expo: _____

Food and Beverage: _____   Tourist Attractions: _____

Local Transportation: _____   Entertainment: _____

Retail Shopping: _____   Other Expenses: _____

FIGURE 14-1   Example of an economic impact survey

The most common method used by facility and event organizations is surveying the participants/customers to determine spending levels while the individual is visiting the community. An example of this method is provided in **Figure 14-1**. If you review the questions carefully, you will see how to ensure you do not violate any of the inviolable principles. For instance, the questions listed will determine who should be considered a local versus a nonlocal person, whether the person should be considered a casual or time-switching visitor, and how much the person spends on various activities during the trip. Once the data are collected, services such as IMPLAN (which stands for IMpact analysis for PLANning) are utilized to generate the multipliers to estimate the impact of the initial spending. For a full explanation of how to perform an economic impact analysis, review Howard and Crompton's *Financing Sport*, which is listed in the references.

Environmental Impact Analysis

The large numbers of people who participate in our events or use our facilities generate an **environmental impact**. Additionally, the construction,

environmental impact The negative effect the construction of or the existence of a facility or event has on the local environment.

VIGNETTE 14-1

Economic Impact of a Small-Town Marathon

In the city of Wenatchee, Washington, event organizers recently hosted their twelfth annual marathon. Originally considered only a local event, the organizers have really created an exciting atmosphere in conjunction with one of the toughest courses available. The event's uniqueness is demonstrated with the colder than average temperatures, challenging hill climbs and descents, energetic volunteer staff, bands at every mile, and other entertainment activities. Because of these factors, the marathon has grown exponentially over the past six events to a current participation level of 12,500 runners. While the event would like to continue to grow, it has potentially maximized its resources. To gain more resources, the organizers have requested additional funding and support from the City of Wenatchee, which has been met with a great deal of resistance.

To improve their position, the organizing committee enlisted the services of a consulting firm to measure the impact the event has had on the local community. The consulting firm attained responses from almost 1500 participants who indicated a zip code outside the designated local area, approximately a 45-mile radius from the city center. Those individuals reported an estimated $3,492,347 in direct spending. Using the IMPLAN multipliers, the consulting firm estimated an indirect impact of $1,193,478, induced impact of $825,194, and total impact of $5,511,019. These values were used to calculate the impact of the event on local labor income ($1,893,383.43) and the total number of new jobs created from the event (38.2 jobs). The consultants notated the number of jobs created may include both part-time and full-time positions. In addition, they cautioned that the nature of the event would suggest the majority of the positions created would likely be part time. Armed with this information, the event organizers were able to garner additional support for the event. The hopes for next year's event will be to increase the number of participants to 15,000, thus maintaining the strong impact for the local community.

maintenance, and resources our facilities use to operate may have a deleterious impact on the local environment. The chemicals and fertilizers we use to maintain the green spaces (e.g., fields, golf courses) may also negatively impact the environment. Moreover, the larger events hosted within our communities cram several thousand people into small areas, and the travel, trash, noise, and other by-products generated by these individuals may harm the local environment. Some events may harm the local flora and fauna through erosion and negative effects on the watershed. For instance, a cyclocross event may damage the local environment because of the repetitive flow of riders following the same path, and the spectators walking along the course may have a similar impact. This trampling of the grasses and underbrush may lead to greater erosion of the soil.

When evaluating the environmental impact of a facility or an event, it is important to remember there is no such thing as a zero impact. Every facility and event will have a negative impact on the local environment, so it is imperative that event and facility managers develop strategies to minimize or counterbalance the impact. For example, a 5K fun run hosted in a local community will have individuals traveling to the event, which will release greenhouse gas emissions. Trash from the event, including the cups at the water stations, will be placed in the local landfills, along with countless other by-products of the event. In this situation, the event could support mass transportation options to reduce the number of individuals traveling to the event or give a reward to those who carpool. The cups used at the water stations could be recycled as long as they are paper and do not have a wax coating. These strategies would not negate the event's impact on the environment but would at least lessen it.

The event may employ other strategies to decrease environmental impact. For example, facilities could reduce their energy consumption by using energy-efficient lighting and cooling/heating systems. Those facilities that use chemicals to treat their green spaces or pools could adopt environmentally safe products that would reduce the harsh chemicals normally used. Facilities may also provide electronic options for ticketing, marketing, and other facility operations that utilize a tremendous amount of paper. When paper must be used, the organization should make sure it is recyclable and print on both sides to minimize the total number of pages.

To further manage the environmental impact of the Olympics, the International Olympic Committee (IOC) created the IOC Sport and Environment Commission. This was established in 1995 in response to the 1992 Albertville, France, Winter Olympics. In those Games, the construction and running of the events associated with the Games had a devastating impact on the local community. The conditions outraged several environmental groups, prompting the IOC's response. In addition to the creation of the Sport and Environment Commission, the IOC added the environment as the third dimension of Olympism (along with sport and culture). For more information and to learn more helpful environmental protection strategies, visit the IOC Sport and Environment Commission website (www.olympic.org/sport-environment-commission).

SOCIAL IMPACTS

Recently, owners have begun to evaluate the impact their facilities and events have on the local community's social norms, roles, and customs. Facilities and events have been found to generate both positive and negative impacts for the host community. Similar to environmental and economic impact analyses, **social impact** analyses are important for organizations to employ so they have a strong understanding of local communities' perceptions of their organizations. It is integral to the success and sustainability of the organization to maintain a positive social impact on the community. Outlined next are some of the potential negative and positive social impacts facility and event organizations may have on the host community.

social impact The effect facilities and events have on the local community, social norms, roles, and customs.

Evaluating the impact of hosting mega-events, such as the Summer and Winter Olympic Games or the International Federation of Association Football (FIFA) World Cup, on the host community, researchers have largely pointed to two negative outcomes: crime and displacement of the working poor. Factors that may contribute to increased levels of crime include the following:

- The nonlocals do not have a strong understanding of the formal mechanisms of social control.
- These visitors also do not act as good guardians of the rental properties.
- Criminals may choose to go to the area because of the perception of "easy marks."

Evaluation of the 2002 Winter Olympics hosted by Salt Lake City, Utah, demonstrated the opposite impact of hosting. In their investigation, Decker, Varano, and Green (2007) found a brief reduction in the crime levels during the event, and once the games concluded, crime rates returned to their normal levels. Alternatively, other research studies have demonstrated that local residents perceived the crime rate to have increased during the event, and their perception (whether accurate or not) may be more meaningful in generating local support for the event.

The second major concern of hosting mega-events is the negative impact on the working poor and the housing available to these groups. When determining where to build the stadiums and other facilities to host such events, communities typically turn to the most affordable land options. Additionally, the pressure of meeting fixed deadlines leads to the bypass of normal decision-making processes, which leads to the demolition of "eyesores" and the displacement of many urban poor (Lenskyj, 2002, p. 228). In doing so, individuals are relocated from these areas, and those who are not directly impacted by the construction of the facility may be forced from the community because of the increasing costs of living in the area.

Facilities and events may also have negative impacts on the local residents' daily lives. For instance, facilities and events typically generate greater levels of noise, traffic, pollution, crowding, and other undesirable variables. These activities may lead to less support from local residents because their routines have been hindered due to the hosting of the event. For instance, individuals who live near a soccer complex may have increased levels of frustration when the facility hosts an annual tournament. With the increased traffic in the community and individuals parking along the streets, the local residents may become frustrated with the event organizers because they are not able to navigate the area as they normally would.

The effects of a facility or event on the local community need not be negative, however. Through proper management, facilities and events may generate a positive social impact within the local community. One example of a positive impact is psychic income. With the lack of economic impact found in most facility economic impact studies, organizations have turned to the notion of psychic income to bolster community support. Psychic income is the method by which the city expresses its identity, personality, and status to the rest of the world. Generated in the local community through the production of major facilities and events, psychic income has a strong social bonding impact on the local community because it develops a shared identity that breaks through all other social barriers (e.g., race, sex, political affiliation, religion). Facilities and events can enhance psychic income through (1) increasing social interactions between the community and the facilities or events through community-specific events, (2) cultivating common group interests through small events in which various stakeholder groups may interact, and (3) developing a strong and trusting relationship between the facility and event managers and the local community. Each of these strategies costs the facility or event organization very little, yet may have a significant impact on the local community. For instance, a local recreational facility adds a rock-climbing wall. To generate a buzz, the facility owners decide to allow nonmembers access to the facility to check out the new equipment. Rather than just having anybody come in, the facility should send invitations to those in the area who may be adversely impacted from the other large events they host. Treat them to a meal and maybe a small instructional session about rock climbing. This open-door invitation will demonstrate to the local residents that the facility understands them and their needs and is attempting to reach out.

Additional social outcomes generated from facilities and events include community cohesion, educational development, support from families, and regional development. These outcomes will engender greater support from the local residents because they feel that hosting such events is of value to the local community. For instance, the city of Indianapolis, Indiana, has made large investments in their sport facility infrastructures. They now host several major sport events (e.g., National Football League [NFL] Combine, National Collegiate Athletic Association [NCAA] men's and women's basketball tournament championships, the Indianapolis 500), two professional franchises (the NFL's Colts and National Basketball Association's [NBA's] Pacers), and a minor league baseball team. This does not include the level of investment made in the local parks and recreation system as well as other sport events hosted in the community. With this level of events in one community, the city of Indianapolis has enjoyed considerable support for investing in additional sport facilities and events by those who see the positive impact generated from hosting such national and worldwide spectacles.

The social return on investment (SROI) model provides a framework for facility and event managers to understand the social impact they have on the local community. The purpose of the SROI model is to estimate the financial amount of social value generated from the facilities or events in the host community. The basic formula to calculate the SROI model is to divide the value of the social impacts by the value of spending. To do so, Rotheroe and Richards (2007) outline four distinct areas on which organizations should focus to determine the level of social impact. The first is stakeholder engagement, which is the level to which stakeholders' objectives are identified and integrated into the organizational processes. Secondly, the event analysis is centered on the stakeholders' interests (i.e., materiality). For example, if sponsors and local residents are considered integral to the success of the event or facility, then measurement of their perceptions of the event would be paramount to other stakeholder groups. Next, organizations will develop an impact map that depicts the pathways to understand how the facility or event causes changes in the external environment. Finally, facility and event managers should develop an appreciation of deadweight. This calculates the proportion of outcomes that would have occurred in the community regardless of the existence of the facility or event.

An alternative approach to the SROI model is the basic social impact assessment. These assessments measure the local residents' attitudes, perceptions, and behaviors as well as the health standards of the local residents, number of local fitness organizations, and lifestyle of the local residents based on a facility or event. The social impact analysis is derived directly from the objectives of the facility or event operations. For instance, in 2011 a small group of individuals hosted the first marathon in Bryan–College Station, Texas. In its inaugural event, they attracted approximately 2000 runners. While this may seem like a relatively small impact, since hosting the event, the community has added two running stores and the organizers have added (and filled) various training and healthy-living workshops directly related to the event.

VIGNETTE 14-2

Small Event, Big Impact: Social Impact of a Local 5K Race

In the spring of 2010, the Grad Sport Society at Northern Illinois University decided to host a 5K fun run to raise money for their group and to complete a class project. The group of 25 students organized the entire event from scratch, including bringing in partners for the event. The title sponsor was a local healthcare organization that was quite pleased with the turnout and the quality of the event. Prior to the event, participants had a chance to meet with the partners of the event and learn more about the services they provide. With more than 100 runners registered for this first-annual event, all involved were satisfied with the results.

One part of the story the students, partners, and participants did not realize was the event had a significant social impact on at least one individual. The main contact for the title sponsor was an integral part to the event. She fired the starting gun, cheered on participants during the run, and helped with the awards ceremony at the end of the event. Completely astonished by what she saw people accomplish, she decided to make a change. In the following year, she completed seven 5K races of her own and lost more than 70 pounds during that time. While only one individual may have been impacted by this local 5K fun run, several of the larger events attempt to achieve these life-altering goals and cultural shifts in the local community.

SUMMARY

Facility and event managers should evaluate performance through a continuous and multifaceted approach. Outlined in this chapter are various strategies and sources of information organizations can use to measure how well they are performing in terms of their overall business objectives. These different measurement approaches allow facility and event managers to better understand the impact of the event on customers and participants and on the organization's internal and external business operations. This type of evaluation is consistent with the triple bottom-line approach to measuring organizational performance. This approach enables the organization to generate a much fuller understanding of the various factors that may impact its performance within its environment and community.

DISCUSSION QUESTIONS

1. Explain the importance of measuring the facility's or event's performance, and outline the basic strategies managers may use to continuously measure performance.

2. Who are the different stakeholders who can give the organization information to determine its performance? What approaches could be used to measure these aspects?

3. How can an organization alter the Scale of Service Quality in Recreational Sports (SSQRS) to determine the satisfaction level of the users of the facility or participants in an event?

4. What measurement approaches can be used to determine the financial performance of a facility or event? What are the strengths and weaknesses of the different approaches?

5. What are the five inviolable principles of an economic impact study, and how can a facility or event avoid violating these principles?

6. What adverse environmental impacts could events and facilities have? What strategies can managers employ to minimize these impacts?

7. Explain the positive and negative social impacts an event may create for the local community. What strategies can event organizers use to maximize the positive impacts while minimizing the negative?

Case **STUDY**

Defining Success for a Nonprofit Event: Measurement and Evaluation of a Local Sport Facility

Nestled in the foothills of the Appalachian Mountains in Tennessee, Knoxville is known for its quality outdoor activities, modern nightlife, rich culture, and natural beauty. To capitalize on the city's location and proximity to more than 50% of the population in the United States, city commissioners decided to build a sportsplex that could host a multitude of events. The new sportsplex has 5 open fields, which can host up to 10 soccer matches at one time, 4 baseball diamonds in a clover design, and 16 tennis courts. Since opening in 2012, the facility has bid on and won several national, regional, and state tournaments in a variety of sports, including baseball, soccer, lacrosse, tennis, softball, and ultimate Frisbee. The director of the parks and recreation department has been very excited about the success of the facility and thought he could use the success to get more support from the local government.

The director knew the importance of demonstrating the economic impact the facility is having on the community and commissioned an economic impact study. The research firm he employed conducted several survey-based studies of a dozen events hosted at the facility during the peak season, the summer months. The research reported the facility was having a major impact on the community, even with their conservative approach to the calculations. In terms of overall impact, they reported the facility generated approximately $25 million annually in new revenue to the community, which accounted for roughly $5.7 million in income growth. They also reported the facility created 20 new jobs due to the new economic activity, but cautioned officials that the majority of these positions were likely part time. The parks and recreation director saw this as a win and realized he could utilize this information to garner more financial support for the fields.

In addition to the economic impact investigation, the director conducted his own survey of event owners to develop an understanding of their satisfaction with the facility. He was pleasantly surprised to find that the event owners thought the location was great because it provided a significant number of hotels, restaurants, and entertainment options for their participants. The event owners reported that the staff and volunteers at the facility were very informative and provided high-quality customer service. They also reported that the facilities were a great size for the current event scope, but they were not as pleased with some of the amenities (e.g., concessions and restrooms) the facility provided, which the parks and recreation director thought would be a great investment for the facility to improve its services.

Using the economic impact report and satisfaction survey as sources of information, he solicited from the city commission an extra amount of investment to expand the facility. He was hoping the positive impact on the community and the demonstrated need for improvement would make this an easy negotiation with the county commissioners. However, the county commissioners quickly turned down the proposal. They cited the local residents' displeasure with the increased traffic, the lights being left on late at night, and the overcrowding of the restaurants. Additionally, they highlighted that while the facility was in use and did well for the local community, it was not performing as well as they had hoped financially and any new investment would end in a loss.

The parks and recreation director, feeling defeated, returned to his office and immediately called the consulting firm. Together they discussed the various issues with the local residents in search of ways to better handle the issues they were having with the facility. In addition, they decided to evaluate more functions of the organization to determine how they could improve organizational efficiency. Acting as the consulting group for the parks and recreation director, complete the following tasks:

1. Establish three new key performance indicators that could be utilized to determine the facility's efficiency.
2. Based on the new indicators, outline who the appropriate stakeholders would be to determine the current organizational performance.
3. Outline the steps and instrumentation you will use to measure this group of stakeholders.
4. Provide a few strategies based on your expected results that the parks and recreation director can use to improve the facility's efficiency and overall financial performance.

REFERENCES

Behn, R. D. (2003). Why measure performance? Different purposes require different measures. *Public Administration Review, 63*, 586–606.

Bitner, M. J., & Hubbert, A. R. (1994). Encounter satisfaction versus overall satisfaction versus quality: The customer's voice. In R. T. Rust, & R. L. Oliver (Eds.), *Service quality: New directions in theory and practice* (pp. 72–94). Thousand Oaks, CA: Sage.

Decker, S. H., Varano, S. P., & Green, J. R. (2007). Routine crime in exceptional times: The impact of the 2002 Winter Olympics on citizen demand for police services. *Journal of Criminal Justice, 35*, 89–101.

Getz, D. (2007). *Event studies*. Oxford, UK: Butterworth-Heinemann.

Hall, C. (1992). Adventure, sport and health tourism. In B. Weiler & C. M. Hall (Eds.), *Special interest tourism* (pp. 141–158). London: Bellhaven Press.

Howard, D. R., & Crompton, J. L. (2005). *Financing sport* (2nd ed.). Morgantown, WV: Fitness Information Technology.

Ko, J. Y., & Pastore, D. L. (2007). An instrument to assess customer perceptions of service quality and satisfaction in campus recreation programs. *Recreational Sports Journal, 31*(1), 34–42.

Lenskyj, H. J. (2000). *Inside the Olympic industry: Power, politics, and activism. SUNY series on sport, culture, and social relations.* Albany, NY: State University of New York Press.

Rotheroe, N., & Richards, A. (2007). Social return on investment and social enterprise: Transparent accountability for sustainable development. *Social Enterprise Journal, 3*(1), 31–48.

CHAPTER 15

Sustainability and Legacy

KOSTAS KARADAKIS, TREVOR BOPP, AND
THOMAS J. AICHER

CHAPTER OBJECTIVES

Upon the completion of this chapter, the reader will be able to:

1. Demonstrate a comprehensive understanding of the immediate and long-term impacts, or legacies, of events

2. Account for and give consideration to the numerous and integrative infra-structures and developments that can accompany the hosting of medium- and small-scale events

3. Capitalize on the economic, social, emotional, promotional, and capital benefits to be derived from the proper management of medium- and small-scale events

CHAPTER OVERVIEW

Facilities are too often left empty or underutilized, and many events do not make it past the inaugural year. This chapter will outline the strategies and techniques organizations employ to create sustainable facilities and events that have a positive impact on the facility, event, and community.

Industry VOICE

John Capella—Race Director, Flying Pig Marathon

The Flying Pig Marathon in Cincinnati, Ohio, is designed to provide a premier running event open to athletes of all abilities and is centered on creating a community celebration. Beginning in 1998, the Flying Pig weekend has grown from its original half and full marathon distances to include a Kids' Marathon, the Little King's Mile, and 5K and 10K races during the marathon weekend. In addition, we have added the Christian Moerlein Beer Series (a series of three road races held throughout the year), and the Queen Bee Half Marathon (a women-only event). We also strive to assist the community through our philanthropic endeavors, raising more than one million dollars for charities during our latest event. As the current race director, my role is to manage the operations of each of the running events that we host throughout the year to ensure that we put on high-quality and fun events.

Getting to where I am today started when I entered a graduate program in sport administration at Xavier University. As part of the curriculum, I completed an internship at Game Day Communications, a small public-relations firm located in Cincinnati. After graduation, I was offered a full-time position that I remained in for 7 years. During that time, I transitioned into a volunteer course director role for the Flying Pig Marathon until I was able to earn my current full-time position.

For someone interested in reaching my type of role, I would say that internships and volunteering are the two biggest things you can do. I learned a lot and gained invaluable experience through my internships, and they helped me get my foot in the door of the sport marketplace. Volunteering in general is also huge, and in the racing industry it is rather easy to find opportunities. For instance, there is a 5K race virtually every weekend in one neighborhood or another, and all of these events need help managing their operations and will likely need volunteers. Doing so will help individuals learn the pace and hours of this type of industry as well as the needed flexibility to deal with the issues that arise. Of course, it will also help get your name out there and allow you to prove yourself to the industry leaders.

When looking at a resume, I look at past experience first. I place more weight on where applicants have worked and volunteered than on their educational background. However, it is important that their professors and instructors know them and think highly of them because I will call and ask for a reference or recommendation from those individuals. Once candidates get to the interview, I evaluate their communication skills and their attitudes about working in this type of industry. I am really looking for someone who has a positive attitude and is willing to work hard. Specific knowledge of the marathon events is not as important because we can help develop this in individuals.

The sport event industry is rapidly changing, but one of our biggest challenges is not owning our venue. We are subject to road construction and other city planning projects that may impact our route. In addition, we have to work within the structure of the city, which is a major challenge as our event continues to grow. With the smaller roads in the city of Cincinnati, we have to make sure to space individuals out at the start so the potential overcrowding does not impact their overall experience. Another issue for our organization is that marathons are not growing in popularity; half marathons and ultramarathons are growing, but not the full distance. We need to determine how to transition a runner from the shorter distances and "unruns" events into the marathons. Finally, the events at the Boston Marathon have changed everything we do to try to make the event safe. Rather than working with just our local officials, we have begun working with local, state, and national levels of security to assist with developing more comprehensive security, which in turn, impacts our event's budget.

The future of the running industry overall seems very bright. The increasing number of MOB events (mud runs, obstacle runs, and beer runs) has led to an increase in the overall number of runners, and this is a potential opportunity for us to increase the number of runners in our events. Distance relays and ultramarathons also seem to be growing in popularity as individuals are looking for that next way to challenge themselves. Finally, female-specific events are becoming more and more popular as the number of women participating in half and full marathons has continued to increase over the past 5 to 10 years.

Introduction

Countries, states, communities, and local residents vie to host sporting events for a variety of positively perceived reasons (e.g., prestige, awareness, economic profitability, increased tourism activity, infrastructure development). However, being awarded a sport event is almost certain to result in both positive and negative impacts on the host community and its residents. Positive impacts can include new and updated roads, entertainment venues, and other infrastructures, as well as increased tourism revenue, media exposure, commercial appeal, and civic pride. Negative impacts can include overcrowding and increased travel concerns, disruption to the local environment, the building or renovating of uneconomical and unsustainable infrastructures, and unfavorable perceptions of the host community. Whether positive or negative, the greater the social, economic, and environmental impact of a sport event and the longer lasting its residual effects, the more likely a sport event legacy is to be created.

What Are Legacies?

Legacies are "the material and non-material effects produced directly or indirectly by the sport event, whether planned or not, that durably transform the host region in an objectively and subjectively, positive or negative way" (Chappelet & Junod, 2006, p. 84). Furthermore, legacies include "all planned and unplanned, positive and negative, tangible and intangible structures

legacy The lasting direct or indirect effects generated from hosting an event that may positively or negatively impact the community.

tangible legacy
Observable, easily identified or physical changes to the host community that remain upon conclusion of the event.

intangible legacy
Nonphysical changes associated with the transfer of knowledge, governmental reform, and emotional capital for residents, participants, and spectators, as well as psychological improvements to the city's image and social structure.

created for and by a sport event that remain longer than the event itself" (Preuss, 2007, p. 211). Legacies may be **tangible** or material, such as sports facilities, or they may be **intangible** or nonmaterial, such as sociocultural development. Tangible legacies, as indicated by the name, are easy to recognize, whereas intangible or nonmaterial legacies are more of a challenge to identify and measure (Chappelet, 2008).

As you can see from these descriptions, the term legacy is broadly defined and can encompass all facets of hosting an event. Examining the legacy of an event can be problematic in that different regions, cultures, and industries consider various outcomes of the event when examining legacies and the subsequent impacts. Simply put, legacies are the "things" left behind upon the completion of an event. These things can be tangible, such as roads, venues, and housing, or intangible, such as memories from attending the event or the perception that the host community/region is a capable and experienced locale to host future events. Legacies can be small or large, valuable or worthless, positive or negative, and can last an indeterminate amount of time, from days to years. Legacies can result from any and all sport events, ranging from small-scale (e.g., local charity race) to mega (e.g., Olympic Games or International Federation of Association Football [FIFA] World Cup) events.

Irrespective of size, community leaders believe hosting a sport event can be the spark needed for urban development and, as a result, have pursued hosting various types and sizes of sport events to use as a platform to attract investors and tourists and to benefit their residents (Misener & Mason, 2008). Thus, the ultimate objective for event organizers and community leaders should be to determine how to develop and market sport events in ways that promote a host city (Misener & Mason, 2009). The resultant impact of such development and marketing efforts could lead to the establishment of sustainable sport venues and events in the local community, increases in sport tourism, improved infrastructure, and the progression of a legacy for both the sport event and host city/community.

Growth in Sport Tourism

As interest in sport and the consumption of sport have increased, so too has the need for more sport options, whether as a participant or as a spectator, when traveling. The tourism industry, as well as the sport industry, has witnessed growth in vacations in which a sporting event, ranging from youth recreational leagues up to the professional ranks, is the main attraction or catalyst for the trip. In fact, a number of sporting events, such as the Daytona 500, National Collegiate Athletic Association (NCAA) national championships, FIFA World Cup, and Olympic Games, have themselves become vacation destinations. Sport event tourism has played a primary and central role for host destinations, evidenced by the

inclusion of sport events in their tourism marketing plans (Chalip & Leyns, 2002; Higham & Hinch, 2002). However, the type (i.e., size) of sport events that take place in certain destinations is often contingent upon the ability of the host community to accommodate the influx of tourists, the current or prospective infrastructure, and the desired impact(s). Sport events can range from mega-events such as the FIFA World Cup and the Olympic Games, to large- or medium-size sport events such as national championships and college and high school tournaments, to small-scale events such as local charity walks/runs and recreational sport leagues. Again, it is important to consider the size of each event because of its impacts on the community (Chalip & Costa, 2005).

Sport Event Sizes

The size of a sporting event is an important consideration in the discussion of legacies. As various events range in sizes, so too does their impact on the host community, participants, and spectators. Mega-sporting events garner the most attention and media exposure on a global scene, and as such, could be argued to result in the greatest and most impactful legacies. Given the large number of spectators, often a worldwide audience, it is understandable for event organizers and host communities to expect positive, long-term impacts from their investments. For instance, anecdotal evidence supports the claim that the cities of Sydney, Australia (host of the 2000 Summer Olympic Games), and Vancouver, British Columbia, Canada (host of the 2012 Winter Olympic Games), witnessed positive legacies regarding their cities as sport-event and tourist destinations. Specifically, one of the lasting legacies used on a daily basis by Vancouver residents and tourists is the new Sea to Sky Highway that has made it faster and safer for individuals to travel from Vancouver to Whistler. However, mega-sporting events have been critiqued in recent years regarding the sustainability of their positive legacies (Smith, 2009). The best support of this argument would be the 1976 Summer Olympic Games hosted by Montreal, Quebec, Canada. The city of Montreal amassed millions of dollars of debt and fell so far behind schedule that the construction of one of the primary venues was not completed until after the games. In fact, it took the city 30 years to pay off the debt for Montreal's Olympic Stadium, with residents finally paying it off in 2006. Additionally, the Athens Organizing Committee did such a poor job of planning for the postevent use of the venues developed for the 2004 Olympic Games hosted in Athens, Greece, that many of them are empty and go unused and have become **white elephants**. Thus, scholars have suggested that the hosting of medium- and small-scale sporting events could be more beneficial in the pursuit of a positive legacy (Higham, 1999; Gibson, Kaplanidou, & Kang, 2012; Misener & Mason, 2006). As such, the primary focus of this chapter will center on medium- and small-scale events.

white elephant In reference to event legacy, a stadium, arena, or other facility constructed to host an event that remains underutilized after the event has occurred.

Medium- and Small-Scale Events

Medium- and small-scale events are currently being utilized more often in community development strategies as host communities are becoming more proactive in the planning and managing stages of hosting an event to ensure they allow for and attain the numerous potential benefits of doing so. Event hosts and organizers have recognized the opportunities to advance their image via increased media attention, promote their community's distinguishing features, draw tourists (as well as participants), and enhance investment opportunities for outside and local businesses (Misener & Mason, 2006). Not only is the size of an event an important consideration, but so too is the type of event.

Depending on the event, host communities may need to plan for an influx of spectators or participants, each bringing with them different needs, expectations, and outcomes. Higham (1999) suggests that there is more tourism development potential in small-scale events given that some of these small-scale events will draw spectators, while others, such as marathons, due to their features (i.e., competition) are more likely to attract participants. Furthermore, Higham (1999) suggests that small-scale sport events can have more positive impacts for residents, as they "comply with the principles of **sustainable tourism**" (p. 87). That is, because the infrastructure to host the event already exists, such events require minor investment of public capital, and the resultant negative impacts (i.e., crowding and congestion) are more manageable.

sustainable tourism Development of the infrastructure in the host community to generate a continuous flow of tourist activity.

While economic benefits appear to be of prime consideration when discussing the expected benefits of any event, social benefits can be extremely important to local and small-scale events. Small-scale events can often bring about a sense of civic pride, allowing local residents and volunteers to claim a sense of ownership and responsibility for the event. Walo, Bull, and Breen (1996) report that residents were more likely to volunteer for events that were perceived as bringing the community together, demonstrating the potential bond that can exist between a small-scale or local event and the host community.

Why Is Legacy Important?

Given the increases in sport event destination traveling and sport tourism, interests have turned to the impacts of hosting a sport event on the local community. The potential legacy that can be left with the host community, as well as with a particular sporting event, has drawn substantial consideration in the planning and organization of a sport event. Furthermore, investments made toward hosting an event have become an important component of community resources and infrastructure development. As a result of this increased awareness and desire to host events, experts have become more interested in gaining a better understanding of how to measure legacies so as to maximize positive legacies and minimize negative legacies. Additional interests lie in helping communities and event hosts to better plan sporting events and sport tourism destinations, as well as to address questions with regard to the postevent use of infrastructures and facilities developed or improved for the event (Karadakis & Kaplanidou, 2012).

VIGNETTE 15-1

Lake Myrtle Sports Complex

In 2009, the city of Auburndale, Florida, opened a multipurpose sports complex consisting of soccer and baseball fields with the capabilities of hosting a variety of sport events such as lacrosse, rugby, and flag football. The sports complex is used to attract tourists by hosting various sporting events organized by the Polk County Tourism and Sports Marketing Headquarters. Some of the reoccurring events that are hosted include Florida State Soccer Association's Florida Classic, RussMatt Central Florida Baseball Invitational, and Florida State Soccer Association's State Cup. The sports complex also is home to the Florida Youth Soccer Association headquarters and host to the Florida Sports Hall of Fame. The sports complex provides the city of Auburndale the opportunity to host various sporting events to attract local communities as well as tourists to attend tournaments. By hosting regular tournaments, the city of Auburndale and the organizers can leverage the tournaments to create an economic impact for the community. Furthermore, the complex provides an opportunity for residents to volunteer at the various sporting events, provides children a place to play sports, and allows residents to come together and get to know one another, either through volunteering or by watching the children from the sideline. Thus, the complex provides residents of Auburndale a social, economic, and infrastructure legacy. Students should do some research to determine who is in charge of their state's and county's tourism and sport event initiatives to identify which sporting events occur on a regular basis in their given communities. Doing so will provide them with the opportunity to identify any legacies generated from hosting events in their community.

It has been suggested that event organizers are responsible for utilizing sport events for the long-term development of a host community, which has directed attention toward the legacy phenomenon (Weed & Bull, 2004). For instance, when awarding the Olympic Games, the International Olympic Committee (IOC) is concerned with the lasting impacts to the host city. More specifically, the IOC has indicated three reasons that generating positive legacies is important to a variety of sport events:

- To prevent the host community from criticizing the organizers of the event for any potential shortcomings
- To substantiate the use of public resources for the potential sport-event-related infrastructure(s)
- To stimulate interest for the community and/or surrounding communities to host future events, helping to ensure the continuity of the event

As it relates to the sport industry, the term legacy is fairly new, and there is no clear definition of what legacy means in the sport event framework (Preuss, 2007). The IOC explains that difficulties in defining the term legacy can be attributed to the fact that different cultures can, and oftentimes do, interpret the meaning of legacy in a variety of ways. As defined previously, legacies are "the material and non-material effects produced directly or indirectly by the sport event, whether planned or not, that durably transform the host region in an objectively and subjectively, positive or negative way" (Chappelet & Junod, 2006, p. 84). Similarly, Preuss (2007) offers a similar definition: "Irrespective of the time of production and space, legacy is all planned and unplanned, positive and negative, tangible and intangible structures created for and by a sport event that remain longer than the event itself" (p. 211).

Notice in these definitions that a legacy consists of effects that are tangible and intangible, are planned and unplanned, have a direct or indirect outcome, can be assessed objectively as well as subjectively, and can be both positive and negative. The contradictory nature of this definition clearly demonstrates the complexity associated with attempting to determine just what a legacy entails and just how it is produced. Thus, Preuss (2007) further explicates that there are five dimensions of legacy incorporated into its definition:

- Degree of planned/unplanned structure
- Degree of positive/negative structure
- Degree of tangible/intangible structure

- Duration and time of a changed structure
- Space affected by changed structure

Components of Legacy Impacts

At this time, it is important to note a component of legacies that seems ambiguous but covers a spectrum of resultant impacts of hosting an event: tangible and intangible legacies. Tangible legacies are observable, are easily identified, include programs and initiatives, are measured by infrastructure (consisting of infrastructures either related to sport or not), consist of technological and environmental improvements to the community/city, and offer networking opportunities for local and international businesses to expand. Looking back at the 1996 Olympic Games in Atlanta, Georgia, infrastructure developed for the Games such as the Athletes' Village was given to the local university to serve as dorms for the students once the games were over. Furthermore, relationships and networking established during the Games resulted in 280 more international businesses in Atlanta (International Olympic Committee Factsheet, December 2013).

Conversely, intangible legacies are a little more difficult to identify and measure. Intangible legacies can be associated with the transfer of knowledge, governmental reform, and emotional capital for residents, participants, and spectators, as well as psychological improvements to the city's image and social structure. According to Kaplanidou and Karadakis (2010), examples of emotional capital experienced at the Vancouver Olympics

> included inspiration, pride, can do attitude, feelings of empowerment, excitement and feelings of togetherness, and gratitude for created opportunities for business and collaboration. As indicated by the Tourism BC Vice President of 2010 and Corporate Relations, "What a great way to build confidence in Vancouver for us, that we could pull off something this big. It builds an air of confidence and, you know, it can only be good for us." (p. 115)

Legacy Event Structures

While it may be difficult to determine exactly which tangible and intangible legacies to expect from hosting and/or organizing an event, there are several types of legacies that are more substantive. In examining characteristics of legacy types and in an attempt to classify the variety of legacies, Preuss (2007) suggests six event structures that can be created as positive offshoots from host-ing an event: (1) infrastructure, (2) know-how, (3) networks, (4) culture (cre-ated both during the preparation stages of hosting the event and postevent), (5) emotions, and (6) image. The following section will present further details on each of the various event structures (from Gratton & Preuss, 2008, p. 1926).

INFRASTRUCTURE

Infrastructure refers to the sport facilities and subsequent surrounding areas needed for training and competition. Depending on the size of the event, this may include improvements and developments to airports, roads, hotels, telecommunication networks, housing (for athletes, media, and officials), entertainment facilities, fairgrounds, parks, etc. Organizers should fit all these different types of infrastructures into their plan, as they will remain long after the event has passed. For example, an upcoming cycling race in a local community may request that roads be resurfaced to ensure riders can safely ride along the route, or the postrace venue may receive significant upgrades to improve the appeal and amenities of the facility.

infrastructure The sport facilities and subsequent sur-rounding areas needed for training and competition.

KNOWLEDGE, SKILL DEVELOPMENT, AND EDUCATION

As sport events take place, local area residents and other stakeholders are exposed to the necessary knowledge and skills associated with organizing an event. Furthermore, employees and volunteers associated with the host organization should have the opportunity to develop skills and knowledge that may be used for future event organization, human resources manage-ment, security, hospitality, service, and other industries. In addition, the spectators, participants, and volunteers are afforded the opportunity to use public transportation (potentially recently developed or improved) and might enjoy increased awareness of different projects, such as environmen-tal sustainability. Lastly, opportunities to boast and inform people about the local community's/city's history and culture can be recognized. For example, in Alachua County, Florida, the Gainesville Sports Commission annually facilitates more than 30 sport events. Through its staff and trained volun-teers, the organization has successfully hosted numerous events, contribut-ing more than $20 million to the local economy. Volunteers who gain skills from hosting these events can move on to other sectors and apply what they have learned, such as volunteer and event management.

IMAGE

Hosting a sport event can produce symbolic meaning, lead to change, or even help to establish the local city's image. When successful, this can provide positive imagery. However, host cities and communities must concern themselves with potential negative impacts. For instance, potential problems such as hooligans, unfriendly local residents, an unwelcoming atmosphere, and organizational shortcomings can have a negative impact on a host's image. Similar to positive imagery, negative perceptions can last for years to come. For example, when people are asked about the Atlanta Olympic Games, they think of the traffic problems that occurred and still associate Atlanta with poor transportation infrastructure. Looking back at the Montreal Olympic Games, people think of the debt that Olympic Stadium cost the local citizens for 30 years. However, there are positive images that can be generated as well, and hosting events can serve as a way to change a city's image. For example, Turin, Italy, was able to rid itself of its long-standing reputation of being little more than an industrial city and became viewed as a tourist and business destination as a result of hosting the Winter Olympic Games in 2006 (International Olympic Committee Factsheet, December 2013).

EMOTIONS

There is also a psychological dynamic to hosting a sport event. When a community or city hosts a sporting event, it is afforded opportunities to create local pride, develop identification, and promote positive vision, optimism, and motivation for the residents. As with image, negative emotions can also be felt, and host organizations and cities need to be cautious of this detrimental outcome. For instance, residents and local area constituents may develop negative emotions toward the event if the construction of new facilities exceeds time expectations and/or displaces local citizens, potentially resulting in the local residents feeling as though they lost their social environment.

NETWORKS

For an event to be successfully organized and executed, numerous organizations need to be involved from the beginning, working together and supporting one another. Depending on the type and size of the event, these organizations can include international sport federations, media, local tourism departments, and political groups, to name a few. The positive impact or legacy of successful networking among these organizations and the host community can lead to the development of grassroots coaching programs, new or improved educational facilities, the advent of sport programs designed for all ages and skill levels, and the potential to host additional sport events. Additionally, individual employees, volunteers, and participants might have the opportunity to socialize and grow their interpersonal networks.

CULTURE

When discussing legacies, culture is a concept that includes the creation, development, potential enhancement, and promotion of local ideas, identity and products. Hosting a sport event allows the host city to showcase its cultural identity, which can produce positive image, increased awareness, new infrastructure, and additional tourist products. This notion of culture as an event structure can be witnessed in the Olympic Games. The opening ceremonies have been grounds for the host country to educate viewers on its history, promote positive characteristics of the country and its residents, and showcase the country's culture and history. Local events may also represent the community's culture. For instance, in some southern U.S. communities, adult softball is a big part of the culture. Several fields, teams, and leagues exist to meet the demands of these individuals. Therefore, hosting a championship tournament through the United States Specialty Sports Association may have a positive impact on the community's cultural identity.

Beyond the event structures discussed previously, researchers have identified and classified legacies with some common themes. Cashman (2005) has suggested that event legacies are not generic and can be organized into six specific categories: (1) sport, (2) economics, (3) infrastructure, (4) information and education, (5) public life, politics, and culture, and (6) symbols, memory, and history. Similarly, Chappelet and Junod (2006) suggest there are five types of legacies, categorized by their effects: (1) sporting, (2) urban, (3) infrastructural, (4) economic, and (5) social. More recently, Karadakis and Kaplanidou (2012) have made use of six themes in researching legacies: (1) economic, (2) tourism, (3) environmental, (4) sociocultural, (5) psychological, and (6) knowledge development.

What is common in all of the proposed sets of legacy themes is that they center on sport as a means to promote and encourage development of infrastructure, improve psychosocial aspects of the host city/community, increase awareness and knowledge of culture, and produce a positive economic return. As can be seen by the numerous studies that have classified legacies, the three pillars of sustainability are always present (i.e., economic, social, and environmental legacies).

Pruess (2007) also recognizes the need to distinguish among legacies, using the terminology of "hard" and "soft" legacies in his classification of event structures. Preuss suggests that **soft structures** include knowledge (e.g., organizational, security, technological), networks (e.g., political, sport federations, security), and cultural goods (e.g., cultural identity, cultural ideas, and common memory). He categorizes **hard structures** as those consisting of primary structure (e.g., sport infrastructure, training sites), secondary structure (e.g., villages for athletes, technical officials, media), and tertiary structure (e.g., security, power plants, cultural attractions, telecommunication networks).

As the discussion thus far has shown, there are numerous examples of the positive legacies produced by a sport event, including those that are easy to identify (e.g., urban planning, sport infrastructure) and those that are difficult to identify (e.g., urban regeneration, increased tourism, improved public welfare, opportunities for city marketing, renewed community spirit, improved inter-regional cooperation, production of cultural values, opportunities for education, emotional experience). However, as the various definitions of legacy indicate, hosting a sport event can produce negative legacies, including debts from construction, opportunity costs, unneeded infrastructure, temporary crowding, and loss of returning tourists (Cashman, 2005; Gratton & Preuss, 2008; Mangan, 2008; Preuss, 2007; Solberg & Preuss, 2007).

Measuring Legacies

Now that we have discussed the broad definition of a legacy, examined the many ways in which a legacy can be manifested through event structures, and introduced the three pillars of sustainability, it is time to provide insight into how legacies are measured. In other words, how do we quantify lasting effects of a sport event? Measuring legacies involves examining the changes that occur as a result of having hosted or through the continuous hosting of a sporting event over time. This section will discuss three traditional methods of measuring legacies—benchmarking, the top-down approach, and the

soft structure An element of event legacy relating to knowledge, networks, and cultural goods that are developed from the hosting of an event.

hard structure An element of event legacy relating to primary structure (e.g., sport infrastructure, training sites), secondary structure (e.g., villages for athletes, technical officials, media), and tertiary structure (e.g., security, power plants, cultural attractions, telecommunication networks).

nontraditional bottom-up measure. Traditionally, measuring legacies has been carried out by conducting economic impact studies. This approach was once deemed the method of choice due to its tangible components and its use of easily defined dollar amounts. Furthermore, an economic impact study was seen as a means to help justify the use of public resources for infrastructure development related to the event (Preuss, 2007). However, most case studies currently aimed at measuring legacies make use of benchmarking and/or a "top-down" approach.

BENCHMARK AND TOP-DOWN APPROACHES

In accordance with the **benchmark approach**, there are three scenarios under which legacies can be produced: (1) the same city hosts the same sport event over time, (2) the same city hosts different sport events over time, and (3) the same sport event is hosted by different cities over time (Preuss, 2007).

benchmark approach A method of evaluating an event's legacy in which an event held in one city is compared to an event held in another to determine the impacts generated from the events.

In the first scenario, the same host city can develop different legacies as a result of hosting the same event twice or on a regular basis. Depending on the size and frequency of the event, new infrastructure or improvements to existing infrastructure may be needed.

In the second scenario, different events in the same city can also create different legacies. Having a portfolio of events that a community hosts may require additional infrastructure requirements, as well as address varying social concerns, and allow for the use of the distinguishing geographical characteristics of said location in developing a legacy unique to the event. Furthermore, if an event strategy is present, the organizers can leverage other events to create a similar legacy for both the host community and the event. Preuss (2007) suggests "synergistic effects are possible when a legacy of one event is a prerequisite for another event (e.g., sport facilities)" (p. 214).

The same event in different cities can create different legacies as every community is unique and may have different infrastructure needs and community agendas, resulting in different legacies from the same event. The intent here is to consider the characteristics of a community when developing a legacy. There are caveats with using a benchmark approach, in that this manner of measurement attempts to compare an event held in one city with an event held in another. This is a difficult task because sport events are unique and complex and occur in a fast-paced changing environment, making it difficult for benchmark studies to identify and measure legacies for future events (Preuss, 2007).

top-down approach
A method of evaluating an event's legacy that compares the economic indicators of the event with the same indicators of the host city if the event had not taken place.

Conversely, the **top-down approach** of measuring an event legacy aims to isolate event-related impacts from general municipal developments that may occur even if the event were not to be held. Thus, the top-down approach aims to compare the economic indicators of the event with the same indicators of the host city if the event had not taken place (Preuss, 2007). The legacy is essentially the difference between these two indicators (having hosted the event versus not having hosted the event).

CONTROL-CASE APPROACH

control-case approach
A method of evaluating an event's legacy in which attempts are made to compare the infrastructure developments a city or community would incur as a result of hosting an event to the potential alternative infrastructure development the city would undertake if the event were not to occur.

A similar approach to, or subset of, the top-down method is that of the control case. In the **control-case approach**, attempts are made to compare the infrastructure developments a city or community would incur as a result of hosting an event to the potential alternative infrastructure development the city would undertake if the event were not to occur. In this situation the legacy would result from the difference found between the event case and the control case (Preuss, 2007). Likewise, there are caveats to using this approach. Legacies are not limited to just economic growth for a host city. Sport events are complex, multifaceted events that go beyond economic impacts. As such, it is important to consider intangible sporting, recreational, political, psychological, and promotional outcomes from hosting an event that are difficult to measure (Preuss, 2007).

BOTTOM-UP APPROACH

bottom-up approach
A method of evaluating an event's legacy in which all relevant changes to infrastructures and the host city are considered as well as potential long-term development for the city.

The **bottom-up approach** responds to the limitations of the other legacy-measuring methods in that all relevant changes to infrastructures and the host city are considered as well as potential long-term development for the city (Preuss, 2007). Recall from earlier in the chapter that sport events have both "soft" and "hard" structures. Two soft structures that are considered in this approach are image and emotions—primarily because they undoubtedly have an impact on the host city. Image has the ability to form, reposition, or strengthen the image of a city, while emotion can instill pride and motivation for residents (Preuss, 2007). Thus, using the bottom-up approach to measure a legacy takes into consideration the fact that structures created for the events may have different and sometimes conflicting goals. For example, trying to improve the city's tourism industry requires increased media coverage, flawless organization, and extraordinary sport facilities.

However, the building of sport facilities does not always take into account use of the facilities after the event and into the future. Therefore, it is important to develop a clear strategy of how legacies will be developed and why it is important to understand legacies, because what may seem to be a positive legacy for organizers may actually be a negative legacy for residents (Preuss, 2007).

An additional point to be made about development plans is that they can result in three types of legacies. First, the host city can develop event structures more expeditiously because of the event. Second, a political consensus is often needed to finalize development plans, and thus helps ensure investments from public resources. Lastly, resources for the development of city infrastructure and/or event infrastructure can be funded by autonomous capital suppliers such as sport federations, central government, or private firms (Preuss, 2007, p. 219). This means that in some cases independent corporations or organizing bodies take the burden to build infrastructure that will be used for an event. This occurred in 1984, when Los Angeles held the Summer Olympic Games. To pay for the Los Angeles Olympic Games, organizers relied on corporate sponsors and the use of existing facilities to host the event. This resulted in a profit being generated and influenced the model used for bidding and hosting the Olympic Games today.

SUMMARY

As demonstrated in this chapter, hosting a sport event requires specific "soft" and "hard" structures and infrastructure that remain after the event. These developments have been found to have the ability to change the quality of the host city as well as leave a positive and/or negative legacy (Gratton & Preuss, 2008; Preuss, 2007) in the minds of the host community, spectators, participants, and other stakeholders, including the general public. Legacies of events are complex; they can be influenced by various local and global factors. Most publications focus on single event legacies or, at best, focus on only one or two legacies resulting from an event (Preuss, 2007). Despite the multifaceted uniqueness of legacies, the most common legacy that is cited and researched centers on the resultant sport facilities (Chalip, 2002) and transportation infrastructure developed for an event. Thus, it is imperative that host communities and event organizers strategically plan for legacies. In doing so, the long-term development of the host community must be at the forefront of any projects. If not, justifying the use and investments of public funds and resources may be difficult (Bohlmann, 2006).

It is possible for the impacts of a legacy to diminish overt time and ultimately disappear if long-term efforts are not taken seriously and infrastructures (both hard and soft) are not maintained (Terret, 2008). Thus, an objective of studying legacies is to attempt to ensure and secure benefits from hosting a sport event that will not fade away long after the event is over (Gratton & Preuss, 2008). This is why studying and understanding legacies is such a critical component of the sport tourism industry. In order to identify if legacies have a lasting effect on the host cities, it is recommended that studies be conducted 15 to 20 years after the event has occurred (Gratton & Preuss, 2008). However, there are few studies that try to scientifically measure these long-term benefits.

To date, there has been no attempt to conduct a research study to evaluate the net, long-term legacies of a sport event. This deficiency can be the result of three critical issues that need to be addressed. First, it is extremely difficult to factually determine potential projects a city would invest in had it not hosted the event. Instead most studies focus on the "gross" legacy. Second, it is difficult to distinguish whether a legacy is positive or negative. While this may not affect the tangible measurement of the legacy, how a legacy is interpreted is important to perceptions of the host community. There is always the potential for discrepancies between perceptions of a legacy for a host community's event organizers and investors when compared to the realities of the legacy for a city's residents. The third issue deals with measuring a legacy over time (Preuss, 2007). Preuss (2007) introduced the "bottom-up" approach, which helps identify a legacy that is left after an event has passed, but the difficulty that is common in all legacy studies is determining the particular impacts of a legacy over time. Consider that a legacy is what remains long after an event has passed, studies must continuously be conducted in an attempt to measure and evaluate the definitive impacts, or even the perception, of a legacy.

DISCUSSION QUESTIONS

1. How different and similar are the two legacy definitions suggested in the literature of this chapter? Using both definitions, discuss/create your own definition of the term legacy.

2. What legacy aspects are more useful in the marketing of a sport event to a host city, the tangible or the intangible? Explain your answer.

3. If you were the chief operating officer for the bid committee for an event, what legacy aspects would you focus on to market this event successfully to stakeholders, such as the federal or state/provincial governments or the public, to gain their support?

4. How can you incorporate the concept of legacies in solicitation of sponsorships, ticket sales, and license merchandizing for a sporting event? (It is probably more beneficial to focus on large-scale events for this question such as the Super Bowl, FIFA World Cup, or Olympic Games.)

5. Develop a model of the potential legacies that can be generated in a given city from hosting a sport event. Can the model be applied to other cities that are planning to host sport events? Or do you think it should change from city to city? What should one take into account?

6. Are there legacies that are unique to the Olympic Games versus other sport events? Are legacies easier to identify/plan for in mega-events, medium-scaled events, or small-scaled events? Explain your answer.

Case **STUDY**

Legacy Impact of RAGBRAI

In 1973, a group of friends got together for a casual ride across the state of Iowa. This inaugural event was organized by two newspaper column writers who were also avid cyclists and thought of the expedition as a potential idea for a column. The event was rather disorganized as no one had prepared the course or developed campsites or rest areas along the way. The two columnists simply selected five different cities throughout the state of Iowa to serve as overnight resting destinations. In total, approximately 300 individuals started the ride and 114 finished the entire event. Currently, the race, now known as Register's Annual Great Bicycle Ride Across Iowa (RAGBRAI), limits the number of riders to 8500 to ensure that they do not overwhelm the host communities.

The event has grown over the years and has received major national and international attention. In the late 1980s, for instance, *NBC Nightly News*, the *Today Show*, and *CBS News* broadcast features about the race and highlighted some of the host communities. In the 1990s, the ride had reached international appeal and was broadcast on a television station in Germany. These broadcasts and the newspaper and other media outlets reporting on the event not only helped increase the awareness and levels of participation for the event, but also highlighted the wonderful state of Iowa.

From a tangible outcome perspective, the event has led to the increase in bicycle lanes throughout the host communities, which rotate every year of the event. The roads are repaved for the safety of the riders, and part of the expense is shared by the state and the event. There are also various charitable organizations associated with the ride, enabling people to raise thousands of dollars each year. Finally, 10 different bike shops across the state are affiliated with the ride, and they each see an increase in riders and provide new riders with helpful tips, bike maintenance training, and ride training plans. Overall, this event has established a positive long-term legacy in its 42-year existence.

RAGBRAI has demonstrated both positive tangible and intangible legacies, as have other events, some likely in your community. Knowing the importance of legacy, you will want to make sure your event is a financial success and a credit to your community, not just now but long into the future. Review a local facility or event in your community to determine if it has developed a positive or negative legacy for the community. The following exercises will help get you on the right track:

1. Select either a sport event or facility and review the history of the event.
2. Evaluate the event's or facility's long-term impact on the host community, including both tangible and intangible benefits.
3. Identify methods you would use to evaluate the success of the legacy of the event.
4. Outline two new strategies you would use to create an additional legacy for the event or facility.

REFERENCES

Bohlmann, H. R. (2006). *Predicting the economic impact of the 2010 FIFA World Cup on South Africa*. Pretoria, South Africa: Department of Economic, University of Pretoria.

Cashman, R. (2005). *The bitter-sweet awakening. The legacy of the Sydney 2000 Olympic Games*. Petersham, Australia: Walla Walla Press.

Chalip, L. (2002). Using the Olympics to optimise tourism benefits: University lecture on the Olympics [online article], from Barcelona: Centres d'Estudis Olimpics (UAB). International Chair in Olympism (IOC-UAB). Retrieved from http://olympicstudies.uab.es/lectures/web/pdf/chalip.pdf

Chalip, L., & Costa, C. A. (2005). Sport event tourism and the destination brand: Towards a general theory. *Sport in Society, 8*(2), 218–237.

Chalip, L., Green, B. C., & Hill, B. (2003). Effects of sport event media on destination image and intention to visit. *Journal of Sport Management, 17*, 214–234.

Chalip, L. & Leyns, A. (2002). Local business leveraging of a sport event: Managing an event for economic benefit. *Journal of Sport Management, 16*, 132–158.

Chappelet, J.-L. (2008). Olympic environmental concerns as a legacy of the Winter Games. *The International Journal of the History of Sport, 25*(14), 1884–1902.

Chappelet, J.-L., & Junod, T. (2006). A tale of 3 Olympic cities: What can Turin learn from the Olympic legacy of other alpine cities? In D. Torres (Ed.), *Proceedings of workshop on major sport events as opportunity for development* (pp. 83–90). Valencia, Spain: Society for the Advancement of Library & Information Science; Madras School of Social Work; and United Nations Educational, Scientific, and Cultural Organization.

Gibson, H., Kaplanidou, K., & Kang, S. (2012). Small-scale event sport tourism: A case study in sustainable tourism. *Sport Management Review, 15*(2), 160–170.

Gratton, C., & Preuss, H. (2008). Maximizing Olympic impacts by building up legacies. *The International Journal of the History of Sport, 25*(14), 1922–1938.

Higham, J. E. S. (1999). Sport as an avenue of tourism development: An analysis of the positive and negative impacts of sport tourism (Commentary). *Current Issues in Tourism, 2*(1), 82–90.

Higham, J., & Hinch, T. (2002). Tourism, sport and seasons: The challenges and potential of overcoming seasonality in the sport and tourism sectors. *Tourism Management, 23*, 175–185.

International Olympic Committee. (2003). Report of the IOC Evaluation Commission. Retrieved from http://www.olympic.org/Documents/Reports/EN/en_report_706.pdf

International Olympic Committee Factsheet (December, 2013). *Legacies of the Games*. Retrieved from http://www.olympic.org/Documents/Reference_documents_Factsheets/Legacy.pdf

Kaplanidou, K., & Karadakis, K. (2010). Understanding the legacies of a host Olympic City: The case of the 2010 Vancouver Olympic Games. *Sport Marketing Quarterly*, *19*, 110–117.

Karadakis, K., & Kaplanidou, K. (2012). Legacy perceptions among host and nonhost Olympic Games residents: A longitudinal study of the 2010 Vancouver Olympic Games. *European Sport Management Quarterly*, *12*(3), 243–264.

Mangan, J. A. (2008). Prologue: Guarantees of global goodwill; Post-Olympic legacies—Too many limping white elephants? *The International Journal of the History of Sport*, *25*(14), 1869–1883.

Misener, L., & Mason, D. (2006). Creating community networks: Can sporting events offer meaningful sources of social capital? *Managing Leisure*, *11*, 39–56.

Misener, L., & Mason, D. (2008). Urban regimes and the sporting events agenda: A cross national comparison of civic development strategies. *Journal of Sport Management*, *22*, 603–627.

Misener, L., & Mason, D. (2009). Fostering community development through sporting events strategies: An examination of urban regime perceptions. *Journal of Sport Management*, *23*, 770–794.

Preuss, H. (2007). The conceptualisation and measurement of mega sport event legacies. *Journal of Sport & Tourism*, *12*(3–4), 207–227.

Smith, A. (2009). Theorizing the relationship between major sport events and social sustainability. *Journal of Sport & Tourism*, *14*, 109–120.

Solberg, H. A., & Preuss, H. (2007). Major sport events and long-term tourism impacts. *Journal of Sport Management*, *21*(2), 213–234.

Terret, T. (2008). The Albertiville Winter Olympics: Unexpected legacies—failed expectations for regional economic development. *The International Journal of the History of Sport*, *25*(14), 1903–1921.

Walo, M., Bull, A., & Breen, H. (1996). Achieving economic benefits at local events: A case study of a local sports event. *Festival Management and Event Tourism*, *4*, 95–106.

Weed, M., & Bull, C. (2004). *Sports tourism: Participants, policy and providers.* Oxford, UK: Elsevier.

act of God   An instance of uncontrollable natural forces (often used in insurance claims).

activation   A specific action taken toward leveraging the sport–sponsorship relationship.

administration domain   The event management domain that includes the finance, human resources, information, procurement, stakeholders, systems, and time elements of an event.

affective dimension of experience   The emotional response to the experience.

ancillary event   An event that occurs in conjunction with another type of event.

ancillary revenue   Income generated from goods and services that enhance the primary product or service; examples include concessions, parking, and merchandise.

arms race   As it relates to the sport event industry, the competition between sport organizations to have the best facilities, resources, revenue-generating amenities, and other event features to ensure an advantage in the marketplace.

behavioral involvement   The action one takes in sport, whether as a participant or a spectator.

benchmark approach   A method of evaluating an event's legacy in which an event held in one city is compared to an event held in another to determine the impacts generated from the events.

bid   A competitive process in which the objective is to win the right to organize a specific sporting event.

bond　A debt security in which the issuer owes the bondholder a designated amount; payment, interest, and maturity date details are provided.

bottom-up approach　A method of evaluating an event's legacy in which all relevant changes to infrastructures and the host city are considered as well as potential long-term development for the city.

breakeven analysis　An assessment used to determine at what point the event can cover all the expenses and begin to make a profit.

capital　Funds needed to finance an organization's assets.

capital project　A long-term investment project that will increase the organization's assets.

checklist　A preventive control tool that ensures that each individual is performing all tasks essential for the success of the event.

closure/shutdown phase　The final stage of event planning to ensure nothing is lost, equipment is returned properly, and the flow of those involved occurs seamlessly.

cognitive dimension of experience　The making sense of an experience through awareness, perception, memory, learning, and judgment.

cognitive involvement　The acquisition of information/knowledge about a sport.

commitment　The frequency, duration, and intensity of attachment to sport.

communitas　A special place where event attendees share a heightened sense of community and belonging.

community event　A relatively small-scale event that appeals to a specific geographic region.

competitive factor　A rivalry or event meant to measure ability in relation to another.

conative dimension of experience　The behavior, or physical responses, of event attendees.

concessionaire　An entity given the rights to operate and sell goods or services on premises that belong to another. Venues often enter into agreements to sell parking and food concessions on their premises.

consumer involvement　A blend of the individual's interest in sport and the degree of importance sport has in his or her life.

consumption   The active use of a product or service.

control-case approach   A method of evaluating an event's legacy in which attempts are made to compare the infrastructure developments a city or community would incur as a result of hosting an event to the potential alternative infrastructure development the city would undertake if the event were not to occur.

core product   The main product that is made by the company for the customer (i.e., the sport event or contest).

critical path   An analysis of the most efficient scheduling of tasks and subtasks.

cue   A feature or element of the event that is perceived and interpreted by the attendee with the intended outcome of a lasting (hopefully positive) impression or memory.

customer profile   A description of the customer or set of customers based on their demographics, psychographics, media preferences, and purchasing behavior.

data-based marketing (DBM)   A comprehensive system that captures critical demographics, psychographics, media use, and purchasing behavior information on customers and potential customers in order to enable direct marketing strategies.

demographics   The categorization of consumers based on age, gender, ethnicity, education, income, socioeconomic status, profession, geographic location, religion, type of sport played, and other such identifiers.

design domain   The event management domain that contains the event's content, theme, program, environment, and production, entertainment, and catering needs.

differential pricing   Differences in pricing of a seat based on quality, time, and place. Quality refers to reputation, strength, and draw of the opponent. Time corresponds to the day of the week, time of day, or part of the season. Place is determined by location of seat.

differentiation   The positioning of a product in the minds of the consumer by highlighting the important attributes and benefits.

direct objective   A business and marketing action specifically crafted toward increasing sales.

discretionary income   Monies left over once all financial obligations have been attended to by an individual or family.

divestment   The disposal/removal of the items associated with consuming a product or service and/or the ceasing of the relationship with the organization altogether.

domain   As used by the International Event Management Body of Knowledge, a division of the labor required at an event.

duration (of experience)   The length that the experience stays present for the individual.

dynamic pricing   A process of pricing that is similar to differential pricing but concerned with the fluctuation of the price of a seat for an event based on demand. Determinants of dynamic pricing may include weather, quality of opponent, promotional offerings, or day of the week.

economic impact   The amount of new money (financial gain) entering a region that can be attributed to a sporting event or facility.

emotional factor   The excitement, enjoyment, and self-fulfillment individuals gain from participating in sport.

emotional involvement   The affect that a sport event produces in the individual.

environmental/destination factor   The attractiveness of a destination or the environment in which an event is hosted that can impact individuals' motivations to attend or participate in an event.

environmental impact   The negative effect the construction of or the existence of a facility or event has on the local environment.

Environmental Protection Agency (EPA)   The U.S. federal agency responsible for protecting the environment and human health as it relates to the environment.

event feasibility   The likelihood that an event can be executed at the desired level given the resources at the event organizer's disposal.

expectation   A set of beliefs about an event.

experience   In the sport event industry, the meaning attached to the event through the perception of the competition, atmosphere, social interactions, food, and entertainment, among other factors.

experience economy   The consumer's reaction to an event beyond the goods or services of the event alone.

feasibility study   An assessment that is conducted to determine key market characteristics.

financial measurement   An outcome used to determine how well the organization is contributing to the bottom line.

fixed cost   An expense that does not change as a function of the business activity.

floor plan   An illustration of where equipment or items are to be placed within the event venue.

flow diagram   A graphical representation as to how attendees will move through the event and venue.

formal communication   Information generated by the facility or sport event owner.

Gantt chart   A bar chart that illustrates the various tasks that must be completed for the event in a time-sequence order.

gate receipt   The sum of money received from ticket sales for a particular event.

general obligation bonds   Bonds that are secured by state and local governments' authority to levy income, property, or sales taxes.

generic experience   An experience that is commonly found at every event.

geotechnical report   A report of the soil conditions that dictate what materials are necessary to support the foundation for the proposed building as well as provisions for drainage of surface and runoff water that can affect the drying time of certain materials.

gift   A donation provided to an organization to finance a project that is tax deductible.

guerrilla marketing   A marketing strategy that uses unique methods to gain large effects at low expenses.

hard cost   A direct cost specifically related to the project.

hard structure   An element of event legacy relating to primary structure (e.g., sport infrastructure, training sites), secondary structure (e.g., villages for athletes, technical officials, media), and tertiary structure (e.g., security, power plants, cultural attractions, telecommunication networks).

heterogeneous   Relating to perceptions of an experience that are widely dissimilar.

heterogeneous experience   The uniquely subjective experience that a person will have at an event; no two people will have the same experience at the same event.

human resource measuresment   An outcome that allows the organization to better develop an understanding of an employee's perception of the organization.

impervious surface   A surface, such as cement pavement, that prevents precipitation from naturally soaking into the ground, causing water to run rapidly into storm drains, sewer systems, and drainage ditches.

implementation phase   The execution of the event plans.

incremental budgeting   Budgeting system that makes slight changes to the previous period's actual revenues and expenses.

indirect objective   An outcome other than achieving immediate sales or gains such as increasing awareness to new market segments or a campaign to reposition a brand.

informal communication   The information we receive from our friends, family, or groups of people we interact with socially.

infrastructure   The sport facilities and subsequent surrounding areas needed for training and competition.

initiation phase   The stage in event planning that allows sport event organizers to define the event, set objectives, and determine the sport event's feasibility.

in-kind payment   An exchange of something of value other than cash currency for the purpose of entering a business relationship between a sports property and a sponsoring company.

intangible legacy   Nonphysical changes associated with the transfer of knowledge, governmental reform, and emotional capital for residents, participants, and spectators, as well as psychological improvements to the city's image and social structure.

integrated marketing communication (IMC)   A delivery strategy that ensures brand positioning, personality, and key messages are delivered synergistically across every element of communication.

intensity (of experience)   The strength of the experience.

jewel box   A stadium design characterized by the two-tier grandstand; steel, wood, or concrete support beams left exposed and incorporated into the design; seats that are traditionally green; and an unconventionally shaped outfield.

leadership   The process of influencing individuals or groups of people to work toward a shared goal.

learning factor   The desire to learn about or explore the facility or destination of a sport event.

LEED certification   A green building certification program that recognizes best-in-class building strategies and practices. LEED stands for Leadership in Energy and Environmental Design.

legacy   The lasting direct or indirect effects generated from hosting an event that may positively or negatively impact the community.

leveraging   The process of ensuring the sponsorship relationship is known to the target markets through strategic marketing and business actions occurring after the rights fees have been exchanged.

liability insurance   A form of general insurance that protects the insured from risks of liabilities imposed by lawsuits or similar claims.

liminal zone   A zone within a sacred, ritualistic event that creates meaning that transcends the person and creates meaning outside of normal everyday life.

liminoid zone   A zone within an unsacred, secular event that creates meaning that transcends the person and creates meaning outside of normal everyday life.

line-item budget   Revenues and expenses are estimated and grouped together into categories.

management   The process of accomplishing the organization's goals while dealing with resource constraints.

marketing domain   The event management domain comprised of the event's marketing plan, marketing materials, merchandize, promotions, public relations, sales, and sponsorship.

mastery factor   A factor relating to the skill, learning, and personal challenge of participating in sport.

matchup hypothesis   In reference to property and sponsorship, the belief that the more congruent the relationship, the more effectively the brands will connect in the minds of the consumers (e.g., a tire company sponsoring a racecar series).

meaning   The perception and interpretation of the event elements that make the event significant.

media preference and use   The categorization of consumers based on the type of media consumed and how it is consumed.

mega-event   The most complicated type of event to execute because it is often international in nature and requires years of planning to implement.

memorabilia   Tangible goods that support theme cues and that are available for purchase or as free takeaways.

memorability   The ability of an experience to remain an intense and enduring memory.

mission statement   A statement defining the purpose of the organization (or event).

money-back guarantee   An agreement between the ticket seller and buyer that the buyer will receive a full refund if the event does not meet a standard of satisfaction for the patron.

monitoring and control system   The controls that are implemented to ensure that performance standards are achieved as the sport event is executed.

municipal bonds   Tax-exempt bonds issued by the local or state government to support capital projects.

naming rights   The nonsport entity's (sponsor's) exclusive ownership of the name of the venue where sport events occur (i.e., the stadium, arena, or ballpark); used interchangeably with "title sponsorship."

need   A state of perceived deprivation.

pervious material   A material that allows water to soak naturally into the ground.

operating budget   Authorizes the funds necessary for the day-to-day operations of the facility or event.

operation and maintenance manual (O&M manual)   A collection of documents that contain pertinent information to maintain the building by providing detailed information on the management of the new systems in addition to the maintenance and repair of equipment.

operations domain   The event management domain that consists of communications, event infrastructure, logistics, the venue, technical needs, participants, and attendees.

organizational factor   An element that differentiates one event from another and influences a participant's motivation to attend an event.

performance measurement   An outcome that describes how well the organization is using its internal and external inputs to produce the desired output.

peripheral product   An element of the core product that complements its existence (e.g., concessions, merchandise, dance teams).

personal seat license (PSL)   A paid license that affords the buyer the right to buy season tickets for a specific seat in a stadium. The license is transferable and seat rights may be sold to another person once the owner decides not to purchase season tickets.

place   The location of the sport product where the product is distributed; the geographic location of the target market and other channels that might be relevant to the sport product.

planning phase   The proactive and dynamic stage in event planning in which the various options suggestion in the initiation phase are reviewed for the best course of action and preparation of the event.

positioning   Developing and delivering a product that is perceived as more valuable than and distinctly different from other products.

postevent analysis   Measurement of a specific variable of interest after the event has occurred.

price sensitivity   Susceptibility to variations in price.

pro forma   A statement that summarizes the projected future status of a company and that is used as the foundation for financial planning for an organization or project.

product extension   An additional event component that creates an atmosphere and experience for an event.

program budget   Funds are allocated for specific programs or projects.

program evaluation and review technique (PERT) chart   An illustration of the tasks, duration, and dependency information, which can be useful in defining the critical path for the project.

project   A temporary and one-time venture undertaken to create a unique product with specific outcomes and benefits.

project management   The dynamic process of organizing and managing appropriate resources in a controlled and structured manner to deliver the clearly defined work required to complete a project within the given scope, time, and, often, cost constraints.

project management triangle   The cost, time, and scope constraints that impact the final quality of an event.

promotion   The communication of the marketing message.

promotion mix   The varied use of a number of promotional methods to create a message.

property   In reference to sport sponsorship, the sport organization or entity being sponsored.

psychographics   The categorization of consumers based on the consumers' interests, beliefs, and attitudes.

purchase   The act of making a final selection.

purchasing behavior   The frequency with which individuals consume a product and the manner in which they use the products and services.

qualitative   Research methodology used to develop more in-depth description of behaviors and experiences.

quantitative   Research methodology used to provide a numeric analysis of the organization's performance.

realtor   An expert in real estate who can assist in identifying land options, demographics, and traffic volumes of an area, as well as zoning requirements for specific areas.

recurring event   An event that happens on a regular basis; it is the "easiest" type of event to execute because it occurs consistently.

referendum   A direct vote in which an entire electorate (i.e., voting public) is asked to accept or reject a proposal put forward by the community leadership.

relationship marketing   A marketing strategy that seeks to develop and maintain relationships with customers, while using information gathered from them to attract new customers; the client–consumer relationship is emphasized over a more purely transactional behavior.

retained earnings   Revenues generated by the sport organization that are reinvested to finance improvements and additions.

revenue and expense statement   Financial statement that presents budgeted and actual revenues and expenses in summary form for a given period of time.

revenue bonds   Issued for a specific project and are secured through the project's revenues.

revenue growth and mix measurement   An outcome used to denote how well the organization is performing toward organizational objectives such as market share, increased markets, or expanding its revenue sources.

rights fees   The amount charged by the property to the sponsor for the sponsor's legal commercial use of the sports organization's protected copyrights, trademarks, logos, and the like.

risk   The probability that a hazard will lead to a loss.

risk analysis   Categorization of the levels of risks based on the severity and likelihood of occurrence.

risk avoidance   A method of managing risk that involves discontinuing the component of the activity considered to be a risk.

risk domain   The event management domain that consists of compliance issues, emergency plans, health and safety plans, insurance needs, legal concerns, security needs, and any risk-related decisions.

risk evaluation   A process of determining the acceptability of the risk through a cost–benefit analysis.

risk identification   Evaluation of the environment, structures, and marketplace to determine the sources of risk associated with the sport facility or event.

risk management   A sound framework to minimize the potential and severity of the risk.

risk acceptance   A method of managing risk that involves preparing for the risk through budgeting, deductibles, or self-insurance.

risk monitoring   The continuous assessment of the risk associated with facilities and events, as well as the management strategies to reduce those risks.

risk reduction through proactive measures   A method of managing risk that involves establishing a series of controls to reduce either the likelihood of occurrence or the consequences associated with the risk.

risk retention   A method of managing risk in which the organization does not employ any risk management strategies.

risk transfer   A method of managing risk that involves moving the risk to another entity.

risk treatment   A method of managing risk that involves minimizing the impact and/or occurrence of the risk.

run sheet   A detailed schedule of the sequencing and timing for each element of the event.

schematic drawing   A drawing that exhibits the size of the facility and assists in defining the maximum capacity of land needed to build.

securitization   When sport organizations use contractually obligated income as collateral for debt.

segmentation   The breaking of consumers into smaller clusters or groups identified by certain characteristics rather than attempting to sell to everyone.

silt fencing   Temporary fencing used to keep any debris from passing from the site to any areas beyond the construction zone.

SMART goals   An acronym used to describe the goals of an event; stands for specific, measurable, attainable, relevant, and time-based.

social identity   A sense of belongingness or membership to a wider social group.

social impact   The effect facilities and events have on the local community, social norms, roles, and customs.

socialization   The process whereby individuals learn skills, traits, values, attitudes, norms, and knowledge associated with the performance of present or anticipated social roles.

soft cost   A cost that is not directly related to the physical construction of the project and commonly occurs prior to the project; also called indirect cost.

soft structure   An element of event legacy relating to knowledge, networks, and cultural goods that are developed from the hosting of an event.

special tax bonds   Bonds that are secured by local taxes. Typically in the form of bed, car rental, or sin tax.

specific expectation   An expectation or belief one holds about an event.

sponsor   The organization purchasing rights from the sport organization. This company may be a sport-oriented organization itself (e.g., sporting goods company) or may not be (e.g., financial entity).

sponsorship   A legal contract between a sport property and another entity exchanging something of value, whether cash or an in-kind service/product, wherein the sport property allows the sponsoring organization the rights to commercialization of its brand and the resulting benefits derived from these actions.

sponsorship inventory   Any place or location, whether physical or digital, that can be exchanged for something of value (cash or in-kind service/product) with the purpose of a sponsoring organization being able to achieve its sponsorship objectives.

sport management   The academic discipline that teaches and trains individuals who have a desire to work on the business side of the sport industry.

sport manager   The individual who is responsible for the planning, organizing, staffing, directing, and controlling functions that are completed for the organization.

stakeholder   A person or entity that has a vested interest in the event.

strategic management   The formulation and implementation of the major goals and initiatives taken by a company's top management on behalf of owners, based on consideration of resources and an assessment of the internal and external environments in which the organization competes.

subjective experience   A unique and personal venture undertaken by an individual, who attaches his or her own meaning.

sustainable tourism   Development of the infrastructure in the host community to generate a continuous flow of tourist activity.

SWOT analysis   A tool used to assess the internal and external strengths and weaknesses of an event; SWOT stands for strengths, weaknesses, opportunities, and threats.

tangible legacy   Observable, easily identified or physical changes to the host community that remain upon conclusion of the event.

target market   The consumer most likely to purchase the product or service.

television blackout   The National Football League's policy stating that if the nonpremium or luxury suite tickets have not been sold out, then the game will not be televised in the local market.

theming   Alteration of the attendees' sense of time and reality through tangible and memorable cues that leave lasting impressions.

title sponsor   See *naming rights*.

top-down approach   A method of evaluating an event's legacy that compares the economic indicators of the event with the same indicators of the host city if the event had not taken place.

topographical report   A survey of the land that identifies any existing buildings, site surface evaluations, and availability of electrical, sewer, water, and gas services.

traveling event   An event that occurs on a regular basis but in various locations.

triple bottom-line approach   A method of measuring organizational performance focused on the impact the event has on its consumers, internal business operations, and external business operations.

variable cost   An expense that changes based on the volume of business activity.

viral marketing   The use of social networks to increase brand awareness through self-replicating processes.

vision statement   A statement of what the organization would like to achieve or accomplish.

want   The form taken by human needs as they are shaped by culture and individual personality.

waste diversion   The prevention/reduction of generated waste through recycling, reuse, or composting.

white elephant   In reference to event legacy, a stadium, arena, or other facility constructed to host an event that remains underutilized after the event has occurred.

work breakdown structure (WBS)   Project tasks broken down into manageable parts.

zero-based budgeting   Requires each line-item from a previous budget be reviewed and approved and starts from a zero amount.

© Stockbyte/Thinkstock

Note: Page numbers followed by *f* or *t* indicate material in figures or tables respectively.